Contents

Scott Basham

Working Men's College
Library & LRC
tel: 0207 255 4736
e mail: libstaff@wmcollege.ac.uk

In easy steps is an imprint of In Easy Steps Limited
4 Chapel Court · 42 Holly Walk · Leamington Spa
Warwickshire · United Kingdom · CV32 4YS
www.ineasysteps.com

Notice of Liability
Every effort has been made to ensure that this book contains accurate
and current information. However, In Easy Steps Limited and the
author shall not be liable for any loss or damage suffered by readers
as a result of any information contained herein.

Trademarks
Microsoft® and Windows® are registered trademarks of Microsoft
Corporation. All other trademarks are acknowledged as belonging to
their respective companies.

In Easy Steps Limited supports The Forest Stewardship Council (FSC),
the leading international forest certification organisation. All our titles
that are printed on Greenpeace approved FSC certified paper carry the
FSC logo.

MIX
Paper from
responsible sources
FSC® C020837

Printed and bound in the United Kingdom

ISBN 978-1-84078-573-9

10 Tools for reviewing   191

Index   211

1 Finding your way around

This chapter quickly gets you started with Word 2013. It shows you how to launch Word and explains all the main areas in its screen layout. You'll try some basic text editing as well as the main controls and how they are organized and accessed.

Introduction

Word processing was one of the first popular applications for the modern personal computer. In the early days it provided little more than the ability to enter and change text on the screen. Today many more people have computers and tablets at home and in the office; virtually all of these use a word processor regularly. As the years have passed, the capabilities of the computer and its software have dramatically increased, far beyond the expectations of the first generation of users back in the 1970s and 80s.

Almost since the beginning, Microsoft Word has been acknowledged as a leader in its field. It is one of the best-selling software applications in any category. It grew in complexity from a program with a handful of menu commands to one with a sometimes bewildering array of features.

In creating Word 2013, Microsoft has built logically on the foundation of the previous versions. Rather than relying on complex menus, Word works with tabbed visual controls that reconfigure themselves to suit what you're currently doing. Accordingly, this book works as a graphical teaching guide – wherever possible, pictures and worked examples are used to demonstrate the concepts covered. It's not intended to replace Microsoft's documentation; instead you should view it as a way of getting up to speed quickly in a wide range of useful techniques.

The full range of Word's features is covered in this and the following chapters – from creating and editing simple text-based documents to tables, graphics and research tools as well as more advanced techniques such as viewing and editing documents on the web.

How to use this book

To gain maximum benefit from this book, make sure you're first familiar with the Windows operating environment (using the mouse, icons, menus, dialog boxes and so on). There are a number of books in the In Easy Steps range that can help you here.

It is a good idea to start off by going through chapters one and two fairly thoroughly, since these introduce basic concepts on which later examples depend. Once you've done this you can then dip freely into the other chapters as you like.

Don't forget

It's very important to experiment using your own examples – trying techniques a few times on test documents will give you the fluency and confidence you'll need when working for real.

The New icon pictured above indicates a new or enhanced feature introduced with the latest version of Word.

Starting Word 2013

The way in which you start Word depends on whether you're using a desktop PC or a tablet, and the operating system version.

From the Windows 8 Start screen

Hot tip

In Windows 7 you can run Word from the Start menu, clicking on All Programs if necessary.

1 If your Start screen includes a tile for Word 2013, as in the illustration below, then simply click with the mouse or tap with your finger if you're using a touchscreen

2 Alternatively, activate the Charms bar by pressing Winkey + C then click the Search icon

3 Enter "word" to see a list of matching applications

Hot tip

You can also activate the Charms bar by swiping inwards from the right edge of the screen (if using a touchscreen), or moving the mouse to the top right corner of the screen.

4 Click on Word 2013

...cont'd

Don't forget

For more details and help on accessing and organizing applications and documents check the range of books in the In Easy Steps series. There are a number of books covering each version of the Windows operating system.

10

Hot tip

Choosing "Open file location" from the Apps bar will take you to a folder containing the shortcut icons for Word and other Office applications. If you don't want Word on the Taskbar, then consider copying the shortcut(s) to the Desktop for quick access.

Installing Word in the taskbar

If you use Word regularly then it might be a good idea to have a quick way of launching it from the Desktop.

1　From the Start screen, or via the Search option in the Charms bar, locate Word 2013

2　Select either by right-clicking or, if you have the appropriate hardware, touching and dragging downwards a small distance. The Apps bar appears

3　Click the button "Pin to taskbar" then press the Winkey to switch to the Desktop

4　You can now launch Word directly from the Taskbar by clicking on its icon. To remove it, again right-click on the icon and choose "Unpin this program from taskbar"

Opening a document directly from Windows

On most PCs, Word document files will be recognized and shown with a distinctive icon as shown below.

1　Locate your Word document using the Charms bar search or the File Explorer

2　Clicking on a search result, or double-clicking in File Explorer will launch the associated program (in this case Word) and automatically open the file

The initial screen

If you launched Word directly (not via a document) then you will see the following screen.

1. To start working with a simple blank page, click the "Blank document" option as shown above

2. If you already have a document to view or edit, then check to see if its name and location are in the Recent list in the left side of the screen

3. If your document is there, click or touch to open it

4. If you cannot see your document then click the Open Other Documents link in the lower left corner

5. The Open dialog box allows you to look for files in Recent Folders, or you can use the Browse button to find a document in any available location

11

The main screen

Once Word is up and running, you should see the following screen – with all the elements illustrated here:

Quick Access Toolbar · Command tabs · Document title

Mini Toolbar

scrollbar

Status bar · Main page · View icons · Zoom

You can resize Word's window in the normal way by dragging on its border (if it's maximized then you'll need to click the ⊡ Restore Down button first).

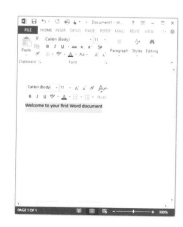

As you can see from the two illustrations on this page, Word automatically resizes and reconfigures its workspace and controls to make the best use of the space available. If you can't see the icon or control you want, simply make the window larger or click the ▼ symbol to see what's been hidden.

The Ribbon

Near the top of the screen is the Ribbon, which gives you access to most of Word's controls within a few mouse clicks. It's divided into a number of tabs, only one of which is active at any time. In the example below, the Home tab is showing basic text editing and formatting features.

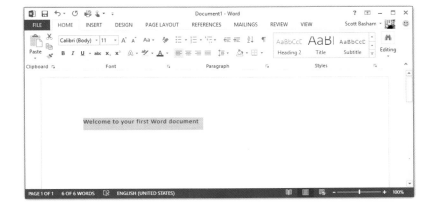

In this example the highlighted text changes its appearance as the controls in the Ribbon are used. It is currently formatted using the style "Normal". As the mouse hovers over the style "Title" the text temporarily changes its format to preview this style. For more about text styles see Chapter Two.

Using different tabs in the Ribbon

1 Click on the Insert tab's title to activate it. You'll see it's subdivided into ten sections

2 Each section contains groups of related controls. Let your mouse hover over one of these to see a brief explanation of its function

...cont'd

Hot tip

If you click on the new ⊞ icon in the top right of the screen you can change how the Ribbon and tabs will display:

3 Double-click on the currently-active tab to hide the ribbon temporarily. This is useful if you want to maximize the amount of screen space available for viewing and editing your document

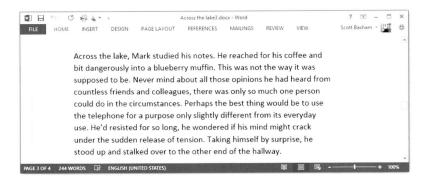

4 When the Ribbon is hidden in this way, clicking on a tab heading will temporarily reveal its contents. Double-click on a tab to restore the Ribbon permanently

5 Click on the File tab to see document information, together with other options for managing documents including printing, sharing and exporting. There is also a range of global options and account tools

Don't forget

Word 2013 integrates seamlessly with a range of connected services such as SkyDrive and YouTube, provided you are logged on to a valid Microsoft online account. See Chapter Eight for more on this topic.

The Mini Toolbar

Whenever you have some text selected the Mini Toolbar will appear nearby. It gives you immediate access to the most commonly-used text formatting options.

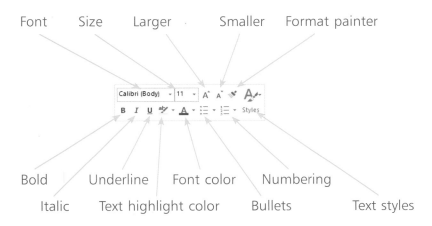

Font   Size   Larger   Smaller   Format painter

Bold   Underline   Font color   Numbering

Italic   Text highlight color   Bullets   Text styles

Hot tip

Some of the Mini Toolbar's controls have keyboard shortcuts. For example, bold can be set on and off by typing Ctrl + B, and italic with Ctrl + I. To find out if a control has a shortcut simply hover over it with the mouse pointer for a few moments. There is a handy reference table of keyboard shortcuts in the inside front cover of this book.

Using the Mini Toolbar

1 Type some text and then select it by dragging across it with the mouse

2 Gradually move the mouse pointer upwards (do not click the button at this point). The Mini Toolbar will fade into view just above the text, as in the illustration below. As you move up towards the Mini Toolbar, it will become more solid

Jasper took a long look at his shoes' reflection and decided to call it an afternoon. Swaying slightly with the unfamiliar extra weight he ploughed a silent unwelcome furrow through the still-damp concrete and made it to the municipal buildings. He allowed himself several lungs of cold air then turned around

3 Click on one of the controls within the Mini Toolbar to change the appearance of your selected text

4 Repeat the process with other selected areas of text

Hot tip

If the Mini Toolbar fails to appear when you hover over selected text with your mouse, try right-clicking. A pop-up context menu will appear with the Mini Toolbar immediately above.

Hot tip

If you click the small downward-pointing triangle next to the touch/mouse mode tool you can choose between the best control layout for mouse or touch input. Touch input adds more space between commands and controls; this makes it easier to operate Word 2013 with a touchscreen.

Optimize spacing between commands

Mouse
Standard ribbon and commands.
Optimized for use with mouse.

Touch
More space between commands.
Optimized for use with touch.

Hot tip

If you use the Quick Access Toolbar's Undo button then a Redo button becomes available. Undo and Redo together allow you to step backwards and forwards through your actions.

The Quick Access Toolbar

The Quick Access Toolbar is the small collection of tools at the top of the screen above the File tab.

Save   Undo   Repeat   Touch/mouse mode   Customize

Customizing the Quick Access Toolbar

1   Click the Customize icon on the Quick Access Toolbar and select a command or choose More Commands... to see the full list. Note there is also an option to place the Toolbar below the Ribbon

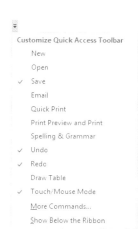

2   In the dialog box that appears, select from "Choose commands from" to see a list of Word commands

3   If you want your customizations to be global, make sure "For all documents" is selected in the top right corner

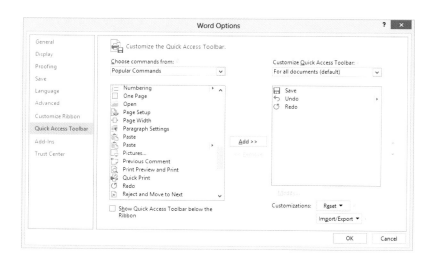

4 Add icons by double-clicking in the left-hand list, or click once to select and then choose Add>>

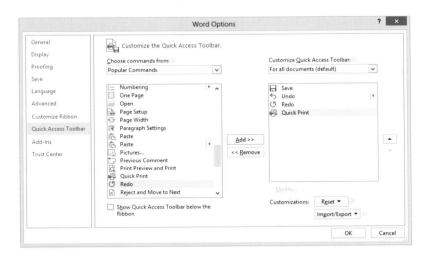

5 Remove icons by double-clicking in the right-hand list, or click once to select and then click on the Remove button

6 You can control the order in which the icons appear in the toolbar. To do this, select a command in the right hand list then use the up and down buttons to change its position. The top item in the list will appear as the first icon at the left of the toolbar

7 Click OK when done, or Cancel to abandon your changes. The Quick Access Toolbar will now show the icons you've selected

From the Customize Quick Access Toolbar dialog box you can reset the toolbar to its initial state by clicking the Reset button. It's also possible to import and export your customizations to a file.

The Status bar

The Status bar is the horizontal strip at the bottom of the Word screen. It normally shows details of general settings and display options, and can be used for adjusting the zoom level.

Customizing the Status bar

1 Right-click anywhere on the status bar to call up the Customize Status Bar menu

2 All the Status bar options are listed along with their current values. For example, in this illustration we can see that the Vertical Page Position is 0.9 inches – even though this is not normally displayed in the Status bar

3 A tick beside an item means it's displayed in the Status bar. Click on this to toggle the setting on and off

4 Click anywhere other than the menu to close it when you have finished

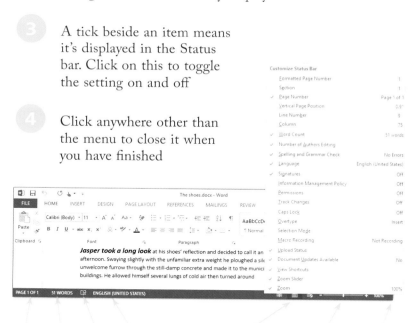

Current page

Spelling & grammar check

Page views

Drag here to resize the main window

Number of words

Dictionary

Zoom level

Getting help

1 Move your mouse over a command in the Ribbon. After a few moments a super tooltip appears, showing you the name of the command (useful if it's displayed only as an icon in the Ribbon). You'll also see an explanation of its function

2 The ⌐ icon indicates that a dialog box will open if you click on it. If you just hover over it with the mouse, however, the super tooltip will include a preview image of the dialog box – as in this example

3 For more information about any of Word's features, press the ⓘ key and a pop-up window will appear

4 For more detail click on the ❓ "Tell me more" icon or press the F1 key. If your mouse was not pointing at any controls when you pressed F1 then a general searchable help window appears

Hot tip

Clicking the "more" icon will take you to the Microsoft support website where there is a wide range of learning resources.

Text editing

Text editing in Word is no different to other programs such as Notepad, Wordpad, Outlook or PowerPoint. If you're already familiar with the basic skills then you might want to skip ahead to the next section.

Getting started

1. Start up Word so that you have a new blank document. If Word is already open then click on the File tab, then choose New, then "Blank document" and click Create

2. Enter some example text, enough for a line or two. Don't worry if you make mistakes as these will be easy to correct later on. Look for the flashing vertical line, known as the insertion point, which indicates where any new text will appear

3. You can easily move the insertion point anywhere in your text by clicking with the mouse. The arrow keys will also let you move up, down, left and right within the existing text. Move your insertion point so that it is somewhere in the middle of your text

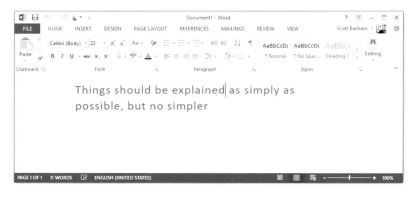

4. If you type more text now it will be inserted at your current position. To remove text, use the Backspace key to delete the character to the left of your current position, or the Delete key to remove the character to the right. If you hold down either of these keys for more than a moment they will repeat and start deleting more characters

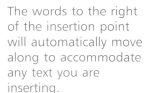

Don't forget

The words to the right of the insertion point will automatically move along to accommodate any text you are inserting.

Hot tip

Word automatically works out when to start a new line without breaking words. If you want to force a new line, for example to begin a new paragraph, press the Return or Enter key.

Selecting text

Basic techniques

Selecting text is almost always the first step when formatting or editing, so it's worth knowing all the different techniques.

1 Click and drag over the text you want to select. This is quick and easy for small amounts of text

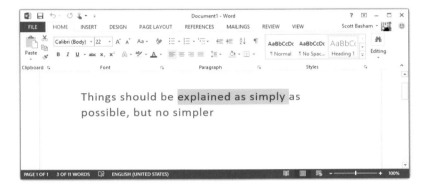

Don't forget

Using the arrow keys, or a mouse click, or a tap on a touchscreen, allows you to reposition your insertion point anywhere within the text. If you try to move beyond the existing text you'll find that the insertion point refuses to move. One way around this is to move just to the right of the last character and then add more text.

2 If the wrong text is highlighted click anywhere in the text-editing area to cancel the selection, then try again

3 Double-click on a word to select it. Triple-click to select a paragraph. If you're using a touchscreen, tap twice to begin selecting then drag the circular handles to adjust the start and end of the selection

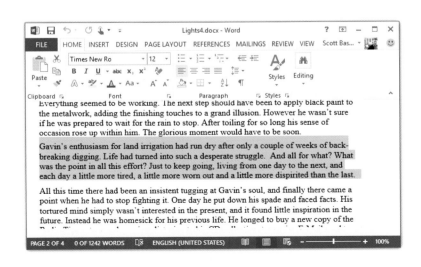

Beware

Don't be tempted to add extra spacing by pressing the spacebar many times. Although this will work up to a point, it's not the most flexible way of controlling spacing. You'll learn much better techniques for this in the next two chapters.

Hot tip

You can quickly select all the text in your document by clicking on the Select option in the editing section of the Home tab, and choosing Select All. The keyboard shortcut for this is Ctrl + A.

More advanced techniques

It's worth experimenting with these. Once you've practised for a while you'll be able to choose instinctively the best method each time you need to select text.

1. Move your mouse into the left margin area. You can tell that you are in the correct area if the cursor turns into an arrow pointing to the right instead of to the left

2. Drag vertically to select whole lines of text

Start dragging here

Finish dragging here

3. The easiest way to select larger amounts very precisely is to click the mouse at the start of the text

4. Locate the end of the area, scrolling if necessary

5. Hold down the Shift key and click. All text between the start and end will be selected. If you accidentally clicked at the wrong endpoint simply Shift + click again

Hot tip

If you hold down the Shift key when clicking in the left margin area the current selection will be extended up to the point where you clicked.

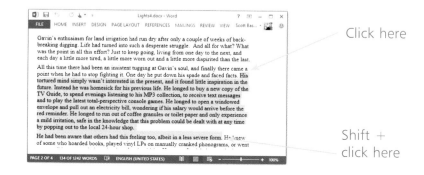

Click here

Shift + click here

Discontinuous text selection

1 Select some text using any of the previous techniques

2 Now hold down the Control key, click and drag across some text that is separate from your original selection

3 Repeat this process to add more areas to your selection

Beware

Anything you type, even a single character, will normally replace all selected text. For example, if you have three paragraphs selected and you accidentally press the spacebar, then all that text will be replaced with the space. If this happens, simply use the Undo button in the Quick Access Toolbar or type Ctrl + Z.

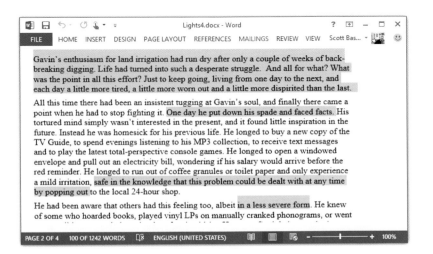

Selection with the Alt key

If you click and drag while holding the Alt key down you can select all text in a rectangular area. This is fun, although of questionable practical use.

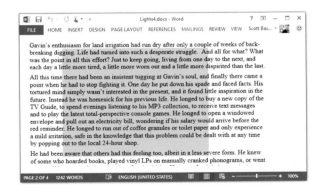

Working with files

Chapter Seven will look at file manipulation in detail, so for now we'll just concentrate on the simplest way to store and retrieve your work.

Starting a new document

1. When you start up Word you'll automatically be shown options for beginning a new document. If you're already using Word and are ready to create another new document select the File tab and click New

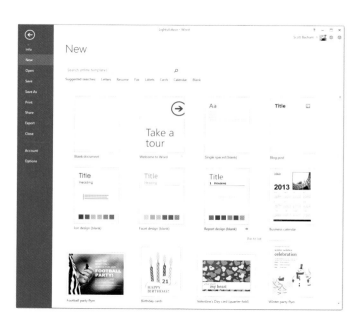

Hot tip

If you accidentally shut down Word you might still have a chance to recover your work. When you reopen the latest version of the document a message may appear, giving you the option of using the most up-to-date version of your document.

Saving your work

1. If you attempt to close down Word without saving you'll see the following message. Click Save if you want to save your work before quitting

2   Another way to save your work is to click on the Save
     icon in the Quick Access Toolbar. If you had saved the
     document before, Word simply saves using the same name
     and file location as before. If this is the first time for
     saving the document you'll see the following dialog box:

3   Click on one of the Places listed then choose a folder by
     clicking or using the Browse button, then click Save in
     the next dialog box

Opening a saved document

1   Select the File tab then click Open

2   Under Places choose from Recent Documents, the online
     storage options, or Computer to access a local file

3   Choose a folder then select a file in the standard
     Windows dialog box which appears

Click and type

Provided you are in Word's Print Layout or Web Layout view you can easily add text anywhere on the page.

1 First make sure that Print Layout view is selected from the Page View icons in the Status bar at the bottom of the screen

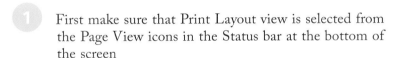

Print Layout view

2 Move over a blank area. The pointer icon will indicate to you whether new text will be aligned left, right or centered. The example below shows the icon for centered text. Double-click to establish a new insertion point

Don't forget

If click and type doesn't appear to work click on the File tab and choose Options. Select Advanced and make sure that the option "Enable click and type" is activated.

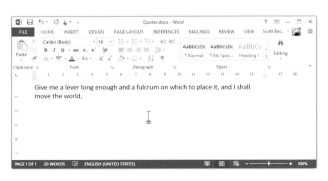

3 Type in some new text. Word will create any new blank lines necessary to allow the text to be positioned correctly. It also applies the correct form of alignment

Hot tip

You'll learn more about left, right and centered text in the next chapter.

Basic navigation

When your text is too large for the document window, you'll need to use one of the following navigation methods:

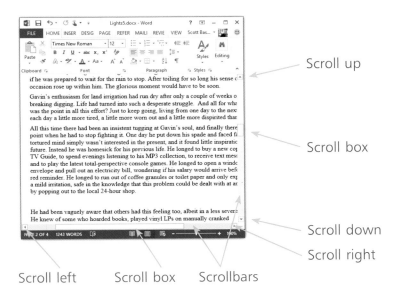

Scroll up

Scroll box

Scroll down

Scroll right

Scroll left   Scroll box   Scrollbars

Hot tip

The scroll boxes' positions let you know where you are in a document. When the vertical scroll box is at the top of the scroll bar you are looking at the top (the beginning) of the document.

Quick ways to scroll

1. Drag the scroll box directly to a new position

2. Click in the scrollbar to either side of the scroll box. The document will immediately scroll in that direction one screen at a time

3. As you move your insertion point with the arrow (cursor) keys, Word will scroll so that it can always be seen

4. If your mouse has a wheel, this can usually be used to scroll vertically through your document

5. The PgUp (Page Up) and PgDn (Page Down) keys will move you up and down one screen at a time

6. If you have a touch-enabled screen, place your finger inside the text area and swipe up or down to scroll

Hot tip

As you scroll down, the scroll box moves like an elevator down a shaft. The size of the box indicates how much of the document you can see (if the box occupies one third of the scroll bar, then you're viewing a third of the document).

...cont'd

Zooming

This allows you to control the level of magnification on screen. The zoom controls are in the bottom right corner.

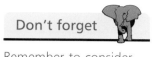

Don't forget

Remember to consider the size of Word's main window – in most cases it should be maximized. Note, however, that in this book we often use smaller windows so that we can concentrate on a particular part of the screen or set of controls.

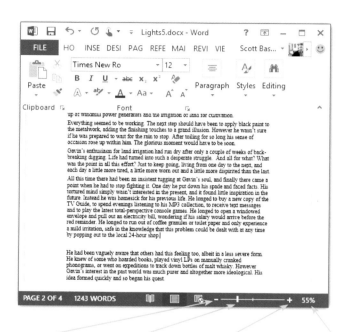

Zoom out   Adjust zoom level   Zoom in   Current level

The Zoom dialog box

1. Click on the "current level" icon (displayed as "55%" in the example above) to open the zoom dialog box

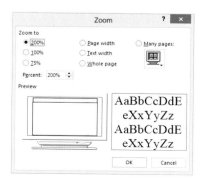

2. Choose one of the options, or enter a percentage value directly. In this example "Text width" is a good option if you dislike horizontal scrolling

3. Click OK to apply the zoom level

28

2 Basic editing

Now that you know your way around we'll look at the most common techniques for text editing and formatting.

The Clipboard

The Clipboard is a temporary storage area that can hold text or even other items such as graphic images. It can be used to help you move or copy text you have selected. It's also usually possible to use it to transfer text between different applications.

Cut and paste

1 Select the text to be moved. Right-click on the selected text, and then choose Cut

30

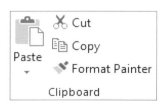

2 The text is removed and put onto the Clipboard. Now place your insertion point at the desired destination and right-click. A pop-up menu appears which offers you a choice of three paste options

Keep source formatting   Merge formatting   Keep text only

3 The source text was 18 point Calibri bold. If you want to use these attributes, click on the Keep Source Formatting option. If you want to use the attributes already at the destination, click on Keep Text Only. In the following example we right-clicked in an area of 11 point Calibri normal text and chose Keep Text Only

Even after you've pasted text you can still change your mind about the paste formatting options.

Altering paste options after pasting

1 After you've pasted text you'll see the Paste Options icon nearby. Either click the icon or press the Ctrl key to review the available paste options

2 In the example below we chose the second option: Merge Formatting. The font and size are that of the destination, but the bold effect has been taken from the source

3 The Paste Options are available to you until you start typing, at which point the icon disappears

4 If you change your mind after this then click Undo until you've gone back to the point just before pasting, then paste once again. The Paste Options icon should appear once more

Hot tip

You can also cut and paste using the keyboard shortcuts Ctrl + X and Ctrl + V respectively.

...cont'd

Copy and paste

1 Select the text you want to copy, right-click and choose Copy from the pop-up menu

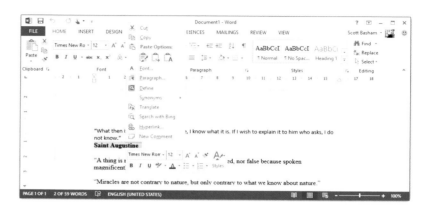

Don't forget

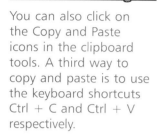

You can also click on the Copy and Paste icons in the clipboard tools. A third way to copy and paste is to use the keyboard shortcuts Ctrl + C and Ctrl + V respectively.

2 Place the insertion point at the destination for the copied text, right-click and choose the appropriate paste option

3 Pasting text doesn't actually remove it from the clipboard, so you can paste the same text many times

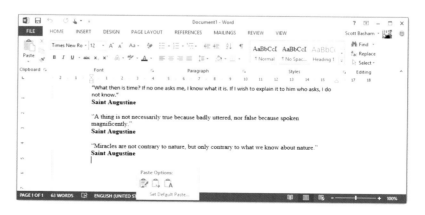

4 If you select some text before pasting, then the pasted text usually replaces what's selected (this feature can be switched on and off from File > Options > Advanced)

The Spike

The Spike is similar to the clipboard in that it's a temporary storage area for text. The main difference is that you can add more and more text onto the Spike with a keyboard shortcut.

1 Select some text and type Ctrl + F3. The text disappears. It has been 'impaled' on the Spike

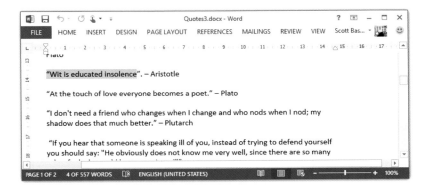

2 Move to a second piece of text and repeat the process: select then type Ctrl + F3. It too will disappear as it has been added to the Spike

3 If you want to add even more text to the Spike, then repeat the previous step as many times as you want, working through your document

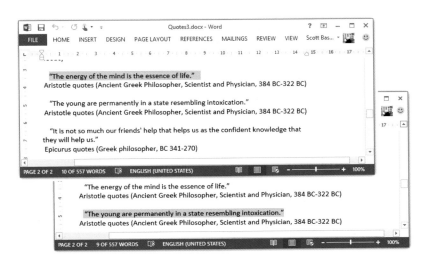

...cont'd

34

4. Finally, position the insertion point at the destination for the text and press Ctrl + Shift + F3. The text is pulled off the Spike and placed back into the document

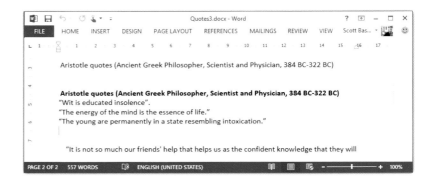

Multiple Clipboard items

Pasting will normally just give you back the last item that was placed on the Clipboard. However, Word's Clipboard actually has space for up to 24 items.

1. Select some text and choose either Copy or Cut using one of the techniques shown earlier

2. Repeat this with more text so that you have several items on the Clipboard

3. Click on the ⌐ icon in the lower right corner of the Clipboard Tools. The full Clipboard appears to the left of the text area

4. Click directly on any item to paste it back into your document. Alternatively, hover over the item to see a small downward-pointing arrow. If you click on this you will see a pop-up menu with options to either paste or to delete the item from the Clipboard

The Format Painter

The Format Painter gives a very easy way to copy attributes from one place to another.

1 Select a sample of text that has the desired attributes

2 Click the Format Painter icon in the Clipboard section of the Home tab. This "loads" the icon with the attributes of the selected text

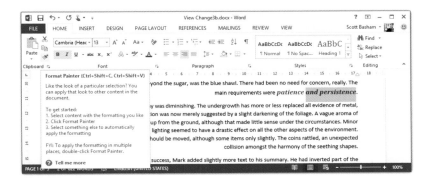

3 Note that your mouse pointer has changed to show that you have attributes loaded. Now use it to drag across your target text. The attributes are applied to the text

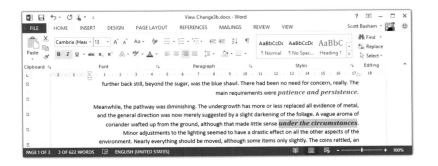

Hot tip

To copy formatting to more than one destination simply double-click on the Format Painter icon. You can then apply the formatting to as many pieces of text as you wish. When you've finished, either click back on the icon to discharge the loaded attributes or press the Escape key.

This normally just copies character-level attributes. However, if you select an entire paragraph, click the Format Painter, then select an entire destination paragraph, all attributes (including paragraph settings such as alignment) will be copied. This is a very powerful feature so remember you can always click Undo if the results are not what you wanted.

Formatting characters

The Home tab contains the controls you'll use most often in Word, so it's selected by default whenever you open or create a document.

As you can see, it's organized into five areas: Clipboard, Font, Paragraph, Styles and Editing controls. We'll start by looking at the Font Controls, as the others will make more sense once you've seen how to change the basic appearance of text.

Choosing the font with the Mini Toolbar

The terms "fonts" and "typeface" come from traditional typography, and describe the visual design of letters and other symbols. Most people will be familiar with popular typefaces such as Arial or Times New Roman. Strictly speaking, a font is an instance of a typeface at a certain size and variant such as normal, light, bold or italic. These days the term font is often used in place of typeface, so in Word we might select a font of "Arial Black", then choose a size of 12 and finally apply an effect of italic.

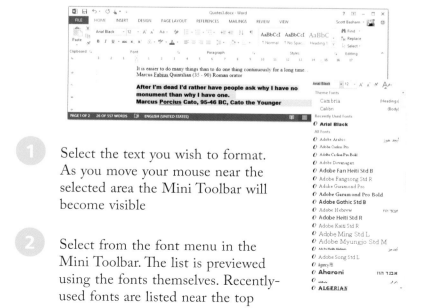

1. Select the text you wish to format. As you move your mouse near the selected area the Mini Toolbar will become visible

2. Select from the font menu in the Mini Toolbar. The list is previewed using the fonts themselves. Recently-used fonts are listed near the top

36

Formatting with the Home tab

The Font section of the Home tab gives you access to more ways of controlling the appearance of characters.

1 Select some text. Change font, size, and other attributes by selecting from the Font section in the Home tab

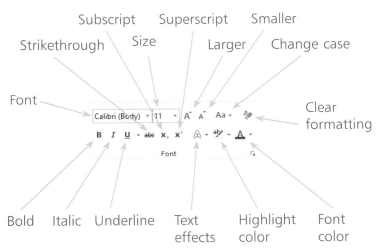

Hot tip

The keyboard shortcuts for Bold, Italic and Underline are Ctrl + B, Ctrl + I and Ctrl + U respectively.

37

2 Whenever you select text, the Font area will show you its current settings (if there are mixed settings within the text you've selected then the value will show as blank)

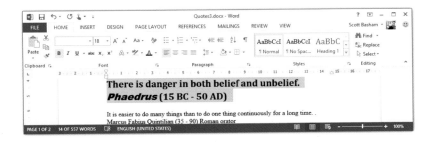

Hot tip

If the settings show as blank then try selecting a smaller portion of text.

3 In this example, all the selected text is 18 point in size, and bold. However, since it uses more than one font, the area which usually displays the font name is blank. Selecting just the word "Phaedrus", or even part of that word, would cause the Font area to show "Arial Black"

...cont'd

The Font dialog box

You can call up the Font dialog box to get full character-level control over the appearance of your text.

1 Select some text. Click on the dialog icon in the lower right corner of the Font area, or press Ctrl + D

Open Font dialog

2 You now have access to additional effects, such as double strikethrough and a variety of underline styles. The Preview box near the bottom gives you an indication of how the text would appear if you clicked OK

Hot tip

Clicking the Text Effects... button will take you to a dialog box where you can apply a wide range of visual effects to your text. These include fills, outlines, shadow, reflections and 3D formats. You can apply some (but not all) of these directly from an icon in the Home tab of the Ribbon, as you will see in an example on page 40.

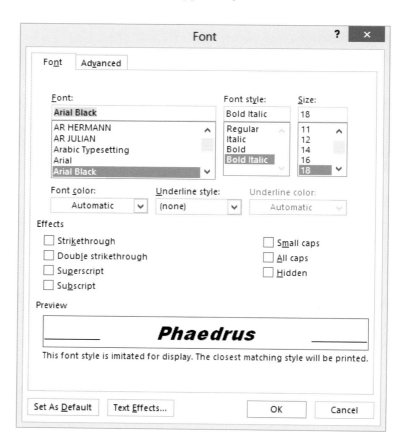

3 Click on the Advanced tab to control the precise positioning and scaling of the selected characters

Kerning

Kerning is a process used to adjust the space between certain combinations of characters. For example, when the letters "T" and "o" occur next to each other, normal spacing appears too wide. If you activate kerning then they will be brought closer together to create the illusion of normal spacing. Since kerning can slow down screen redrawing you might want to activate it only for larger font sizes (where spacing is more noticeable).

Ligatures

The Advanced dialog box also has the ability to access a range of OpenType features. OpenType allows font designers to make use of features such as special small caps, ligatures, number forms and spacing. Ligatures are combinations of characters designed as a single entity. In this example you can see that applying ligatures affects the two consecutive "f" characters, which are displayed as a specially-designed single character.

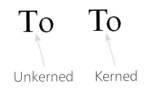

Unkerned   Kerned

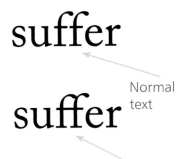

Normal text

Ligature applied to the pair of f characters

Beware

Scaling allows you to stretch or compress text horizontally. While this can sometimes work well for large titles it's not recommended for use on main text as the results are often unreadable. If you need narrower or wider text then try using a different font that is already the desired shape.

Don't forget

You might not notice any changes in the appearance of your text when you activate ligatures, as this setting will only make a difference if you are using a font which has been specially created with ligature information.

...cont'd

Text effects

Word gives you a wide range of effects for adding to your text, and by using the Toolbar you'll get an instant preview.

1 Select some text. Click on the "Text Effects and Typography" button within the Font Tools to see a menu of popular effects. As you hover over an item your text will temporarily preview the effect. Either move to a different effect or, if you are happy with your selection, click once on the effect to apply it permanently

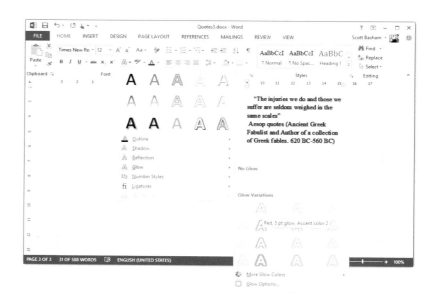

Hot tip

The Text Highlight Color and the Font Color buttons also give you an instant preview of how the text will look as you hover over each color in their pop-up menus.

2 You can use the submenus to access more options within the individual effects of outline, shadow, reflection and glow. Note that you can apply several effects at once, although just one from each category. For example, an outer shadow, a green glow and a medium reflection can all be applied to a single piece of text, as in the following example:

Aesop quotes

Formatting paragraphs

The Mini Toolbar gives you the ability to switch centering on and off, adjust the left indent, or create a bulleted list. For most paragraph-level attributes, however, you'll use the Paragraph section of the Home tab.

Paragraph

Alignment

1 If you want to change just one paragraph then simply click anywhere within it. If you want to change multiple paragraphs then select them using any of the techniques we looked at earlier

Don't forget

Remember that a heading is regarded by Word as a single-line paragraph.

2 Click on one of the alignment icons to choose left, centered, right or justified alignment. There is an example of each type illustrated below

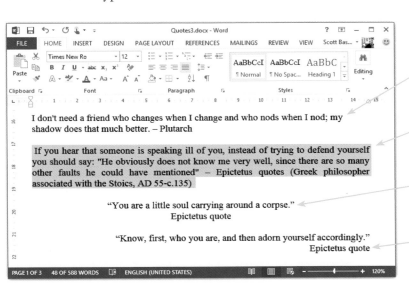

Left(normal)

Justified

Centered

Right

3 To see more paragraph controls, click the small open dialog icon ⌐ in the lower right corner of this section. The dialog box which appears has two tabbed pages: "Indents and Spacing" and "Line and Page Breaks". These give you accurate control over attributes such as line spacing, indentation and hyphenation

Hot tip

Justified text is aligned to both the left and the right margins, so that both have a straight edge (apart from the final line in a paragraph). To achieve this, the spacing between words is automatically adjusted.

4 Click OK to the dialog box to view the changes to the text

Bulleted lists

1. Enter the text for your list, pressing the Return key after each item. Select this text

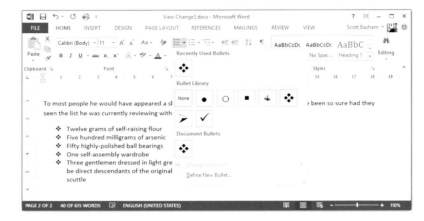

2. Open the Bullets pop-up menu in the Paragraph area of the Home tab

3. Choose the desired type of bullet. If you don't like any of those displayed then choose Define New Bullet. From this dialog box you can select any symbol or picture

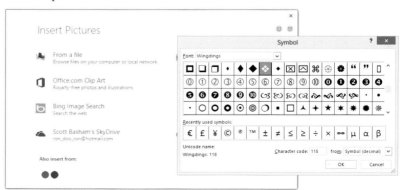

Numbered lists

1 If you enter a new line of text beginning with a "1." then Word will automatically start to create a numbered list for you. When you press Return, the next numbered line will be created for you automatically, and so on until you press Return twice to indicate the end of the list

2 This behavior may not always be what you want. If it is not, then click on the AutoCorrect icon that appears by your text. You can then undo the automatic numbering just for this example, or disable the feature for future lists

3 Another way to create a numbered list is to enter your text with no numbers, and then select it in the normal way and open the Numbering pop-up menu in the Paragraph section of the Home tab. As you hover over the different format options you'll see a preview of how your text will appear

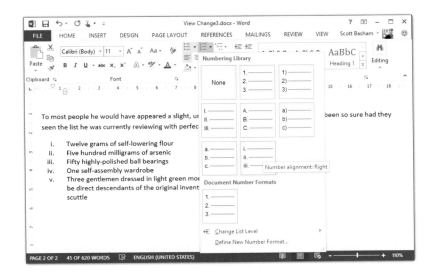

43

...cont'd

Sorting lists

1 Select your list, then click Sort in Paragraph tools

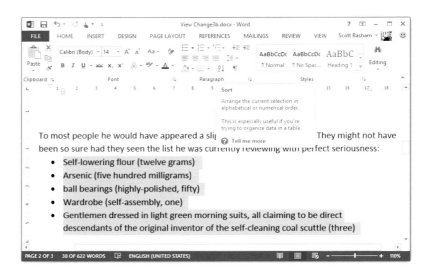

2 The following dialog box appears. Choose the appropriate sort type (in this case, text) then click OK

Hot tip

You can also sort multilevel lists (see the next page for creating this type of list). The Sort Text dialog box allows you to specify a sort order for up to three levels.

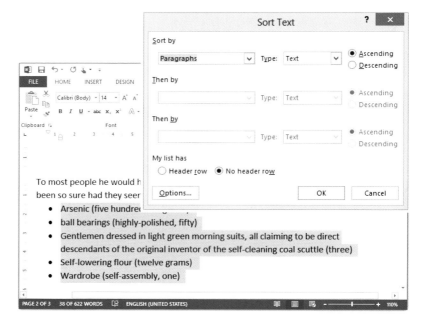

Multilevel lists

1 Create the text for your list. Press the Tab key at the beginning of a line once for each level of indent

2 Open the Multilevel pop-up menu in the Paragraph section and select the desired style

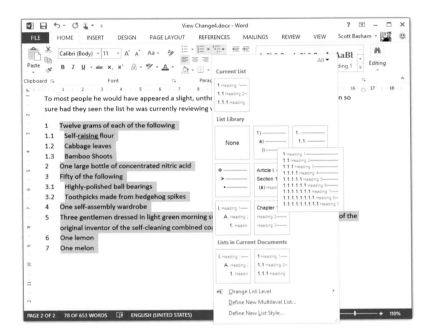

Hot tip

You can use the Change List Level option in the Multilevel pop-up menu to move an item to a higher or lower level. Alternatively, click at the beginning of a line and use Tab to move right or Shift + Tab to move left.

45

3 If you want to choose your own custom settings then select Define New Multilevel List...

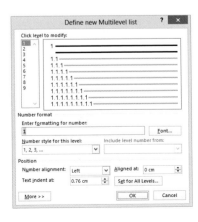

4 By clicking the Font... button in this dialog box you can control the appearance of the number at each level of the list, separately from the main text

Styles

Styles help you to apply a consistent set of formatting attributes to main text, headings and other elements of your document. Once you start using styles you'll be able to control your document's presentation with the minimum of tedious manual editing. Word comes with a set of styles for you to use straight away (in an area of the Home tab called the Styles Gallery), but it's also easy to create your own. There are two main types of style:

Paragraph styles

These can contain information about virtually any text attribute, e.g. font, size, alignment, spacing and color. They are called paragraph styles because they are applied at the paragraph level. In the Styles area paragraph styles are marked with a ¶ symbol.

Applying a paragraph style

1. Choose the paragraph of text you want to format by clicking anywhere within it, or multiple paragraphs using any of the techniques covered in the previous chapter

2. If you hover over a style from the Styles Gallery in the Toolbar you'll see a preview of your text using the style. Choose one of the styles marked with a ¶ symbol. To see the full list of available styles use the scrollbars or the ⏷ symbol in the bottom right of the Styles tools

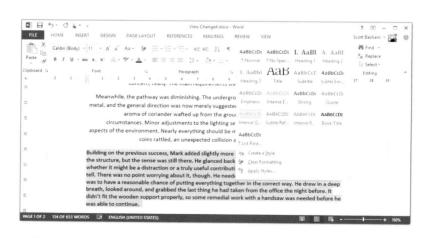

3. Click once on the style to apply it to your text

Don't forget

A paragraph of text can only have a maximum of one paragraph style applied to it at any time. If you select a single word and apply a paragraph style to it, then the whole of the surrounding paragraph will be affected.

46

Hot tip

There is a third type known as a Linked style. This can contain both character and paragraph level attributes. See page 54 for more about this.

Character styles

These can contain information about character-level attributes only, e.g. font and size, but not alignment (which is a paragraph-level attribute). They can be applied to any amount of text, even individual characters or words. Character styles have no ¶ symbol.

Applying a Character style

1 Select the text you want to change

2 Look for a style which doesn't have a ¶ symbol and hover over it with the mouse. Your text will temporarily preview the selected style until you move the mouse elsewhere

Beware

It is very easy to accidentally override all your carefully-chosen text settings simply by clicking on a style in the toolbar. If this happens choose Undo from the Quick Access Toolbar.

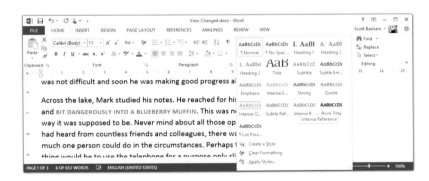

3 Click directly on a style to apply it permanently to the selected text

Removing the style from Text

1 Select the text in question

2 Click the ⊡ symbol in the bottom right of the Styles tools to see the full list of styles plus a menu below these

3 Choose Clear Formatting. This will reset the text to a style called Normal, which uses "plain text" settings. It's possible to redefine Normal to anything you like, as you will see in the next few pages

...cont'd

Creating a style

1 The easiest way to create a new style is to select some text that already has all, or most, of the attributes you want to use

2 Open the Styles panel by clicking the ⌐ icon in the lower right corner of Styles area

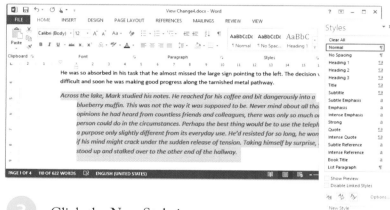

Hot tip

You can apply a style to text using the keyboard shortcut Ctrl + Shift + S. An Apply Styles window will appear – type the first few letters of the style's name. If the desired style appears then click the Apply button; if not then select from the list.

3 Click the New Style icon ⁣ at the bottom of the panel

4 Note that the dialog box shows you a preview of the style you're about to create. If this does not look correct then click the Cancel button and examine the text you selected. If necessary, alter its formatting or select a different sample of text

5 If you're already happy with the style's attributes then click OK, otherwise select Modify... to edit the settings

Modifying a style using the dialog box

1 Right-click the style in the Toolbar and select Modify...

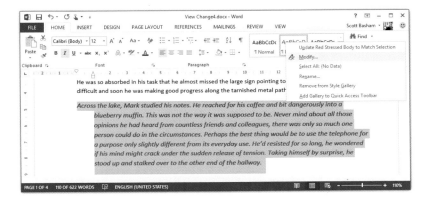

2 The following dialog box appears. From here, you can rename the style or alter attributes such as font, size or effects including bold and italics

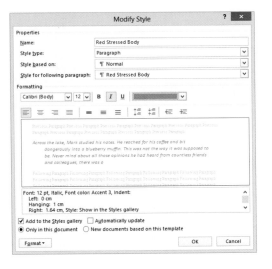

Many other useful settings can be made from this dialog box. If you click the Format button, you can access dialog boxes for Font, Paragraph, Tabs and several other categories.

3 When you're happy with your settings click OK. If there's any text in your document already using this style then it'll be automatically updated

49

...cont'd

Modifying a style using document text

One problem with modifying styles via the dialog box is that you don't see the results until you return to the main document. The following method doesn't suffer from this drawback:

1. Select text that already uses the style you plan to modify, and make the desired formatting changes

2. Right-click on the name in the Styles area and choose the "Update... to Match Selection" option

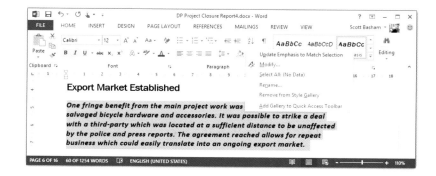

Collapsing and expanding headings

A new feature with Word 2013 allows you to hide or reveal text below any headings which were formatted with the built-in styles.

1. Click the small triangle ▶ to the left of a heading

2. Click again to toggle the display of the contents on/off

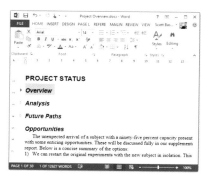

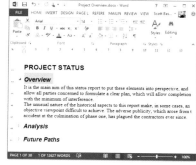

3 Editing in more depth

This chapter covers more advanced text editing, including manipulation of styles, using the Ruler and Tabs to help with precision layout, and special effects.

The Styles panel

In the last chapter you started to use styles. You can create more advanced types of style from the Styles panel.

1 Open the Styles panel by clicking on the ⌐ icon in the bottom right corner of the Styles area

2 You'll see a list of recommended styles

Paragraph-level style

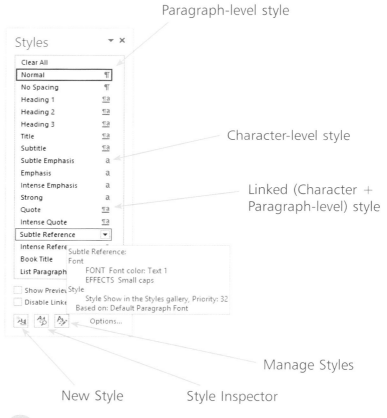

Character-level style

Linked (Character + Paragraph-level) style

Subtle Reference:
Font
  FONT Font color: Text 1
  EFFECTS Small caps
Style
  Style Show in the Styles gallery, Priority: 32
Based on: Default Paragraph Font

Manage Styles

New Style

Style Inspector

3 If you allow your mouse to hover over a particular style name, a summary box will appear. This lists the essential attributes of the style

4 Click on Options... to select which styles should be shown in the Styles window. You can also control how they are displayed and sorted

Paragraph-level styles

Creating a new paragraph-level style

1 Make sure the Styles panel is open. If it isn't, click on the ⌐ icon in the bottom right corner of the Styles area

2 Click the New Style button near the bottom

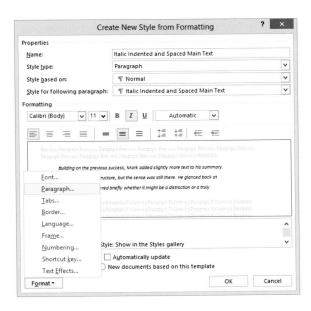

3 Enter a style name, and choose a Style type of Paragraph

4 Select the other formatting options as appropriate. When you click OK your new style becomes available in the Styles area. Note the ¶ symbol next to its name

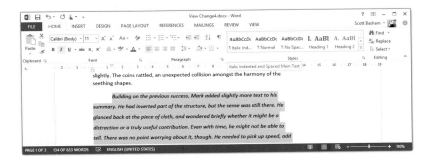

Linked styles

A linked style can be used at either the paragraph or the character level, depending on the amount of text selected when it's applied.

Creating a new linked style

1. Open the Styles panel by clicking on the ⌐ icon in the bottom right corner of the Styles area. Click the New Style icon

2. Give your style a name. For "Style type" select "Linked (paragraph and character)"

3. Select the other formatting options as appropriate. In this example we've chosen green, italic text with individual words underlined. You can set the word underline feature by clicking Format and choosing Font...

4. Click OK when you're done. Your new style is now available. In the Styles panel the name is followed by a ¶a symbol to indicate it's a linked style

54

5 Select a whole paragraph of text (the quickest way to do this is to triple-click anywhere inside the paragraph), locate your new style in the Home tab and apply it

6 Now select an individual word in a different paragraph and apply the style

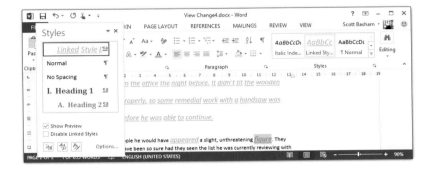

7 To modify a style, click on the ⋅ symbol next to the style's name in the Style panel and select Modify... Note that the style type setting is now grayed out. Once a style has been created its type cannot be changed

Hot tip

Although you can't change a style type once created, you can always create a new style based on another – to do this simply select the style in the Style panel then click the New Style button. You can now set the type for the new style.

Mixing styles in a paragraph

Character-level and paragraph-level styles can be used in the same paragraph. In this case the character-level style's attributes take precedence. The following example is a good illustration of this.

1 Select an entire paragraph and apply a paragraph-level style to it. In this example a style called "Green stressed body" was used. It's Arial, 10 point, green, italic, centered text

2 Now select a small group of words within the paragraph and apply a character-level style. Here we've used a style called "Blue underline char style", which is 12 point, underlined and blue. The style definition has no font name built in so the font remains the same as that for "Green stressed body"

Don't forget

The selected words in this example still follow the attributes of the paragraph style, except where they have been overridden by the character-level style. So, if you edited "Green stressed body" to make its font Times New Roman this would affect all the text. If, however, you made "Green stressed body" a darker green color, the text seen highlighted here would still be blue.

3 Note that the character-level style's attributes override those of the paragraph-level style

4 Now, with the same group of words selected, adjust the size to make it larger

5 Now open the Styles window and click on the Style Inspector icon:

This panel shows you exactly how the text was formatted.

Using style sets

If you've been using Word's built-in styles, or if you've created your own by editing them and keeping the same names, then you can switch the style set to redesign your document completely.

1 Make sure the Design tab is active and hover over a style set to see a preview of how your document would look with the new design

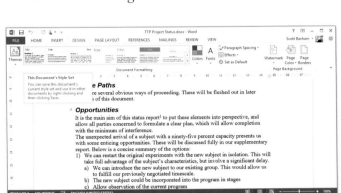

2 To see more options click the ⬇ icon in the lower right corner of the style set area. Select an option to make the change permanent

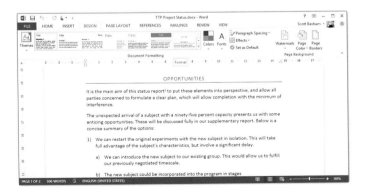

Don't forget

As your documents grow you will want to check your formatting and overall design is consistent and easy to change, so make sure you use styles rather than formatting directly in the page.

3 Each style in the style set will replace the style of the same name in your current document. Any text which used these styles will be automatically reformatted. This allows you to give even long documents a new and consistent design with the minimum of fuss

The Ruler

Text that is laid out neatly with accurate horizontal positioning greatly helps to give your documents a professional look. Effective use of white space, including tabulation, is the key to this.

Making the Ruler visible

The horizontal ruler can be displayed in most page views. However, the vertical ruler displays in Print Layout view only.

1. Make sure that you are in Print Layout view. Activate the View tab and make sure that the Ruler option in the Show area is active

| Left indent for the first line of each paragraph | Left indent for subsequent lines | Drag here to move both left indents at once | Right indent |

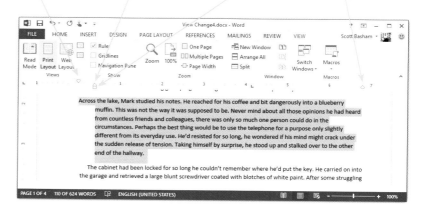

2. Experiment by moving the left and right indent markers on the Ruler and observe what happens on the page. It helps if you have several lines of text selected

You can change the measurements system from the File tab by choosing Options and then Advanced. In the Display section go to the option "Show measurements in units of:" and choose a different value. Points and Picas are sometimes useful as they match font sizes.

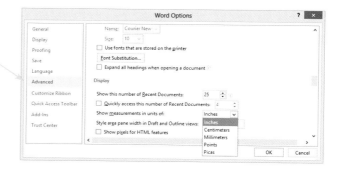

Tabulation

Tab stops are paragraph-level attributes that define what happens if the Tab key is pressed when entering text. If you select a paragraph and examine the Ruler you'll see any tab stops that have been defined. If no tab stops have been defined for this paragraph then the default tabs apply. These are marked in the Ruler as small vertical lines, spaced out at regular intervals in its lower section.

Overriding default tabulation

1   Click the Show/Hide ¶ button in the Paragraph section of the Home tab. This will allow you to see where you've pressed the Tab key – shown as a small arrow pointing to the right

Don't forget

When you click the Show/Hide ¶ button, paragraph marks also appear visibly as the ¶ character.

2   Type in some text similar to the example below. Note that each text element is separated from the next by a Tab character. Don't worry about how far across the screen the Tab takes you – this will be altered soon. Make sure you only press Tab once between one element and the next

3   Also make sure that you press Return once at the end of each line. This will show up as a ¶ character as in the illustration above

4   Now select all the text you just entered

...cont'd

5 Make sure that the ∟ icon is visible at the left side of the Ruler. This means that when you create a tab stop it will use left alignment. If it looks different, then click on it until it changes to the correct symbol

6 Click in the Ruler around the 1 inch mark to create a new left tab. Drag it left or right to adjust its position

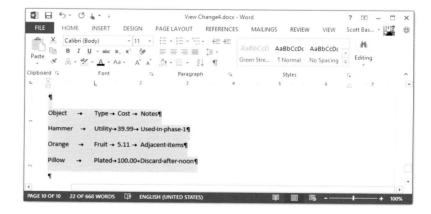

7 The characters should move so that the text following the first tab lines up vertically along its left edge. Making sure that your text is still selected, create some more tab stops

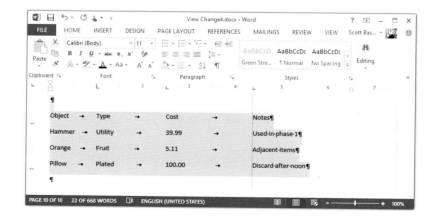

Note that the text automatically moves to follow your new design.

Different types of tabs

1 Keeping your text selected, delete the right-most tab by dragging it downwards from the Ruler until it disappears

2 Now click on the ∟ symbol until it changes into a ⌐

3 Click in the Ruler near the right edge of the page. The text is moved so that it lines up along its right edge

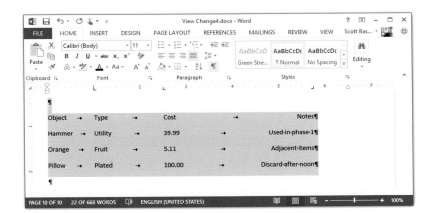

Hot tip

When you click on the ∟ symbol the icons cycle between left, center, right and decimal-aligned tabs. After these there is the bar (vertical line) icon, followed by first-line indent and hanging indent icons.

61

4 If the text fails to line up correctly then adjust the tab positions by dragging them left or right. You can call up the Tabs dialog box by double-clicking directly on any tab:

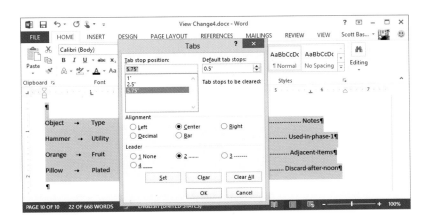

5 Select a tab from the list. You can now change its type, add a leader (in the below example, we lead into the third tab with a line of dots), set new tabs, or clear tabs

6 In this example, bar tabs were created at 4 inches and 6 inches. These create vertical lines:

Don't forget

Tabulation can be built into a style definition, and so used consistently throughout a document.

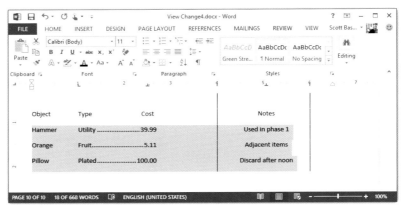

7 Sometimes the first line, since it contains headings, needs a slightly different form of alignment compared with the main text. In this example, the first line was selected on its own so that the word "Cost" could have a centered tab rather that the decimal tab with the leader of dots. Then the remaining lines were selected so that the formatting of the main text could continue

8 When you're done, click the Show/Hide ¶ button in the Paragraph section of the Home tab. This makes the hidden characters invisible again so that you get a better idea of the appearance of the final result

Removing all Tabs

1 Make sure all the relevant text is selected, then double-click on a tab to summon the Tabs dialog box

2 Click Clear All, then OK

Editing controls

The right hand side of the Home tab contains the Editing area with its Find, Replace and Select tools. These sometimes work in conjunction with the Navigation and Selection panes which you'll see later on.

The Find button

1 Press Ctrl + F or click the Find button in the Toolbar. If you click on its pop-up menu rather than the main part of the icon you'll see three options, one of which is Find

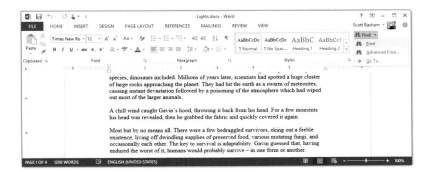

2 The Navigation pane appears along the left side of the screen. Enter your search text

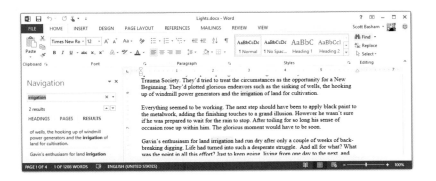

3 Word will immediately highlight all matches in the document, and also list them in the Navigation Pane. If you scroll through these and click on an item the main page will automatically move to that particular instance

Hot tip

If you click the pop-up menu icon (the small black triangle) next to the search text you can ask Word to find other elements such as graphics, tables or equations. See Chapter Five for more on pictures and graphics.

Advanced Find

Although the Navigation Pane is useful for instant searches, you may want to use the Advanced Find feature to access more flexible and powerful options.

1 Open the pop-up menu next to the Find icon in the Editing area and choose Advanced Find...

2 Click the More >> button to see the full set of options

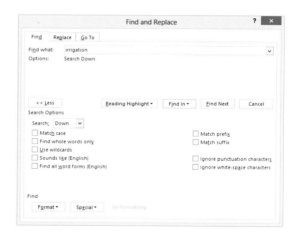

3 Enter the search text in the "Find what" box

4 Note the option to match case – keeping this switched off means that searches are not case sensitive

5 By clicking the Format button you can base your search on text attributes such as font or size. If you set some attributes and also enter text in the "Find what" box then Word will look for that particular text but only if its attributes match what you've specified

6 To go ahead and run the search click the Find In button and choose Main Document. If you happen to have selected some text within your document it's also possible to search just the selection

Find and Replace

Word can be instructed to search through your document, or selected text, and automatically substitute text, text attributes or even a combination of the two.

Hot tip

You can also summon the Replace dialog box by using the pop-up menu in the Navigation pane, if available.

1 To access the Find and Replace dialog box you can either click directly on the Replace icon in the Toolbar or use the keyboard shortcut Ctrl + H

2 Enter the search text in the "Find what" area. While the cursor is still in this field you can also, optionally, click the Format button to specify search attributes

3 If you want to replace with new text then enter this in the "Replace with" area. This example is a formatting change rather than a text substitution. Remember to ensure the cursor is inside the "Replace with" box rather than "Find what" before you click the Format button

...cont'd

4 You can now either use the Find Next and Replace buttons to check each substitution one at a time or, if you're confident to do it all at once, click Replace All

5 A message tells you how many changes were made. If this number worries you at all then use the Undo button (or Ctrl + Z) and then step through the changes one at a time with the Find Next and Replace buttons

6 In the above example all instances of the word "irrigation" were made bold, red and underlined

Go To

The pop-up menu on the Find button in the Toolbar has a Go To option which summons this dialog box. It lets you jump easily to another location in the document, using a range of target options.

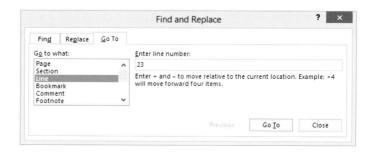

Using special characters

The Find and Replace dialog box also allows you to work with special characters such as paragraph markers or wildcards. It can even match words which sound similar to the search text.

1 Type Ctrl + F to open the dialog box and enter your search text. Click Special to see a list of special search characters

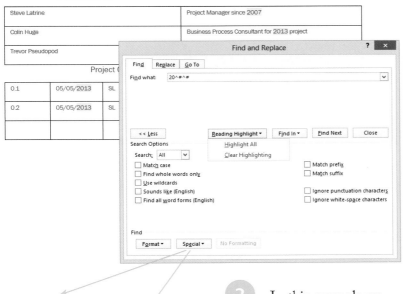

2 In this example we selected "Any Digit" twice to insert the special code "^#" into the "Find what" box. The pattern "20^#^#" tells Word to look for the literal text "20" followed immediately by any two digits. As you can see in the yellow highlight, it has found "2007", "2009" and two instances of "2013"

Hot tip

If you activate the "Use wildcards" checkbox then the Special pop-up menu contains some different options which can help make your searches very powerful. The illustration on the left shows both versions of the menu.

Advanced text effects

WordArt lets you present text using a wide range of visual effects.

Using WordArt

1 Select your text and then click on the WordArt icon in the Text area of the Insert tab

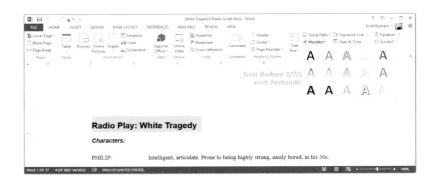

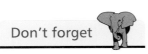

Don't forget

Initially the new WordArt object is independent of the main text, so you can easily move it by dragging. You can make it part of the main text by right-clicking, choosing Wrap Text then "In Line with Text".

2 Choose an effect from the gallery

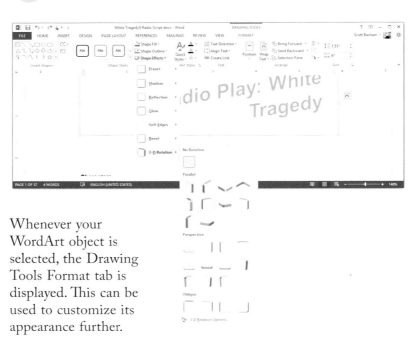

Whenever your WordArt object is selected, the Drawing Tools Format tab is displayed. This can be used to customize its appearance further.

3 There's a set of WordArt tools in the Drawing Tools/ Format tab. Click on the symbol in WordArt Styles

4 Select or change an option to see the results in your document. You can resize the text box for the new object by dragging on its corner handles, or rotate using the top handle

If you spend a lot of time creating an effect, consider saving the result to the Quick Parts Gallery – see page 85 for details on how to do this.

Creating a Drop Cap

1 Click anywhere inside a paragraph, then on the Drop Cap tool to select a Drop Cap style. This will affect the first character in the paragraph

2 The first letter becomes an object which can be resized by dragging on its handles, or reformatted as text

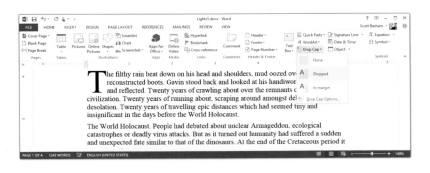

Equations and symbols

Creating and editing an equation

Equation Symbol

Symbols

1 Click the Equation icon in the Symbols area of the Insert tab, and select one of the prebuilt equations, or choose Insert New Equation to enter one manually

2 The equation appears as a new object on the page

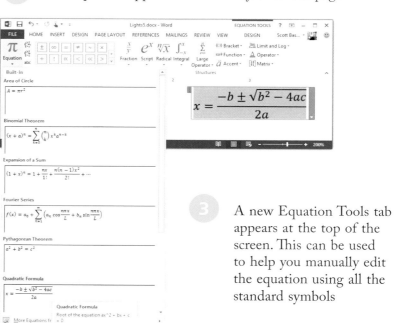

3 A new Equation Tools tab appears at the top of the screen. This can be used to help you manually edit the equation using all the standard symbols

Inserting a symbol

1 Click on the Symbol icon in the Symbols area of the Insert tab to open the pop-up menu

2 If the symbol you want is in the display of commonly-used items, simply click to insert it into your document, otherwise click on More Symbols for a larger selection

4 Structured documents

Now that we've examined a range of editing techniques it's time to look at features which make it easier to work with longer, more structured documents. Most of what we'll see is found in the Design tab of controls.

The Pages tools

The Pages area, on the left hand side of the Insert tab has three controls for working with pages.

Adding a blank page

Normally you don't need to do anything to add pages to your document – as you add text and other objects, Word automatically makes room for them by creating new pages as necessary. Sometimes, however, you may want to force Word to create a new blank page in a specific part of your document.

1   Click the Blank Page icon to add a new blank page

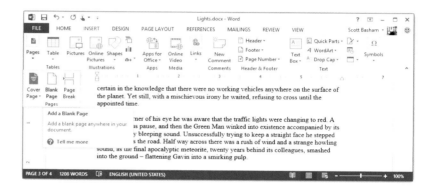

Note that in Web Layout view the concept of pages is very different, as the whole document will exist in a web browser as a single page. In this case your new blank page will show up as a few blank lines.

2   Any text before your insertion point will remain on its own before the new blank page. Any text after the insertion point will be moved after the new blank page

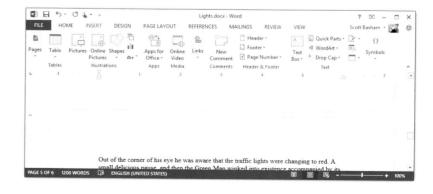

Adding a page break

1 Click the Page Break icon. Everything after the current cursor position will move to the next page

2 If the ¶ tool in the Home tab is active you'll be able to see the page break as a visible marker

Hot tip

When you're entering text you can type Ctrl + Return to insert a page break.

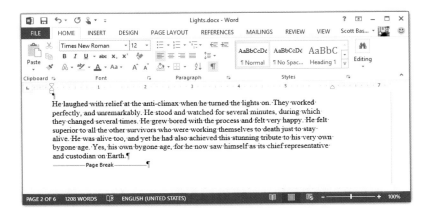

Hot tip

Like any other character, the page break can be selected and deleted if necessary.

Adding a cover page

1 Click the Cover Page icon and select from the gallery of styles available. The new page is inserted at the start

2 Select the placeholder text and type in your own

Don't forget

In this example, since you are replacing text, the original formatting is kept. This maintains the look and feel of the cover page design.

Tables and illustrations

These tools in the Design tab allow you to add graphical elements to your document. As soon as you start working with tables or pictorial items a new tab with relevant controls appears – this will be covered in detail in Chapter Five.

Always check to see which display mode you're using. If it's set to Draft or Outline then you will not see any graphical elements at all (you will see the text contained within tables but not the tables themselves). For graphical editing work you should use the Print Layout view, available from the Status bar.

Print Layout

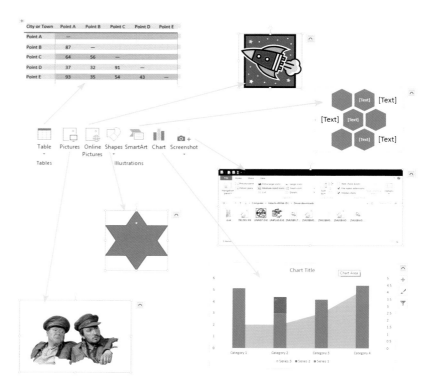

Note that some of the predesigned cover pages seen earlier contain graphic elements. If you use one of these it's possible to edit and format its pictorial components just as if you'd added them yourself.

The Links tools

This section of the Insert tab lets you add hyperlinks, bookmarks and cross-references.

Bookmarks

Defining bookmarks at key places in your document makes it easy to navigate to them, or even create hyperlinks from other areas.

Creating a bookmark

1 Navigate to the appropriate position in your document. Click on the Bookmark icon in the Links area

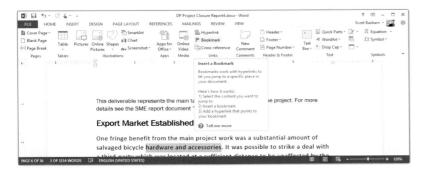

2 The Bookmark dialog box appears. Enter a name for your bookmark and click on the Add button. Note that spaces are not allowed in the name

3 You can now use the Go To dialog box to move instantly to a bookmark

Hot tip

This quickest way to get to the Go To dialog box is to type Ctrl + G.

...cont'd

Hyperlinks

A hyperlink is usually presented as colored and/or underlined text. Clicking on a hyperlink will normally transport you somewhere else – perhaps to a web page, a different document, or a different position within the current document.

Creating a hyperlink to a document on disk

1 Place your insertion point wherever you want the hyperlink to be added

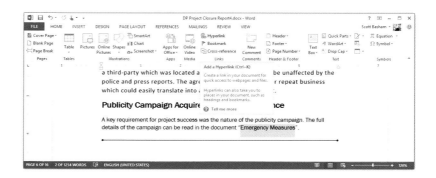

2 In the Links area of the Insert tab, click Hyperlink – or press Ctrl + K

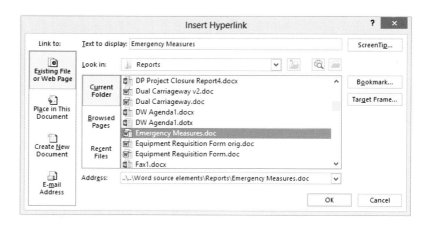

Don't forget

This hyperlinking feature works in much the same way across all Microsoft Office applications.

3 For "Link to" choose "Existing File or Web Page" and locate the desired document. Select this and click OK

The hyperlink is inserted into your document. To follow it to its destination hold down the Ctrl key and click the link.

Cross references

Sometimes you'll want your text to refer to another location, e.g. "see page 89 for more information". If you actually type in the number "89" then you'll need to go back many times to check to see if the reference has changed, perhaps because you've added more pages or edited some text. You can avoid this problem by creating automatic cross references in Word.

1 Place your insertion point wherever you want the cross reference to appear, then click the Cross Reference tool

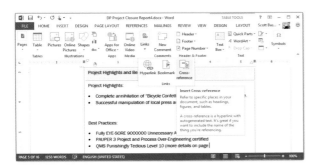

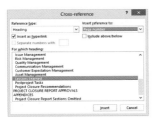

2 Choose the reference type and pick from the list of targets. Click Insert to see your reference

Hot tip

You can cross-refer to a range of possible targets including headings, bookmarks and tables.

Hot tip

In the Cross-reference dialog you can also choose the form of the reference. For example, if your reference type is a heading you might want to use the heading number, the heading text itself, or the page number.

Header   Footer   Page
▾   ▾   Number ▾

Header & Footer

Headers and footers

Headers and footers appear at the top and bottom of each page. There are built-in items available with standard designs for these.

Adding a header or footer

1   In the Header & Footer area of the Insert tab click Header or Footer as appropriate

2   Select the design you want. The header or footer will be added to your document

Editing a header or footer

1   Double-click on the header or footer to enter edit mode. A new set of Header & Footer tools will appear

Hot tip

When you're finished working with headers and footers, simply double-click in the main page area to reactivate normal editing. Alternatively, click the "Close Header and Footer" button.

2   You will now be able to edit directly in the header or footer area of the page. With the Header & Footer tools you can adjust the position of the header and footer, add graphic items, and decide whether headers and footers should be separately defined for odd and even pages (this is useful if your document will be printed double-sided)

3   There is also a Navigation area in the tab, which allows you to switch between header and footer. If your document is divided into sections then headers and footers can be defined independently for each section

Hot tip

See page 101 to learn how to divide your document into sections.

Inserting a date and time

1   Place your insertion point then click Date & Time

2   Choose from one of the formats listed in the dialog box, and then click OK

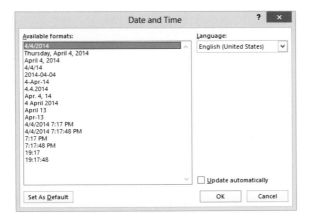

Hot tip

If you select the "Update automatically" option in this dialog then the date/time value is updated when the document is saved or printed.

3   The current system date and/or time taken from the computer clock will be inserted into the current position in your document:

4/4/2014

The Text tools

These tools in the Insert tab let you add a variety of objects.

Text Boxes

These give you a lot of freedom in positioning and formatting small amounts of text. Text can also be flowed automatically between boxes, which can help with more advanced page layouts.

Using Text Boxes, Building Blocks and Quick Parts

1 Click the Text Box icon to access the pop-up menu

Text boxes, like other shapes, can have text wrap applied to them. This is useful if you have a text-filled page – you can decide how the main text will flow around the edges of the text box. See page 120 for more on text wrap.

In the gallery that appears you see examples of Building Blocks. These are components that can be used in any document. You can define your own Building Blocks or download more from the Office.com website. Other types of Building Blocks are headers, footers, page number styles, cover pages, watermarks and equations.

 2 If you hover over a design you'll see a ToolTip with a brief explanation. Click on one of the designs to insert it into your current page

The Text Box appears on the page in whichever is the default position for this particular design.

3 To resize the Text Box drag on one of its square handles, either in the corner or half way along each edge

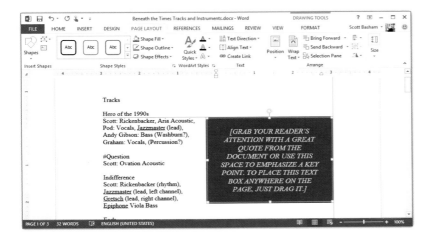

Hot tip

As you drag an object, horizontal and vertical alignment guides may appear. These are called alignment guides – see page 123 for more on how to activate these.

4 If you want to move the Text Box, then drag somewhere on its edge but not on any of its handles

5 The Text Box comes with some sample dummy text. Select this and enter your own

6 You can change the appearance of the text, or the box itself using the controls in the Home tab or the Quick Access Toolbar

7 If you've enhanced or changed the design and would like to reuse it later on, make sure the Insert tab is active, click on the Quick Parts tool and choose "Save Selection to Quick Part Gallery..." Give your design a name then click OK

Creating a Text Box manually

1 Make sure the Insert tab is active. Click the Text Box icon and choose Draw Text Box

2 Drag a rectangular area to define the box perimeter

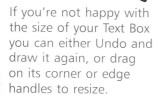

3 Click inside to enter the text within the box. You can use all the normal editing and formatting controls, and the techniques you learned in earlier chapters

4 When the Text Box is selected the Format Tab will be available. You can use this to control the line and fill style of the box, as well as to change the layering (using "Bring to Front" and "Send to Back") or to apply effects such as shadowing or 3D boxes

Sometimes the box may be too small for your text. If this happens you can either increase the box size, reduce the text size, or create more boxes and link them using text flow. We'll see how to use text flow next.

Flowing text between boxes

1 Locate a Text Box that has too much text to display within its defined area

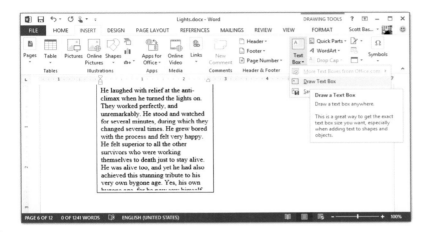

Text flow works not just on Text Boxes, but on any shapes that are capable of containing text. See Chapter Five for more details.

2 Click on the Text Box icon in the Toolbar and, in the popup menu which appears, choose Draw Text Box

3 Click and drag to define the second Text Box

4 Select the first Text Box and make sure the Format tab is visible. Click the Create Link button

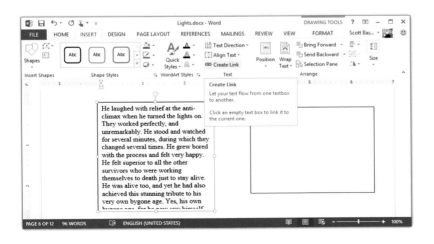

Hot tip

You can reverse this operation by selecting the first Text Box and then clicking on Break Link. All the text will be moved back into the first box. You will now need to edit the text, change its size, or change the size of the Text Box to see all the text once more.

5 Now click anywhere within the second Text Box. The text that didn't fit into the first box will automatically flow into the second

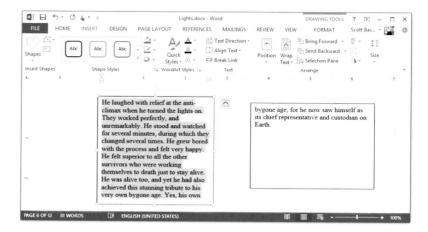

6 If there is still too much text, or if you decide to add more text, you can repeat this process to create a longer sequence of Text Boxes with the same text continuously threaded through them

7 The text remains linked, so changing the size and shape of any box will automatically cause the text to reflow

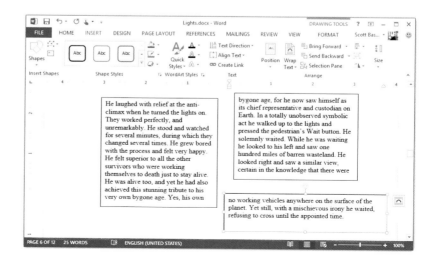

Creating your own Building Blocks

As we saw a few pages ago, you can select any text or other objects within Word and make these into new Building Blocks.

1 Create and format the content which will become your new Building Block

2 Select your content, then click Quick Parts and select "Save Selection to Quick Part Gallery"

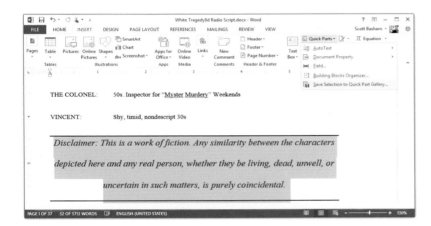

3 The Create New Building Block dialog box appears. Enter a name and select a gallery to use (in most cases this should be the Quick Parts Gallery)

4 Choose a category and enter a text description

5 Next choose the Word template that will store the building block. If you select "Building Blocks.dotx" then the building block will be available to all documents

6 The Options available are "Insert content only", "Insert content in its own paragraph" and "Insert content in its own page". Choose the appropriate option and then click OK. Your Building Block is now installed and ready for you to use from the Quick Parts icon

Using your own Building Blocks

Once you have created your own Building Blocks you can use them in the same way as the others.

1 Navigate to the part of your document where you want to add your Building Block and click an insertion point

2 Click the Quick Parts button and select your Building Block from its gallery. It will be added at the current position

Editing an existing Building Block

If you have an example of a Building Block somewhere in your document, then you can edit this and reattach it to the gallery.

1 Make the necessary changes to the content, then select it

2 Click the Quick Parts button and make a careful note of the name of the Building Block you're planning to edit

3 Click on Quick Parts and choose "Save Selection to Quick Parts Gallery..."

4 If you enter exactly the same name and gallery as before then the original Building Block's definition will be overwritten

Don't forget

To replace an existing Building Block, you must enter precisely the same name in the Create New Building Block dialog.

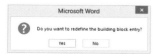

The Building Blocks Organizer

Building Blocks can be very flexible, and there are many different types. In this chapter we have seen tools such as Cover Page, Header, Footer, Page Number, Text Box and the more general Quick Parts. Each of these has its own gallery containing a particular type of Building Block. Here we'll see how to manage all these objects in one place.

Don't forget

The Quick Parts tool is in the Insert tab, as are most of the tools covered in this chapter.

1 Click on the Quick Parts tool and choose Building Blocks Organizer to see this dialog box

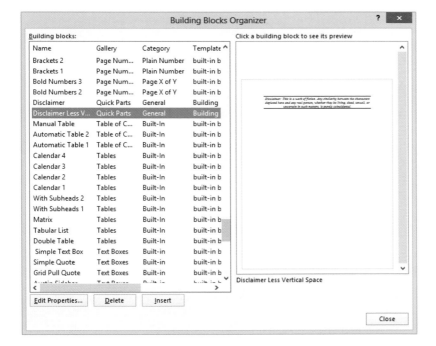

2 If you scroll down through the predesigned elements you should be able to find Quick Parts objects you created yourself. Click Edit Properties... to change an item's attributes

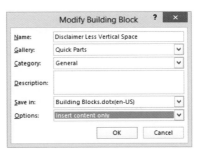

Hot tip

If you previously saved a customized text box as a Quick Part you might want to use this dialog box to change its Gallery attribute to Text Boxes. It'll then appear directly in the pop-up menu which you see when you click on the Text Box tool.

Tables

Tables allow you to organize and manage text in rows and columns. They provide a more visual way of working than you would have with normal text formatted via tab stops.

Inserting a table

Click on the Table icon in the Insert tab

In the grid that appears, click and drag to define an initial table size. Don't worry too much about getting this right first time, as it's easy to change size later on

Hot tip

If you already have some text formatted using tab characters, then it's easy to convert this to a table automatically. To do this select the text, click the Table icon and choose "Convert Text to Table".

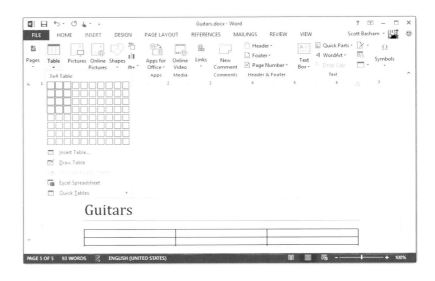

Alternatively, if you click the Table icon and then choose Insert Table from the submenu, this dialog box appears. You can then specify the table dimensions numerically. Click OK to go ahead and create the table

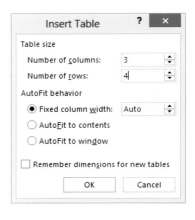

Resizing a table

1 Click and drag on the boundary between rows or columns to resize them. Your insertion point will turn into a double-headed arrow as you do this

Drawing a table

You may prefer to use the table drawing tool to create tables. This gives you more flexibility, particularly when you're trying to create irregularly-shaped tables.

1 Click the Table icon and choose Draw Table

2 Click and drag to draw a rectangle which defines the overall table size

The rectangle you drew represents the table perimeter. Your next task is to draw in the rows and columns. The special Table Tools/Layout tab is automatically activated and its Draw Table tool is selected ready for you to start work.

Insert Table

⊞ Insert Table...

📝 Draw Table

▤ Convert Text to Table...

🗷 Excel Spreadsheet

⊞ Quick Tables ▶

Draw Table   Eraser

Draw

3 Click and drag horizontally across the table to draw in the rows. As you drag, a dotted or red line appears, giving you a preview of the new line. If you accidentally draw the line in the wrong place simply use Ctrl + Z to undo and then try again

Don't forget

All these features are still available to you even after you add text into the cells of your table. Sometimes it's useful to see how much text you need before you finalize the table's dimensions.

4 Now drag vertically to draw in the column boundaries

5 You can even drag diagonally to create a new line that will divide cells in two, as in the example below

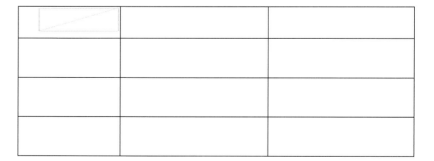

Note that if you drag from inside to an area outside of the table, then the table will be extended automatically. However, if you begin and end dragging completely outside the table then a new independent table will be created.

6 Sometimes you will want to remove lines to create an irregular table where some of the cells are much larger. To do this select the Eraser tool and then click directly on the part of the line you wish to remove

A single click will normally remove the shortest segment at the current mouse position.

If you want to remove larger sections of a line, or even a whole line, then click and drag over the desired area.

7 Once you have erased a fairly large area switch back to the Draw Table tool. You can now add in more lines to this area

8 In the example below you can see how flexible this technique is, allowing for a complex patchwork of odd-sized cells to be created

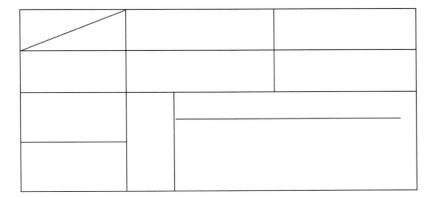

Table cells are normally filled with text, and can have their background shaded and different line styles applied. It's also possible to place other items such as graphics inside a table cell.

...cont'd

Formatting your table

You can use all the formatting techniques learned in earlier chapters on your table text. Often you will start by dragging across an entire row or column to select it prior to formatting.

Name	Type	Price
Rickenbacker 330	Hollow Body Electric	$1871.00
Epiphone Viola	Bass	$499.99
Squire Telecaster	Solid Electric	$283.65

Inserting and deleting rows or columns

1. To insert a row, first select an existing row either just above or just below the place where you want to position the new line

2. To the left of the row, a circular icon with a plus sign inside will appear. Click this icon, and the new row will appear in the desired position

Guitars

Name	Type	Price
Rickenbacker 330	Hollow Body Electric	$1871.00
Epiphone Viola	Bass	$499.99
Squire Telecaster	Solid Electric	$283.65

3. To insert additional rows, keep clicking on the icon

4. To add multiple rows in a single action, first click and drag to select the number of rows you wish to add. When you click the circular icon Word will add this number of rows

5. You can add columns in a similar way. Select one or more columns then move your mouse to the top left, or top right of the area you've selected. The circular Add icon will appear, allowing you to add in the columns

Merging cells

Each cell can contain text that is formatted and aligned independently of other cell text (if desired). Sometimes it's useful to group or merge cells together so that they behave as a single cell.

1 Select the cells you wish to merge. Note that these must be next to each other

2 Right-click and choose Merge Cells

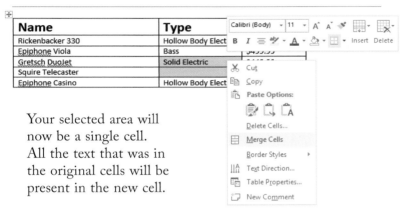

Your selected area will now be a single cell. All the text that was in the original cells will be present in the new cell.

3 Select the new cell, then make sure the Layout tab in the Table Tools is active. In the Alignment area choose Align Center. Note that the centering acts across the whole area, so it really is behaving as if it were a single cell

Table Properties

From the Cell page of the Table Properties dialog you have individual control over the vertical alignment of text within each cell. Horizontal text alignment can be controlled via the Paragraph area in the Home tab, or both together from the Alignment area of the Table Tools Layout tab.

1. Make sure your insertion point is somewhere inside the table (or select part or all of the table), right-click and then choose Table Properties

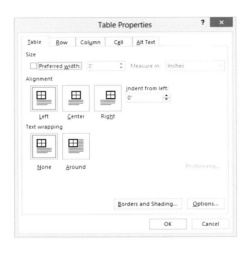

From this dialog box you can define properties for the entire table, or at the row, column or cell level.

You can also use the "Borders and Shading..." button to set the visual properties for the whole table.

Table styles

1. Select, or click within, your table to make sure the Table Tools tab is active. Make sure the Design sub-tab is selected and look for the area named Table Styles. As you hover over each style you'll see a preview of your table

2. Click on the style to apply it permanently to your table

Word 2013 includes a wider selection of preset table styles, helping you to quickly apply an effective design without spending hours fiddling with formatting settings.

94

The Table Design controls

1 Click anywhere in your table and make sure the Table Tools Design tab is active

2 Select one or more cells to apply background colors via the Shading icon

3 Choose a Border Style to activate the Border Painter. This turns your cursor into a paintbrush which you can use to change the border style of any lines in your table

The Table Layout controls
If you activate the Layout controls you'll see that there are tools for operations on tables, rows, columns and individual cells.

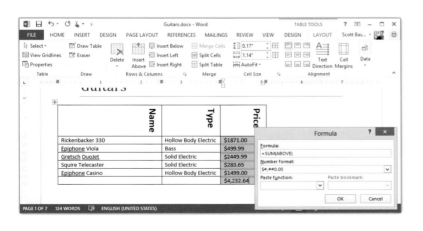

In this example the Formula button was used to calculate the sum of the values in the cells above the one selected

Hot tip

Many of the features in the Table Layout controls are also present in the pop-up menu when you right click within a table.

Themes

Themes can control your overall document design by defining its main colors, fonts and effects. If you use a Theme's colors, for example, then changing Theme will change these automatically.

Selecting a Theme

Themes

1   Make sure the Design tab is active

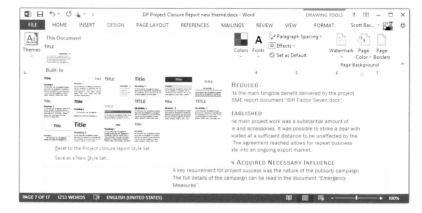

96

2   Click the Themes button and browse through the Themes in the Gallery. As you hover over a Theme your document will preview its settings. Click once to set the Theme

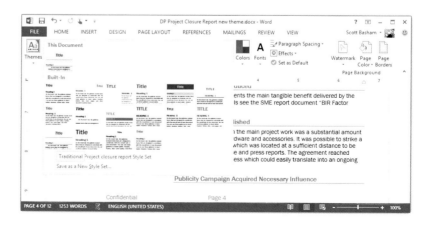

3   All aspects of the document under Theme control will be updated to reflect your choice

Using a Theme's colors

1. To change just the colors that belong to the Theme, click on the Theme Colors icon in the Themes area. A gallery of color swatches appears

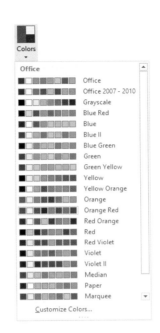

2. Choose a different option. If your document used Theme colors then these will be changed automatically

3. From now on, whenever you select a color you will be able to choose one from the Theme's current selection

Using a Theme's effects

1. You can also change a Theme's effects independently of its fonts and colors. To do this, click on the Effects button in the Themes area and select a different option

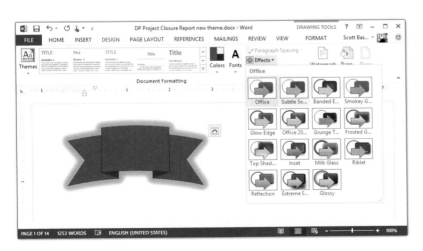

...cont'd

Using a Theme's fonts

1 Make sure the Design tab is active, then click on Fonts in the Document Formatting area. Each option contains one font for headings, and a second one for main body text

2 Choose a different option. If your document used Theme fonts then these will be changed automatically

3 Now switch back to the Home tab and open the Fonts menu. At the top you will see the two Theme fonts. If you use these you can easily switch Themes later – your text will change accordingly

4 It's a very good idea to make sure your text styles are defined using Theme fonts – if your document uses those styles throughout then it's very easy to experiment with different designs

Page Setup

This set of tools includes controls for margins, size and orientation as well as line numbering, adding breaks, and hyphenation.

Margins and columns

1 Click the Page Layout tab. In the Page Setup area click on the Margins icon to choose from the gallery, or click Custom Margins to define these via a dialog box

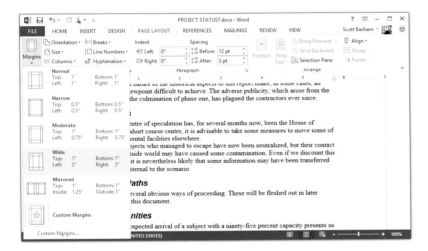

2 By default, your text is set out in a single column spread across the page. To change to a multi-column layout click the Columns icon and choose the number you want. Your text will be reformatted in the new layout

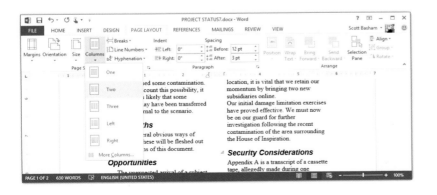

Breaks

Different types of break

At the start of this chapter we saw how to add a simple page break. The Page Layout tab also has a tool for this, but it's much more powerful.

1. Position your insertion point then click the Breaks tool

2. As you can see there's a number of different options. To help organize our document we'll create a section break – choose the Continuous type

3. At first sight nothing seems to change. However, if you click on the ¶ tool in the Home tab you'll see the break

4. Now click in the text after the break and change the number of columns. Note that this affects just the current section, i.e. the text after the break

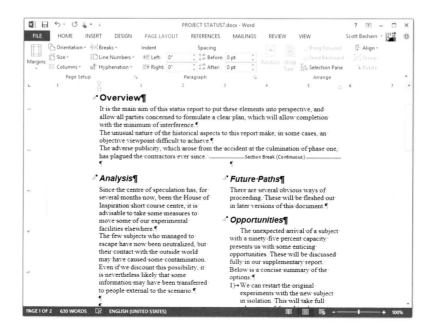

Sections

Dividing a document into sections

It's useful to divide your document into sections using the Next Page section break, so that the next section starts on a new page. This helps organise your work, and different sections can have their own page numbering, plus different headers and footers.

1 Divide your document into sections by clicking the Breaks tool and choosing a Section break. On the first page after a section break, double-click anywhere within the footer to see the Header and Footer Tools

2 Click the Link To Previous icon to deactivate it. You can now set a different footer for this Section

3 If you have an automatic page number, then right-click on it and choose Format Page Numbers

4 Change the Page Numbering option to restart at page 1

Hot tip

It's worth spending some time customizing each section. In this example the footer text in the new section has been changed. Note that the previous Footer is "Overview, page 38" while the current one is "Essential Information, page 1".

Line numbers

You can add line numbers to your whole document or to sections, and you can also switch this on and off for individual paragraphs.

1. Either select your whole document or just click within a section, depending on where you'd like line numbering

2. Click on Line Numbers and select an option

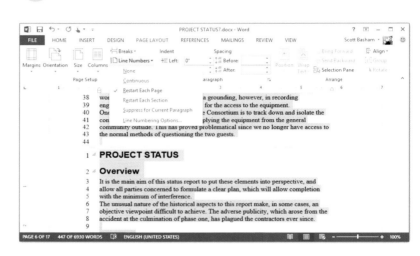

The Page Setup dialog

1. Click on the small ⌐ icon in the lower right corner of the Page Setup tools area

2. This dialog box contains controls for adjusting the margins and page orientation as well as advanced settings for setting multiple pages per printed sheet

3. Click the Paper tab to define the size and printing options

4. The Layout tab lets you make settings for either the whole document or individual sections. You can also access line numbering and border options

Hyphenation

Word can automatically hyphenate your text for you. This can allow more text to fit on the page, particularly if lines of text are not very long. You can also choose manual hyphenation, where Word will prompt you for each potential instance. Hyphenation is more useful when you are working with a layout that uses many columns such as a magazine or newspaper design.

Hot tip

Click the Hyphenation tool and choose Hyphenation Options... to see the following dialog box. This gives you finer control over exactly how much hyphenation takes place.

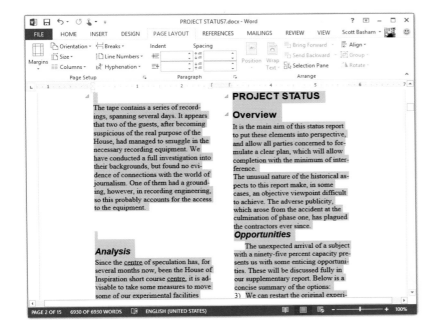

Watermark Page Page
         Color ▾ Borders
Page Background

Page design

These controls can be found at the right side of the Design tab.

Watermark

1 Click on the Watermark icon and either choose one of the preset designs or click on Custom Watermark…

2 From this dialog box you can either use your own text or a graphic. For text click on the option "Text watermark", for a graphic click on "Picture watermark" and locate the appropriate file

Hot tip

To delete the watermark click on the Watermark icon and select Remove Watermark.

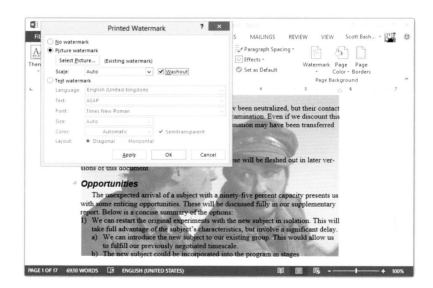

3 Choose a scale – Auto is probably best if you want to fill the entire page

4 It's usually a good idea to select Washout. This lightens the image considerably, which means that the page's text and other elements will still be easy to read

Page color

1 In the Design tab click on the Page Color icon and choose a color from the range of defined Theme Colors

2 For a more interesting effect click the Page Color icon and choose Fill Effects...

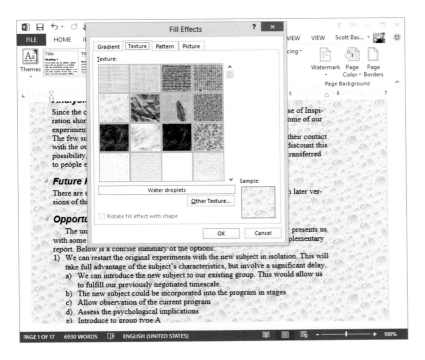

3 From this dialog you can choose a gradient (where one color slowly changes into another), a texture, a pattern or even a picture from a file on disk

4 In this example the "Water droplets" texture was chosen. A texture is a small image which is repeated across and down to fill the page. A well-designed texture will join or "tile" seamlessly, so that it's impossible to see exactly where one tile begins and another ends. If you're able to design your own texture (perhaps in a dedicated graphics program) then click Other Texture and locate its file

Page borders

Word gives you a range of options for adding borders to the edges of your page.

1 Click on the Page Borders icon in the Design tab

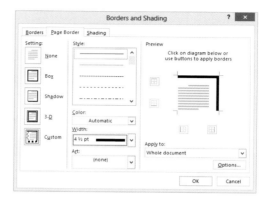

2 Choose your setting and experiment with the line style, color and width. The Art pop-up lets you select from a range of graphic designs. As you work, the Preview section on the right will give you some visual feedback

Hot tip

The Shading tab in this dialog box allows you to apply a background shading to the current paragraph.

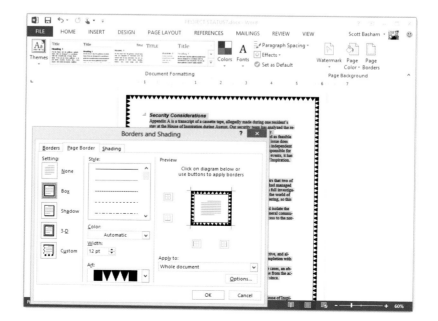

5 Pictures and graphics

This chapter looks at Word's graphical features, from photos and video through to charts, diagrams and screenshots.

Pictures

The Illustrations area

The Illustrations area of the Insert tab allows you to add a range of different graphical objects.

108

Adding a photo from a file on disk

In this example we'll import an image created by a digital camera. We'll assume that we have some photo files available on the hard disk or other storage medium.

1   Navigate to the appropriate part of your document, then click on Picture in the Illustrations area of the Insert tab

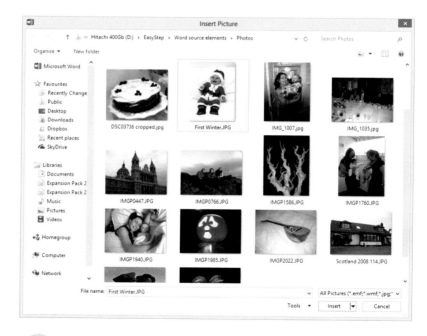

2   Use the standard Windows controls at the top and the left of the dialog box to locate the photo files

3   Once you have found the image you want, select it and then click the Insert button

④ The image is brought into the current page. Note that it has eight square "handles", which can be dragged around if you want to manipulate the image

Drag the circular arrow icon to rotate the image; any other handle will resize it

Drag directly on an edge (not on a handle) to move without resizing

⑤ Sometimes you'll want to cut away unnecessary parts of the picture. Click on the Crop tool and you'll see some heavy black corners and edges. Dragging inwards on these will prepare the image for cropping

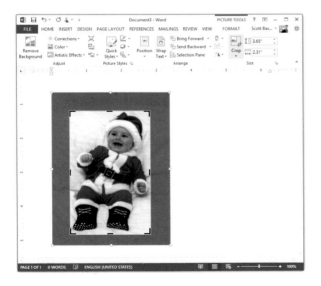

⑥ When you're happy with your adjustments click on the Crop tool again and choose Crop to apply the changes. If you change your mind later simply reselect Crop and drag the black handles outwards again

Remove Background

If your photo has a prominent main object which is easily distinguishable from its background, then you can get help from Word to remove the background automatically.

1 Select the photo then click the Remove Background tool in the Adjust area of the Picture Tools Format tab

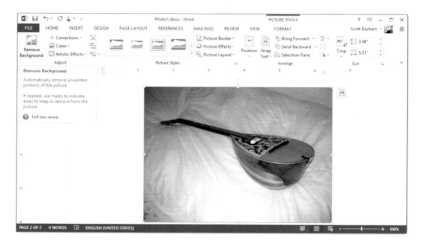

2 The magenta-colored area indicates Word's guess at what is the background. If it hasn't got it quite right then use the "Mark Areas to Keep" and "Mark Areas to Remove" tools to subtract from or add to the magenta area

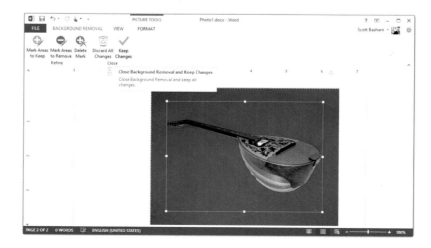

...cont'd

3 When you're satisfied that the correct area is defined, click the Keep Changes icon and the background will be removed

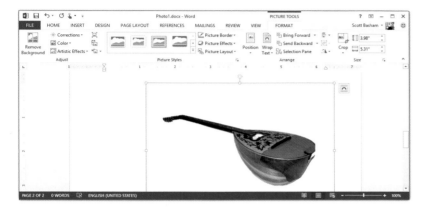

Don't forget

Most of the tools described here are in the Picture Tools/Format tab. If you select a picture, the tab, although available, may not be currently active. In this case simply click on the tab title (depicted below) to select it.

PICTURE TOOLS
FORMAT

111

Photo corrections

Although Word isn't a fully-blown photo manipulation package, it does have a range of tools for both creative and corrective work

1 Select the photo and click the Corrections tool

2 The pop-up menu contains options for sharpening/ softening and for adjusting brightness and contrast. If you hover over an option you'll see a preview of the effect

The Adjust tools

There are some useful tools in the Adjust area of the Picture Tools/Format tab, although three don't have captions

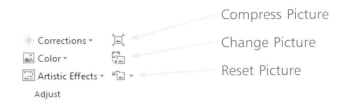

Compress Picture gives you the opportunity to reduce the file size used for your image (and consequently reduce upload and download time if copying across the web or via email). You can do this by permanently removing cropped-out areas, or by changing the detail level (resolution).

Change Picture lets you substitute in a new picture file, whilst preserving the attributes such as size and crop information.

Reset Picture removes all the formatting, effectively returning the image to how it was when first imported.

Picture styles

The Picture Styles area lets you easily apply a wide range of visually-interesting effects such as shadow, glow, reflection, rotation or a combination of these in a preset style.

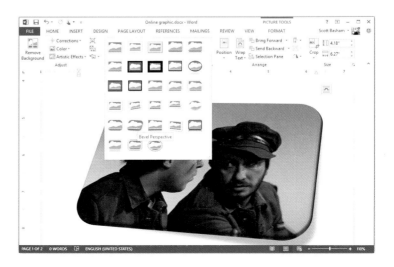

The Format Picture pane

As well as the tools in the Format tab, there is a task pane window which gives you more control over your picture settings.

1 Select the photo and click the Picture Effects button

2 Choose Shadow then Shadow Options... The Format Picture task pane will appear with its Shadow tab active

Scroll down the Format Picture pane to see a wide range of controls. Use the small black triangles to reveal and hide settings.

Hot tip

The Format task pane's controls will change to reflect what is currently selected. If, for example, you select some text then it turns into a Format Text Effects panel.

Don't forget

Side panels can be undocked, simply by dragging on their title away from the current position. Once free from the main window, they can be positioned and resized easily. To re-dock simply drag onto the left or right side of the tabbed controls area.

Online pictures

Accessing elements from online services

Word can access pictures from a variety of online sources, including services such as SkyDrive, Flickr, Facebook and Twitter.

1 Go to the File tab, and click on Account

The Connected Services are associated with your Microsoft login. This is normally the account used for logging in to Windows (if you're running Windows 8 or above). Within Word you can log in explicitly or switch the login user by clicking on the small downward pointing arrow beside the current login name (located in the top right corner of the main screen).

2 You can see your list of Connected Services on the left side of the dialog which appears

3 Click the "Add a service" button to see the options. If you use Flickr, for example, you can link your account so that Word is able to import directly from your online set of photographs or pictures

4 If you need to add a service, make sure you have your login details to hand, and then click on the service you wish to add. For Microsoft services such as SkyDrive or Office 365 SharePoint you may find the service has already been added for you automatically

5 If you're happy with the Connected Services, return to the main editing screen by clicking on the white arrow in the top left corner: ⬅

Importing online pictures

Once your services are set up, it is easy to import pictures.

1 Move your insertion point to the place in your document where you'd like to put the picture. Note you don't need to get this exactly right as it's very easy to move your imported pictures later on

2 Go to the Insert tab, and click the Online Pictures icon

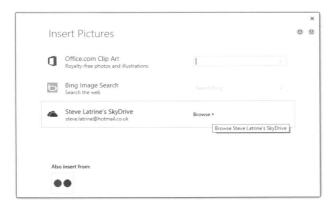

3 Choose the picture source. In this example we've clicked on the Browse button for the SkyDrive service

4 You will see a preview of the available images. Make your selection and then click Insert

5 The picture is imported into the current position. It can now be manipulated just like the photos you brought in from local disk file earlier

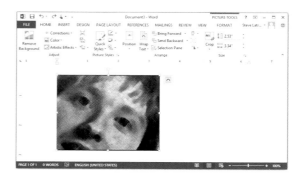

6 In this second example look for some standard ClipArt. Click on Online Pictures then enter some search text in the Office.com Clip Art section

7 If there are matching images, then you'll see them presented as a scrolling list. Select then click Insert

Adding a draw-type picture from a file on disk

In this example we'll import and manipulate a draw-type object.

Pictures

1 Navigate to the appropriate part of your document, then click on Pictures in the Illustrations area in the Insert tab

2 Once you've found a suitable draw-type graphic select it and then click the Insert button

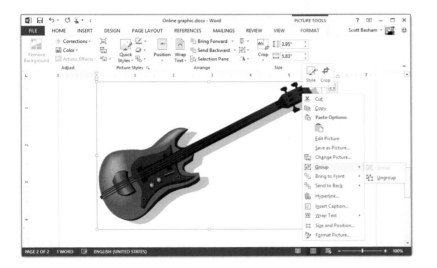

Don't forget

Draw-type graphics can generally be edited with no appreciable loss in quality, as they are stored as a set of mathematical objects. Using the Online Pictures button try searching the Microsoft clipart, as in the previous example, with "WMF" in the search criteria. This stands for Windows MetaFile, and is a widely-used standard for draw-type graphics.

3 If the graphic consists of a number of shapes, then it's usually possible to edit its individual components. To do this right-click to access the pop-up menu. Click on Group to see a sub-menu and select Ungroup

4 If you see the dialog box pictured above click Yes

117

5 Often this will be sufficient for you to start editing individual elements. Experiment by clicking on different areas of the graphic to see what you can select. Once an element is selected it can usually be moved, resized, rotated or formatted using color or line styles

Beware

Paint-type graphics cannot be manipulated in this way. They are represented as a grid of rectangular pixels (picture cells) rather than mathematical objects. This means they cannot be broken down into simpler objects.

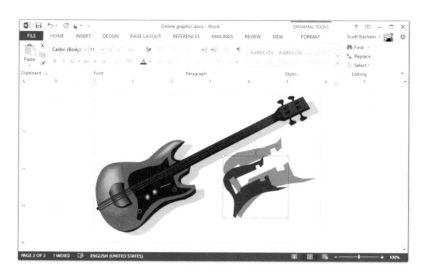

6 Sometimes a draw-type graphic consists of items that are grouped together. If it does you can break it down further by right-clicking and choosing Grouping and then Ungroup

7 The graphic is now split into a set of smaller objects

8 Experiment by editing one or two objects. You can use the Format Tab to apply new borders, color or styles

Hot tip

The easiest way to select all the objects within the general graphics frame is to click on one (to establish selection within the frame) then type Ctrl + A for Select All.

9 When you have finished you might want to select all the small objects then right-click, choose Group and select Group from the sub-menu. The graphic will behave as a single item once more

Shapes

Word offers a large selection of standard graphic shapes that can be drawn and then customized.

1 Click on the Shapes icon in the Insert tab. A gallery of standard shapes appears

2 Select one of these. This example uses "Down Arrow Callout"

3 Now click and drag diagonally on the page to create the initial shape. Don't worry if it's the wrong size or position, as both of these can be changed easily

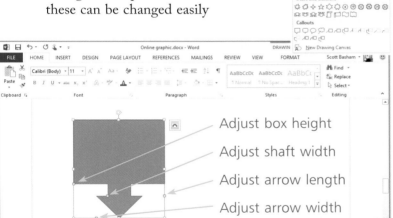

Adjust box height
Adjust shaft width
Adjust arrow length
Adjust arrow width

4 You can move the object by dragging directly on it. Drag on a white square handle (corner or edge) to resize it

5 Drag on a yellow square handle to change a single aspect of the shape. Precisely what this changes depends on the shape you drew, so it's worth experimenting to see what you can do in each case. In the above example the yellow handles let you customize the dimensions of the box and the arrow part individually

Don't forget

Since Shapes are draw-type graphics you can resize and manipulate them in other ways without any loss in quality.

Hot tip

Right-click on a shape and choose edit points. You'll then be able to change the shape by dragging its vertices. Click and drag along a line to add a new point. Right-click a point to choose between Smooth, Straight or Corner.

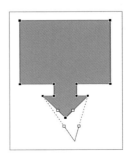

Layout options

Hot tip

The Layout Options icon appears to the top right of any object you select, and provides a quick way of controlling how it interacts with its surroundings.

1 Select any object and then click on the Layout Options icon ⌐ to see the following settings

2 If your object overlaps text you may be interested in text wrap. "Tight" is sometimes all you need for the surrounding text to closely follow the contours of the shape

3 Right-click on the object and a menu will appear. Choose Wrap Text then Edit Wrap Points. You'll then see the text wrap border defined as straight black lines connected by small black squares which work as handles

Hot tip

The Arrange Tools on the right of the Format tab can be used to align objects, and move them in front of or behind other objects.

4 Drag one of these handles to move the boundary line. If there's text nearby then you'll see it move so that it's always outside the perimeter

Hot tip

To delete a text wrap handle hold down the Ctrl key and click directly on the handle.

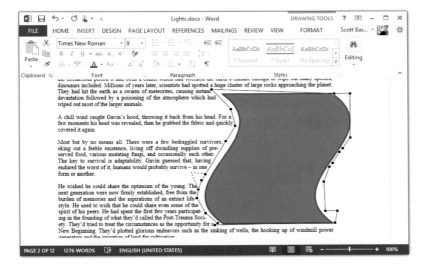

5 Click and drag on the border, but not on an existing handle, to create a new handle. Using these controls you can alter the way text flows around any irregular shape

6 If you click on an object's Layout Options icon then choose "See more..." Word will show you a dialog which gives you more numeric control over position, text wrapping and size. Some of these options are also available from the Page Layout and Format tabs

Adding text inside a shape

Most shapes can be used as text boxes, and all the normal text formatting options are available within these.

1 If there's currently no text in the shape, then right-click and choose Add Text

2 Enter the text (or paste from the Clipboard)

3 Format using the Mini Toolbar or the other tools

4 You can still apply effects to the shape itself. If you rotate, for example, the text will rotate as well (when you edit the text it will temporarily switch back to horizontal so you can easily read what you are trying to change)

Text within a shape can be formatted using the same controls as those you would use for ordinary text. Sometimes it is easier to prepare the text elsewhere and then copy it to the clipboard. This is a good idea if the shape is irregular or otherwise difficult to use for text editing.

Canvas objects

When you ungroup a complex object it will by default become a series of smaller items within a rectangular canvas object. You can move the whole thing or set layout options by clicking on the canvas border, or manipulate the individual items inside by selecting them in the normal way.

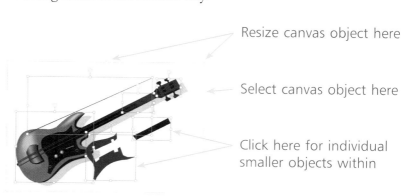

Resize canvas object here

Select canvas object here

Click here for individual smaller objects within

Controlling layout

Alignment guides

1 Go to the Page Layout tab, click Align and make sure Use Alignment Guides is selected

2 Move an object to see temporary vertical and horizontal guides – these assist with alignment to other objects

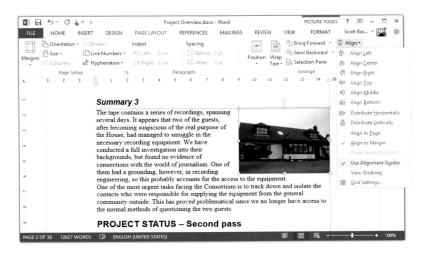

Live layout

Word 2013 introduces a real-time preview of your document as you move, resize or rotate a picture – so you can see exactly the effect of your changes without any delay.

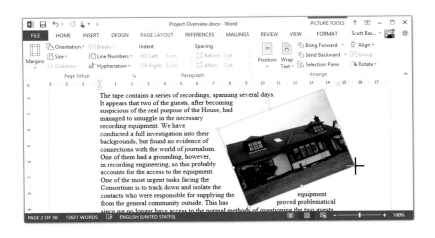

Video

As long as your machine is online, you can now easily add video to your documents, from a variety of sources.

1 Click on the Online Video icon in the Media area of the Insert tab

2 The Insert Video dialog box appears. Either click to run a Bing Video Search or copy an embed code from a web-based site such as YouTube

3 The Video object is inserted at the current location. You can move, resize, or play by clicking the white triangle

SmartArt

SmartArt graphic items allow you to present concepts and information in a visual way.

1 Click on the SmartArt icon in the Insert tab. The following dialog box appears. Choose an item and click OK

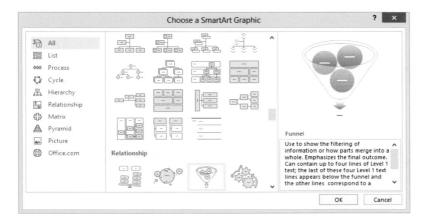

2 Click on Text Pane in the Create Graphic area of the Design tab to make it visible. Enter your text in the window on the left, and it will appear in the diagram

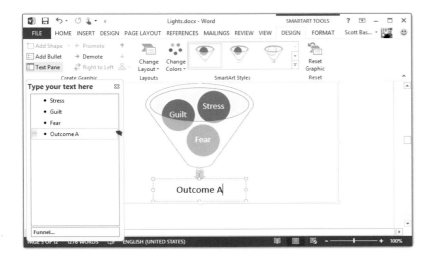

Hot tip

You can radically change your design at any time by changing the selection from the Layouts and SmartArt Styles in the Design tab.

3 You can work on parts of the object by selecting individual items and then editing

The SmartArt tools
Whenever SmartArt objects are selected the SmartArt Tools appear, divided into two tabs: Design and Format.

1. In the Design tab make sure the text pane is activated by clicking on the icon. This lets you edit the text easily. You can use the Tab key to add indented items

Don't forget

SmartArt objects are ways of presenting text lists in graphical form. Often you'll edit the text directly on the object, but sometimes it's useful to view and change it in the separate text pane.

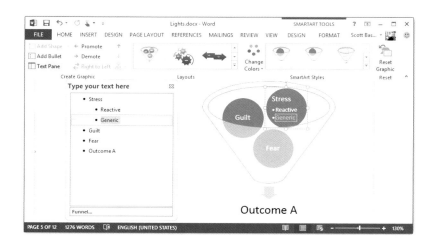

2. Activate the Format tab to experiment with different visual effects. Depending on what you select, these controls can apply to the whole object or individual parts

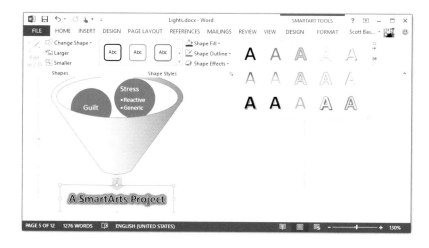

Charts

If you've used Microsoft Excel you may be familiar with the concept of presenting tables of figures in chart form.

1 Click on the Chart icon in the Insert tab. The following dialog appears, with a large selection of chart variants:

2 Choose a chart type and click OK

3 A default chart appears. You can select and customize this using the Chart Tools tab, which appears automatically

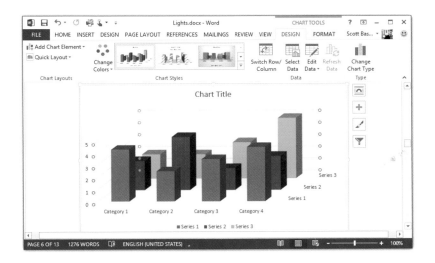

A separate window opens displaying some sample chart data. You can edit this so that the chart uses your own text and figures.

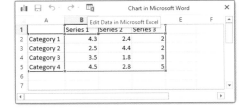

Don't forget

If you don't like the chart type you selected it's easy to go back and select another, so enjoy the freedom to experiment.

Hot tip

If Excel is installed on your machine you can click the "Edit Data in Microsoft Excel" button to access its full range of features.

Screenshots

Many technical and training documents make use of screenshots, which are images taken directly from the computer screen, perhaps demonstrating a particular task within a program. Some people use the PrtScn key, which places an image of the entire current screen in the Clipboard (Alt + PrtScn snapshots just the currently-selected window). Since this functionality is rather limited, others might use special utility software. However, there's also support for doing this directly within Word.

1 Click on the Screenshot icon in the Insert tab. The pop-up will show you the thumbnails of the current windows – either choose one of these or Screen Clipping

Hot tip

If you choose Screen Clipping then you'll be able to click and drag to define a rectangular area to crop within the screen display area.

128

2 The screenshot is inserted as a picture into your document. Note this is a bitmap (rather than a draw-type) graphic so be careful if you plan to resize it. If you increase its size too much then the image will become "blocky" with the pixels clearly visible

3 Repeat the process if you need to include a series of screenshots

6 Document views

Here we'll look at five different ways of viewing your document, plus some additional viewing features.

Read Mode

Word 2013 has a greatly-enhanced Read Mode, which is best if you're viewing (rather than writing or editing) a document.

Activating Read Mode

Don't forget

In Read Mode Word reformats the entire document to make the best use of the available screen space. Material is organized into screens rather than pages, so a break between pages may not be in the same place as a break between screens.

1. Make sure the Read Mode icon (shaped like a book) in the Status bar is selected

Hot tip

Read Mode is ideal when working with a tablet or touchscreen-enabled machine, as the left and right arrow icons are easy to operate with your finger. You can also use a swipe left or swipe right gesture to move through the document.

2. Use the left and right arrow icons to move between screens, or the scroll bar at the bottom

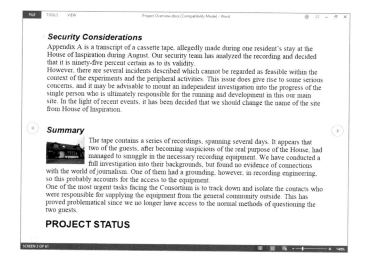

Hot tip

In Read Mode you can type a number then press Enter to jump immediately to that page, e.g. 6 + Enter to move to page 6.

3   There is a Reading Toolbar in the top-right corner. As well as the usual minimize, maximize and restore controls, you can also click ⊞ to auto-hide the toolbar and menus. This maximizes screen space, as in the example below

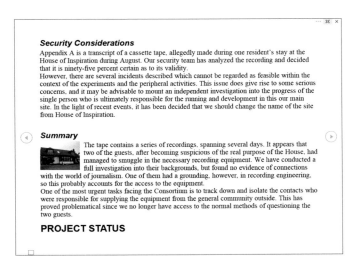

4   Pictures will normally be displayed at a small size so you can concentrate on reading. Double-clicking with the mouse, or a double tap on a touchscreen will enlarge an image. Tap or click elsewhere to return to normal

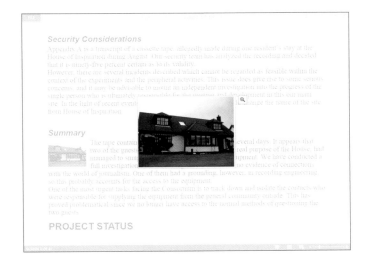

5 If you close and then later reopen your document, Word remembers the location, so that you can carry on reading from where you left off. To do this, click on the message which automatically appears

Welcome back!
Pick up where you left off:

Summary
4 minutes ago

6 If you select and then right-click (or double-tap on a touchscreen) then you'll see a pop-up menu of useful options including looking up a word's definition, translating text, or performing a web search. You can also add comments or highlights

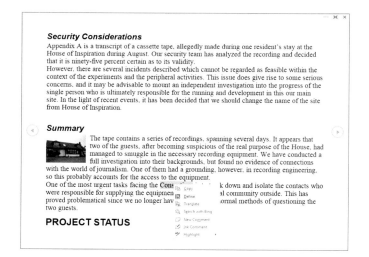

7 You can use the zoom slider in the bottom right corner to scale the text anywhere from 100-300% in size

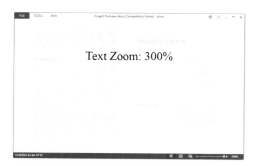

Accessing the other views

As you've seen already, you can use the View icons in the Status bar to switch views. However, this only gives you access to the three main views: Read Mode, Print Layout and Web Layout. There are two other views: Outline and Draft. To access any of the five views you need to go to the View tab.

Print Layout View

1 Go to the View tab and select Print Layout from the Views area, or click on the Print Layout icon in the Status bar

2 This is the best view for general work as it gives you the full range of editing controls, together with a very accurate preview of how everything will look when printed. Scroll through your document and make some changes

3 Temporarily switch to Read Mode to see how both the display and the available controls change

4 When you save your document, Word will make a note of which of the main views (Read Mode, Print Layout or Web Layout) you used most recently, and switch to it the next time you open the file

...cont'd

Web Layout View

Web Layout View gives you a good idea of how your document would look if saved as a web page and then viewed in a browser such as Internet Explorer.

1 Go to the View tab and select Web Layout from the Views area, or click on the Web Layout icon in the Status bar

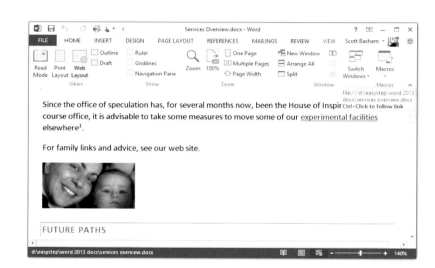

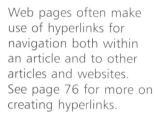
2 To turn this into a web page, make sure you choose Web Page (*.htm, *.html) as the file type when saving

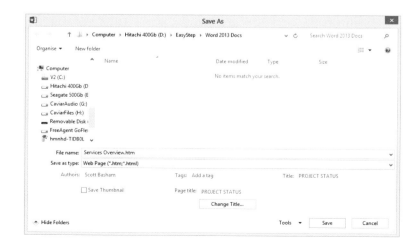

Hot tip

Although you've created a page, for it to be available on the Web it must be copied onto a server run by a web-hosting service or Internet Service Provider. If you have an account with one of these then the company will be able to give you instructions on how to upload your files to its site.

Outline View

1 In the Views area of the View tab, click the Outline icon

Outline view is useful if you structure your document using headings and subheadings which are allocated to indented levels. The controls in the Outlining tab let you change levels, move lines up/down, or "collapse" items so that lines on lower levels are temporarily hidden from view.

Beware

Outline view is only suitable if your document uses at least two levels of heading and subheading – otherwise there is not enough structure for it to add any real value. Remember Word 2013's Print Layout view can also collapse and expand standard headings.

Draft View

1 In the Views area of the View tab, click the Draft icon

The screen now shows a simplified view of your text, with elements such as headers and footers not visible.

2 This view is useful if your computer is slow, or if you just want to concentrate on the text with no distractions

3 You can continue to edit your text in this view. However, if you wish to see how your document will look when printed make sure that you return to Print Layout view by clicking the appropriate icon in the Views area of the View tab (or in the Status bar)

Gridlines

Defining and customizing gridlines

Gridlines are useful for helping you to align objects and resize them in a regular way.

1. When you're working with a drawing element the drawing tools appear automatically. Make sure the Format tab is active, click the Align icon in the Arrange area, and then choose Grid Settings...

2. Here you can set the size of the grid using "Grid settings". You can also control how many visible vertical and horizontal lines will be displayed. For example, if you set "Vertical every" to 2 then a visible line will appear for every second actual grid line. This is useful if you don't want your page cluttered with too many grid lines

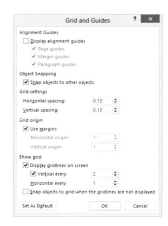

3. Select "Display gridlines on screen" and then click OK

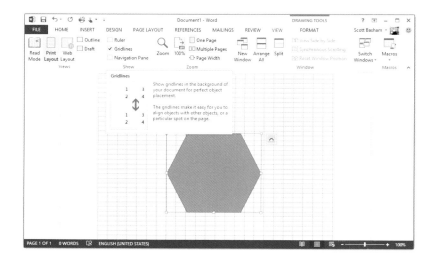

The Navigation pane

The Navigation pane can use the headings in your document to create a structured list located to the left of the main page area. This can be used to navigate easily through a long document.

Activating the Navigation pane

1 In the Show area of the View tab, click the Navigation Pane checkbox to switch it on

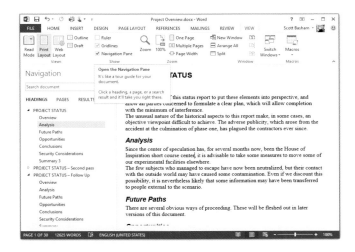

2 The Navigation pane appears, with its own scroll bars. It has three tabbed pages, so make sure the first of these is active. This will list any headings or subheadings. If you click on one of these then the main document window will automatically move to this line, scrolling if necessary

3 The second tabbed page will display the pages in your document as Thumbnails (small images) so you can scroll visually through the document

4 The third tabbed page allows you to search based on text or objects such as pictures, tables or equations

5 When you're finished with the Navigation pane either click the close icon in its top right corner or switch off the option in the Show area of the View tab

Don't forget

A quick way to summon the Navigation pane with the Results tab active is to type Ctrl + F as this is the shortcut for Find.

...cont'd

The Navigation pane can be used in a variety of ways. Here we'll see some advanced examples using a document which has been structured with several levels of headings.

Browsing Headings

138

1. Make sure the Navigation pane is visible. If not, select the View tab and click on the checkbox labelled Navigation Pane

2. Make sure the first of the three icons is selected at the top of the pane. This lists just the headings in your document

3. The network of headings and subheadings is displayed as a tree structure. If you click on the small triangle in this area the sub-structure beneath this line will be collapsed (hidden) and revealed in turn

4. You can drag headings up and down to a different location, effectively restructuring your document very easily

5. Right-click on a heading to see options for adding, deleting, promoting, demoting, selecting and printing headings

Browsing pages

1 Make the Navigation pane visible then click the second icon labelled Pages near its top. This allows you to browse by scrolling through small thumbnail images of each page

2 You can resize the Navigation pane by dragging horizontally on the vertical border between it and the main page. Also you can drag on its title bar to make it a free-floating window

3 If you click on any page icon the main window will scroll to that page

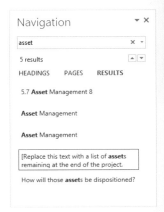

Browsing search results

1 If you click the small triangle beside the magnifying glass at the top of the pane you can browse through objects such as graphics, tables or equations as well as text

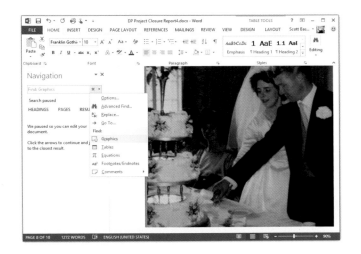

Hot tip

If the Results tab is active, and you're searching for text, you can see your results in context. Click on one of these and the main page will scroll to the appropriate location.

The Document Inspector

Before distributing your document to others, it's a good idea to check its content carefully. Sometimes your document might contain hidden information, or details you'd rather not include. The Document Inspector can help you with this.

1 Click on the File tab

2 The Info screen should appear by default (if not then click on Info). Click on the "Check for Issues" button then select Inspect Document from the pop-up

The Document Inspector dialog box appears. It lists different categories of content worth checking, some of which may be hidden but would be readable to someone with good technical knowledge.

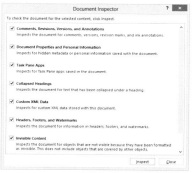

3 Click the Inspect button. The Results window appears

4 If you have any found items, you can get rid of them by clicking on the Remove All button. Click on Reinspect to verify the current state of play, then Close when done

7 Files and settings

In this chapter we'll see that the File tab looks very different to the others. It lets you take a step back and consider Word files as opposed to working within the contents of a document.

Info

1   With a document open, click on the File tab

2   By default you see the Info screen. This gives you a useful summary of your current document's properties – listed along the right hand side

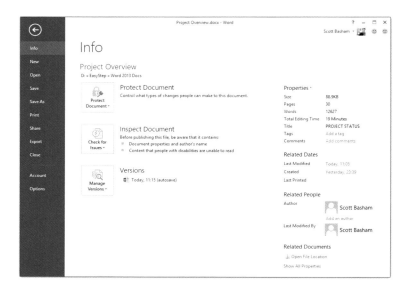

3   In the central part of the screen there are controls for changing the permissions, checking for issues before sharing or distributing, and clearing up any draft versions of your document which may have been created automatically

4   If your current document is in a format for an older version of Word, you'll be missing out on some of the new features. If you want to upgrade it to the latest format, click the Convert button:

Beware

If you do convert your document to Word 2013 format, others using earlier versions prior to Word 2010 may not be able to open it. If you need them to work on your document then use Save As and select "Word 97-2003 Document" as the file type (see page 143).

Save to local file

1 Choose Save As, then select Computer to see this screen:

Hot tip

With Word 2013 you have the option to save to the Cloud, using a service such as SkyDrive. This means you'll be able to access documents wherever there's an internet connection. See Chapter Eight for more details on sharing features.

2 To select a location choose the current folder, one of the recently-used folders, or click the Browse button

3 Open the "Save as type" pop-up to see a list of file types. Useful types are PDF, Web Page, Plain and Rich Text

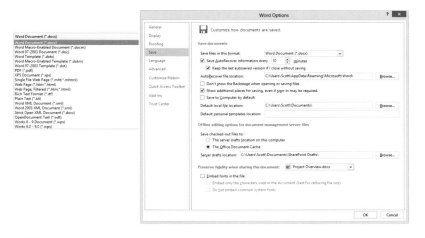

Hot tip

Plain Text is the simplest type – there's no formatting but your file will be readable on virtually any system.

4 Click on Tools and choose Save Options to control default settings such as file format and locations

5 Click OK and then Save to save your document

Recently-used files

1 Exit Word (if it's running) then start it up again

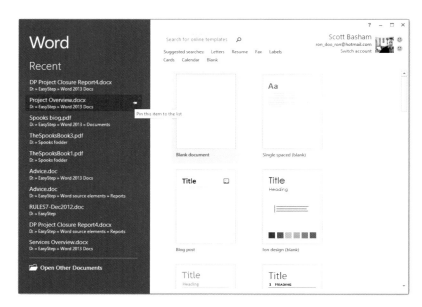

2 The left side of the screen will list your recently-used documents, so in most cases you'll just click one of these to resume work

3 If you hover over one of these a small pin icon ⬛ appears. If you click this then the document will be "pinned", i.e. permanently added to the list

4 The item will move to the top of the list, above a horizontal line, and the icon beside it will have changed to a vertical pin: 🛋. Click this to "unpin" the item

5 If the document you want to open is not in the Recent list then choose Open Other Documents at the bottom of the screen

Opening local files

If Word is already running you can still use the File tab to open documents, although the screen design is slightly different.

1 Go to the File tab and choose Open

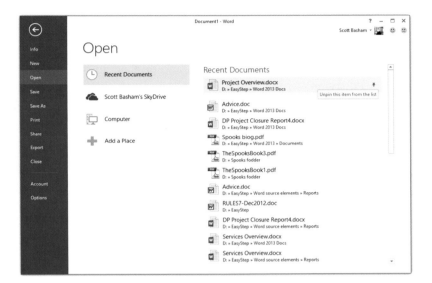

2 There are four main options for locating your file. By default, Recent Documents is selected. On the right hand side you'll see the same list as in the previous example, with any pinned items at the top

3 If the document you want isn't there then click on Computer

4 You'll now see a list of recently-used folders, so either select one of these or click Browse to manually navigate to your file's location. You can also use the Search Documents feature via the Browse icon

Don't forget

These examples assume that your documents are stored as local files rather than online. For guidance on accessing online documents, see Chapter Eight.

145

Hot tip

The list of Recent Folders also has a pin/unpin facility, so you can make sure that your favorite locations are always easily accessible.

Opening other file formats

Word 2013 can open a range of file types, including .doc (the native type for older versions of Word) and .rtf (rich text format) which is a cross-platform standard for text including a reasonable set of formatting features.

1 Click on the File tab and choose Open

2 In this example, we've located and opened an old document which was stored in the .doc format

For many such files, Word will present you with a read-only copy. In this case it automatically defaults to Read Mode. Furthermore, if you look in the title bar you'll see that Compatibility Mode is active.

3 Go to the File tab and examine the Info screen

If you don't need your document to be edited in older versions of Word, then you should use the Convert feature to upgrade it to the .docx format. You will then have access to the full range of Word 2013's features.

Note the indication that this is a read-only document. Also, Word's Compatibility Mode restricts available features to those present in earlier versions of Word. This means you can save a copy and send it to someone using older software.

4 Click Save As to create an editable copy. The .doc file type is used by default but you can change this easily

Opening PDF files

Adobe Systems' Portable Document Format (PDF) is a very popular file format for read-only documentation. A new feature with Word 2013 is the ability to open these and convert them into an editable format. You can then save in Word's own format, or re-export to PDF.

1 Click on the File tab and choose Open

2 Using any of the techniques covered in the previous examples, locate a PDF document

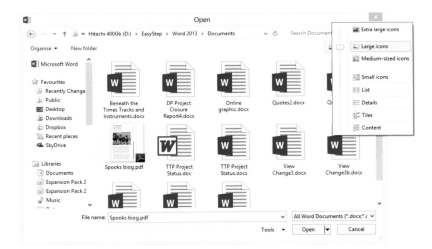

147

3 When you click Open the following message will appear

4 Click OK. A progress bar will appear at the bottom of the main window while Word is performing the conversion

5 If the conversion is successful the document will display in Print Layout view

...cont'd

6 Have a good look through the document and, if possible, compare what you see with the same document opened in the Adobe Acrobat viewer. There may be some differences, particularly with the positioning of graphics or special text effects

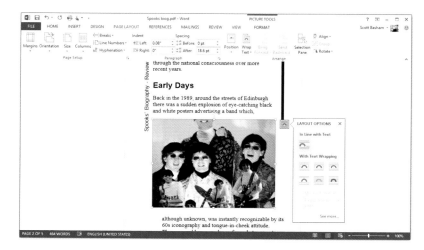

7 You can now work with this as a normal Word document, with the full range of editing features

8 Next time you save, Word will default to saving as a .docx file, although you can change "Save as type" to PDF

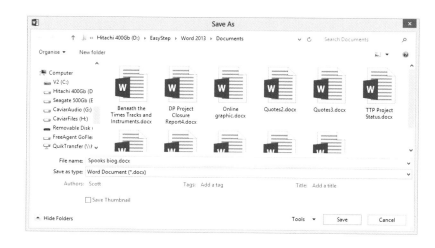

Hot tip

The .docx file type is Word 2013's native format and so is the best choice for important documents, especially if you might need to edit them further. Saving and opening foreign formats such as PDF always require a conversion process and so may not be 100% accurate or reliable. In this example the best policy is to save your "definitive" file as a .docx, and then (if required) you can create a PDF copy.

Printing

1 Make sure you have an open document. Choose Print from the File tab

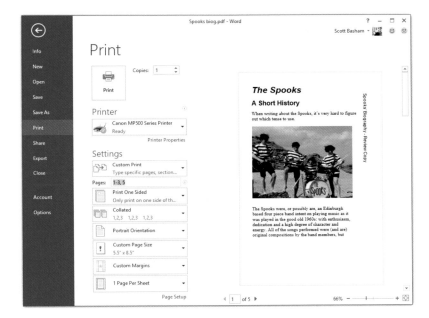

2 You'll see a preview of the current page, which is useful for checking margins and text flow. Click on the forward and back arrows at the bottom to move through the pages

3 Make sure the correct printer is selected, and that it is online. If your printer isn't listed choose Add Printer

4 Review the other settings listed. If you don't want to print all pages then there are a number of other options available. In the example above, a discontinuous range has been chosen (pages 1 to 3, followed by 5)

5 You can click on the Printer Properties link, or Page Setup, to access more detailed dialog boxes

6 Finally go back to the top of the dialog box, check the number of desired copies and then click Print

Hot tip

If you're printing on special paper then it's always worth clicking on the Printer Properties link. This will display the settings dialog box for your particular make and model of printer, and will almost certainly contain controls for specifying paper type.

Using templates

Word 2013 has access to a new range of templates, and has an improved interface for locating the right one for your needs.

1 Click on New. In this screen you will initially see a selection of the most commonly-used templates

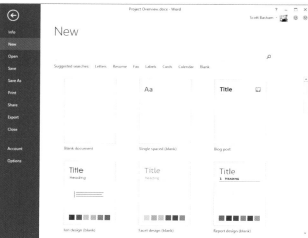

 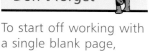
2 Click one of the suggested searches or enter your own search text. The example below searches for "agenda"

3 Scroll through the results and select a template

4 If you right-click on a template a small pop-up menu appears. Choose Preview to learn more about the selected template

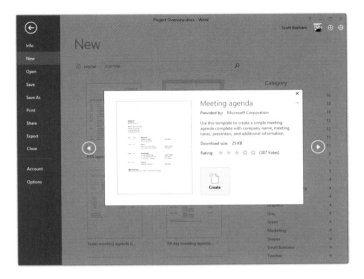

When previewing in this way you can use the left or right arrow icons to go to the previous or next template in the list.

5 If you're happy with your choice click the Create button, or click on the background to return to the main screen

6 Once you open a template you can edit and add to the sample text, then save the document under a new name

Although you're free to change settings such as font, size, spacing and color, it's usually best to stay with what was provided by the template. Most templates have their own particular design in order to allow you to concentrate just on the content.

...cont'd

Creating your own templates

A template is just an ordinary Word document saved as a special file type, and usually in a special location.

1 Create your document in the normal way. It may be worth using dummy placeholder text. When it's ready, choose Save As from the File tab and select a location

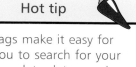

Hot tip

Tags make it easy for you to search for your templates later on. In this example the words "Agenda" and "Business" are being added as tags, so that any searches using one of those words will return this template (plus any others with similar tags).

2 In the dialog box, for "Save as type" choose Word Template (*.dotx). It's also good to set a title, and add some tags

3 Note that Word will, by default, save the file in a special Custom Office Templates directory (it's best not to change this if you want to be able to easily access your template in future). Click Save

4 Go to the File tab and choose Close. Then go back to the File tab and this time choose New

5 Click on the Personal heading to see your new template

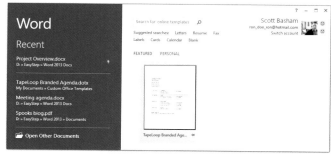

Options

We've already seen how to change certain options when we customized the Ribbon in Chapter One. All these options and many more are available in one place via the File tab.

1 Make sure the File tab is active then click Options. The dialog box that opens is organized into ten sections, with General options displayed at first

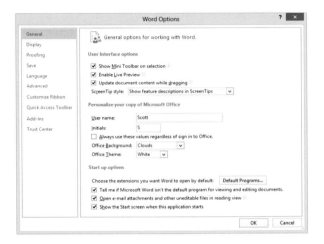

153

2 Unless your computer is very slow, keep on the options "Show Mini Toolbar on selection" and "Enable Live Preview". The latter controls what happens when you hover over a formatting feature, e.g. hovering over a style in the Style Gallery will temporarily show selected text in that format. "Update document content while dragging" enables the live preview when dragging objects

3 Click on the Trust Center section, then Trust Center Settings. This gives an overview of security and privacy settings, and also links to Microsoft policies and guidance

Hot tip

If you get an error message when attempting to open documents which were sent via email attachments, or were downloaded from the Web, then first check you're sure they came from a reputable source. If you are, then go to the Trust Center Settings, click on the Protected View section, then clear the three checkboxes shown in the illustration on the left.

4 Click on the Display section to control whether Word displays non-printing characters such as Tabs and Paragraph marks

5 This dialog box also has printing options so you can, for example, elect to print without drawings created in Word. This will speed up printing and save on printer ink – simple blank boxes will be printed in place of the graphic

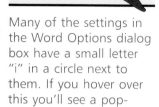
154

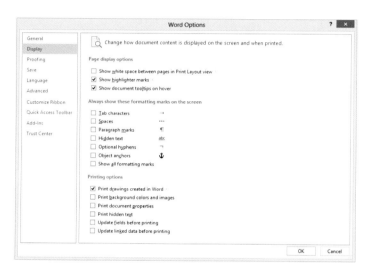

6 Have a look at the other sections. The largest of these is Advanced which contains extra settings for editing, display, printing and saving

8 Sharing features

In this chapter we'll see how Word 2013 places a much greater emphasis on portability and sharing.

Roaming documents

An exciting feature, introduced with Word 2010 and greatly enhanced in Word 2013, is the ability to view and edit documents directly on the Web, even if Word isn't installed on your computer. This means you're able to work on your files from any machine with internet access, provided you've saved your document to a shared area such as a Microsoft SharePoint server or Windows Live's SkyDrive.

Using a shared area from Word

1 First it's a good idea to review the services associated with your online account. Go to the File tab and then click on Account

For best results Word 2013 needs to know who you are. Normally the active account will be taken automatically from your Windows login. If this is not the case then the first time you use Word you will be prompted for your user name and password.

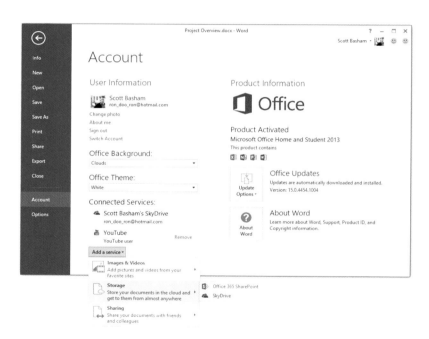

2 Check the account name and login listed under User Information. If this isn't you then click Switch Account and enter your details

3 Now look to see what is listed under Connected Services. Word may have already connected you to your SkyDrive or Office 365 SharePoint service if linked to your login

4 If there are no storage services connected, then, provided you have an appropriate active account, you can add one in. Click the "Add a service" button

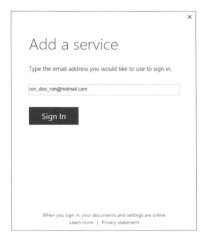

Hot tip

Anyone with a Hotmail account will have access to a SkyDrive area for shared document storage. Log in to Outlook.com to see this for yourself. If you do not have an account then it's free to set one up, or for an annual subscription fee you can sign up to an enhanced service with more storage space.

5 Once you have a connected service for storage you can use it very easily. With a document open, go to the File tab and choose Save As

6 In this example, the current account has a SkyDrive connected service. Your account may be different to the above, so look for the cloud icon, which indicates an online shared area available to you. If you click on this then the right hand side of the dialog will display folders you have accessed recently, plus a general Browse option. Click Browse to specify where your file will be saved

...cont'd

Don't forget

This is still the standard Windows Save As dialog box, so you have access to the normal features for searching, navigating and displaying files as well as viewing icons with preview if available. The file path shown at the top will depend on how your connected service is set up – in some cases it will be a local directory on your hard disk, which your system will automatically keep in sync with its online equivalent.

Beware

Don't be tempted to change file type at this stage, unless you have a specific reason for doing so. Word's web-editing features will require you to use the standard native file format.

7 You will now see the directory structure of your online storage area. Double-click to move into a sub-directory

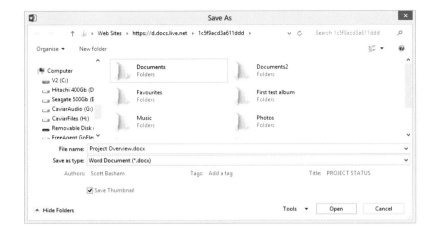

8 When you've found the right location, enter your filename and click Save

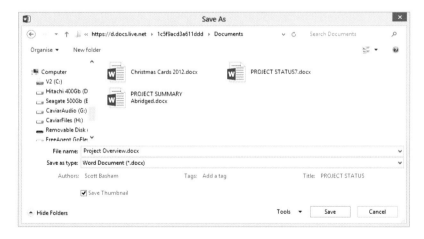

9 Now you can close your document, or carry on editing. If you edit it and then Save, the online location will be updated just the same as for a local file on your disk. As long as your machine is always online, you can use the cloud storage as your main repository for documents and, as we shall see, this has quite a few advantages

Accessing documents from the Word Web App

Imagine you're away from your main PC or tablet, and do not have access to Microsoft Word. The Word Web App gives you the ability to read and edit documents directly within a web browser. In the following example, we'll access the Word document that was stored in SkyDrive in the previous page.

1 Start up a web browser and log into your account on Outlook.com

2 At the top left of the screen click on the downward arrow beside the Outlook icon to see the following four options:

3 Click on SkyDrive to see your top level of folders and files, some with small preview images. The folders are listed first and have a number in the bottom right to indicate the number of files within. Click to enter a folder and view its files

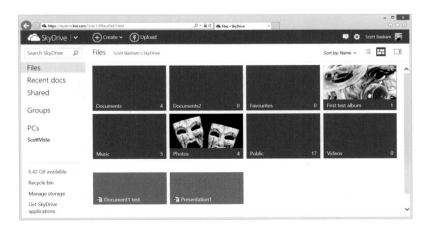

4 In this example we can see along the top of the screen a set of controls including options for creating, uploading and opening documents. A quick way to access a document is to click inside its blue tile

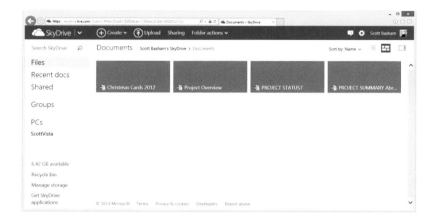

5 The document opens in a read-only mode, giving you an accurate preview and the ability to add comments by selecting and right-clicking areas of text

6 Click Edit Document then "Edit in Word Web App"

Hot tip

If you hover over the document's blue tile you'll see a small checkbox in its top right corner. You can click on this to select and deselect. If you have one or more documents selected then a Manage menu appears allowing you to delete, move or access the properties for everything you selected.

7 Now you'll see a simplified view of your document where you are able to edit the text. You can also access a subset of Word's normal editing and formatting features

8 Once you've made some edits, click on the File tab

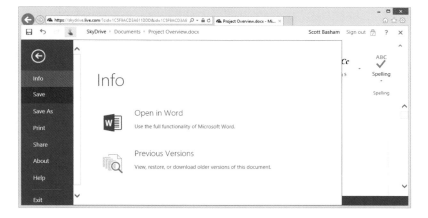

9 If the machine you're using has the full version of Word installed, you can choose to "Open in Word" and access its full functionality

10 Click Save to write your changes back to the online storage. Note that the File tab also lets you access other features such as Save As and Print

Creating new documents from the Web

1 If the Word Web App is still running go to the File tab and choose Exit

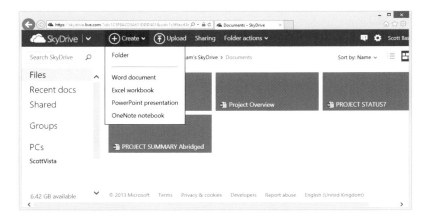

2 You should be returned to the view of your online files and folders. Navigate to the location for your new document, then click Create and choose "Word document"

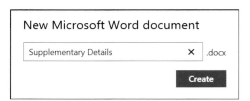

3 Enter a name for your document then click Create

4 The Word Web App opens in Edit mode with a new blank document. In this example we'll go to the Insert tab and add a Picture

5 You might need to wait while the picture is uploaded. Enter some text, and also experiment by adding a table

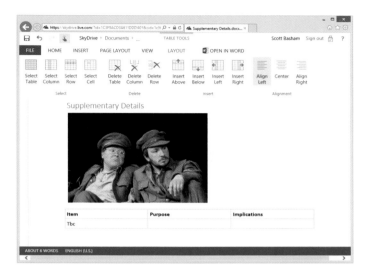

While you can add and manipulate images to a certain extent, the range of features on the Web version of Word is more limited. To see an example of this, right-click on the picture to see a pop-up menu offering a simple Grow and Shrink option plus access to a smaller range of Styles.

6 Save the new document and then close down the browser

7 On your main PC or tablet, start up Word 2013 and open the newly-created online document

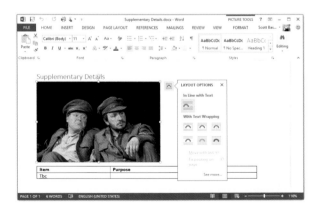

If you were using the same machine for Word 2013 and the Word Web App, then in this example it's easier to choose the Open In Word option to move between the App and the full program.

8 Make sure Layout View is selected. Now you are back to a full preview of the document whilst being able to access the complete range of editing features at the same time

Working together

Once you have a document in a shared area such as SkyDrive you can collaborate with a number of co-authors. It's even possible for multiple users to work on the same document at the same time, the key restriction being that only one person can edit a particular paragraph at one time.

Preparing to share

1 In this example we'll take a locally-stored document and go through the process of setting it up for online collaboration. Go to the File tab and choose Share

2 First we must save to a shared location, so click the Save To Cloud button

3 The standard Save As screen appears. Choose your online location from the list of recent folders or click Browse

4 Enter the filename and click Save

5 Word returns you to the File tab, so click on Share again

Don't forget

If you enter names rather than email addresses, Word will try to locate each person from your list of Contacts.

165

6 Now, under Invite People, enter the name or email address of another person who will access the document

7 On the right hand side you can choose whether to set "Can edit" or "Can view" for this person. In this example we'll allow editing

8 Click the large Share button near the bottom. Word will send an email to the person you nominated, similar to the example below. Repeat this process for each person who will be working with you on the document

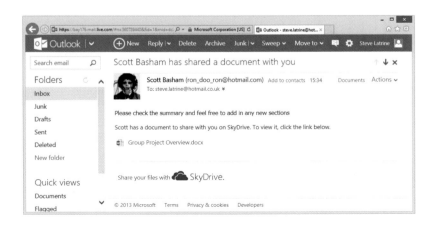

Multiple users working on one document

In the previous example, a user named Steve received an email advising him that he could work on our file. The email contained a hyperlink which would take Steve straight to that document. There he would have the choice of using the Word Web App or the full version of Word 2013 or Word 2010 (depending on what's available to him) to start editing. In this example, we'll look at an interesting scenario where we start editing the document at exactly the same time as Steve.

1 Open your shared document either in the full version of Word or the Word Web App

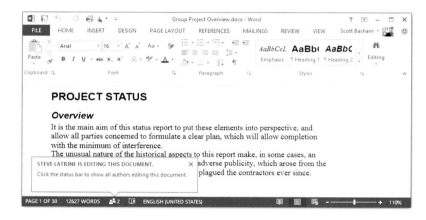

Beware

Coauthoring only works for Word 2010 version and above. Also bear in mind that not all of Word's features are available in the Word Web App.

2 A pop-up message appears, letting you know that Steve is currently editing this document

3 The Status bar now contains an icon reminding you that there are two people working on this file. If you click on the icon you'll see their names

4 Start making some edits to your document, but keep a look out for any sign of Steve's activity. You'll see an example of this on the next page

5 Word operates a paragraph-locking mechanism on a first-come first-served basis. So, if Steve starts editing a paragraph before you, the following message will appear

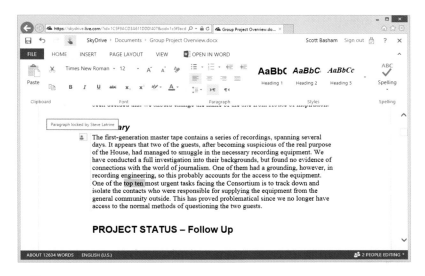

6 The vertical dotted line represents the paragraph you are editing, while the sold line shows you that Steve is working on the paragraph above. When you each save the file the changes will be merged together

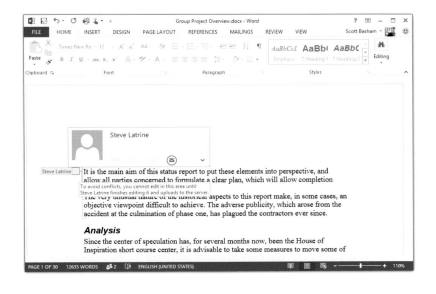

Hot tip

If you hover over the message next to the paragraph locked by the other user, Word will show you their details and also available methods of contacting that person. In this example the only option to contact Steve is via an email message.

Email

Many people like to attach Word documents and other types of file to email messages. If you have email client software, such as Microsoft Outlook, installed on your machine you can send emails directly from Word.

Sending from Word

168

1 Once your document is ready for emailing, it's a good idea to Save first of all

2 Go to the File tab and click Share

3 Select Email and then choose the option "Send as Attachment"

4 Provided your email client software is correctly installed, it will open with a new blank message. The Word document will automatically be added as an attachment

5 Note you can also send in other formats such as PDF

Present Online

With Word 2013 you can easily present your document to a group of people via the Web.

1 Open the document and scroll through to check what you'll be presenting

2 When you're ready, go to the File tab and choose Share. Click on Present Online

Hot tip

This feature is also available, more appropriately, in Microsoft PowerPoint – also part of the Office 2013 suite.

3 The document is sent to a Microsoft website, which acts as a free hosting service for the presentation. Once preparation is complete, you'll see a message similar to this one below

4 A URL (hyperlink) is generated. If you have a client email program (such as Outlook) installed, you can click on "Send in Email" to send this to your intended participant(s). Otherwise, copy and paste the Link into an email message or instant messaging system

5 Once you have given your audience the URL, click Start Presentation. You can now see your document with a special Present Online tab of controls

Hot tip

If you have Microsoft OneNote installed you can click on Share Meeting Notes to let your audience see notes you've prepared.

6 Anyone receiving your email or message can click on the URL to view the live presentation

Hot tip

Sometimes email client software doesn't support clicking on a URL for going automatically to a web page. If this is the case then the URL can simply be copied to the Clipboard then pasted into the URL or Web Address area of the chosen browser.

7 As you move through your document the people viewing will see their screens move in the same way

8 During the presentation you can make changes to the document if you first click the Edit button in the Present Online tab

9 You can send out additional invites by clicking the Send Invitation button. This shows the dialog box we saw previously so you can access the URL and then send it to them

10 When you have finished, click End Online Presentation to see the dialog box below. You can either Cancel to resume presenting, or click "End..." to close and return to Word's normal screen

Blogging

Blogs are websites which consist of a number of entries, or posts. These are usually arranged and presented in date order with the most recent first. To publish your own Blog, you need to set up an account with a provider such as WordPress or Blogger. Often these are free to set up, although you can pay for a premium service with more storage and options to customize formatting.

Posting to a Blog

1. Create and edit a document in the normal way

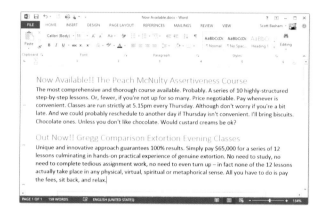

2. When you're ready, go to the File tab and choose Share

3. Click "Post to Blog" to see the following dialog box

172

4 A new document will be created in Blog post format, and your text copied in. Replace the text [Enter Post Title Here] with a suitable title

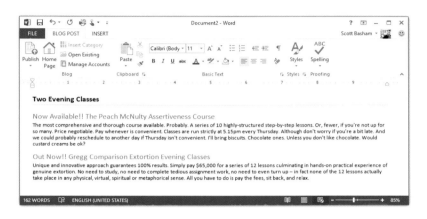

173

Hot tip

If you save this document it will retain its Blog Post property, so you can use it as a starting point for re-posting. Also, when you manually create a new document, if you search the Templates list for "Blog" you'll be able to use the "Blog post" blank template. This will give you a pre-formatted document with the Blog Post tab already available.

5 If you haven't used Blogging before, click on the Manage Accounts button in the Blog tools then click New

6 In the New Blog Account dialog choose your Blog provider then click Next

7 Fill out your Blog Post URL, user name and password (and select Remember Password if you'd prefer not to enter it every time you post) then click OK

Hot tip

You should have been given a user name and password by your Blog Service Provider. If you're not sure what to enter for Blog Post URL then click the "Help me fill out this section" hyperlink for guidance appropriate for each Provider.

...cont'd

8 Click Yes to the Warning dialog box which appears. If your account details were correct you'll see the following confirmation message

9 A new entry will be listed in the Blog Accounts dialog box, so posting to your blog will be very easy from now on. Click Close to return to the main document

10 Back in the main window click the Publish tool in the Blog Post tab. A message will appear near the top confirming the date and time of the post

Don't forget

Now is a good time to go to your Blog website and have a look at the new post. If you need to change anything you can edit in Word then click Publish again. Alternatively, most Blog Service Providers will allow you to edit posts via their own site.

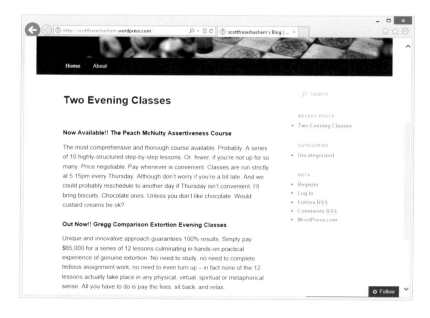

9 References and mailings

In this chapter we'll look at more formal documents, covering indexing, tables of contents and other types of references. Also we'll look at ways of creating a range of standardized documents.

Table of Contents

You can automatically create a Table of Contents by asking Word to look for instances of particular styles, or by using entries that you create manually.

Creating a Table of Contents

1 Open a suitably-long document which uses a structure of style headings. Make sure the References tab is active so you can see the Table of Contents controls on the left

2 Click the "Table of Contents" button and choose one of the available preset styles

3 Word looks through your document and uses the headings to generate the Table of Contents. It calculates the correct page number reference and adds it to each entry

4 The entries in the Table of Contents behave like hyperlinks: Ctrl + Click on any of these to jump straight to the relevant page

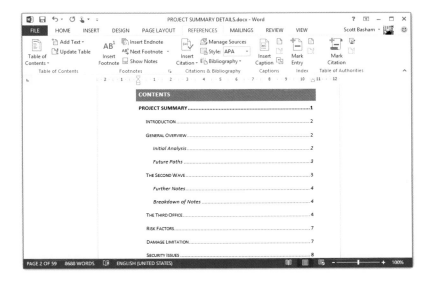

Manually adding or removing items

1 Select some text which is not already in the Table of Contents, then click the Add Text button and choose a Level number

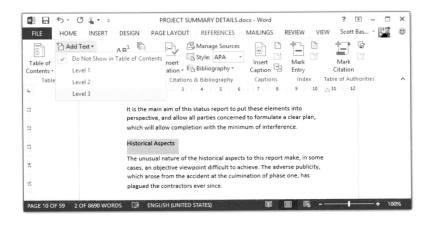

2 To remove an item, select some text which is already in the Table of Contents, then click the Add Text button and select "Do Not Show in Table of Contents"

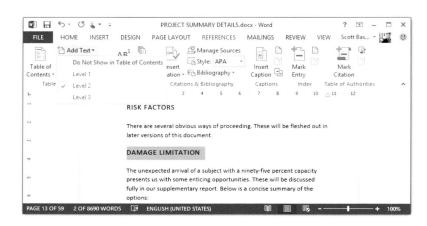

You can check at any time whether a piece of text is currently included in the Table of Contents. To do this, select the text then click the Add Text tool to see if it's currently assigned to any particular level.

178

Customizing your Table of Contents

1 Select a line in the Table of Contents and use the Styles Inspector to view its style. If you redefine this style then you automatically change all the entries of the same type

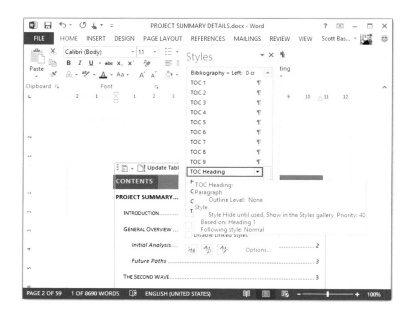

Updating your Table of Contents

1 As you continue to work with your document, text may move to different pages, pages may be inserted or deleted, and new headings may be added

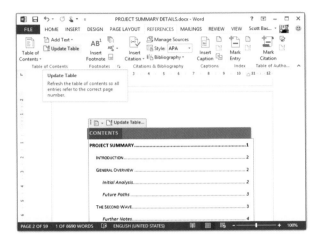

2 Click Update Table to rebuild the Table of Contents. You'll be given the choice of updating the entire table or just the page numbers of the existing entries

Don't forget

If you've added or removed items for your Table of Contents then make sure you select "Update entire table" rather than "Update page numbers only".

Manually defining your Table of Contents

When you click the "Table of Contents" tool to create the Table of Contents, as well as the predefined styles there's an option "Insert Table of Contents". This will display a dialog where you can choose which text styles to use.

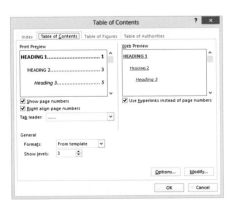

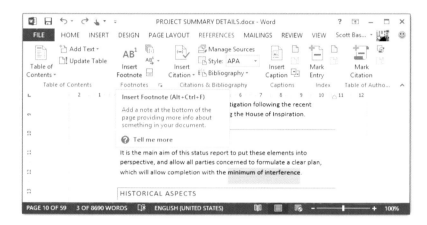

Footnotes and endnotes

These allow you to add a superscript number to a word or phrase which relates to explanatory text at the bottom of the page (for footnotes), or the end of the document or section (for endnotes).

Adding a footnote

1. Select the desired text and click Insert Footnote or press Ctrl + Alt + F

2. Next, add the footnote text at the bottom of the page

3. Note that the text you'd highlighted now includes a superscript footnote number. If you hover over this text the footnote will temporarily appear as a pop-up

Don't forget

If you add new footnotes earlier on in your document, Word will automatically renumber the rest so that numbering is continuous.

Adding an endnote

① Select the text and click Insert Endnote

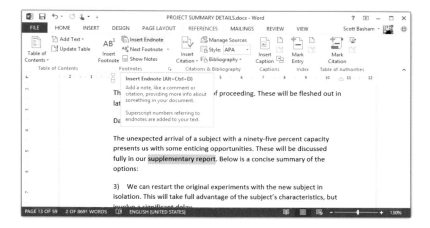

Hot tip

The keyboard shortcut for Insert Endnote is Ctrl + Alt + D.

② Enter the text for your endnote in the space provided

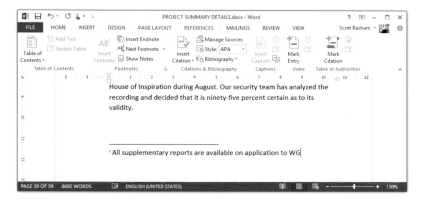

Hot tip

When you insert a footnote or endnote the display automatically scrolls to the footnote or endnote area, ready for you to type in the text.

③ The Show Notes button will take you from the footnote back to the related text in the main part of the document

④ If you click the button a second time you will be taken to either the footnote or the endnote area

...cont'd

Navigating through footnotes and endnotes

1 Click the Next Footnote icon to see its pop-up menu

2 There are four options, allowing you to jump straight to the next or the previous footnote or endnote

The Footnote and Endnote Dialog

1 Click the 🔽 icon in the lower right corner of the Footnotes area to see the Footnote and Endnote dialog

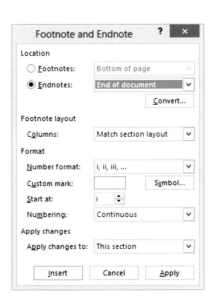

Here you can specify where the notes are positioned – endnotes can go either at the end of the document or just the end of the current section.

The number format defaults to Roman numerals for endnotes, but there are other options available.

You can also have different dialog settings for each section if you need that level of control.

Hot tip

Click the Convert... button to switch around footnotes and endnotes, or to convert all notes to just one type.

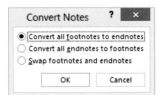

Citations

Citations are useful if you need to add a reference to another author or publication within your text. Later on you can compile a standard bibliography that collects together all your citations.

Adding a citation

1 Click just after the reference in your main text. Click the Insert Citation button and choose Add New Source...

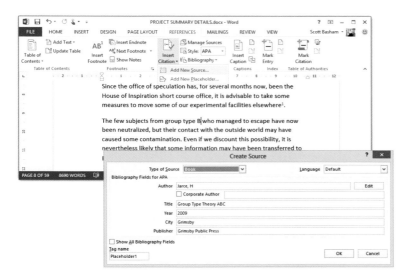

2 The Create Source dialog box appears. Choose the source then enter the details and click OK

3 A short citation reference now appears next to your text. If you need to change any of the details you entered then click the Manage Sources button

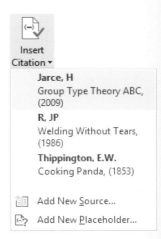

Captions

Insert Caption

Insert Table of Figures
Update Table
Cross-reference

Captions

Hot tip

You can also add captions to equations and tables – follow exactly the same procedure.

1 Select your element then click on Insert Caption

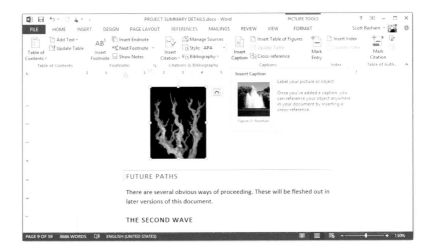

2 Add the caption text in the dialog. There are three label options – Equation, Figure and Table (you can also use the New Label... button to add more options). Choose Figure for this example

3 Captions will normally be numbered 1, 2, 3 and so on, but this can be changed by clicking on Numbering... Repeat the process to add more captions

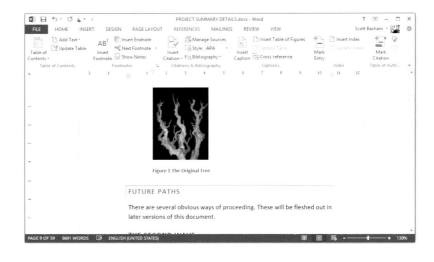

Tables of figures

Once you've created captions throughout your document you can ask Word to build a Table of Figures.

1 Make sure your insertion point is placed where you want the Table of Figures

2 Click on Insert Table of Figures

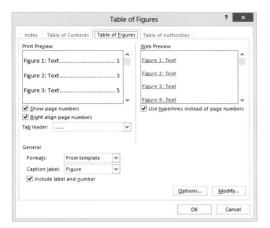

The Table of Figures dialog box appears as shown.

3 Choose a format from the pop-up list. The Print and Web Preview areas will show you how this will look. Click OK to generate the table

4 If you make changes to your document you should probably refresh the table. To do this click Update Table

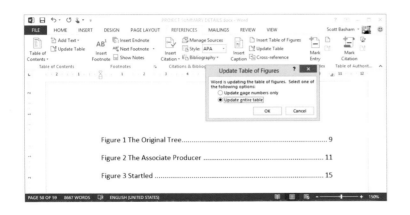

Don't forget

As with footnotes seen earlier, Word automatically renumbers captions as you add to or delete from your document.

Indexing

Longer documents benefit greatly from a well-organized index. Word makes the process of creating an index fairly easy.

1. Select the text to add to the index, and click on Mark Index Entry (References tab) or press Shift + Alt + X

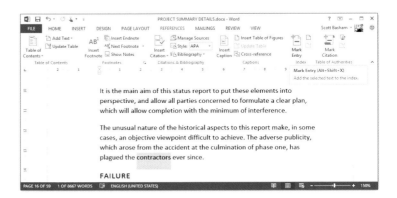

2. You can now edit the entry text, add a subentry, and choose whether the index will show the current page, a range of pages or a cross reference to another index entry

3. Use the Bold and Italic checkboxes if you want your index entry to be emphasized

4. When you have finished making your settings click Mark, or Mark All if you want to mark all instances

5. This dialog box is *non-modal*, which means that you can continue to work on the main page with the dialog box still open. In this way you can go right through your document, quickly and easily marking new entries, without having to continually reopen the dialog box

6 As soon as you mark an entry, Word switches on the Show/Hide ¶ feature so you can see your index entries marked clearly

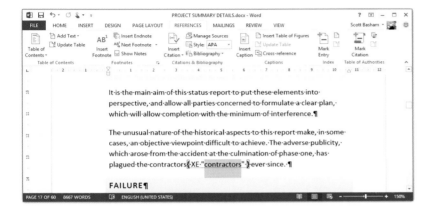

7 Place your insertion point where you'd like the index, then click Insert Index to see the finished result

8 Click in one of the entries in the new index then use the Style Inspector to see how it is automatically formatted

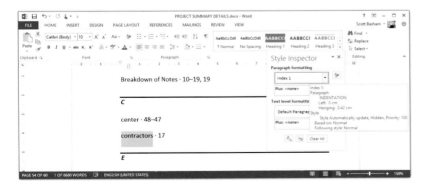

9 Word uses special styles (Index Heading, Index 1, Index 2, and so on) to control the formatting. If you edit these styles, rather than the index text directly, then your formatting decisions will be preserved even if you rebuild the index later on

Don't forget

You can toggle the Show/Hide ¶ feature on and off with Ctrl + *.

Don't forget

You can display the Style Inspector with the following: type Alt + Ctrl + Shift + S to summon the Styles panel then click on the 🔲 icon at the bottom.

187

Hot tip

If you edit your document so that the page numbers have changed, or if you have added more index entries, then you will need to rebuild the index. To do this, select the index and then click on Update Index.

Envelopes and labels

Creating envelopes

Envelopes Labels

Create

1. Activate the Mailings tab and, in the Create area, click Envelopes. The following dialog box appears:

2. Enter the delivery address and, optionally, the return address. Click the Options button to select the envelope's design and dimensions from a list of standard sizes

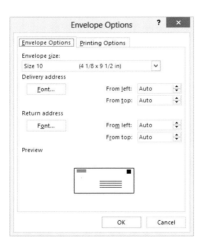

Hot tip

As well as the Envelope Options, this dialog box has a tab for Printing Options. This lets you tailor the settings to match the way you load envelopes into your printer.

3. Click Add to Document

4. If you entered a return address you'll be shown a dialog box asking you whether you want to make this the default return address. If you click Yes then you won't need to retype it the next time you create an envelope

5. Once you've dismissed the dialog box your envelope will be generated on a new page

188

Creating labels

1 Click the Labels tool. The following dialog box appears

2 Enter the text (usually an address) and choose between creating a single label or a full page of the same label

3 Click the Options button and select the label vendor and then the label from the product numbers listed

4 Click the Details button to review the attributes of the currently-selected label

5 If you can't find the right label then click Cancel to return to the Label Options dialog box, then click on Create New Label

6 Click OK to return to the Envelopes and Labels dialog box then choose New Document to generate your labels

7 Your labels will be generated on a new page

Mail Merge

There are several ways of setting up mail merging in Word, but the easiest is to use the Wizard, which guides you through the various stages of the process.

Using the Mail Merge Wizard

1 Click Start Mail Merge (in the Mailings tab) and select "Step-by-Step Mail Merge Wizard..."

2 The Mail Merge window appears at the right-hand side of the screen. If you drag on its title bar you can make it into a floating window. Select the document type then click Next to be guided through the steps

3 You'll be prompted to specify a list of addresses. This can be taken from a variety of data sources, such as your Outlook contacts, or can be entered manually

4 You can then write your document using special fields or placeholders, which are then substituted with values from each address before printing

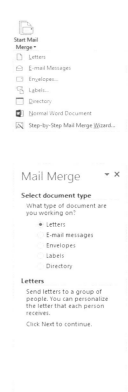

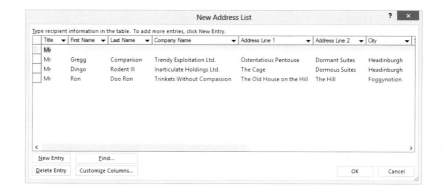

10 Tools for reviewing

This chapter looks at various ways of checking your work. We'll see how to manage changes that may need to be done on your own or in collaboration with others.

Spelling and grammar

Word can access a number of English and non-English dictionaries, which it uses when running spelling checks.

1 As you type, Word will automatically check your spelling using its default dictionary. Any suspect words will be underlined in red with a wavy line. Right-click on each word to see your choices

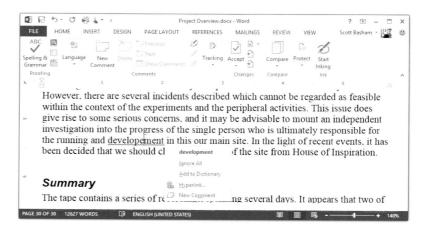

2 Any suggestions will be shown. Click on one of these to substitute in the correction

3 Click Ignore All if you'd like the highlighted word to be exempt from spell checking. Alternatively, click "Add to Dictionary" to add in the highlighted word

4 To run a check on your whole document click the Spelling and Grammar button in the Proofing area of the Review tab. A Spelling panel will appear with all the necessary controls and information

 Hot tip

Rather than the whole document, you can also check just some text by selecting it in the normal way before clicking the Spelling and Grammar button.

5 Once you've made a decision to change, ignore or add to the dictionary, Word will resume its search for mistakes. If it finds a problem with grammar then the Spelling pane will be replaced with the Grammar controls, as in the example below

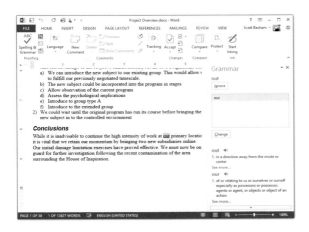

6 Review Word's suggestion and either click the Ignore or the Change button as appropriate. Or you might prefer to simply manually edit the text then run the check again

7 When Word has finished looking through the document it will display a "check complete" message

Hot tip

Another useful proofing tool is Define. You can access this either from the Proofing area of the Review tab, or more directly by right-clicking on a word and choosing Define from the pop-up menu. Word will use its installed dictionary to display the definition.

Hot tip

Your initial installation of Word may not include dictionaries for word definitions – if so the Grammar pane will inform you of this. Click the "Get a Dictionary" link at the bottom to download one from an online source.

Translation

There are a number of built-in bilingual dictionaries, which allow you to see translations of words or sentences.

Translating selected text

1 Select one or more words and then right-click and choose Translate from the pop-up menu

2 In the Research pane which appears choose English in the From field, and the target language in the To field

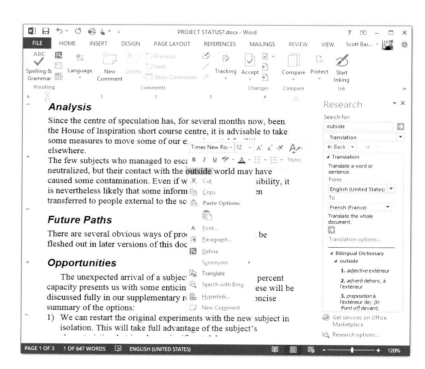

Hot tip

Once the Research pane is visible you can open the pop-up menu underneath the "Search for" criteria to change from "Translation" to one of the list of sources below:

All Reference Books
  Encarta Dictionary: English (U.S.)
  Thesaurus: English (United States)
  Thesaurus: French (France)
  Thesaurus: Spanish (Spain)
  Translation
All Research Sites
  Bing
  Factiva iWorks™
  HighBeam (TM) Research

3 The translated text appears in the lower half of the Research Pane

4 If you'd like to use the translated text click Insert

5 When you've finished close the Research pane

Thesaurus

1 A Thesaurus is a collection of synonyms (words with identical or similar meanings). Select a single word and then click on the Thesaurus icon in the Proofing tab

2 The Thesaurus pane appears – this can be moved or resized simply by dragging with the mouse. It contains a list of synonyms for the word you selected

3 Scroll though and select one of the options. The word will be moved to the main field at the top, and the list will now show you synonyms of that word

Hot tip

A quicker way to access the Thesaurus is to select a word, right-click, then choose Synonyms from the pop-up menu.

4 To go back one level click the ⊙ icon.

5 If you right-click in the list, from the pop-up menu that appears you can choose to insert the selected item, or copy it to the Clipboard

Comments

Adding a comment

1. Select the text to which you'd like to add the comment

2. Make sure the Review tab is active then click the New Comment icon in the Comments area

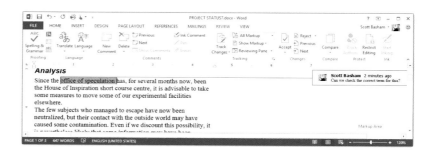

3. Add the comment text in the Markup Area at the right

4. Repeat this process to add more comments

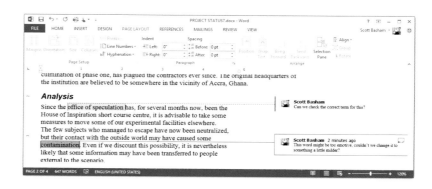

5. To delete a comment, click on it and then the Delete icon

6. You can move through the comments in your document using the Previous and Next buttons

7. Choose Delete All from the Delete pop-up to remove all comments

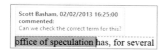

Scott Basham, 02/02/2013 16:25:00
commented:
Can we check the correct term for this?
office of speculation has, for several

Multiple users adding comments

We saw in Chapter Eight that many users can access the same document, sometimes even at the same time if the file is in a shared area. In Word 2013 the comments feature has been greatly enhanced to take account of this.

1 In this example, Steve, our second user, has logged in to Word and is editing the document we saw on the last page. Take a look at one of his comments

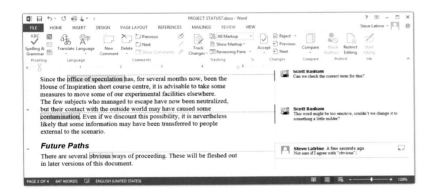

2 We can clearly see which comments are made by which person. Steve can also click the 🗨 icon to respond to a comment made by the first user as you can see below

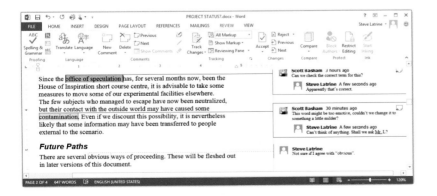

3 This process can repeat, with the original user commenting on Steve's comment, and perhaps even a third and fourth user commenting on the others

Marking a comment as done

Once an exchange of comments has ended to a satisfactory conclusion, you might want to mark them as "done". This will change them to a light-gray color so that they are less distracting, although you can still see them in case you need to change your mind later on.

Hot tip

You can also delete comments from this pop-up menu.

1 Right-click on a comment to see the pop-up menu shown on the right

2 Choose Mark Comment Done to indicate it's no longer active

3 If you change your mind, simply click again so that the option is deselected

Simple Markup

Word 2013 has a new way of looking at comments, which lets you see where they are without cluttering the screen too much.

Simple Markup
Simple Markup
All Markup
No Markup
Original

1 From the Review tab Tracking area, open the pop-up menu to select Simple Markup

2 Comments now show as a balloon icon in the margin

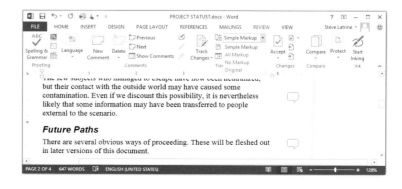

3 Click on a balloon to view or edit the comment

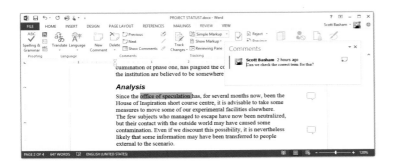

4 If you switch to Read Mode then comments will always be shown in this minimal way. As before, just click or tap on the balloon icon to reveal the comment

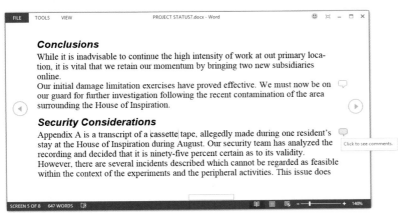

5 You can also add comments in Read Mode. Select some text and then right-click to display the pop-up menu, then choose New Comment

6 To delete comments or mark them as done you'll need to return to Page Layout View

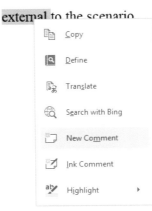

Ink

Adding comments using Ink

If you have access to a pen input device, you might find it much easier to hand-write comments and annotations to the document. Word 2013 supports this using the Ink tools and Ink Comments. In this example we'll see how to add comments using Ink.

1 Open a document in Print Layout view. Make sure the Review tab is active

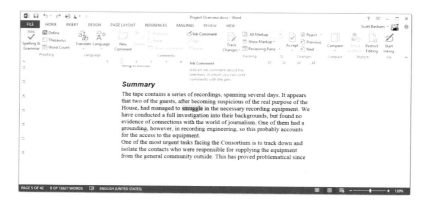

2 Look for the Ink Comment icon 🖉 in the Comments area. Select some text then click Ink Comment

3 Use your pen to write your comment in the area provided on the right hand side. Just like a normal comment this will be timestamped and logged under your name

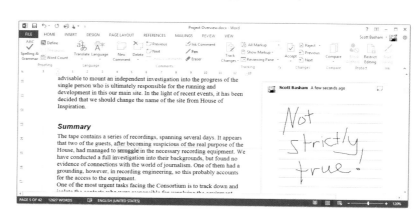

4 In this example another user opened the document and added his own comment

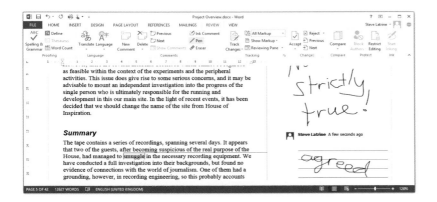

Editing Ink Comments

As well as the Ink Comment icon, there is a Pen and an Eraser tool available in the Comments area.

1 Click on an existing Ink Comment to make the tools accessible

2 Select the Pen tool and write in the comments area

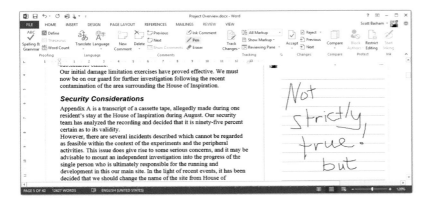

3 Now select the Eraser tool and click on the writing to remove it

Beware

Be careful with the Eraser tool. Word will have organized your written material as a series of discrete "elements", so rather than erasing one pixel at a time, each click will remove one element. For this reason it's best to erase using clicks (or taps) rather than the "scrubbing" technique which you may intuitively use. Remember you can Undo using Ctrl + Z if you make mistakes.

...cont'd

Inking

Word has a more general Inking feature which allows you, if you have a pen device, to use it to scribble all over the main page.

1 Open a document in Print Layout view. Make sure the Review tab is active

2 Click the Start Inking tool and get your pen ready. The Ink Tools tab appears as below

Start Inking

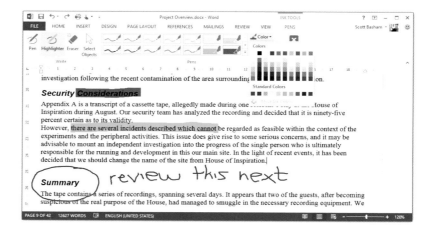

3 Use the Pen tool to write anywhere on your document, even directly over the text

4 Select the Highlighter tool then drag over various areas. You can change color and styles with the Pens tools

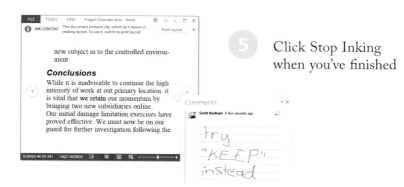

5 Click Stop Inking when you've finished

Don't forget

If you switch to Read Mode these ink annotations will not be displayed (Word will show you a message under the title bar to remind you of this). However, you can still add Inked Comments as shown in the previous example.

Tracking

Sometimes it's useful to track changes you make to a document, so that someone else can see exactly what you have done. It may even be necessary for someone to approve or reject those changes before they become permanently incorporated into the document.

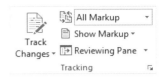

1 To activate change tracking, click the Track Changes icon in the Tracking area of the Review tab

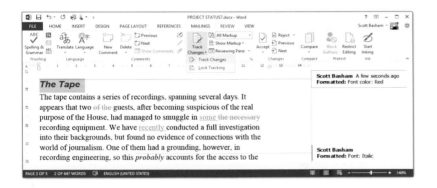

Don't forget

Deleted text can be shown in a different color with a horizontal line running through it, or noted in the right margin. A vertical line in the margin indicates that changes were made in this area.

2 Now your edits will be shown visually. Experiment by deleting text, adding in some new text, editing existing text, changing format and then finally using copy and paste to move a phrase, sentence or paragraph to a different part of your document

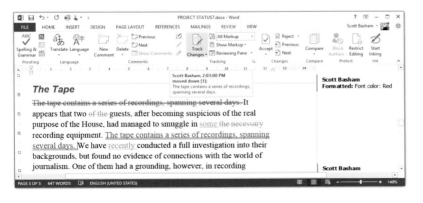

Don't forget

If you rest your mouse over any changed text, then the name, type of change and date/time appears as a ToolTip.

3 The Markup area to the right of the main page is used to show you who has been making changes. On the next page we'll ask Word to add to this information

4 Click on the Show Markup icon in the Tracking area, choose Balloons and then "Show Revisions in Balloons" to see all the revision details in the Markup area

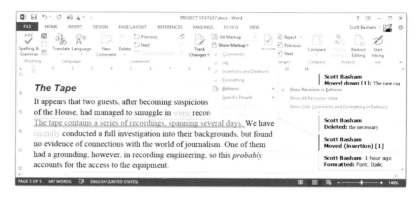

Hot tip

Just below its title, the Reviewing pane shows you the total number of revisions. Clicking the ✔ icon beside it will toggle on and off a more detailed summary.

5 Click on the Reviewing Pane icon in the Tracking area, and choose one of the two options (Vertical or Horizontal) to make it visible

6 Make some more changes to your document and watch what happens in the Reviewing pane

7 The Reviewing pane contains a comprehensive summary of all the comments and revisions made. Clicking on an entry in the main list will take you to its location in the main document

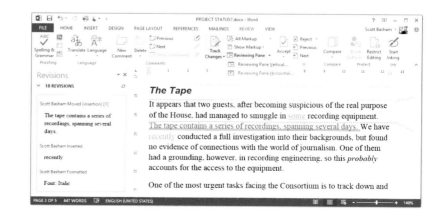

8 Close down the Reviewing pane, either with its ✕ icon or from the Tracking area of the Review tab. Make sure All Markup is selected from the Show Markup pop-up control in the same area

9 Scroll through your document until you find a section with both comments and revisions (or make some new comments and revisions yourself)

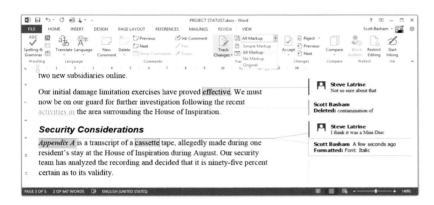

10 Now switch to Simple Markup so that you can appreciate the difference. It's much easier to read – but you can still see comments by clicking on the balloons

11 Click on one of the vertical colored lines to see revisions, then click again to hide the Markup area

All Markup ▾
Simple Markup
All Markup
No Markup
Original

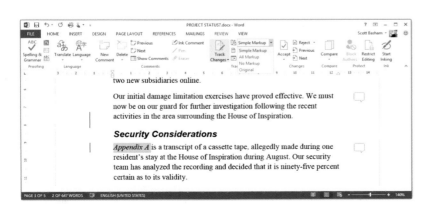

Locking tracking

If you'd like to insist that tracking is switched on when you collaborate with others then you can lock it using a password

1. Open the pop-up menu attached to the Track Changes icon in the Tracking area of the Review tab

2. Choose Lock Tracking

3. Enter a password, then once more to confirm and click OK

Changes

Now, if there are some changes in your document, you can take on the role of someone who reviews those changes. The tools in the Changes area let you work through your document looking at each change in turn – using the Previous and Next icons.

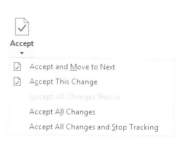

1. If you click the Accept button then the change is permanently applied to the document

2. If you click Reject, the change is removed and the text reverts to its original state

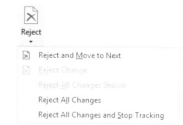

Protecting a document

Word allows you to protect your document in a number of ways. You can control which aspects may be edited: for example, you may allow a user to add comments but not to edit the text directly. If you are sharing your document you can also restrict permissions to certain users. Furthermore, you can set protection on the document as a whole.

Creating a document password

1 Make sure you have your document open. Go to the File tab – the Info section is displayed by default

2 Click Protect Document then "Encrypt with Password"

3 Enter a password, click OK, then enter it a second time to confirm

4 Save the document in the normal way. Make sure you remember the password you set

After you've set the password, the Info section in the File tab will remind you that a password is required to open the document.

Mark as Final

When you have finished editing your document you can "Mark as Final", which indicates to anyone who opens it that this is the definitive version and should not be changed.

① Go to the File tab and make sure the Info section is displayed

② Click Protect Document and then "Mark as Final"

③ Save the document. The following message appears

Opening a protected document

① Go to the File tab and open the document you saved previously

② A dialog box appears prompting you for the password. Enter the password then click OK

③ If the document was marked as final then Word will automatically select Read Mode. If there were any inked annotations or comments then at the top of the window you'll see something similar to this:

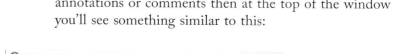

Beware

Although "Mark as Final" is a good way to let people know you are not expecting them to edit your document, it is not enforced. Anyone clicking the Edit Anyway button will be able to make changes. On the next two pages you'll see a much better way of ensuring your document is read-only.

4 Go to Layout Mode and try to make some changes. You'll find you cannot change things and instead you'll see a message in the Status bar

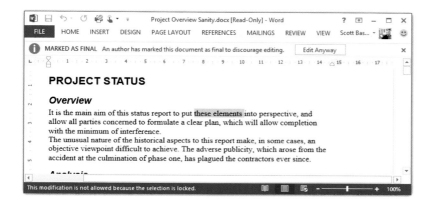

Restrict Editing

This offers better control over access to your document.

Restrict Editing

1 Click the Restrict Editing tool in the Protect area on the right hand side of the Review tab. The Restrict Editing pane appears

2 Switch on "Limit formatting to a selection of styles" then click on Settings

3 From this dialog box you can choose which styles are allowed. By default they're all enabled, so either review each one or, if you want to use just a few, click "None" then reselect the styles you wish to allow. Click OK when you've finished this

...cont'd

4 You may see the message below, asking you what you'd like to do with the styles you've forbidden

5 Alternatively, you can limit users' activities in several other ways by choosing an option for Editing Restrictions. "Tracked changes" means that tracking is compulsory and cannot be switched off. Choose "No changes (Read only)" to fully protect your document

Hot tip

If you're sharing your document online, you can manually lock the other authors out of certain areas. Select the text you'd like to reserve and then click the Block Authors icon in the Protect area of the Review tab. To release this area reselect and click the icon a second time, then save the document.

6 Make any last-minute changes to your document then, when you're ready, click "Yes, Start Enforcing Protection"

7 Enter a password, and then once again to confirm

8 Save and close the document

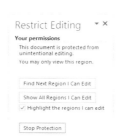

9 Now re-open the document to check the level of protection

The Restrict Editing panel will remind you that the document is protected and you cannot make edits. If you change your mind you can click Stop Protection and enter the password to proceed.

Index

Working
with
Feminist
Criticism

Working with Feminist Criticism

Mary Eagleton

BLACKWELL Publishers

First published in 1996
2 4 6 8 10 9 7 5 3 1

Blackwell Publishers Ltd.
108 Cowley Road
Oxford OX4 1JF
UK

Blackwell Publishers Inc
238 Main Street
Cambridge, Massachusetts 02142,
USA

British Library Cataloguing in Publication Data
A CIP catalogue record for this book is available from the British Library.

Library of Congress Cataloging-in-Publication Data
Eagleton, Mary.
    Working with feminist criticism/Mary Eagleton.
        p.   cm.
    Includes bibliographical references and index.
    ISBN 0-631-19441-X (alk. paper : hardcover).
    - ISBN 0-631-19442-8 (alk. paper : pbk.)
    1. Feminist literary criticism.   I. Title.
  PN98.W64E24   1996
  801' .95'082—dc20   95-39954
                                                                  CIP

Typeset in Ehrhardt in $^{11}/_{12}$ pt
by Ian Foulis & Associates

Printed in Great Britain by T. J. Press limited, Padstow, Cornwall

This book is printed on acid-free paper

Contents

Acknowledgements

I should like to acknowledge my debt to the following friends, students and colleagues (not always separate categories): to my students who, with forbearance, acted as guinea-pigs for some of this material and to Judy Giles who piloted certain sections with her own students and passed on much helpful advice; to Joyce Smith, Liz Sourbut and, especially, Sarah Lawson Welsh who came to the rescue with missing references; to the Librarian and library staff of the University College of Ripon and York St John and to Andy Sawyer of the Science Fiction Foundation Collection, the University of Liverpool; to the Research Management Group and my colleagues in Literature and Women's Studies, both of the University College of Ripon and York St John, who gave the necessary financial and practical support to allow me to finish this project. I am particularly grateful to Julia Dunphy who with characteristic generosity gave of her time to read and comment on several sections; her care and attentiveness were greatly valued. As ever, the professionalism of the Blackwell team, especially Simon Prosser and Jill Landeryou, eased any problem. I am also very indebted to Connie Hallam and Thelma Gilbert for their help with permissions, to Zeb Korycinska for her indexing work and, above all, to Alison Truefitt whose editorial skill proved exemplary.

My deepest thanks are always to David and Matthew but this book is for Matt now that he's old enough to understand and, hopefully, appreciate what I'm doing.

We are grateful for permission to reproduce the following copyright material:

Margaret Atwood: extract from *The Handmaid's Tale* (1987) reprinted by permission of Virago Press, Houghton Mifflin Company and the Canadian Publishers, McLelland & Stewart, Toronto; and 'A Paper Bag' from *Selected Poems 1966-1984*, Copyright © Margaret Atwood 1990, reprinted by permission of Virago Press, Houghton Mifflin Company, and Oxford University Press Canada. **Judith Barrington**: 'Naming the Waves' from *Naming the Waves:Contemporary Lesbian Poetry* edited by Christine McEwen (Virago, 1988), reprinted by permission of the publishers. **Jean 'Binta' Breeze**: 'I Poet' from *Spring Cleaning* (Virago 1992), reprinted by permission of the publishers. **Church Times**: '100 Years Ago' article from *Church Times* 18.12.92, reprinted by permission. **J. M. Coetzee**: extracts from *Foe*, Copyright © 1986 J. M. Coetzee, reprinted by permission of Viking Penguin, a division of Penguin Books USA Inc, and Murray Pollinger. **Helen Dunmore**: 'Three Ways of Recovering a Body' from *Recovering a Body* by Helen Dunmore (Bloodaxe Books, 1994), reprinted by permission of Bloodaxe Books Ltd.

The Guardian: graphic from *The Guardian* 12.10.93, Copyright © The Guardian. **Safiya Henderson-Holmes**: 'Rape: A Class Act' from *Madness and a Bit of Hope* (Harlem River Press, 1990), reprinted by permission of Writers and Readers Publishing Inc. **Maxine Hong Kingston**: extracts from *The Woman Warrior: Memoirs of a Girlhood Among Ghosts* (Picador, 1981), reprinted by permission of Macmillan Publishers Ltd and Random House Inc. **Joan Larkin**: 'Rape' from *A Long Sound* (Granite Press, 1986). **Liz Lochhead**: 'Men Talk' from *True Confessions and Clichés* (Polygon, 1985), reprinted by permission of Polygon. **Máighréad Mebdh**: lines from 'Easter 1991' first published in *Feminist Review* 44, Summer 1993, reprinted by permission of the author. **Elma Mitchell**: 'Thoughts After Ruskin' Copyright © Elma Mitchell, from *The Poor Man in the Flesh* (Peterloo, 1976), reprinted by permission of Peterloo Poets. **NATE**: chart from *Gender Issues in English Coursework* (1988) reprinted by permission. **Grace Nichols**: 'Of Course When They Ask for Poems About the "Realities" of Black Women' from *Lazy Thoughts of a Lazy Woman* (Virago, 1989), Copyright © Grace Nichols 1989, reproduced by permission of Curtis Brown Group Ltd, London on behalf of Grace Nichols. **Sylvia Plath**: extract from *The Bell Jar*, reprinted by permission of Faber & Faber Ltd and HarperCollins Publishers Inc. **Fahmida Riaz**: 'Image' From *We Sinful Women* (Women's Press, 1991), translated and edited by Rukhsana Ahmad, reprinted by permission of The Women's Press and Rukhsana Ahmad. **Adrienne Rich**: lines from 'Cartographies of Silence' from *The Dream of a Common Language: Poems 1974–1977* by Adrienne Rich, Copyright © 1978 by W. W. Norton & Company, Inc, reprinted by permission of the author and W. W. Norton & Company, Inc. **Diane Richardson and Victoria Robinson**: chart and extract from 'Publishing Feminism: Redefining the Women's Studies Discourse' in *The Journal of Gender Studies* 3:1, 1994, reprinted by permission of Carfax Publishing Company, P O Box 25, Abingdon, Oxon OX14 3UE. **Routledge**: Contents page of *Gender and Women's Studies* Catalogue 1995, reprinted by permission. **May Sarton**: lines from 'My Sisters, O My Sisters' Copyright 1948 and renewed © 1976 by May Sarton from *Collected Poems* 1930–1993, Copyright © The estate of the late May Sarton, reprinted by permission of W. W. Norton & Company, Inc, and A.M. Heath & Company Ltd, Authors' Agents. **Anne Stevenson**: lines from 'Re-reading Jane' from *Fiction Makers* (OUP, 1985) and lines from 'Letter to Sylvia Plath' from *The Other House* (OUP, 1990), reprinted by permission of Oxford University Press. **Margaret Walker**. 'Lineage' and 'Kissie Lee' from *For My People* (Yale University Press, 1942). **Yorkshire Evening Press**: article by Kevin Bostock, 22.7.94 reprinted by permission of Press Agency (Yorkshire) Ltd.

Despite every effort to trace and contact copyright owners prior to publication this has not always been possible. We apologize for any apparent infringement of copyright and if notified, we will be pleased to rectify any errors or omissions at the earliest opportunity.

Introduction

Aims of the book

If you have recently entered higher education to study literature, or women's studies, or cultural studies, if you are planning to do so, or if you have an interest in how critical debates have developed in recent years, then at some stage you will confront the significant body of materials produced in the last thirty years in feminist literary criticism – an encounter which I hope you undertake with the appropriate mixture of excitement and trepidation. Engaging with feminist literary criticism is a large project but, at the same time, endlessly challenging. The aim of this book is to help with the process in a variety of ways.

In 1973 French critic, Roland Barthes published a book about reading called *The Pleasure of the Text*. So let us start with the idea of pleasure – pleasure in the intellectual provocation of the ideas you will find in feminist criticism and, sometimes, pleasure in the recognition of a kindred spirit, a writer saying just what you have always thought or just what you wanted to hear. I believe that the ideas discussed in this book are important to literature, important to women's lives and important to men who care about women's lives. I hope you experience a similar sense of immediacy and relevance.

The book does not intend to be exhaustive. You will find here only a fraction of what is available, lined on acres of bookshelves. But what the book should do is introduce you to some of the central ideas and approaches that have preoccupied feminist critics. As a teacher of this material I feel I am always running to stand still, guiltily aware of what I have failed to read. My students tell me how overwhelmed they can feel by the quantity and, sometimes, the difficulty of the criticism. This book provides you with, at least, a starting point.

I am trying to encourage an active involvement with the material in the belief that the more one does the more one understands. Thus, in each section, I ask you to find out, to think, to review, to jot down, to compare, to evaluate, to research, to discuss ... There is a temptation to avoid following any of these requests and simply deduce where the process is leading. I ask you to resist such a temptation if you can since by taking a full part in the process you will learn more and you will become increasingly at ease with the concepts.

I hope the book will function also as a resource. I include many extracts from different critics and writers and I trust that at least some of them will intrigue you sufficiently to want to discover more about the author's work. The sections contain advice for further projects and reading, so once you feel confident about the basics, you can move on to other materials. I like to think that the book will be a useful adjunct to your future work in feminist criticism, a convenient source to which you can return for names, titles, ideas, quotations.

Your responses

For those of you who are new to higher education or returning to academic work after a break of some years, following the activities and guidelines given in each section should help in developing the analytical and research skills you will need also in other areas of study. Later in this Introduction I list some of the kinds of reference material you will find useful. In the sections themselves you will encounter two kinds of question:

- those which ask you to think widely, laterally, intuitively
- those which ask you to organize, systematize, focus.

Both kinds of question are essential to any research process: the first stimulates a diverse and creative response to ideas; the second helps you to direct the hetero-geneous response for the purpose of producing an essay, a seminar paper, a presentation. Don't feel that you have to conjure up instantly profound comments. To remind yourself of the obvious is a handy way of getting clear in your mind the basics of the debate. Secondly, try not to censor yourself. Those thoughts we dismiss as 'wrong', 'probably irrelevant', 'off the wall' are often the start of genuine perceptions. Be attentive to your own responses, nurture them; don't short-change them in your haste to get to the nearest critic or 'authority'.

If you look to this book for answers then you will be disappointed. There are few correct answers in feminist criticism – or, indeed, in any other form of criticism. Obviously it is better to make clear that *Pride and Prejudice* was written by Jane Austen rather than Barry Manilow but, once one gets beyond that baseline, there is a plurality of critiques, interpretations, ways of reading. This is not to say, however, that every opinion is as valid as every other. There are ways in which one can illustrate that George Eliot's use of imagery is more complex than Barbara Cartland's and fans of Miss Cartland will just have to eat humble pie. But quite how the reader interprets George Eliot's imagery seems to me to be open to long-term debate. Thus, I would encourage you to pursue questions beyond your initial thoughts to further, more perceptive analysis; your first response is important but, if you keep working on the material, you will find other responses to add to that first one.

Although there are no neat answers, I do provide hints as to productive avenues, or I start a response and ask you to continue, or I begin a checklist of points and ask you to complete it, or I give my response and then ask you to comment on it or to give yours. This is because I recognize that students who feel unsure of their capabilities or who are coming new to the area value guidance. On the other hand, if you want to experiment freely, then redefine the guidelines in ways that suit you.

Dealing with difficulty

My own students have been the enthusiastic, willing and, occasionally, less than willing experimenters with this material over many years and their responses and comments have carefully guided me. In one area, though, I have to admit that I have not completely followed their advice, in that I have not removed from the text all the bits which they told me were 'difficult', 'inaccessible', 'obscure'. This is not because of any particular malice on my part and I have, indeed, tried to make the text as lucid as possible. However, not only is it beyond my capabilities to make this text transparently clear for every reader, it is also not my desire so to do. I do not want to control all possible meanings; I want to leave spaces for readers to produce their own – sometimes novel, sometimes idiosyncratic – interpretations. The result is that, from time to time, the reader has to struggle with difficult materials. This will mean that you, like me, will repeatedly return to material, sometimes over a long period, to glean what it has to say. It will mean that you, like me, will have to admit, on occasions, that you cannot make sense of something, or cannot at the moment. The main point is not to be put off by difficulty, not to see it as a sign of your 'failure'. It isn't. Trying to find your own way through difficult material is an important aspect of intellectual development; it is part of what study is about. Equally, don't dismiss all difficult material as pretentious nonsense. Sometimes it may be that, but it can also be a writer trying to express complex and subtle ideas or a writer experimenting with a new approach. You have to work with the author to elucidate those ideas.

How can one 'work with the author'? If you are faced with material which you find hard to understand, try the following strategies:

➤ List what seem to you some of the important points and then amplify each one in your own words.

➤ Select points with which you agree, disagree, or about which you are unsure. Explain why in each case.

➤ Write a synopsis of the argument as far as you can take it.

➤ Select an aspect that interests you and produce a list of questions that you would like answered about that aspect.

➤ Can you think of other material (critical, imaginative or from other cultural forms) that in some way – maybe obliquely – connects with the passage you are studying? Have you come across some aspects of the argument elsewhere? If so, follow up your references and compare what is being said.

➤ Are there phrases, sentences, structures in the writing, tones, rhythms which intrigue you or strike you? Are there terms you don't understand which you need to look up in a dictionary or a glossary of literary concepts?

➤ Try taking issue with the parts of the argument you understand; give a contrary view or dispute the terms or premises.

➤ As always, if you can share notes with a friend, your understanding will be greatly increased.

Following these and similar strategies does not mean that all will be laid bare as a consequence but they will give you a way in to a text which, at first, may have appeared mystifying.

Ways of reading the book

My intention is that the book is both structured and open, though I realize that I risk missing both goals in trying to do the impossible. Each section has defined structure. There is an introduction which outlines the aims of the section; my observations on material are marked with a bullet, thus: •; points which demand a response on your part are indicated by ➤. Sections conclude with a reading list of all the texts mentioned in the section and other related material (full publication details are given in the list of works at the end of the book).

There is also a rough logic to the sequence of the sections:

- Since the ability to take up a place in public discourse is the foundation of all women's writing, the first section considers women's relation to both speech and silence, while the second section also considers language by focusing on the problems of definition. The openness of feminism to investigating and re-defining its terminology is notable throughout this text; many terms have layers of meanings and associations.

- Sections 3–5 consider the position of the woman author and the development of a tradition of women's writing.

- Sections 6 and 7 look at issues of genre and literary form and how they might relate to gender and the field of possibilities for the woman writer.

- Sections 8–10 examine publishing, strategies for reading and the practices of feminist criticism, in other words – what happens to the text once it leaves the desk of the woman author.

- Sections 11–15 concentrate on some of the key theoretical problems that have preoccupied feminist writers and literary critics.

- The final sections are a Conclusion, indicating ways forward for future study, and a list of all the texts that have been cited in the earlier sections.

However, there is no necessity to read the sections consecutively. You *can* approach them that way and, in so doing, you will cover a spread of the major preoccupations in contemporary feminist literary criticism or you can simply dip into sections that appeal to you.

Sections vary, somewhat, in length – some issues take longer to explore than others – and material varies in complexity. As I noted above, the individual reader can work in her own way on these different levels of material, immediately responding in some cases, undertaking further reading and thought in others. Some material is approachable for students with no knowledge of feminist criticism; some, while not presuming a detailed knowledge, is certainly easier to grasp if you have experience of feminist criticism or a willingness to acquire that experience. If you are working in a group or in an institutional setting, this multi-level approach aims to provide something, not for everybody all the time, but for a good number of potential readers for a fair amount of the time.

Some questions demand a personal response but, in gathering information or testing out hypotheses, a group approach is often helpful. When working in groups try not to come to a too-easy consensus or to be swayed by the most authoritative voice. Keep questioning yourself and each other; be alert to contra-dictions and inconsistencies in the argument; develop the most creative and suggestive elements in the debate.

If you are studying in higher education, you could use the book as supportive reading within a course: indeed, your tutor might direct you in this. One section might be useful preparation for a seminar, another might reinforce what was said in a lecture, a third might feed in to research for an essay – and so on.

It helps if you make links between the material in different sections. At some stages I advise the reader to look at another section but you may find other links, comparisons and contrasts that I have not anticipated. Such links reinforce ideas and open up new avenues.

Think also about interrelating the approaches. There may be certain kinds of questions which you find particularly productive. In that case, apply those questions in other sections you read. You will get most out of the book if you use if flexibly – establish dialogues, carry over ideas, see if comments from one section relate elsewhere, adapt it to suit your needs and interests.

Are you the reader I have in mind?

Narrative theory talks about someone called the 'implied reader'. (We shall discuss this figure further in the section on Feminist Reading.) This is not the real, living reader of the book but a creation of the book itself, the kind of reader the book needs so as to be understood. Thus, with this book, for instance, the implied reader would have to take feminist ideas seriously. This does not necessarily mean you have to be a feminist and certainly not that you have to show a solemn reverence for every feminist proposition; rather, what is needed is a willingness to debate feminism as a valid literary and political critique. If the reader thought the ideas of feminism were something akin to those of the Flat Earth Society – I hope I am not unintentionally insulting all my Flat Earth readers here – then the whole project would be a non-starter.

Narrative theory discusses also the 'narratee' who is the person to whom a book's narrator is speaking. Sometimes the narratee can be directly addressed as in that famous moment in *Jane Eyre* when the narrator says, 'Reader, I married him.' This workbook is clearly not, in any conventional sense, a narrative but I do have a strong sense of the person I am addressing and my 'narratee' is female. When I say 'you', I am thinking of a female 'you' and my focus is on *women* writers, experiences common among *women* and issues of femininity. This is not to say that men cannot read the book and that it has nothing to say about/to men, experiences common among men and issues of masculinity. Let me clarify:

Visibility of women	Readers and practitioners of feminist criticism are more likely to be female. So, one could say that on pragmatic grounds a female narratee is suitable. That may be the case but, for me, the political argument is more fundamental. If feminists do not try to make women visible, the historical record shows that nobody else will. My experience indicates that it is still necessary to remind the world that women exist. My emphasis on 'she' is a gesture in that direction.
Gender is a major issue	Literary feminists are very conscious of how gender affects the processes of reading and writing: authors are

not neuters speaking to neuters. Whether you agree or not with my insistence on 'she', I am raising the issue simply by being explicit about the female sex of my narratee. I suspect that many studies you read, whether in literature, history, the social sciences etc., fail to consider gender as a relevant factor: that silence is as resonant as speech. You might also ask why many people still believe that using the pronoun 'he' all the time is 'normal' while using the pronoun 'she' all the time is 'ideological'. If this is a topic that you find interesting and/or contentious, you could look especially at the material in this book on Feminist Reading and at the recommendations for further reading.

For male readers

If my 'you' is female, then how might a man read this book? The answer – which is not at all flippant – is, in any way he thinks best. Some suggestions are:

➤ to consider the difference of a woman-to-woman writing/reading experience
➤ to approach material through the perspective of a mother, sister, female friend
➤ to link issues of femininity to issues of masculinity
➤ to become more conscious of the issues of gendered reading, of what it means to read 'as a man'.

Research and reference

A developing sub-genre in recent fiction is the novel about academic life; the 'campus' novels of David Lodge or Malcolm Bradbury would fit within this group as would Tom Sharpe's *Wilt* (1976). Of interest to me are those novels which discuss specifically 'feminist academic research and/or the experience of investigating a woman's history. I am thinking, for instance, of the end of Margaret Atwood's *The Handmaid's Tale* (1987) when the heroine's life and words become research material for male academics; or of the research processes undertaken in Alison Lurie's *The Truth About Lorin Jones* (1988) and Antonia Byatt's *Possession: A Romance* (1991), where the discovery of 'lost' women artists leads to profoundly unsettling reassessments; or of the search for a woman's history across space and time in Bharati Mukherjee's *The Holder of the World* (1994). One thing that these texts point to is that research is far from being the disinterested activity academic mythology might like us to believe. Political, economic and ideological pressures, complex personal motives, unconscious desires, academic rivalry, plain error all render the research process imperfect.

For feminists, that imperfection has shown itself most starkly in the absence of reference material on women's lives and work. A research process aspiring to both impartiality and general application had seemingly overlooked half the human race. Which names, what meanings and material should be included in reference volumes; how is this data to be selected; how is it to be prioritized; how is it contextualized? For example, is Dorothy Wordsworth an author in her own right

Cartoon by Carolyn Hillyer, Women's Studies International Forum, *Pergamon Press*

with a separate bio/bibliographical entry or is she, merely, sister and helper of William with a sentence to herself at the end of his entry?

Much of the material I list here, as an aid to your research, has been published in the last ten years, which is a measure of both the gap that needed to be filled and the considerable amount of research work that has been done in our time. It is difficult to put limits on this material since women's writing and feminist criticism have interconnected easily with many other critical discourse and subject disciplines. Thus, volumes of feminist literary criticism readily link with material in cultural criticism, with feminist thought generally, with related studies in history and the social sciences, with political theory ... and so on. In an attempt to keep some kind of grip on the material, I have confined myself as far as possible to:

- works concerned with language, women writers and feminist criticism
- works readily available in Great Britain and North America.

The texts are divided into seven categories:

- dictionaries
- biographical dictionaries of women writers
- bibliographies of research on women
- anthologies of women's writing
- introductions to feminist criticism
- journals and magazines

- handbooks, guides, others.

The happy news is that we can now, at least, start putting together bibliographies of reference material on the history of literary women. Fifteen years ago, reference material would have been mostly limited to the 'star' names – Austen, the Brontës, Dickinson etc.

Dictionaries

These dictionaries follow three main tacks: tracing the etymology of words to discover earlier meanings of interest to women; redefining existing terms; coining new terms and meanings. Kramarae and Treichler define their terms through copious quotation; thus, the dictionary becomes also an excellent guide to further reading. Humm's dictionary, as the title indicates, confines itself to terms from feminist theory.

> Mary Daly and Jane Caputi, *Webster's First New Intergalactic Wickedary of the English Language*

> Maggie Humm, *The Dictionary of Feminist Theory*

> Cheris Kramarae and Paula A. Treichler, *Amazons, Bluestockings and Crones: A Feminist Dictionary*

> Rosalie Maggio, *The Bias-Free Word Finder: A Dictionary of Nondiscriminatory Language*

> Jane Mills, *Womanwords: A Vocabulary of Culture and Patriarchal Society*

> Monique Wittig and Sandie Zeig, *Lesbian Peoples: Materials for A Dictionary*

See also, Raymond Williams, *Keywords: A Vocabulary of Culture and Society*. It is a shame that, even in this revised edition of his 1976 and 1983 work, Williams barely addressed feminism. Neither 'feminism' nor 'gender' appear as keywords; 'women's liberation' gets a passing reference under 'liberation'. Nevertheless, this book does trace the etymology of many words that are central to an understanding of our culture and that are frequently employed in critical theory – feminism included.

Biographical dictionaries

These studies give details of the biography and literary achievement of each woman author. In addition they may include material on the author's social and historical context, details of the reception of the author's work, advice as to further reading, introductory essays etc. The term 'literary' is interpreted in its widest sense: novelists and poets are found alongside the authors of hymns, household manuals, guides to midwifery, political tracts. These volumes are a useful starting point for research, especially for a new project when you have little knowledge on which to build.

> Maureen Bell, George Parfitt, Simon Shepherd (eds), *A Biographical Dictionary of English Women Writers, 1580–1720*

> Virginia Blain, Patricia Clements, Isobel Grundy, *The Feminist Companion to Literature in English: Women Writers from the Middle Ages to the Present*

Claire Buck (ed.), *Bloomsbury Guide to Women's Literature*

Anne Crawford et al., *Europa Biographical Dictionary of British Women*

Frank M. Magill (ed.) *Great Women Writers: The Lives and Works of 135 of the World's Most Important Women Writers from Antiquity to the Present*

Lina Mainiero, *American Women Writers: from Colonial Times to the Present*

Paul Schlueter and June Schlueter (eds), *An Encyclopaedia of British Women Writers*

Joanne Shattock, *The Oxford Guide to British Women Writers*

Janet Todd (ed.), *A Dictionary of British and American Women Writers 1660–1800*

Janet Todd (ed.) *Dictionary of British Women Writers*

Jennifer Uglow and Frances Hinton, *The Macmillan Dictionary of Women's Biography*

Ann Owens Weekes, *Unveiling Treasures: The Attic Guide to the Published Works of Irish Women Literary Writers*

Bibliographies of relevance to women

Bibliographies and bibliographical essays are an excellent way of rapidly surveying the field, getting a quick idea of the research that has been done and where it would be most profitable for you to concentrate your efforts. Bibliographies of Women's Studies obviously consider a wide range of women's concerns but the literary, linguistic and cultural are always among them. Think also of bibliographies of individual writers. Well-known women writers – Austen, Eliot, the Brontës, Woolf, Katherine Mansfield, Sylvia Plath etc. – have reference material on their work. Similarly, it is useful to research bibliographies of particular areas of writing – American literature, the novel, the Gothic etc. – since women practitioners are included.

Patricia K. Ballou, *Women: A Bibliography of Bibliographies*

Gwenn Davis and Beverly Joyce, *Personal Writings by Women to 1900: A Bibliography of American and British Writers*

Gwenn Davis and Beverly Joyce, *Poetry by Women to 1900: A Bibliography of American and British Writers*

Gwenn Davis and Beverly Joyce, *Drama by Women to 1900: A Bibliography of American and British Writers*

Maureen Ritchie, *Women's Studies: A Checklist of Bibliographies*

Patricia E. Sweeney, *Biographies of British Women: An Annotated Bibliography*

Related to bibliographies are abstracting periodicals which give synopses not only of books but of articles in journals. See:

Studies on Women Abstracts

Anthologies

Anthologies of women's writing are now in plentiful supply. Some collections are devoted to particular groups of women writers (mothers and daughters, Jewish women); some to particular historical periods; to particular countries; to particular forms of writing (collections of short stories, modernist writing). What I offer here are more general anthologies covering a wide historical and/or geographical spread. If you feel your experience of women's writing is limited, spending time with one of these large anthologies is an easy and pleasurable way to get a sense of the range of women's writing and to discover new women authors.

Marian Arkin and Barbara Shollar, *Longman Anthology of World Literature by Women: 1875–1975*

Aliki Barnstone and Willis Barnstone (eds), *A Book of Women Poets from Antiquity to Now*

Louise Bernikow, *The World Split Open: Four Centuries of Women Poets in England and America, 1552–1950*

Sandra Gilbert and Susan Gubar (eds), *The Norton Anthology of Literature by Women: The Tradition in English.*

Olga Kenyon, *800 Years of Women's Letters. The Tradition in English.*

Carolyne Larrington, *Women and Writing in Medieval Europe: A Sourcebook*

Ann Allen Schockley, *Afro-American Women Writers, 1746–1933: An Anthology and Critical Guide*

Dale Spender and Janet Todd, *Anthology of British Women Writers: From the Middle Ages to the Present*

Introductions to feminist criticism

If you are new to feminist criticism I suggest you look first at some of the surveys, readers and collections of essays that have been produced in this area. These will give you a sense of the scope of feminist criticism and of the way in which it has contributed to and learned from other critical positions. *The Lesbian and Gay Studies Reader* has a wider remit than the literary but I include it here as sections on representation and writing do feature and other concerns, such as concepts of subjectivity and experience, are relevant to our focus. All these texts have suggestions for further reading so it you find a feminist approach or critic that interests you, you can follow the reference.

Henry Abelove, Michèle Aina Barale, David M. Halperin (eds), *The Lesbian and Gay Studies Reader*

Catherine Belsey and Jane Moore (eds), *The Feminist Reader: Essays in Gender and the Politics of Literary Criticism*

Mary Eagleton (ed.), *Feminist Literary Theory: A Reader*

Mary Eagleton (ed.), *Feminist Literary Criticism*

Maggie Humm (ed.), *Feminisms: A reader*

Maggie Humm, *A Reader's Guide to Contemporary Feminist Literary Criticism*

Toril Moi, *Sexual/Textual Politics. Feminist Literary Theory*

Pam Morris, *Literature and Feminism: An Introduction*

K. K. Ruthven, *Feminist Literary Studies: An Introduction*

Elaine Showalter (ed.), *The New Feminist Criticism: Essays on Women, Literature and Theory*

Robyn R. Warhol and Diane Price Herndl (eds), *Feminism: An Anthology of Literary Theory and Criticism*

Journals and magazines

European Journal of Women's Studies (Sage Publications Ltd.).

Everywoman (Everywoman Publishing).

Feminist Review (Routledge).

Feminist Studies (University of Maryland).

Journal of Gender Studies (Routledge).

Signs: Journal of Women in Culture and Society (University of Chicago Press).

Trouble & Strife (Collectively produced; distributed by Central Books).

Women: A Cultural Review (Oxford University Press).

Women' Studies: An Interdisciplinary Journal (Gordon and Breach).

Women's Studies International Forum (Pergamon Press).

Most of the above are academic journals, published three or four times a year and available in academic libraries. If you find a journal that particularly fits your interests and want your own copy, it would be best to subscribe, as newsagents are usually unable to supply. (Details of subscription are always included with each issue.) Though the stock is often limited, academic and radical bookshops are another source, particularly for special issues. *Everywoman*, which is published monthly, counts as a magazine and is often available through newsagents. *Trouble & Strife* (twice yearly) has an attractive, readable format which bridges the academic and a wider market. If you are unfamiliar with feminist journals, it is worth spending some time getting to know them. There is much variety in terms of academic level, critical approach, range of disciplines covered, national or international perspective.

Recent years have been an unsettled time for publishing and journals and magazines are particularly susceptible to the vagaries of the market. No longer published but still available in libraries and Women's Centres are:

m/f

Spare Rib

Women's Review

Remember also that feminist critiques are now integrated into many mainstream literary and cultural journals so it is worth researching widely in the periodical sections of libraries. Keep a look out for special issues on feminist topics.

Handbooks, guides, others

Loulou Brown et al. (eds), *The International Handbook of Women's Studies*. This handbook contains not only details of women's studies course, but also lists of research resources and publications which usefully supplement the lists given here.

Mary Ellen S. Capek, *A Women's Thesaurus: An Index of Language Used to Describe and Locate Information By and About Women*

Sarah Carter and Maureen Ritchie, *Women's Studies: A Guide to Information Sources*

Margaret Doyle, *The A–Z of Non-Sexist Language*

Carolyne Larrington (ed.), *The Feminist Companion to Mythology*

Rosalie Maggio, *The Beacon Book of Quotations by Women*

Casey Miller and Kate Swift, *The Handbook of Non-Sexist Writing for Writers.*

Editors and Speakers

Elaine Partnow (ed.), *The New Quotable Woman: From Eve to the Present Day*

Susan Searing, *Introduction to Library Research in Women's Studies*

Susan Sellers (ed.), *Taking Reality by Surprise: Writing for Pleasure and Publication*

Anne Stibbs (ed.), *Like a Fish Needs a Bicycle ... And Over 3,000 Quotations By and About Women*

Lisa Tuttle, *Encyclopaedia of Feminism*

Barbara G. Walker, *The Woman's Encyclopaedia of Myths and Secrets*

Francine Wattman, Frank and Paula A. Treichler, *Language, Gender, and Professional Writing*

Elizabeth Wright (ed.), *Feminism and Psychoanalysis: A Critical Dictionary*

Reference material can look intimidatingly weighty and wordy. Yet dipping into volumes and flicking through are as valid as concentrated study and note-taking. Casual reading can stimulate ideas and quickly result in a list of helpful references. It is important, though, when consulting reference works to read carefully the author/editor's introduction in which s/he sets out an agenda and criteria for selection. In this way you make best use of the material that is there and you do not waste time looking for what was never intended to be there. Predictably, the more you use reference books, the more at ease you feel with them. Here are some activities which might help:

➤ Consider some of the issues involved in dictionary making. The introductions to Mills, and Kramarae and Treichler are relevant, as is Alma Graham, 'The Making of a Nonsexist Dictionary', in Barrie Thorne and Nancy Henly (eds), *Language and Sex: Difference and Dominance*.

➤ Compare a selection of texts *within* any section above. Consider how texts are constructed; can you work out the basis on which selections are made; what kind of limitations has the author/editor necessarily put on the project? the dictionaries, most notably, show some interesting variations in approach.

➤ Practise being a lexicographer and trace the etymology of words that are significant for you. The terms in Kramarae and Treichler's title, 'amazons, bluestockings and crones', have a particularly fascinating history. For your chosen terms, uncover old meanings and, if you like, coin new ones.

➤ As an on-going project, it would be useful to make a list of the terms that are likely to feature prominently in this book and in feminist studies generally – female, feminine, feminist, lesbian, gender etc. – and to collect and compare definitions and usage. In this way you will produce your own glossary. You could extend this to critical terms that are current in feminist criticism.

➤ Compare mainstream and feminist dictionaries and biographical dictionaries. At which points do selection, approaches, meanings concur; at which do they differ?

➤ If there are women writers you admire but know little of, use anthologies, bibliographies and biographical dictionaries to put together a bio/biblio-graphical introduction.

➤ Inevitably bibliographies soon get out of date. Do the necessary research to up-date any bibliography you have found useful.

➤ Compiling annotated bibliographies is not only a job for the professional. Get into the habit of keeping a record of every book you read – publishing details and a short synopsis of plot and/or key arguments or themes. Such a record can quickly become a resource for references and secondary material.

➤ Later in this book in the section on Feminist Criticisms we shall be looking at the contents of introductions to feminist criticism and examining the selection process involved. If you want to, look ahead to that section now.

➤ If you are not familiar with the practice of abstracting, you could begin abstracting your own essays as a regular part of your planning and research. To condense the argument of a dozen pages into as many lines means that you have to know precisely what you want to say; in this way, the redundant parts of the essay rapidly become evident.

➤ Read Deborah Cameron's critique of the guides to non-sexist language use by Doyle, and Miller and Swift. See 'Lost in Translation: Non-Sexist Language' *Trouble & Strife* 32 (Winter 1995/6). Would you agree with Cameron's points or would you want to produce a counter argument?

What these exercise should suggest to you is that reference books are neither comprehensive nor unbiased, so readers need to be aware of the limitations – in feminist works as much as any others – while still making good use of the resources within.

Electronic texts

So far we have been thinking about paper resources but a quick tour round any academic library soon illustrates that information is increasingly being accessed electronically. The most enjoyable way to find out about what's available is through hands–on experience, sitting in front of a computer and surfing the information highway. Unfortunately, that is also the best way to lose large chunks of time for no obvious gain: fascinating, compulsive but not always very productive. So advice from professionals in information technology or from computer buffs (there's always one at the next desk) is necessary, and introductions and guides in old-fashioned things called 'books' are also invaluable. Here's just a taster of what's available:

- CD-ROMs of literary texts, databases of journal indexes, newspapers. Think how easily you could search the indexes of numerous journals to find just the article you need. Consider how useful newspapers are for accessing recent reviews or tracing the changing cultural representation of feminism – specifically literary feminism.

- The Internet can give you access to biographical and bibliographical information about women writers or to electronic libraries from which you can download texts so as to work on them. The book that's never on the shelf when you want it thus becomes available. Establishing bibliographies and databases, searching texts for key words, creating a concordance, and all manner of textual analysis can be undertaken with surprising ease. A growing number of bookshops and publishers are also now on–line.

- As the names indicate, discussion lists and bulletin boards enable you to talk to like-minded people about common interests, to obtain up-to-date information, to have queries answered, to get in touch with women's groups, to find out about women's studies programmes etc.

Moreover, the experience of communicating through cyberspace, faceless and voiceless with no necessary markers as to age, race, class, gender etc. adds an exciting dimension to the creation of subjectivity. How we see ourselves in 'real' space and time is not necessarily how we present ourselves in cyberspace. What is involved here and the potential for a new feminist politics and practice are only beginning to be understood.

- For written information see:

  Feminist Collections (University of Wisconsin – a most helpful guide to resources generally. See particularly introductory articles to the Internet by Phyllis Holman Weisbard. 'Gophering Around in Women's Studies' (vol. 15, no. 2 Winter, 1994);' 'More Gophering Around in Women's Studies ...' (vol. 15, no.3 Spring, 1995); 'Web-ster Definitions: A Quick Introduction to the World Wide Web and Women' (vol. 16, no. 2 Winter, 1995)

  Angus J. Kennedy, *The Internet & World Wide Web: The Rough Guide*

  Dale Spender, *Nattering on the Net: Women, Power and Cyberspace*. Spender's bibliography is useful and she provides a necessary context to and cautions about women's experience of technology, particularly computer technology.

However, she has rather less to say about the academic, creative and political potential of the Internet for feminism. For a more enthusiastic introduction, see the work of Sadie Plant. For example, Rosie Cross, 'Cyberfeminism: Interview with Sadie Plant', *geekgirl* (no. 1, 1995).

Endnotes

Don't worry if you cannot immediately comprehend everything you read in this book. Respond to what you do find accessible and then begin to work on what you do not.

Don't pay undue respect to this book. Mould it to suit your needs and interests.

Let me know, c/o Blackwell Publishers, 108 Cowley Road, Oxford, OX4 1JF, what you like and dislike about the book.

I hope you enjoy *Working with Feminist Criticism* – both the book and the activity. I hope it informs and animates you. If it sometimes irritates you too, that is no bad thing!

Speech and Silence

Introduction

> I am Ireland/and I'm silenced
> I cannot tell my abortions/my divorces/my years of slavery/
> my fights for freedom
> it's got to the stage I can hardly remember what I had to tell/
> and when I do/I speak in whispers
>
> from Máighréad Medbh, '*Easter 1991*'

The idea of women as silenced is, at first glance, a curious notion since little girls appear to have no special difficulty in learning a language; indeed, we are often told by educationalists that girls are more verbal than boys. Simply from daily experience we would find it hard to claim that girls and women of our acquaintance are any less fluent than boys and men. Yet, equally, women frequently complain that they feel gagged in certain situations or that what they do say is unheard or misheard or undervalued. The situation is complicated further in that many men would also insist that their relation to language is far from ideal: they, too, are often silenced.

As a way through this conundrum I suggest the following contentions as working principles for this section:

- When women speak of being silenced they don't mean that they are incapable of adequately speaking a language; rather they are referring to social and cultural pressures which undermine their confidence and make them hesitant about speaking.

- This unease in women is, partly, a product of patriarchal power. One location for patriarchal power is language and the public platforms where language is used most prestigiously. Areas of linguistic status in our culture – the pulpit, the bench, the board, and the dispatch box – are associated with men.

- Gender is not the only determinant that affects language. Differences in class, race, sexuality, status, generation etc. also play their part. Hence the working-class man, the Black man, the male child, for example, may also at times feel themselves to be victims of language. As Máighréad Medbh's poem illustrates, national identity can be relevant as well.

- These determinants don't operate separately but interrelate. The woman who is uneasy when speaking at a committee meeting may be experiencing the impact

16

of gender difference. She could equally be experiencing the consequences of being the only Black person in the room, or of being unfamiliar with committee procedure.

The obverse of the debate about silence is feminism's strong exhortation to women to speak. For women to speak, to write, to claim language and use it for their own purposes are aims high on any feminist agenda. Women, as all oppressed groups, find liberation intimately linked with language.

Let us consider further these three key points:

- women's experience of silence
- how gender relates to other determinants in the practice of language
- the significance of speech for women.

The experience of silence

1 Thinking of your own experience and what you have observed, can you find examples of the following?

➤ prohibitions against women's speech, that is, where women's speech is singled out and forbidden

➤ situations in which men's speech is customary and more acceptable; to see a woman speaking on such occasions strikes one as strange or unconventional

Cartoon by Ros Asquith, She *November 1993*

➤ situations where women are free to speak but find it difficult to do so

➤ situations in which women's speech is disregarded.

2 How do you account for the material you have just collected? Select one particular example – it may be the problem girls have in expressing their views in mixed-sex classes or the awkward relationship some women have with their male doctors – and examine as closely as you can the dynamics of that situation and the factors that inhibit the women involved. Which aspects relate to gender; which to other determinants? For example, the woman speaking to a male doctor may talk happily about her sprained ankle but not about her menstrual problems. Or she might feel constrained not by the fact that he is male but by his aura of professional authority. But is that authority linked to has masculinity ... and so on?

3 Commentators often state that the uncertain area for women is *public* discourse: to declare oneself publicly is in various ways unseemly for women,

whereas expressiveness in the private sphere is acceptable. For instance, Lauretta Ngcobo writes:

> Men met regularly in places where women were not expected to attend and they discussed community issues to the exclusion of women. I have distinct memories of those weekly announcements – my grandfather's sombre Sunday voice inviting men to a meeting at some designated spot behind the dipping tank, where they met after dipping their cattle on Thursday mornings. It went without saying that no woman would be there. In a society with sharp divisions of work roles, women did not tend cattle and could not be at the dipping site on a Thursday morning at 10 a.m., when men 'talked'. I puzzled for many years why my grandfather, a very quiet man, could go and 'talk', leaving behind my grandmother who did all the talking around the home and did it most incisively. Hers is the voice I remember most clearly from my youth. Yet she did not attend the Nkwali meetings!
>
> Later, as a grown woman involved in the politics of protest and the struggle against apartheid, I slowly came to realise that mine was a cheering role, in support of the men. I had no voice; I could only concur and never contradict nor offer alternatives.

Lauretta Ngcobo, *Let It Be Told: Black Women Writers in Britain* (1988) pp. 136–7

Cartoon by Cork, Spare Rib *n. 234, May 1992*

Examples of the special places for men's talk in British culture are the working-man's club, the gentleman's club and still, in large measure, the major institutions of government, the law, the church and business.

Yet the problem pages in women's magazines would suggest that in private discourse also – in relations with partners, parents, children – women frequently feel silenced, that they can't focus on themselves and their needs. What do you think? Is speech in the public domain more of a problem for women than in the private? Or is each problematic in different ways?

4 Conversely, think of the contexts in which you can most readily say what you want to say. Is it with your partner, amongst friends, to a family member, in the work situation? For those of you in education or contemplating education, do you find an academic context one which fosters or restricts the speech of women? Try to think specifically of what helps and hinders.

5 Mineke Schipper's collection of writing from women in Africa, the Arab world, Asia, the Caribbean and Latin America is appositely entitled *Unheard Words*. One element in her collection are lists of traditional proverbs, many of which make clear that women should, indeed, be unheard:

> If in times of drought a woman comes and tells you she has found a well, don't listen to her. (Watshi/Ewe, Benin/Togo)
>
> Tie up a woman's tongue and a mule's legs. (Morocco)
>
> Virtuous is the girl who suffers and dies without a sound. (Bengal, India)
>
> A woman's mouth is a fowl's mouth [i.e. she is ungrateful]. (Jamaica)

> Mineke Schipper, *Unheard Words: Women and Literature in Africa, the Arab World,*
> *Asia, the Caribbean and Latin America* (1985) pp. 20, 71, 122, 166

One hopes that whoever coined the first saying was the last to get a drink. The universal nature of these admonitions is striking. Can you think of other cultural examples from proverbs, fairy tales, films, books, jokes – whatever – that suggest that the normative woman and, indeed, the virtuous woman is silent?

6 At the start of her innovative dictionary, *Womanwords*, Jane Mills groups together terms used now and in the past to refer to women. In the category 'Woman and Words' she lists the following:

> anathema; authoress; babble; biddy; bitch; blurb; broad; Cassandra; cat; chatter; cotquean; delphic; fate; fishwife; flibbertigibbet; glamour; gossip; hack; harpy; herstory; madrigal; mother(tongue); nag; nice; pretty; pussy; scold; Sheila; shrew; siren; termagant; testify; trivia; virago; vixen.

> Jane Mills, *Womanwords: A Vocabulary of Culture and Patriarchal Society* (1991) pp. xxi–xxii

What interpretations of the speaking/writing woman are suggested by these words? You could compare Mills's listing with Liz Lochhead's rap 'Men Talk' which gives humorous testimony to the devaluing of women's speech:

> Women
> Rabbit rabbit rabbit women
> Tattle and titter
> Women prattle
> Women waffle and witter
>
> Men Talk. Men Talk.
>
> Women into Girl Talk
> About Women's Trouble

Trivia 'n' Small Talk
they yap and they babble

Men Talk. Men Talk.

Women yatter
Women chatter
Women chew the fat, women spill the beans
Women aint been takin'
The oh-so Good Advice in them
Women's Magazines.

A Man Likes a Good Listener.

Oh yeah
I like A Woman
Who likes me enough
Not to nitpick
Not to nag and
Not to interrupt 'cause I call that treason
A woman with the Good Grace
To be struck dumb
By my Sweet Reason. Yes –

A Man Likes a Good Listener

A Real
Man
Likes a Real Good Listener
Women yap yap yap
Verbal Diarrhoea is a Female Disease
Women she spread she rumours round she
Like Philadelphia Cream Cheese.

Oh
Bossy Women Gossip
Girlish Women Giggle
Women natter, women nag
Women niggle niggle niggle

Men Talk.

Men
Think First, Speak Later
Men Talk.

Liz Lochhead, 'Men Talk' (1985)

The disparaging terms that Lochhead uses here are linked specifically to *women's* language. Is there a parallel vocabulary to describe men's language?

7 Below are two extracts about female silence. The first from Virginia Woolf, the second from Audre Lorde, both speaking of their fear of discussing their sexuality:

> These were two of the adventures of my professional life. The first – killing the Angel in the House – I think I solved. She died. But the second, telling the truth about my own experiences as a body, I do not think I solved. I doubt that any woman has solved it yet. The obstacles against her are still immensely powerful – and yet they are very difficult to define. Outwardly, what is simpler than to write books? Outwardly, what obstacles are there for a woman rather than a man? Inwardly, I think the case is very different; she has still many ghosts to fight, many prejudices to overcome. Indeed it will be a long time still, I think, before a woman can sit down to write a book without finding a phantom to be slain, a rock to be dashed against.

Virginia Woolf, 'Professions for Women' (1942; 1979) p.60

> And of course I am afraid because the transformation of silence into language and action is an act of self-revelation, and that always seems fraught with danger. But my daughter, when I told her of our topic and my difficulty with it, said, 'Tell them about how you're never really a whole person if you remain silent, because there's always that one little piece inside you that wants to be spoken about, and if you keep ignoring it, it gets madder and madder and hotter and hotter, and if you don't speak it out one day it will just up and punch you in the mouth from the inside.'
>
> In the cause of silence, each of us draws the face of her own fear – fear of contempt, of censure, or some judgement, or recognition, of challenge, of annihilation. But most of all, I think, we fear the visibility without which we cannot truly live.

Audre Lorde, 'The Transformation of Silence into Language and Action' (1984) p. 43

Both these essays started life as lectures, Woolf's in 1931, Lorde's in 1977. Woolf's words were prophetic. Nearly half a century after Woolf, Lorde was still fighting Woolf's ghost about the open discussion of female sexuality, particularly about naming lesbianism.

I list here some of the random impressions that come to my mind as I re-read these passages. Before reading my comments, you might like to note a list of your own responses; then you can compare the two.

- the sense of danger, threat, vulnerability in both passages;

- the sense of struggle in both passages;

- What *is* our culture's anxiety about women's words that they have to be so obstructed?

- What price do women pay for speech?

- Do women continue to censor themselves; if so, why? I remember a student writing in her essay, 'Sometimes it seems easier to be silent'. Are we all occasionally guilty of this kind of silence?

- I identify with the fear of revealing in a hostile world an aspect integral to oneself. Better to keep silent.

- What is the difference between the 'lazy' silence – don't bother, leave it to others – and the silence as necessary self-defence? What other kinds of silences are there?

- Men can talk about women's sexuality but women shouldn't be explicit. Does that still hold true? Are there other taboos?

- I regret more the times I failed to speak than the times I spoke out and made a fool of myself.

- 'Speak properly'; 'be polite'; 'don't shout'; 'don't interrupt'; 'be seen but not heard'; 'be quiet'. Do the rules of children's speech continue into adulthood for women?

8   Most of the work on women and silence that I have looked at suggests that silence is a *problem* for women, that they are, in some sense, intimidated into silence and stifled by silence. Yet linguists make clear that no linguistic practice is *intrinsically* good or bad for women, or for anybody else; all depends on the context and interpretation of that speech or lack of speech. Speech can be dangerous. How often did I wish that Mrs Thatcher would hold her tongue since her words were making the lives of most women in Britain immeasurably worse. On the other hand, silence can be persuasive. Have you ever been in an audience that refuses to clap the speaker? Isn't silence and a deadpan expression a compelling response to an offensive joke or comment? The important distinction seems to be the difference between silence as a consciously chosen ploy and silence as a restraint imposed upon one.
   In 'Cartographies of Silence' Adrienne Rich writes:

> Silence can be a plan
> rigorously executed
>
> the blueprint to a life
>
> It is a presence
> it has a history   a form
>
> do not confuse it
> with any kind of absence

from Adrienne Rich, 'Cartographies of Silence' (1975)

And Trinh T. Minh-ha writes:

> Silence as a refusal to partake in the story does sometimes provide us with a means to gain a hearing. It is voice, a mode of uttering, and a response in its own right. Without other silences, however, my silence goes unheard, unnoticed; it is simply one voice less, or more point given to the silencers.

Trinh T. Minh-ha, *Woman, Native, Other: Writing Postcoloniality and Feminism* (1989) p. 83

➤ Think of examples from life and art which suggest that silence can be superior to speech. Again, proverbs offer one possibility: 'empty vessels make most noise'.

➤ Think how the norms concerning speech and silence vary between cultures, classes, different social situations, age groups etc.

➤ How do the observations you've gathered here relate specifically to issues of gender? Is the voluble or taciturn woman viewed in the same way as her male equivalent?

➤ Think about speech and silence being used *strategically* by women. How can women employ speech and silence as part of a feminist politics? See the references to imaginative texts in the 'References and Further Reading' as one way of exploring further this idea of strategic silence.

Language, gender and other differences

9   Lorde's essay illustrates that her battle against silence is not solely a matter of gender. Speaking from a public platform at an academic conference (the essay was first delivered at the Modern Languages Association's 'Lesbian and Literature Panel' in Chicago, 1977), and speaking not only as a woman but as a Black woman and as a lesbian who wishes to declare herself 'a poet', entails a whole series of confrontations with conventional views about who uses certain forms of language, where and in what ways.

Secondly, we need to be careful about how we make connections between language and gender, and language, gender and other differences. The speakers we've considered so far are from varied locations: as I have just noted, a Black American lesbian (Audre Lorde), but also a Black South African in exile in Britain (Lauretta Ngcobo), an upper middle-class, white English woman (Woolf), together with proverbs from around the world. To come are extracts from the lives of three women of working-class origin, a Chinese-American, an African-American and a white English woman. In working with this material we have to be equally aware of the connections and the contrasts, alert to the specifics of the situation. We cannot make easy generalizations and presume that what appertains in one instance will count also for the others.

The three extracts I should like you to think about now are all from women's autobiographies. This in itself is a factor: why should each of these women in telling her lifestory find language an issue? In each case also, language relates to gender but, as strongly, to other determinants. As you read this material, write down any thoughts that come to you concerning aspects of language. Don't worry at this stage about fully-formed arguments: impressionistic words and phrases are as useful. The first extract tells of Maxine Hong Kingston's upbringing as a Chinese-American:

When I went to kindergarten and had to speak English for the first time, I became silent. A dumbness – a shame – still cracks my voice in two, even when I want to say 'hello' casually or ask an easy question in front of the checkout counter, or ask directions of a bus driver. I stand frozen, or I hold up the line with the complete, grammatical sentence that comes squeaking out at impossible length. 'What did you say?' says the cab driver, or, 'Speak up,' so I have to perform again, only weaker the second time. A telephone call makes my throat bleed and takes up that day's courage. It spoils my day with self-disgust when I hear my broken voice come skittering out into the open. It makes people wince to hear it. I'm getting better, though. Recently I asked the postman for special-issue stamps; I've waited since childhood for postmen to give me some of their own accord. I am making progress, a little every day.

My silence was thickets – total – during the three years I covered my school paintings with black paint. I painted layers of black over houses and flowers and suns, and when I drew on the blackboard, I put a layer of chalk on top. I was making a stage curtain, and it was the moment before the curtain parted or rose. The teachers called my parents to school, and I saw they had been saving my pictures, curling and cracking, all alike and black. The teachers pointed to the pictures and looked serious, talked seriously too, but my parents did not understand English. ('The parents and teachers of criminals were executed,' said my father.) My parents took the pictures home. I spread them out (so black and full of possibilities) and pretended the curtains were swinging open, flying up, one after another, sunlight underneath, mighty operas.

During the first silent year I spoke to no one at school, did not ask before going to the lavatory, and flunked kindergarten. My sister also said nothing for three years, silent in the playground and silent at lunch. There were other quiet Chinese girls not of our family, but most of them got over it sooner than we did. I enjoyed the silence. At first it did not occur to me I was supposed to talk or to pass kindergarten. I talked at home and to one or two of the Chinese kids in class. I made motions and even made some jokes. I drank out of a toy saucer when the water spilled out of the cup, and everybody laughed, pointing at me, so I did it some more. I didn't know that Americans don't drink out of saucers.

I liked the Negro students (Black ghosts) best because they laughed the loudest and talked to me as if I was a daring talker too. One of the Negro girls had her mother coil braids over her ears Shanghai-style like mine; we were Shanghai twins except she was covered with black like my paintings. Two Negro kids enrolled in Chinese school, and the teachers gave them Chinese names. Some Negro kids walked me to school and home, protecting me from the Japanese kids, who hit me and chased me and stuck gum in my ears. The Japanese kids were noisy and tough. They appeared one day in kindergarten, released from concentration camp, which was a tic-tac-toe mark, like barbed wire, on the map.

It was when I found out I had to talk that school became a misery, that the silence became a misery. I did not speak and felt bad each time I did not speak. I read aloud in first grade, though, and heard the barest whisper with little squeaks come out of my throat. 'Louder,' said the teacher, who scared the voice away again. The other Chinese girls did not talk either, so I knew the silence had to do with being a Chinese girl.

Maxine Hong Kingston, The Woman Warrior:
Memoirs of a Girlhood among Ghosts (1981) pp. 148–50

The second extract describes how Maya Angelou's grandmother, owner of a small shop, responds to the racially motivated abuse of a group of 'powhitetrash' girls by humming hymns:

Momma changed her song to 'Bread of Heaven, bread of Heaven, feed me till I want no more.'

I found that I was praying too. How long could Momma hold out? What new indignity could they think of to subject her to? Would I be able to stay out of it? What would Momma really like me to do?

Then they were moving out of the yard on their way to town. They bobbed their heads and shook their slack behinds and turned, one at a time:

''Bye, Annie.'

''Bye, Annie.'

''Bye, Annie.'

Momma never turned her head or unfolded her arms, but she stopped singing and said, ''Bye, Miz Helen, 'bye, Miz Ruth, 'bye, Miz Eloise.'

I burst. A firecracker July-the-Fourth burst. How could Momma call them Miz? The mean nasty things. Why couldn't she have come inside the sweet, cool store when we saw them breasting the hill? What did she prove? And then if they were dirty, mean and impudent, why did Momma have to call them Miz?

She stood another whole song through and then opened the screen door to look down on me crying in rage. She looked until I looked up. Her face was a brown moon that shone on me. She was beautiful. Something had happened out there, which I couldn't completely understand, but I could see that she was happy. Then she bent down and touched me as mothers of the church 'lay hands on the sick and afflicted' and I quieted.

'Go wash your face, Sister.' And she went behind the candy counter and hummed, 'Glory, glory, hallelujah, when I lay my burden down.'

I threw the well water on my face and used the weekday handkerchief to blow my nose. Whatever the contest had been out front, I knew Momma had won.

Maya Angelou, *I Know Why the Caged Bird Sings* (1984) pp. 31–2

In the final extract, from Carolyn Steedman's account of her 1950's working-class London childhood, a scene of confrontation is again recounted:

The arrival of the forest-keeper was a dramatic eruption on this scene, jarring colour descending on a shady place, a hairy jacket in that strange orange tweed that park-keepers still sometimes wear, plus-fours, brown boots and a pork-pie hat. He was angry with my father, shouted at him: it wasn't allowed. Hadn't he read the notice, there'd be no bluebells left if people pulled them up by the roots. He snatched the bunch from my father's hand, scattered the flowers over the ground and among the ferns, their white roots glimmering unprotected; and I thought: yes; he doesn't know how to pick bluebells.

My father stood, quite vulnerable in memory now. He was a thin man. I wonder if I remember the waisted and pleated flannel trousers of the early 1950s because in that confrontation he was the loser, feminized, outdone? They made him appear thinner, and because of the way the ground sloped, the forest-keeper, very solid and powerful, was made to appear taller than him. In remembering this scene I always forget, always have to deliberately call to mind the fact that my father retaliated, shouted back; and that we then retreated, made our way back down the path, the tweed man the victor, watching our leaving.

Carolyn Steedman, *Landscape for a Good Woman: A Story of Two Lives* (1986) p. 50

As a way in to our topic about the interrelation of gender with other factors, it might help to think firstly about some of the intriguing textual details in these passages. What do you think is the significance of the following?

➤ 'I enjoyed the silence' (Maxine Hong Kingston). Later, she doesn't enjoy the silence. How do you account for each of these responses?

➤ The black paintings in the Hong Kingston passage.

➤ The use of first names and titles in the Angelou extract.

➤ In what tone would you read, 'yes; he doesn't know how to pick bluebells' (Carolyn Steedman)?

➤ What does it mean for Steedman to say her father was 'feminized'?

➤ Select some words, phrases, single sentences which you find particularly striking.

10 These three scenes focus on potentially traumatic engagements with language. As we have already noticed, the fact that these authors have remembered these events into adulthood is a measure of their impact. Matters of gender difference connect in varying ways with other differences: class difference, generational difference, racial and ethnic difference also feature. To tease out the many strands, it would help to select from the material some relevant examples. I have started the process here, you carry on:

gender	class	generational	racial/ethnic
Kingston sees silence as an aspect of being feminine	Class position of Steedman's father affects his use of language	Children are able to abuse Momma	Kingston sees silence as also an aspect of being Chinese

When you complete the grid – and, of course, enlarge it as much as you like – patterns, links and comparisons should become more clear. For example, it is the racial injustice recounted in Angelou's extract that enables the white girls to ignore generational difference: you don't need to show respect for a Black woman of any age, is their attitude; why not make jokes at her expense? To compensate for their economic poverty, the white girls deny their gender affinity with Momma or any generational deference and assert a racial superiority. Look at the data on your completed grid and try to summarize, as I have with reference to Angelou, several strands of interconnection.

11   The importance of generational difference and how that influences the sense of identity of the author-as-girl is felt in both Angelou and Steedman. Compare their two extracts:

➤ In each case, what are the expectations and the anxieties of the girl with regard to the adult?

➤ In Angelou's story, the grandmother is enhanced and the event becomes for Maya a positive encounter; in Steedman's, the father is reduced and the event becomes a negative memory. Can you account for that contrast?

➤ There are marked differences in tone between these two passages and differences in the way the authors position themselves with respect to the material. Try to describe these differences.

➤ Look specifically at the gender dimension of these extracts. In Angelou, a girl watches a woman in confrontation with girls; in Steedman, a girl watches a man in confrontation with a man. In what ways is it significant that these people are female or male?

12   I want finally to draw your attention to what seems to me one of the most interesting sentences in the three passages. Why does Steedman say, 'I always forget, always have to deliberately call to mind the fact that my father retaliated, shouted back'? We are already aware that *women's* speech is often unheard but why does Steedman cut across the gender and generational norms – regard for the words of men, regard for the words of your parents – and forget her father's speech? I offer two possible interpretations:

• The father has failed in the confrontation. He has become like a woman, subject to a powerful man. The expectation, therefore, is that, like the oppressed woman, he will be silent. Steedman forgets what is somewhat unusual.

• The child is angry at the father's failure to live up to the social norm: he hasn't acted like a 'proper' father. *His* failure is also a failure for her. Vengefully, she represses the contradictions of the scene – that he did actually speak out, however ineffectually – and fixes him a silence. To remember the ambiguities becomes a conscious and painful act of will.

Do either of these interpretations seem satisfactory to you? I'm not sure I'm fully happy with either of them. How do you respond to Steedman's sentence?

The exhortation to speech

13   As a counter to the restrictions on women's speech and the constraints of silence, feminists have emphasized the political and psychological importance of women's speech and exhorted women to speak out. Below is a series of passages which in varied ways encourage women to speak. In working through the following material, jot down alongside each extract what seem to you the positive

factors about women's speech. I've started the process by looking back at the Lorde extract we considered earlier. What comments would you add with reference to the other extracts?

Texts	Comments
a) Lorde's title quoted on p.21	'Transformation' suggests the potential for change; women are not condemned to silence; 'action' suggests that speech can empower women.
b) Lorde's extract quoted on p.21	Language as fulfilling Language providing a sense of wholeness and validation for women Language linked to visibility Silence as corrosive Silence reinforcing your fears
c) I gave a brief talk tonight on 'Sisterhood and Survival', what it means to me. And first off I identified myself as a Black Feminist Lesbian poet, although it felt unsafe, which is probably why I had to do it. I explained that I identified myself as such because if there was one other Black Feminist Lesbian poet in isolation somewhere within the reach of my voice, I wanted her to know she was not alone. Audre Lorde, 'A Burst of Light' (1987) p. 73	
d) But first she would have to speak, start speaking, stop saying that she has nothing to say! Stop learning in school that women are created to listen, to believe, to make no discoveries. Dare to speak her piece about giving, the possibility of a giving that doesn't take away, but gives. Speak of her pleasure and, God knows, she has something to say about that ... Hélène Cixous, 'Castration or Decapitation?' (1981) pp. 50–1	
e) Then out of Ts'ai Yen's tent, which was apart from the others, the barbarians heard a woman's voice singing, as if to her babies, a song	

so high and clear, it matched the flutes. Ts'ai Yen sang about China and her family there. Her words seemed to be Chinese, but the barbarians understood their sadness and anger. Sometimes they thought they could catch barbarian phrases about forever wandering. Her children did not laugh, but eventually sang along when she left her tent to sit by the winter campfires, ringed by barbarians.

After twelve years among the Southern Hsiung-nu, Ts'ai Yen was ransomed and married to Tung Ssu so that her father would have Han descendants. She brought her songs back from the savage lands, and one of the three that has been passed down to us is 'Eighteen Stanzas for a Barbarian Reed Pipe', a song that Chinese sing to their own instruments. It translated well.

Maxine Hong Kingston, *The Woman Warrior: Memoirs of a Girlhood among Ghosts* (1981) p. 186

14 Reviewing this section, how do you now evaluate your own relation to speech and silence? You may not want to make any public declaration; on the other hand you may think it essential to speak what has been unspoken. If so, to whom and about what? In either case, try to clarify the potential of speech and silence for women generally and for yourself in particular.

Cartoon by Cork, Spare Rib *234, May 1992*

References and further reading

Maya Angelou, *I Know Why the Caged Bird Sings*

Deborah Cameron (ed.), *The Feminist Critique of Language: A Reader.*
A section in Cameron's introduction and part one of the collection focus on issues of speech and silence.

Mary Childers and bell hooks, 'A Conversation about Race and Class', in Marianne Hirsch and Evelyn Fox Keller (eds), *Conflicts in Feminism.* Pages 72–4 consider problems of language.

Hélène Cixous, 'Castration or Decapitation?' in *Signs: Journal of Women in Culture and Society*

Hélène Cixous and Catherine Clément, *The Newly Born Woman.* In the final section, 'Exchange', Cixous and Clément debate the political significance of the silence of Freud's patient, 'Dora'. Tony Harrison's poetry constitutes an impressive exploration of the relationship between class and language. Unfortunately, he says very little about gender or racial difference so I haven't included his work in this section. However, feminist readers can fill the gap. See especially 'The School of Eloquence' sequence in *Selected Poems.*

Cora Kaplan, 'Language and Gender' in *Sea Changes: Essays on Culture and Feminism.* A shorter version of this essay is included in Cameron (1990).

Maxine Hong Kingston, *The Woman Warrior: Memoirs of a Girlhood among Ghosts.*

Liz Lochhead, 'Men Talk', *True Confessions and Clichés.*

Audre Lorde, 'The Transformation of Silence into Language and Action', *Sister Outsider: Essays and Speeches*

Audre Lorde, the title essay in *A Burst of Light*

Máighréad Medbh, 'Easter 1991', *Feminist Review*

Jane Mills, *Womanwords: A Vocabulary of Culture and Patriarchal Society*

Lauretta Ngcobo (ed.), *Let It Be Told: Black Women Writers in Britain*

Adrienne Rich, from 'Cartographies of Silence', *The Dream of a Common Language: Poems 1974–7*

Mineke Schipper (ed.), *Unheard Words: Women and Literature in Africa, the Arab World, Asia, the Caribbean and Latin America*

Dale Spender, *Man Made Language.* Chapter 2 is concerned with women's silence.

Carolyn Steedman, *Landscape for a Good Woman: A Story of Two Lives.* For a psychoanalytical interpretation of the scene quoted here see Elizabeth Abel, 'Race, Class, and Psychoanalysis?' in Marianne Hirsch and Evelyn Fox Keller (eds), *Conflicts in Feminism*, p. 192.

Trinh T. Minh-ha, *Woman, Native, Other: Writing Postcoloniality and Feminism*

Virginia Woolf, 'Professions for Women' (1942), in Michèle Barrett (ed.), *Virginia Woolf: Women and Writing*

Two imaginative examples of silence being used strategically by women in defence of women are:

Susan Keating Glaspell, *Trifles* (1916) a one-act play anthologized in Sandra M. Gilbert and Susan Gubar (eds), *The Norton Anthology of Literature by Women: The Tradition in English.* The play was rewritten by Glaspell as an equally successful short story, 'A Jury of Her Peers', (1917) now available in Lee R. Edwards and Arlyn Diamond (eds), *American Voices, American Women.*

Valerie Milner, *Murder in the English Department.*

Defining a Feminist Text

Introduction

The aim of this section is to encourage you to think more closely than, perhaps, you have done hitherto about the meaning of the term 'feminist' when related to a literary text. It is not expected that you will discover a precise ten word definition which will cover all eventualities. Rather the aim of these questions is to highlight both the difficulty of definition and the presumptions which may, unwittingly, have informed your thinking. Work sequentially through the questions since they involve a process of thought which, hopefully, leads you to a sharper awareness. As a focus, I am thinking of a concrete situation, that of buying a book.

1 Suppose you are buying a birthday present for a friend. She has told you that she would like 'a feminist book'. What book might you select for her? Jot down some possible titles – fiction, non-fiction, poetry, a play, a reference book – whatever.

2 How did you decide these books fitted the description 'feminist'? Were you considering:

	Yes	No
➤ the sex of the author	☐	☐
➤ the sex of likely readers	☐	☐
➤ the publisher	☐	☐
➤ a review you read	☐	☐
➤ how the book is marketed	☐	☐

What other factors could lead you to describing a book as feminist?

➤

➤

➤

3 Could the book you choose for your friend be written by a man? If you think so, list some possible titles of male-authored feminist books. Why do you think feminist an apt description for these titles?

4 Would a Jackie Collins or a Jilly Cooper novel be a suitable present? After all the authors are female and the audiences predominantly female.

5 Have you had the experience of reading a book which you expected to be feminist but which, upon reading, didn't seem to be so? Why did you expect the book to be a feminist book and in what ways did the book fail to fulfil your expectations?

6 Conversely, have you had the experience of reading something which you didn't expect to be feminist but which stirred a feminist response in you? Name the title(s) and try to explain the effect.

7 Think about reviews or articles in magazines concerning women's writing. Consider TV or radio programmes about women's writing. Have you noticed in bookshops special promotions of women's writing? Has any of this influenced your understanding of the term 'feminist'?

8 Returning to your original list of titles, do you still want to call each of those titles feminist? Do you want to question or qualify at any point? Are you clearer in your own mind as *why* you are calling those titles feminist?

9 I said at the beginning that the aim was *not* to produce a neat definition but now you may question whether *any* definition – even loose or qualified – is possible at all. Try to construct one. How adequate do you find it? What problems did you encounter in drafting it?

Which of the following statements would you want to include in your definition? Would you want to amend some statements, delete or add others?

➤ Feminist texts are written primarily by women.

➤ Feminist texts have a female audience in mind.

➤ Feminist texts discuss sympathetically the situation of women.

➤ The texts published by women's publishing companies are feminist.

➤ It would be impossible to write a feminist text before the start of the women's movement.

➤ The attitude of the author determines whether or not a text is feminist.

➤ The response of the reader determine whether or not a text is feminist.

10 Here are several attempts at definition from feminist critics: some definitions, or parts of the definitions, are rather prescriptive; others more generalized. Do these relate to your definition? Do you veer towards the specific or the less defined? What aspects of these definitions do you like or dislike?

> To earn feminist approval, literature must perform one or more of the following functions: 1. serve as a forum for women; 2. help to achieve cultural androgyny; 3. provide role-models; 4. promote sisterhood; and 5. augment consciousness–raising.
>
> Cheri Register, 'American Feminist Literary Criticism:
A Bibliographical Introduction' (1975) pp. 18–19

> I used to think that a feminist novel was a novel *written by a feminist* and free from or critical of phallocentric (or masculinist, patriarchal, sexist – pick your term, you know what I mean) thinking and themes. But, seeing

the people who now define themselves as feminist, I reject this as an inadequate and individualistic definition. I now prefer to think of a feminist novel as one *recognized by feminists as feminist*, embraced as it were with recognition by a non-existent, but still observable, consensus feminist reader. I do not mean a novel which all feminists like, even if there were one, but one which the women's movement acknowledges as its own, lays claim to, declares ... A feminist novel is one where the identification (of character, language, concern, imagery or concept) is with oneself, when 'oneself' cannot be separated from 'being a feminist', and where there is some agreement that this is not a private hankering, but is the feeling of other 'selves' who are also feminist selves.

Sara Maitland, 'Novels are Toys not Bibles, but the Child is Mother to the Woman' (1979) p. 204

... it's a book on any subject written by a woman which is informed by a critical analysis of her position in society as a woman.

Carole Spedding quoted in Joan Scanlon and Julia Swindells, 'Bad Apple' (1994) p. 45

My definition of feminist literature is thus a relatively broad one, which is intended to encompass all those texts that reveal a critical awareness of women's subordinate position and of gender as a problematic category, however this is expressed.

Rita Felski, *Beyond Feminist Aesthetics: Feminist Literature and Social Change* (1989) p. 14

11   Some final questions:

➤ Does it actually matter whether we have or not a definition of a feminist text, however imprecise? Is it helpful to a feminist politics to make a distinction between feminist and non-feminist writing?

➤ Can a book be read sometimes as a feminist book and sometimes as a non-feminist book? For example, *Jane Eyre* by Charlotte Brontë could be seen as a feminist novel, a Gothic novel, an adolescent romance. Can you think of other examples of texts that are open to different readings?

➤ Could the definition 'feminist' be seen as a restriction on the text? When Sandra Gilbert and Susan Gubar published their anthology of women's writing, *The Norton Anthology of Literature by Women: The Tradition in English*, Gail Godwin complained of

> ... the retrospective feminist pattern they are attempting to impose which, all too frequently, diminishes the power and scope of the literary art produced by women down through the ages and distorts or undermines the achievements of individual artists.

Gail Godwin, 'One Woman Leads to Another' (1985)

Godwin evidently finds definition limiting. Others would find that applying the term 'feminist' to a text offers a new way of looking at it. How do you respond to Godwin's remark?

➤ If your friend had asked for 'a lesbian book' would the selection process have been any easier. Not according to Bonnie Zimmerman:

The critic will need to consider whether a lesbian text is one written by a lesbian (and if so, how do we determine who is a lesbian?), one written about lesbians (which might be by a heterosexual woman or a man), or one that expresses a lesbian 'vision' (which has yet to be satisfactorily outlined).

Bonnie Zimmerman, 'What Has Never Been: An Overview of Lesbian Feminist Literary Criticism' (1981) p. 208

➤ Or if she had asked for a 'Black feminist text' would you have been on surer ground? Deborah McDowell, here talking of Black feminist *criticism* thinks not:

There are many tasks ahead of these critics, not least of which is to attempt to formulate some clear definitions of what Black feminist criticism is. I use the term in this paper to refer to Black female critics who analyse the works of Black female writers from a feminist or political perspective. But the term can also apply to any criticism written by a Black woman regardless of her subject or perspective, a book written by a Black woman or about Black women authors in general, or any writings by women.

Deborah McDowell, 'New Directions for Black Feminist Criticism' (1980) p. 191

You might repeat with reference to 'a lesbian text' or 'a Black feminist text' the process of attempted definition you have just followed for 'a feminist text'. Are the problems and issues similar or different?

➤ My opening paragraph asked you to think about unwitting presumptions you may have been making in talking about feminist texts. How do you feel about that now? Do you think you were presuming factors which, on closer analysis, look less likely? Are you now more conscious of influential factors and how those factors have been influencing you? Would you now be buying different books for the feminist birthday gift or buying the same books with a different awareness?

➤ See the section on Feminine Writing and Reading. If your friend had asked for a 'feminine' book rather than a 'feminist' book, what questions would that request have raised?

References and further reading

Michèle Barrett, 'Feminism and the Definition of Cultural Politics' in Rosalind Brunt and Caroline Rowan (eds), *Feminism, Culture and Politics*

Rosalind Coward, 'Are Women's Novels Feminist Novels?' anthologized in Elaine Showalter (ed.), *The New Feminist Criticism*

Extracts from both the above are in Mary Eagleton (ed.), *Feminist Literary Theory: A Reader* (second edition)

Rita Felski, *Beyond Feminist Aesthetics: Feminist Literature and Social Change* See particularly pp. 12–17

Sandra Gilbert and Susan Gubar (eds), *The Norton Anthology of Literature by Women: The Tradition in English*

Gail Godwin, 'One Woman Leads to Another', *The New York Times Book Review*

Susanne Kappeler, 'What Is a Feminist Publishing Policy?' in Gail Chester and Julienne Dickey (eds), *Feminism and Censorship: The Current Debate*

Sara Maitland, 'Novels are Toys not Bibles, but the Child is Mother to the Woman', *Women's Studies International Quarterly*

Deborah McDowell, 'New Directions for Black Feminist Criticism' in Showalter (1986). The relevant section is also anthologized in Eagleton (1996).

Cheri Register, 'American Feminist Literary Criticism: A Bibliographical Introduction' in Josephine Donovan (ed.) *Feminist Literary Criticism: Explorations in Theory*. The relevant extract is anthologized in Eagleton (1996).

Joan Scanlon and Julia Swindells, 'Bad Apple', *Trouble & Strife*

Bonnie Zimmerman, 'What Has Never Been: An Overview of Lesbian Feminist Literary Criticism' in Elaine Showalter (ed.), *The New Feminist Criticism*

Creating a Matrilineage

Introduction

The American critics, Sandra Gilbert and Susan Gubar begin their study of nineteenth-century women's writing, *The Madwoman in the Attic: The Woman Writer and the Nineteenth-Century Literary Imagination*, with what must be the most arresting opening sentence in literary criticism:

> Is a pen a metaphorical penis?

The sentence introduces Gilbert and Gubar's response to the influential theories of literary history propounded by Harold Bloom. Bloom describes literary history as an intense, violent Oedipal struggle as each son strives to supplant his literary father. Women enter the creative process as female Muse to the male author rather than as active creators in their own right. Gilbert and Gubar ask:

> Where, then, does the female poet fit in? Does she want to annihilate a 'forefather' or a 'foremother'? What if she can find no models, no precursors? Does she have a muse and what is its sex?
>
> Sandra M. Gilbert and Susan Gubar, *The Madwoman in the Attic: The Woman Writer and the Nineteenth-Century Literary Imagination* (1979) p. 47

What Bloom terms the 'anxiety of influence' is reinterpreted by Gilbert and Gubar as an 'anxiety of authorship'. How can women write at all according to Bloom's model or, if they can, are they supposed to 'prove' themselves by taking an unequal part in a struggle with male precursors?

In contrast to Bloom's patrilineage, many feminist critics and writers have employed the concept of a matrilineage, a literary history of mothers and daughters. The desired relationship between mother and daughter is not one of competitive rivalry but one of nurture and empowerment.

The focus in this section will be on three aspects of this debate:

- Why the constructions of a matrilineage has been important to so many women writers. What practical and emotional roles a matrilineage plays in their writing lives.

- The problems in constructing matrilineages. For instance, the possibility that relationships between women writers might be presented in over-idealized terms. Maternal nurturing or welcomed tutelage are often elusive goals rather than constant realities.

● An indication of how the notion of matrilineage has influenced writing and publishing practices.

The importance of a matrilineage for feminists

1   In *A Room of One's Own*, Virginia Woolf remarks on the difficulty of writing generally and then comments:

> But for women, I thought, looking at the empty shelves, these difficulties were infinitely more formidable.

Later she writes:

> For masterpieces are not single and solitary births; they are the outcome of many years of thinking in common, of thinking by the body of the people, so that the experience of the mass is behind the single voice.

And, then again, she claims that she and other women writers

> think back through our mothers ...

> > Virginia Woolf, *A Room of One's Own* (1929; 1993) pp. 47, 59–60, 69

The debilitating scarcity of women writers (the empty bookshelves), the process by which earlier books can generate later ones, the search for literary foremothers – all these can be seen as reasons for constructing and valuing a matrilineage.

Woolf, like Gilbert and Gubar, is thinking of the woman writer's place within the tradition of western, canonical literature. Trinh T. Minh-ha discusses a different heritage, the historical role in non-western cultures of women storytellers as 'keepers and transmitters' of the story:

> Tell me and let me tell my hearers what I have heard from you who heard it from your mother and your grandmother, so that what is said may be guarded and unfailingly transmitted to the women of tomorrow, who will be our children and the children of our children. These are the opening lines she used to chant before embarking on a story. I owe that to you, her and her, who owe it to her, her and her. I memorize, recognize, and name my source(s), not to validate my voice through the voice of an authority (for we, women, have little authority in the House of Literature, and wise women never draw their powers from authority), but to evoke her and sing. The bond between women and word. Among women themselves ...
>
>   In this chain and continuum, I am but one link. The story is me, neither me nor mine. It does not really belong to me, and while I feel great responsibility for it, I also enjoy the irresponsibility of the pleasure obtained through the process of transferring. Pleasure in the copy, pleasure in the reproduction.

> > Trinh T. Minh-ha, *Woman, Native, Other: Writing Postcoloniality and Feminism* (1989) p. 122

➤ Put yourself in the position of the aspiring woman writer. Perhaps, you do, indeed, have aspirations to be a published writer. In what ways could a matrilineage help in your endeavours? Think of both your psychological and practical needs as a writer. Are these needs likely to lessen or increase as you become an established writer?

➤ Woolf is thinking of a written tradition, Trinh T. Minh-ha of an oral one; in what ways do their comments coincide and differ?

2   Alice Walker's essay 'In Search of Our Mothers' Gardens' (this is also the title of the volume) has become an important text in the study of matrilineages. Walker extends the meaning of 'mother' from her own biological mother, to other female relatives and neighbours, and then to women of strength and significance from whom Walker feels she has learned much. In this particular essay, her concern is how female creativity has been kept alive in varied forms in the most adverse circumstances – hence the significance of the title; the creativity of Walker's own mother was expressed partly in gardening. Furthermore, Walker writes:

> Yet so many of the stories that I write, that we all write, are my mother's stories. Only recently did I fully realise this: that through years of listening to my mother's stories of her life, I have absorbed not only the stories themselves, but something of the manner in which she spoke, something of the urgency that involves the knowledge that her stories – like her life – must be recorded. It is probably for this reason that so much of what I have written is about characters whose counterparts in real life are so much older than I am.

> Alice Walker, *In Search of Our Mothers' Gardens* (1983) p. 240

Again, situate yourself as a woman writer. Can you relate Walker's comments to your own family and cultural situation, and to the passage from Trinh T. Minh-ha?

➤ Create your personal matrilineage. Who are the women to whom you would look as informing/inspiring/guiding your writing? They may be women you have known, women of achievement, historical figures, literary or mythological figures, women with whom you work. In what ways would you see them as helping; what would be the particular contributions of each woman?

➤ Can you discern in your personal matrilineage signs of female creativity which the dominant culture generally may disregard or undervalue? Walker, for instance, often discusses the significance of quilt-making in the lives of Black women.

➤ Walker mentions not only the influence of her mother's stories but 'the manner in which she spoke'. In your matrilineage can you also discover less tangible factors – a tone of voice, a certain personality trait, a characteristic gesture – that have, in some way, impinged on you as a potential writer?

3   Part of Walker's matrilineal involvement has been her on-going quest for the life story and work of Zora Neale Hurston. At times, Walker characterizes the relationship between herself and Hurston in almost mystical terms, as if she created Zora's writing:

> I became aware of my need of Zora Neale Hurston's work some time before I knew her work existed–

and as if Zora predicted the future needs of Walker:

> She had provided, as if she knew someday I would come along wandering in the wilderness, a nearly complete record of her life.

Alice Walker, In Search of Our Mothers' Gardens (1983) pp. 83, 12

Despite the chronology – Walker was only sixteen when Hurston died – Hurston and Walker seem to have become co-authors in each other's work.

Below are some suggestions for research projects which could provide material for essays or seminar papers.

➤ Review Walker's interest in Zora Neale Hurston. (See the relevant essays in Walker's *In Search of Our Mothers' Gardens.*) Why is Hurston so indispensable to Walker? In what ways is it significant that Walker's chosen literary mother is a Black woman?

➤ Compare Walker's preoccupation with Hurston with Tillie Olsen's interest in Rebecca Harding Davis. (See Olsen's collection of essays, *Silences.*) In each of these cases the contemporary author has undertaken a personal crusade to reinstate an almost-lost precursor.

➤ Explore matrilineages in women's poetry. Women poets have been particularly vocal in acknowledging the influence of other women writers, either mentioning them by name in their poems or dedicating poems to them. Why should this be so? Here are some possible titles for you to locate; poems by Anne Stevenson and May Sarton that follow later in this section are additional examples. You might like to research anthologies of women's poetry to find yet more:

- Michèle Roberts, 'Madwoman at Rodmell' (on Virginia Woolf)
- May Sarton, 'Letter from Chicago' (dedicated to Virginia Woolf)
- Anne Sexton, 'Sylvia's Death' (on Sylvia Plath)
- Elizabeth Bishop, 'Invitation to Miss Marianne Moore'
- Adrienne Rich, 'For Julia in Nebraska' (makes reference to Willa Cather)
- Dilys Laing, 'Sonnet to a Sister in Error' (to Anne of Winchilsea)
- Patricia Beer, 'In Memory of Stevie Smith'.

Links and lesions

4   The interconnections between women writers are not always as positive as the maternal metaphor might lead one to think. *In No Man's Land: The Place of the Woman Writer in the Twentieth Century*, Sandra Gilbert and Susan Gubar refer to some of the poems listed above as 'ambivalent eulogies' (p. 211). At times, relationships seem severely affected by Bloomian rivalry and angst. Understandably, this can cause distress to feminists who are hoping to construct models of literary endeavour that are marked by a new kind of sisterly politics. Gilbert and Gubar return to the thesis of Harold Bloom to explain the causes of female rivalry:

In fact, we suspect that the love women writers send forward into the past is, in patriarchal culture, inexorably contaminated by mingled feelings of rivalry and anxiety. Though there is no mythic paradigm of Jocasta and Antigone which would parallel Bloom's archetype of Laius and Oedipus, strong equals at the crossroads, most literary women do ask – as Sylvia Plath did about women poets – 'who rivals', partly because, as Margaret Atwood explains, 'members of what feels like a minority' must compete for a 'few coveted places' and partly because those coveted places signify, as Freud's model tells us, the approbation of the father who represents cultural authority. But the woman writer who engages with her autonomous precursor in a rivalrous struggle for primacy often learns that the fruit of victory is bitter: the approbation of the father is almost always accompanied by his revulsion, and the autonomy of the mother is frequently as terrifying as it is attractive, for – as Woolf's comments about Charlotte Brontë suggest – it has been won at great cost.

Sandra M. Gilbert and Susan Gubar, *No Man's Land:*
The Place of the Woman Writer in the Twentieth Century (1988) p. 195

The material and questions we consider below illustrate that both the concept of constructing a matrilineage and the relationships within that tradition can be highly problematic.

5   Consider these extracts from two poems by Anne Stevenson, the first a response to Jane Austen's epitaph in Winchester Cathedral, the second, written at the end of Stevenson's work on her biography of Sylvia Plath.

> The amazing epitaph's 'benevolence of heart'
> precedes 'the extraordinary endowments of her mind'
> and would have pleased her, who was not unkind.
> Dear votary of order, sense, clear art
> and irresistible fun, please pitch our lives
> outside self-pity we have wrapped them in,
> and show us how absurd we'd look to you.
> You knew the mischief poetry could do.
> Yet when Anne Elliott spoke of *its misfortune*
> *to be seldom safely enjoyed by those who*
> *enjoyed it completely*, she spoke for you.

from Anne Stevenson, 'Re-reading Jane' (1983)

> Dear Sylvia, we must close our book.
> three springs you've perched like a black rook
> between sweet weather and my mind.
> At last I have to seem unkind
> and exorcize my awkward awe.
> My shoulder doesn't like your claw.

from Anne Stevenson, 'Letter to Sylvia Plath' (1988)

Obviously, to appreciate the full complexity of Stevenson's responses to two of her literary mothers, you need to read the complete poems. For the moment, compare these excerpts, similar in some stylistic matters, notably different in tone and attitude. What similarities and differences strike you?

6 With the publication of Stevenson's biography of Plath this particular female, literary relationship became something of a *cause célèbre*. Details in the References and Further Reading (Stevenson herself, Rose, Malcolm) could help if you wanted to make a special study of this instance of female influence.

7 In the two extracts below, May Sarton and Adrienne Rich construct matrilineages and try to situate themselves within long traditions of female poetry:

> Dorothy Wordsworth, dying, did not want to read,
> 'I am too busy with my own feelings', she said.
>
> And all women who have wanted to break out
> Of the prison of consciousness to sing or shout
>
> Are strange monsters who renounce the treasure
> Of their silence for a curious devouring pleasure.
>
> Dickinson, Rossetti, Sappho – they all know it,
> Something is lost, strained, unforgiven in the poet.
>
> She abdicates from life or like George Sand
> Suffers from the mortality in an immortal hand,
>
> Loves too much, spends a whole life to discover
> She was born a good grandmother, not a good lover.
>
> Too powerful for men: Madame de Staël. Too sensitive:
> Madame de Sévigné who burdened where she meant to give.
>
> Delicate as that burden was and so supremely lovely,
> It was too heavy for her daughter, much too heavy.
>
> Only when she built inward in a fearful isolation
> Did anyone succeed or learn to fuse emotion
>
> With thought. Only when she renounced did Emily
> Begin in the fierce lonely light to learn to be.
>
> Only in the extremity of spirit and the flesh
> And in renouncing passion did Sappho come to bless.
>
> Only in the farewells or in old age does sanity
> Shine through the crimson stains of their mortality.
>
> And now we who are writing women and strange monsters
> Still search our hearts to find the difficult answers,
>
> Still hope that we may learn to lay our hands
> More gently and more subtly on the burning sands.
>
> To be through what we make more simply human,
> To come to the deep place where poet becomes woman,
>
> Where nothing has to be renounced or given over
> In the pure light that shines out from the lover,

In the pure light that brings forth fruit and flower
And that great sanity, that sun, the feminine power.

from May Sarton, 'My Sisters, O My Sisters' (1948)

I read the older women poets with their peculiar keenness and ambivalence:
Sappho, Christina Rossetti, Emily Dickinson, Elinor Wylie, Edna Millay,
H. D. I discovered that the woman poet most admired at the time (by men)
was Marianne Moore, who was maidenly, elegant, intellectual, discreet. But
even in reading these women I was looking in them for the same things I
had found in the poetry of men, because I wanted women poets to be the
equals of men, and to be equal was still confused with sounding the same.

I know that my style was formed first by male poets: by the men I was
reading as an undergraduate – Frost, Dylan Thomas, Donne, Auden,
MacNeice, Stevens, Yeats. What I chiefly learned from them was craft. But
poems are like dreams: in them you put what you don't know you know.
Looking back at poems I wrote before I was twenty-one, I'm startled
because beneath the conscious craft are glimpses of the split I even then
experienced between the girl who wrote poems, who defined herself in
writing poems, and the girl who was to define herself by her relationships
with men.

Adrienne Rich, 'When We Dead Awaken: Writing as Re-Vision' (1971) pp. 39–40

Certain factors are common to these extracts; most especially, both raise
fundamental questions about what we, readers and critics, are doing when we link
together women writers to form a female tradition. For instance, compare in the
two extracts:

How the matrilineages are constructed   Who is chosen; why; would you
agree with the choices?

The 'problem' of the woman writer   To whom is she a problem; in what
ways; does the construct of a matrilineage help or hinder the status of the woman
writer?

The position of men   Why do men feature in these discussions; do men and
women constitute separate lineages, or related lineages; how should women writers
relate to male precursors, or male writers to female precursors?

The relation of the younger woman writer to older women.

8   As one explores that final area, the idea that the younger woman writer is
always in a position of either filial devotion or competitive opposition becomes
less and less tenable. A myriad of other, intermediary positions is equally possible:
critical distance, cautious regard, self-aggrandizement, aspiration, a sense of
inadequacy etc. Consider, for example, Margaret Walker's creation of a tender and
hesitant matrilineage:

My grandmothers were strong.
They followed plows and bent to toil.
They moved through fields sowing seed.
They touched earth and grain grew.
They were full of sturdiness and singing.
My grandmothers were strong.

My grandmothers are full of memories.
Smelling of soap and onions and wet clay
With veins rolling roughly over quick hands
They have many clean words to say.
My grandmothers were strong.
Why am I not as they?

Margaret Walker, 'Lineage' (1942)

➤ Return to one or two of the poems you selected when looking through anthologies of women's poetry and reconsider them in terms of mixed, varying or ambiguous responses.

➤ Return to Gilbert and Gubar's comment (point 4). If possible read the complete chapter from which the extract comes. Does this seem to you an adequate explanation for female rivalry? Would you add or dispute any points?

9 Two further passages raise fundamental questions about matrilineal thinking. Jan Montefiore is concerned about the homogeneity of matrilineages:

For however necessary it may be to think in terms of 'the woman poet' or 'the woman writer' in the early stages of constructing feminist criticism, she is entirely mythical; she doesn't exist in real life, any more than 'the archetypal male poet' does. What does exist is an immense variety of women poets, often divided by major differences of class, race and circumstances, and writing in a multiplicity of discourses; and any account of a woman's tradition has to take account of these differences and separations. It is arguable that the necessary task for feminists is not re-creating a 'woman's tradition', but asking 'in *which* tradition, feminine and otherwise, do particular writers belong?'

Jan Montefiore, *Feminism and Poetry; Language, Experience, Identity in Women's Writing* (1987) p. 59

Linda Williams questions both the use of familial metaphors and the presumption, in some forms of matrilineal thinking, that women intuitively bond:

Why do we so often employ familial metaphors to interpret our conceptual and scholarly relationships with each other? What are the power relations at stake in setting up feminist networks of thinking which rely on mother–daughter or sisterly ties? Why are we so reluctant to rid ourselves of the family? These questions focus not only on the problem of mother–daughter relations in history or psychoanalysis, but crucially on the way we have interpreted women's *literary* history as a *family* history, glued together by those 'unknowable' feminine relations … Thus it seems, ironically, that the very force which some writers have drawn upon to signal the breakdown of patriarchal family relations – a feminine communication which disrupts normal epistomologies – has then been used to make coherent an alternative Great (female) Tradition.

Linda R. Williams, 'Feminist Reproduction and Matrilineal Thought' (1992) p. 53

These ideas are complex and the contradictions not open to easy resolution. I've started to gather together some of the material we have covered, dividing it into points in favour of constructing matrilineages and points against. Add to the lists, using your own responses as well as ideas from this section. Reflecting on the arguments raised, where would you now place yourself?

A matrilineage ...

- gives to the woman writer and reader a sense of history and identity;
- makes visible the woman writer and establishes creative links between women writers;
- allows the woman writer to focus on material of particular relevance to women;
-
-
-

or

- falsely idealizes the relationship between women writers;
- imposes a uniformity on women's writing;
- separates women into 'good' supportive writers and 'bad' critical writers;
-
-
-

or do you want to adopt a third position; if so, what is it?

Matrilineage/writing/publishing

10   We can think, finally, how matrilineal ideas have influenced writing and publishing practices. This is evident not only in the number of recently published works – both critical and imaginative – that trace histories of women's writing or concern themselves specifically with mother/daughter relations, but also in attempts to create writing practices which deviate from the concept, outlined at the beginning of this section, of the individual writer in opposition to all other individual writers; for example, writing couples, dialogues, group or collective projects. Lest we harbour, once again, romanticized views of these unions, read these two extracts from Jane Gallop's intensely involved account. She is a rejected sibling in the first passage, the 'disregarded daughter' in the second:

YFS 62 ... opens thus: 'This is a very unusual issue of *Yale French Studies*, in that its guest editor is a seven-headed monster from Dartmouth.' The notion is quite funny: non-human it might be, but nonetheless Ivy League.

Seven Dartmouth faculty women edit YFS 62. The monster is a figure for the seven individuals working together as one body. Appearing in the Introduction signed by the editors, the image is a self-portrait and is followed by a glowing description of their collaboration. The editors are saying: we are horrifying, we are inhumanly ugly. This an ironic way of saying: we are 'very unusual,' we are extraordinary, we are beautiful.

The image of the monster thinly disguises a monstrous narcissism. This reader, for one, recoils from such unseemly self-congratulation. The irony of this irony is that when the editors say that they are ugly to mean they are beautiful, they become ugly....

In 1979 I received a letter from seven Dartmouth women inviting me to contribute to a feminist issue of *Yale French Studies* they were editing. Jumping at the chance to be published in the top journal of what was then my field, I immediately sent them an abstract of a text on Irigaray and Freud. I never received an answer. This absolute lack of response was, for me, worse than rejection. Pointing to the editorial collective's self-regard, I am the disregarded daughter 'watching her look at herself in the mirror.' The seven-headed monster 'rejected (my) efforts to be present in it.'

Jane Gallop, 'The Monster in the Mirror' (1992) pp. 48, 54

➤ Do you read these passages as supportive evidence for Gilbert and Gubar's thesis, or do you read them in some other way?

➤ Gallop was criticized by many feminists for publishing these views. They were considered unsisterly in themselves and imprudent in publication – merely more 'proof' that women are bitchy, incapable of working together and in need of strong men to keep them in check. Would you defend Gallop's right to publish?

11 Happily, other women have found the collective process more creative and, like the authors of *Feminist Readings/ Feminists Reading*, link their work practice to a feminist politics and theory of writing:

Whilst collective work is more time-consuming and difficult than individu-alistic writing, it has been a valuable experience for us all, and, for us, is an important part of a feminist practice. Our discussions and criticisms have been enabling rather than competitive, and in this way have differed radically from the conventional reception of texts, where criticisms are marked in the margin: the blind spots of the argument are located. This is not to suggest that we have been uncritical, but that we have developed more useful ways of discussing the work that others have produced, aiming to create some positive contribution which can help to improve the theory.

Sara Mills, Lynne Pearce, Sue Spaull, Elaine Millard,
Feminist Readings/ Feminists Reading (1989) p. 12

These authors take their organizing model not from the family but from the collective groupings of radical politics, particularly the work in the late 1970s of the Marxist-Feminist Literature Collective.

➤ You could compare the material above with any experience (not necessarily writing experience) you may have of collective work with women.

➤ You could undertake a collective writing project and keep a log/diary of the process.

➤ What metaphor would you use to describe your experience – maternal, sisterly or …?

References and further reading

Sharon Bryan (ed.), *Where We Stand: Women Poets on Literary Tradition*

Jane Gallop. 'The Monster in the Mirror', *Around 1981: Academic Feminist Literary Theory*

Sandra M. Gilbert and Susan Gubar, *The Madwoman in the Attic: The Woman Writer and the Nineteenth-Century Literary Imagination*, see part 1, chapter 2

Sandra M. Gilbert and Susan Gubar, *No Man's Land: The Place of the Woman Writer in the Twentieth Century* vol. 1, 'The War of the Words', see chapter 4

Marianne Hirsch, *The Mother/Daughter Plot: Narrative, Psychoanalysis, Feminism*, see particularly part III

Sara Maitland and Michelene Wandor, *Arky Types*. An optimistic and humorous story of women writing together.

Janet Malcolm, *The Silent Woman: Sylvia Plath and Ted Hughes*

Sara Mills, Lynne Pearce, Sue Spaull, Elaine Millard, *Feminist Readings/Feminists Reading*

Jan Montefiore, *Feminism and Poetry: Language, Experience, Identity in Women's Writing*, see particularly chapter 3

Susheila Nasta (ed.) *Motherlands: Black Women's Writing from Africa, the Caribbean and South Asia*. The second section which discusses metaphorical meanings of the mother-figure in women's writing is particularly relevant to our concerns here

Tillie Olsen, *Silences*, see two sections relating to Rebecca Harding Davis

Adrienne Rich, 'When We Dead Awaken: Writing as Re-Vision', *On Lies, Secrets, and Silence: Selected Prose 1966–1978*

Jacqueline Rose, *The Haunting of Sylvia Plath*, see particularly chapter 3 for a discussion on the literary history of Sylvia Plath and the significance of Anne Stevenson's biography

Dianne F. Sadoff, 'Black Matrilineage: The Case of Alice Walker and Zora Neale Hurston'

May Sarton, 'My Sisters, O My Sisters', *Collected Poems 1930–1973*, also anthologized in Sandra Gilbert and Susan M. Gubar (eds), *The Norton Anthology of Literature by Women: The Tradition in English*

Anne Stevenson, 'Re-reading Jane', *The Fiction-Makers*

Anne Stevenson, *Bitter Fame: A Life of Sylvia Plath*

Anne Stevenson, 'Letter to Sylvia Plath', *The Other House*

Trinh T. Minh-ha, 'Grandma's Story', *Woman, Native, Other: Writing Postcoloniality and Feminism*

Alice Walker (ed.), *I Love Myself When I am Laughing …: A Zora Neale Hurston Reader*

Alice Walker, *In Search of Our Mothers' Gardens*

Margaret Walker, 'Lineage', *For My People*, also anthologized in Sandra Gilbert and Susan M. Gubar (eds), *The Norton Anthology of Literature by Women: The Tradition in English*

Linda R. Williams, 'Feminist Reproduction and Matrilineal Thought' in Isobel Armstrong (ed.), *New Feminist Discourse: Critical Essays on Theories and Texts*

Virginia Woolf, *A Room of One's Own and Three Guineas*, ed. Michèle Barrett

An interesting debate is developing on generational/matrilineal differences between feminists in academic institutions. See:

Alice Jardine, 'Notes for an Analysis' in Teresa Brennan (ed.), *Between Feminism and Psychoanalysis*

Evelyn Fox Keller and Helen Moglen, 'Competition and Feminism: Conflicts for Academic Women'

Madelon Sprengnether, 'Generational Differences: Reliving Mother–Daughter Conflicts' in Gayle Green and Coppélia Kahn (eds), *Changing Subjects: The Making of Feminist Literary Criticism*

The Woman Author: Lost and Found

Introduction: lost

A belief that many women writers have been lost to literary history and a desire to reinstate those writers have been fundamental to much feminist literary research. In 1971 Tillie Olsen, the American author and critic, gave a lecture in which she estimated that, in terms of published 'writers of achievement', the sex ratio was one woman writer for every twelve men. The lecture eventually became an essay included in Olsen's collection, *Silences*. Olsen categorized 'achievement' as:

> ... appearance in twentieth-century literature courses, required reading lists, textbooks, quality anthologies, the year's best, the decade's best, the fifty years' best, consideration by critics or in current reviews ...
>
> Tillie Olsen, *Silences* (1978) p. 24

At the time of the lecture, Olsen was working outside academic circles and made clear that her figures were impressionistic: she did not have access to research facilities which could have made her study more scientific.

Do Olsen's statistics still seem relevant; are *all* groups of women under-represented; are women under-represented in *all* forms of writing? This first part of the section will examine Olsen's basic premise in two ways:

- by updating Olsen's research;
- by surveying the texts used in British schools and higher education institutions.

To consider the school curriculum is, of course, particularly important since school textbooks give children an early and formative sense of who writers are and who has contributed to the history of literature.

Updating Olsen's research

1   As an introduction to the material, try to predict what you imagine *now* to be the ratio of female to male authors. Consider, for example, the following categories. How do you feel the statistics might have changed from Olsen's 1:12?

A JUBILEE REVERIE

MEN WHO HAVE MADE MY GLORY.

Female/Male

- the short list for major book awards
- the best-seller fiction list
- the best-seller non-fiction list
- current anthologies of poetry
- current anthologies of short stories
- current collections of critical essays.

2   Consider the situation in bookshops. In a randomly chosen section from the fiction shelves – a section of approximately 3m in length – what would you predict to be the ratio of female to male authors?

3   Consider the situation in academic libraries. What would you predict to be the ratio of female to male authors in the following three categories?

Female/Male

- eighteenth-century poetry
- nineteenth-century novels
- twentieth-century drama.

4   Now visit as many libraries and bookshops as you can to check your predictions.
➤ In which areas were your predictions correct; in which were they off-target?
➤ Were your correct predictions the product of guesswork or careful deduction? If the latter, what factors were you taking into account? Did you, for instance, remember something abut the importance of women novelists in the nineteenth century?
➤ If you are working with others, pool your evidence. Can you see patterns emerging? Are there variations between the data of different group members? How would you account for these? Tabulate your collective material as follows:

Areas of equality or near equality	Areas of marked inequality	Evidence inconclusive

5 Return to Olsen's data of 1971. Look particularly at the chapter entitled, 'One Out of Twelve: Writers Who Are Women in Our Century'. How do Olsen's findings relate to your contemporary data? Which of her findings still seem relevant? Do you want to qualify Olsen's results at any point? Are there areas in which you need more evidence? Olsen suggests:

> For a week or two, make your own survey whenever you pick up an anthology, course bibliography, quality magazine or quarterly, book review section, book of criticism.
>
> Tillie Olsen, *Silences* (1978) p. 24

You may like to follow Olsen's suggestion.

6 What happens when exclusion on the grounds of gender is linked with exclusion on the grounds of race, class or sexuality? List the names of female authors whom you *did* find represented in your search and check – in critical commentaries, biographies, biographical dictionaries etc. – their racial and class origins and, where known, their sexual orientation. Such data is not always easy to find since some writers wish to define themselves to their public simply as 'writers', rather than lesbian writers, Black writers or working-class writers; others see these self-definitions as part of their writing identity. Still the question is worth asking. Is there evidence that white, middle-class and heterosexual women writers feature more prominently than Black or working-class women or lesbians?

Looking at women's studies textbooks rather than imaginative writing, Bonnie Zimmerman comments:

> Tillie Olsen, in her classic article, 'One Out of Twelve: Writers Who Are Women in Our Century', noted that on gauges of literary achievement, such as courses and anthologies, one woman writer appears for every twelve men. For open lesbian writers in women's studies texts, the figure is close to one out of thirty, forty, or fifty. In the books that structure introductory women's studies course, lesbians are at best tokens, and at worst, invisible. I surveyed twenty paperbacks used in these courses and found that lesbianism is represented by at most one article or a handful of pages. Editors and authors seem to be too uncomfortable with or oblivious to the experience, politics, culture, and oppression of lesbians to seriously include our perspectives in their texts.
>
> Bonnie Zimmerman, 'One Out of Thirty: Lesbianism in Women's Studies Textbooks' (1982) p. 128

If such was the situation in women's studies textbooks, we can presume that the absence was even more pronounced in other forms of writing. Again, Zimmerman's evidence is now some years out of date; how do contemporary statistics compare? Zimmerman was writing of the situation in the States; the situation in Britain, then and now, might be different.

7 Following Olsen's lead, we have confined ourselves so far to the kind of writing most commonly found in academic institutions. Would the findings be different if we widened the research? Return to your tour of bookshops and, this time, include public libraries rather than academic ones. Are there forms of writing in which women predominate or are significantly represented?

The education curriculum

8 The table below compiled by a group of British teachers of English, the Language and Gender Committee of the National Association for the Teaching of English (NATE), compares the representation of male and female poets in poetry anthologies commonly used in secondary schools

	MEN	WOMEN	TOTAL	% WOMEN
HERE TODAY, 1963 Modern Poems introduced by Ted Hughes	44	1	45	2.2
POETS OF OUR TIME, 1965 ed. F. E. S. Finn	11	0	11	0
NINE MODERN POETS, 1966 ed. E. L. Black	9	0	9	0
POETRY 1900–1965, 1967 ed. G. Macbeth	21	2	23	8.7
VOICES 3, 1968 ed. G. Summerfield	83	9	92	9.8
TOUCHSTONES 4, 1971 ed. M. and P. Benton	59	3	62	4.8
TOUCHSTONES 5, 1971 ed. M. and P. Benton	64	5	69	7.2
DRAGONS TEETH, 1972 ed. E. Williams	59	2	61	3.3
WORLDS, 1974 Seven Modern Poets ed. G. Summerfield	7	0	7	0
TELESCOPE, 1974 ed. E. Williams	70	4	74	5.4
THE NEW DRAGON BOOK of VERSE, 1977 ed. M. Harrison & C. Stuart-Clark	92	6	98	6.1
STRICTLY PRIVATE, 1981 ed. R. McGough	50	16	66	24.2
RATTLEBAG, 1982 ed. Seamus Heaney & Ted Hughes	127	10	137	7.8
SPEAKING TO YOU, 1984 ed. M. Rosen & D. Jackson	43	19	62	30.6

Source: *Gender Issues in English Coursework* (1988)
National Association for the Teaching of English, Language and Gender Committee

Visit the children's section of a public library or the teacher training/education section of an academic library to research these anthologies. Which women represent women's poetry in the anthologies? Do there seem to you to be any notable female omissions?

9 Who are the editors of these anthologies? Most are listed here by initial only. Could the sex of the editor be a significant factor in the choice of the contents. The Language and Gender Committee of NATE who compiled this information comments:

Women have very rarely been given the opportunity to select such anthologies. It is important to bear in mind how much taste can account for the lack of inclusion of women's work, rather than any lack of intrinsic merit, or even the availability of work by women.

Gender Issues in English Coursework (1988) p. 10

Would you support this view?

10 Leaving aside *Rattlebag*, it appears that the imbalance between female and male poets was somewhat redressed in the early 80s. What has happened since then? Could you produce an up-to-date list following the format of the one above? Or, alternatively, consider another form of school anthology – short stories, for instance – or texts for examination and see what the situation is there.

11 In 1992 Tim Cook surveyed the literature syllabus in thirty-six higher education institutions in England. Here are some extracts from his report which discuss the prominence of women writers:

... Fanny Burney is now taught in a third of respondent colleges, and other writers such as Mary Wollstonecraft and Sarah Fielding are beginning to feature. A similar trend is indicated by the appearance on at least twelve syllabuses of Mary Shelley's *Frankenstein*, putting her well ahead of her male Gothic rival, Horace Walpole, with Anne Radcliffe third and James Hogg, whom some people put in this category, fourth ...

Emily Dickinson and Walt Whitman are as widely available as Hopkins ... Christina Rossetti and Elizabeth Barrett Browning were written in by several respondents, and are probably increasingly taught.

... there are very few colleges where he (Dickens), Charlotte and Emily Brontë are not available. Jane Austen, George Eliot and Thomas Hardy, in that order, are only slightly less popular with teachers. The first two are compulsory for English majors or specialists in half the participating institutions. Another sign of increasing interest in women's writing is that Mrs Gaskell and Maria Edgeworth now appear on more course lists than Thackeray or Trollope (favourite reading of Tory prime ministers), while Edith Wharton is ahead of them as well as of Melville and Cooper amongst her fellow American writers.

... Other writers appearing twice or more are Ford Madox Ford, Gertrude Stein, Dorothy Richardson (does any student read more than a few pages?) Basil Bunting and, unexpectedly rarely, Katherine Mansfield.

... Seamus Heaney is taught in every college but one, and just beats Philip Larkin, Ted Hughes and Sylvia Plath, though Plath is required reading in more colleges than any other poet ... Other poets with more than 30 per cent of citations are Stevie Smith, Louis MacNeice, Anne Sexton ... Also mentioned several times were Elizabeth Bishop, Marianne Moore ... Other women poets written in, and likely to be taught more widely in future, include Grace Nichols and Adrienne Rich.

Tim Cook, 'Canon Survey Report' (1992)

If you have access to course lists from any higher education institutions, you could check your data against Cook's.

➤ Do the names coincide or differ?

➤ What is the proportion of female to male authors on the course lists you have?

➤ Are there any courses where women predominate or where the ratio is 1:1?

➤ What about recommendations for critical studies? Are the authors mostly male?

➤ If you have a course in which women are significantly under-represented or completely absent, try to construct an alternative course list. Histories of women's writing, bibliographical dictionaries and publishers' catalogues are good sources of information.

➤ Would you be in favour of some form of positive discrimination so as to bring to the fore the writing of underrepresented groups?

➤ Cook's data comes from the new universities. Is there evidence that the older universities are more traditional in their selection of texts? Again, try to locate course descriptions and reading lists so that you can assess the evidence.

12   Olsen's work suggests that women's achievements are deemed minor, are often excluded and marginalized and are retrieved only with difficulty by persistent women. The illustration of Queen Victoria, in which she meditates with an appropriate po-faced solemnity on 'men who have made my glory', indicates another problematic position for the woman of achievement: she becomes a figurehead, secured in her place by the efforts of exceptional men. The graphic summarizing some of the data of Tim Cook's survey presents a third option. Here women writers find themselves in happy equity with men, a ratio of 5:5 for the top ten authors overall, and 5:5 for twentieth-century novelists. Can we say, then, that at least for the woman author the problem of a just representation has been solved or do issues remain?

Top ten authors who are given priority in the new universities

1 Wordsworth
2 Emily Brontë
3 Charlotte Brontë
4 George Eliot
5 Charles Dickens
6 Shakespeare
7 Jane Austen
8 James Joyce
9 Virginia Woolf
10 W B Yeats

Top ten 20th century novelists

1 D H Lawrence
2 James Joyce
3 Virginia Woolf
4 Henry James
5 Angela Carter
6 Toni Morrison
7 Margaret Atwood
8 Alice Walker
9 George Orwell
10 Chinua Achebe

from the Guardian *12 October 1993*

➤ Cook's data indicates that, with the exception of Shakespeare, both female and male writers, pre-nineteenth century, have disappeared from the top ten. Is that a concern specifically for women?

➤ What do you think of the selected twentieth-century women novelists? Are they supposed to be a representative sample of contemporary women's writing? If so, how? Why do you think these particular women writers have become predominant?

➤ Is the equal balance in the academic listings duplicated among the reading public generally? You could check on this by surveying over a period of time the best-seller lists displayed in newspapers and bookshops.

➤ Do you conclude that getting women writers on to course lists is a necessary political activity for feminism? Does it in some ways help the woman reader, the woman writer or the woman student? What significance does the activity have for our understanding of literature generally?

We have been considering here issues from the British educational system but they obviously have a wider currency. If you are familiar with other educational contexts, you could make some useful comparisons in terms of the representation, significance and status of the woman author.

Introduction: found

However you evaluate the material you gathered in the first part of this section, the evidence is clear that women writers *are* now more fully represented than they were when Olsen began her survey. Indeed, some women authors have gained wide coverage and high levels of popularity. This development raises its own set of questions. Should feminists, and women readers generally, be delighted when a woman author becomes acclaimed, even a cult figure? Should we interpret this status as a positive sign of women's achievement and a support for other women writers? Or should we see the book readings, the interviews, the literary prizes as a fatal compromise with a publishing and marketing machinery that serves its own ends and does no real service for women? Or can one take less absolute positions and find both problems and possibilities in the cult of the female author?

   This second part of the section approaches the issue through three perspectives:

• Helen Taylor, Virginia Woolf and Hilary Hinds present different responses to the problem so as to establish some reference points in the debate.

• The comments of Jane Rule and Margaret Atwood illustrate some of the anxieties authors might have about the publicity circus around them. Most importantly, can one promote the individual, successful writer while still supporting the mass of aspiring women writers?

• The particular questions raised by the *visual* promotional material created around women authors.

Views on the cult of the female author

13   Here is a response from Helen Taylor:

   The problem for radical readers and critics is that the obsession with the author rather than the text has been rightly identified as a bourgeois preoccupation which has worked against women's interests. In a much quoted line, Mary Ellmann wrote 'books by women are treated as though they themselves are women, and criticism embarks ... upon an intellectual measuring of busts and hips'. Thus feminists have struggled hard against the phallocratic dismissal or trivialisation of women's work by reference to the author's feminine gender. From the nineteenth century critic's prurient speculations about the identities and personal practices of women who wrote pseudonymously, to the modern critical academy's fascination with each tiny detail of Virginia Woolf's Bloomsbury round or Erica Jong's sexual pursuits, the history of literary criticism is one of special pleading or special damnation of women writers.

So for many feminist critics the obvious escape from gender obsession has been to move towards a text-centredness, focussing on the work itself as a combined product/mediation of a specific historical context, of various historical influences, and of its producer's (rather than 'author's') location in terms of gender, class, race, region, and sexual orientation. Even more liberating has been the recent shift of interest from authorial intention to reader-reception, refusing the hierarchical relationship between text and passive reader in favour of a more democratic dialogue between active, critical reader and a work which then becomes a new text according to each reader's historically specific and variable experience. In teaching, such an approach releases students from that ahistorical question, 'Why didn't Charlotte Brontë give *Jane Eyre* a more radical ending?' and encourages them to see the determinations of contemporary readings in terms of their own class, race, politics, sexual orientation and so on.

So why invite writers to speak in public at all? Should they not be silent, uninterviewed, unphotographed, and allow their works to speak for themselves to each historically specific reader? Why should we want to know how many hours they write each day, who does the shopping in their home, and where they dream up ideas? To what use can we put such knowledge, except for the most suspect kind of heroine-worship or identification with the rich and famous – something *Cosmopolitan* and *Working Woman* already offer in abundance?

Helen Taylor, 'The Cult of the Woman Author' (1986) p. 40

Taylor's reference to Virginia Woolf is apposite since the promotional hype around the successful author is one of the issues she remonstrates about in *Three Guineas*:

Money is not the only baser ingredient. Advertisement and publicity are also adulterers. Thus, culture mixed with personal charm, or culture mixed with advertisement and publicity, are also adulterated forms of culture. We must ask you to abjure them; not to appear on public platforms; not to lecture; not to allow your private face to be published, or details of your private life; not to avail yourself, in short, of any of the forms of brain prostitution which are so insidiously suggested by the pimps and panders of the brain-selling trade; or to accept any of those baubles and labels by which brain merit is advertised and certified – medals, honours, degrees – we must ask you to refuse them absolutely, since they are all tokens that culture has been prostituted and intellectually sold into captivity.

Virginia Woolf, *Three Guineas* (1938; 1993) p. 219

On the other hand, Hilary Hinds begins her essay on Jeanette Winterson's *Oranges Are Not the Only Fruit* with this paragraph:

> Jeanette Winterson's first novel *Oranges Are Not the Only Fruit*, is one of those success stories of which feminists feel proud. From its small-scale beginning as a risky undertaking by the newly formed Pandora Press in 1985, through the winning of the Whitbread Prize for a first novel later the same year, to its much-lauded adaptation for BBC television by Winterson herself in January 1990, the work's reputation, like that of its author, has grown and prospered. Winterson herself is now unquestionably treated as a 'serious' author, highly praised by other 'serious' authors such as Gore Vidal and Muriel Spark; yet she is also a popular success, appearing on Clive James's television chat show and being sympathetically profiled in the press. The 'serious' side of the success story, her qualification as a repre-sentative of high culture, is largely dependent on her literary output: *Oranges* and, more especially, her third novel, *The Passion*; her popular success and high media exposure can be dated to the television adaptation of *Oranges*. That an author who is a lesbian and a feminist should be so successful in such contrasting contexts is seen by other lesbians and feminists as something to celebrate. Whatever misgivings may be felt about the traps and pitfalls of the mainstream, the sight of 'one of us' being given so much approval by the pillars of the establishment, whence usually comes opprobrium, is a source of enormous pleasure.
>
> Hilary Hinds, '*Oranges Are Not the Only Fruit*: Reaching Audiences
> Other Lesbian Texts Cannot Reach' (1992) p. 153

To clarify the arguments above, list the key points and add your own ideas to each listing. Try to think of a good range of valid arguments for each side of the debate. Can you make a judgement as to where you stand on this issue or do you find points from each perspective equally telling?

➤ Hinds believes there is a particular significance in the public acclamation of a lesbian writer; would you agree?

➤ Since Hinds published the above, Winterson's relationship with the media and the media's relationship with Winterson have changed quite markedly. You could research this issue as a fascinating example of how the woman writer is marketed and markets herself.

➤ Woolf's language is impassioned. Note, for instance, the extended metaphor or 'brain prostitution'. You should read *Three Guineas* to get the full import of this argument but, just from this small extract, what do you think is Woolf's case? In what ways does it coincide with Taylor's? Is Woolf offering these comments as a model for the author's conduct? If so, do you find the guidelines relevant for the female author of the twenty-first century?

➤ What about the questions of Taylor's final paragraph? How would you answer these questions? Particularly, are there valid reasons why you might want to know about the personal life of a female author?

Individual stars/collective aspirations

14   Taylor sees the cult of the author as raising problems for cultural and feminist politics. Nicci Gerrard sees what she terms 'the star system' as having detrimental consequences for individual writers. She quotes Jane Rule:

> I do very little publicity. I think you have to be extremely careful that the world doesn't turn you into its terms – I've always said that my business is to write and not to be 'the writer': what the world seems to want of me is to be 'the writer'. The temptation to be successful is in every place in life. I feel very ambivalent about self-publicity because if you live that way then your view of the world gets changed – you get an undue sense of your own importance in the world. And the media does terrible things to people. Once you set them up you have to knock them down. In Australia they say 'we cut our tall poppies down' and in Holland they say 'tall trees get a lot of wind'.
>
> quoted in Nicci Gerrard, Into the Mainstream (1989) p. 51

Margaret Atwood is just as cautious as Jane Rule concerning media hype. The heroine of her wonderfully comic novel, *Lady Oracle*, is an author who, for a short time, enjoys/endures the full media treatment:

> I was reassured by the advance copies of the book, though. It looked like a real book, and there was my picture on the back, like a real author's. Louisa K. Delacourt never got her picture on the back. I was a little alarmed by the jacket blurb: 'Modern love and the sexual battle, dissected with a cutting edge and shocking honesty.' I didn't think the book was about that, exactly; but Sturgess assured me he knew what he was doing. 'Your write it, you leave it to us to sell it,' he said. He also told me jubilantly that he'd 'placed' the most important review.
>
> 'What does that mean?' I said.
>
> 'We made sure the book went to someone who'd like it.'
>
> 'But isn't that cheating?' I asked, and Sturgess laughed. 'You're incredible,' he said. 'Just stay that way.'
>
> **UNKNOWN BURSTS ON LITERARY SCENE LIKE COMET**, said the first review, in the *Toronto Star*. I cut it out with the kitchen scissors and pasted it into the new scrapbook I'd bought from Kresge's. I was beginning to feel better. The *Globe* review called it 'gnomic' and 'chthonic,' right in the same paragraph. I looked these words up in the dictionary. Maybe it wasn't too bad, after all.
>
> (But I didn't stop to reflect on the nature of comets. Lumps of cosmic debris with long red hair and spectacular tails, discovered by astronomers, who named them after themselves. Harbingers of disaster. Portents of war.)
>
> Margaret Atwood, Lady Oracle (1976) pp. 233–4

Atwood might have added that comets also burn themselves out. On the basis of these two extracts, discuss what are the *writer's* anxieties about the star system. What/who are the targets for Atwood's irony?

15   Is the cult of the individual woman author at odds with notions of collectivity and sisterhood? Is the mega-star an inspiration, a dupe, a token ... or what? Taylor suggest:

> It is perhaps time we devised more methods of celebrating and criticising women's writing without isolating or elevating the individual artist.
>
> Helen Taylor, 'The Cult of the Woman Author' (1986) p. 41

How might this be done? Can you produce an action plan for supporting and developing women's writing without 'isolating or elevating the individual artist'? Nicci Gerrard describes one audacious strategy. Discussing the Booker prize, she writes:

> Whatever the merit and originality of the individual winners and runners-up, the tone set by Booker is one of conservatism and caution, and often seems to demonstrate the stranglehold of the literary establishment. When in 1985 the Maori writer Keri Hulme won with *The Bone People*, the announcement was greeted with astonishment, disapproval and some jubilation. Her three feminist editors, who collected the prize on her behalf, wove their way to the platform chanting in Maori and magnificently disrupting the sober and civilised atmosphere.
>
> Nicci Gerrard, *Into the Mainstream* (1989) p. 56

Opportunities for such splendid drama don't arise often. What strategies are possible on a daily basis?

The visual promotion of women authors

16   Inevitably much of the promotion surrounding famous women writers is of a visual nature – calendars, posters, diaries, mugs, T-shirts etc. Do these images strike you as 'the most suspect kind of heroine-worship' (Taylor); or as a 'source of enormous pleasure' (Hinds); or as something else?

17   Should we make discriminations about the *nature* of the image? For example, Taylor talks elsewhere about 'excessively romantic photos' of women authors and admires the image of Keri Hulme for resisting the familiar idealizing, sometimes glamorizing, of the women author. Should we make discriminations about the *use* of the image? I collect postcards of women writers and stick them on my wall; I have a Virginia Woolf coffee mug. Yet I baulk at the Virginia Woolf menu and the thought of a 'Mrs Dalloway Burger'. Is that inconsistent on my part, or mere snobbery, or are there significant differences in the meanings created by these images?

18   Start to put together your own collection of photos of women authors.
➤ What issues about the visual representation of women are raised by the images you collect?

60

Virginia Woolf's

The Hotel Russell is located in Bloomsbury, an area renowned for its association with the writers and artists known as the Bloomsbury Group. The Group used to meet in the early 1900's at 46 Gordon Square, the home of Virginia and Vanessa Stephen and their brothers. Philosophy, religion and the arts were the topics for discussion. Other members of the Group included Lytton Strachey, E.M. Forster, Saxon Sydney-Turner, Clive Bell, Duncan Grant, Maynard Keynes and Leonard Woolf.

Virginia Stephen (1882-1941) married Leonard Woolf in 1912. A 'modernist' writer, her novels, short stories, essays, diaries, biographies and literary criticism have achieved international acclaim.

Virginia Woolf's major works include The Voyage Out, Night and Day, Jacob's Room, Mrs. Dalloway, To the Lighthouse, Orlando, Between the Acts, The Waves, The Years and A Room of One's Own.

HOT STARTERS

Deep fried Camembert	£4.15
Tomato soup	£2.05
Breaded mushrooms	£2.25
Garlic bread	£1.85

COLD STARTERS

Prawn cocktail	£3.90
Avocado vinaigrette	£2.75
Avocado with prawns	£3.90
Mixed salad	£2.25

GRILLS

Our grills are served with either French fries, gratin dauphinoise potatoes or new potatoes. To complement the dish we can offer a choice from our delicious selection of sauces at an extra cost of 50p.

8oz sirloin steak	£10.95	**SAUCES**
12oz T-bone steak	£11.95	Creamy mushroom
Toulouse sausages	£6.85	Pepper
Spicy devilled chicken	£8.95	Bar-B-Q
8oz lamb steak served with mint and yoghurt dressing	£10.95	Provincial

BURGERS

Our half pound burgers are made with the finest beef, grilled to your liking and served with either French fries, gratin dauphinoise potatoes or new potatoes.   £6.95

Philosopher's Choice
Plain & unadulterated

Artist's Inspiration
A choice of melted Cheddar or Stilton cheese

Writer's Dilemma
Topped with our special Bar-B-Q sauce

Mrs Dalloway's
Topped with sauce poivre; cream, brandy, pink and green peppercorns, no bun

Jacob's Burger
Topped with creamy mushroom sauce, no bun

Night & Day
Topped with white wine, tomato, garlic, red and green pepper sauce, no bun

CHICKEN, FISH & VEGETARIAN

The following dishes are served with either French fries or new potatoes.

Deep fried fillet of plaice	£6.85	Vegetable quiche	£5.95
Breast of chicken Kiev	£9.75	Deep fried goujons of salmon with	
Nut cutlet	£6.95	dill and lime sauce	£6.95

PASTA

The following pastas are recommended with their sauce, however, we can serve any combination of your choice   £6.95

Fettucini Finocchi
Broad strips of pasta served with a fennel, mushroom, cheese and cream sauce

Tortellini Vesuviana
Spinach parcels in tomato sauce with herbs and cheese

Leo's Favourite Pasta
Twists of pasta with a basil, bacon and cream sauce

Spaghetti Bolognaise

JUMBO SANDWICHES

(Available until 5.30pm)   £5.95
Served in ciabatta bread with potato skins and garnish

- Tuna & sweetcorn
- Bacon & avocado
- Prawn & Marie Rose sauce
- Mozzarella & tomato
- Ham, cheese & pineapple
- Virginia Club

SALADS

Served either as a starter or main course

	Starter	Main
Spinach, bacon & croutons	£2.85	£4.75
Mozzarella, tomato & avocado	£2.85	£4.75
Poached chicken & avocado		£6.65
Poached salmon salad		£6.95
Mixed salad	£2.25	£3.95
Tuna & cucumber salad	£2.25	£3.95

All dishes are cooked to order, please allow us time to prepare your meal.
All prices include VAT. Gratuities at your discretion.

Menu from the Hotel Russell, London

When you need a break from reading why not write a letter to a friend...? We are delighted to offer this beautiful stationery straight from The National Portrait Gallery...

Stylishly produced stationery wallets containing five cards and matching envelopes, and one blank saddle stitched book suitable for all your notes and small diary entries. Featuring beautiful portraits of Virginia Woolf, Alice Walker or Agatha Christie plus a short biographical note and a quotation from their work, these wallets are a delight.

National Portrait Gallery
+ Hartman Cards £2.95 each
**Book Club Special Offer
£1.95 each**
18H Virginia Woolf **19H** Alice Walker
22J Agatha Christie

Attractive cloth bound note book featuring two photographs of Virginia Woolf (front and back), and 112 blank pages.

20H National Portrait Gallery £3.95
Book Club Special Offer £2.95

Advertisement for National Portrait Gallery materials, in the Women's Book Club Catalogue, 1992

➤ Are these women photographed alone, or within a group; in what setting?
➤ Are Black women represented; are women of all ages?
➤ What modes of femininity are suggested by the photos?
➤ Are the photos constructing women authors as icons or iconoclasts?
➤ What would be your guiding principles if you were photographing a portfolio of women writers?

19   Mary Scott, in her survey of photos of women authors, comments:

> Assume a pretty pic will attract a literary audience and you're only a step away from the recent, peculiar trend for publishers to promote novels on the basis of sex appeal.
>   That's nothing new in the genres. Romance writers have long been posed to appear fluffy and slender with a whisp of lace at the throat; authors of blockbusters sport big hair and fake leopard skin catsuits to reveal a swell of bosom. Both make functional sense – they're a pretty reliable guide to what lies between the covers. But what does a portrait of Candida McWilliam or Donna Tartt, looking delectable, tell you to expect of a 'serious' novel?
>
> Mary Scott, 'Making Faces' (1994) p. 27

Scott suggests that the modes of femininity operating in these photographs are both restricted in number and specific in type. Can you find evidence to support her two main claims

- that different models of femininity are associated with different genres;
- that, even in 'serious' women's writing, the more glamorous author is more marketable?

20 You could research also the recent high media visibility of a particular group

Author Keri Hulme, photo by Michael Scott courtesy of Hodder and Stoughton

of American writers – Camille Paglia, Naomi Wolf, Katie Roiphe, Rene Denfeld. All are critical of feminism or what they see as the dominant forms of feminism; all were aggressively marketed in Britain when their first books appeared; all have been marketed in particular ways with specific audiences and effects in mind. What marketing strategies are you aware of here? What part does the *visual* representation of these authors play in that strategy? Consulting reviews, newspaper and magazine articles would be helpful. More generally, why is anti-feminism or critiques of feminism seen as marketable?

References and further reading

Margaret Atwood, *Lady Oracle*

Tim Cook, 'Canon Survey Report'

Margaret Cooter et al., (Women in Publishing), *Reviewing the Reviews: A Woman's Place on the Bookpage*. This short, readable study examines the representation of women in reviewing, both as reviewers and as authors of books reviewed.

Nicci Gerrard, *Into the Mainstream*, see particularly the chapter on 'The Star System'

Hilary Hinds, '*Oranges Are Not the Only Fruit*: Reaching Audiences Other Lesbian Texts Cannot Reach' in Sally Munt (ed.), *New Lesbian Criticism: Literary and Cultural Readings*

Paul Lauter, 'Working-Class Women's Literature: An Introduction to Study' in Robyn R. Warhol and Diane Price Herndl (eds), *Feminisms: An Anthology of Literary Theory and Criticism*. Lauter's essay contains extensive reference material on working-class women's writing.

Sally Munt, 'Is There a Feminist in This Text? Ten Years (1979–989) of the Lesbian Novel: A retrospective'

NATE Language and Gender Committee, *Gender Issues in English Coursework*

Tillie Olsen, *Silences*. Look particularly at the two sections entitled 'One Out of Twelve'.

Mary Scott, 'Making Faces', *Everywoman*

Helen Taylor, 'The Cult of the Woman Author'

Winterson, Jeanette, *Oranges Are Not the Only Fruit*

Virginia Woolf, *Three Guineas* in the combined volume of *A Room of One's Own and Three Guineas*, ed. Michèle Barrett

Bonnie Zimmerman, 'One Out of Thirty: Lesbianism in Women's Studies Textbooks, in Margaret Cruickshank (ed.), *Lesbian Studies: Present and Future*

The Death of the Woman Author?

Introduction

In 1968 the French critic Roland Barthes published what proved to be a highly influential essay entitled 'The Death of the Author'. In the following year Michel Foucault responded with an equally attention-grabbing title, 'What is an Author?' Despite Barthes's dramatic demands for 'The death of the Author', 'the removal of the Author', 'the destruction of the Author', he is not suggesting mass executions or that writing can be produced mechanically by self-programming computers or rooms of chimps at word processors. What he is questioning is the view of the author as the source of all meaning in the text. As Gayatri Chakravorty Spivak comments:

> Barthes is writing here not of the death of the writer (though he *is* writing, quite copiously, of writing) or of the subject, or yet of the agent, but of the *Author*. The author, who is not only taken to be the authority for the meaning of the text, but also, when possessed of authority, possessed *by that fact* of 'moral or legal supremacy, the power to influence the conduct or action of others'; and, when authorising, 'giving legal force to, making legally valid' (OED).
>
> Gayatri Chakravorty Spivak, 'Reading *The Satanic Verses*' (1993) pp. 104–5

Similarly, Foucault's question is neither bemused nor a sign of some inexplicable ignorance on his part. Both writers are using a rather hyperbolic rhetoric as a way of establishing a debate on the significance and function of the author in our culture, particularly, as Spivak indicates, on the relation between the author and notions of authority. Foucault looks at the history of this figure, how the author has been constructed in culture and functioned in culture. He stresses that an authorless world (note Spivak's caveat, *not* writerless) is a vision for the future, not a description of the present. We could create a different concept of writing, though the writer would never function without constraint.

Neither writer is concerned – at least in these essays – with issues of gender. Barthes, on one occasion, refers to the author as 'the man or woman'; Foucault uses the work of Ann Radcliffe as one of his examples. However, generally, both name the author as 'he' and neither shows any interest in the specific situation of the *woman* author. Foucault ends his essay with the question:

> What difference does it make who is speaking? (p. 160)

His proposition here is to get away from the person and life of the author as the ultimate explanation for the text. I would suggest, though, that for the feminist reader the sex of the author and the cultural and historical position of the woman author might continue, for the foreseeable future, to make a lot of difference. To consider these issues further:

- Firstly, we shall try to clarify some of the central points in Barthes's and Foucault's arguments.

- Secondly, we can relate their arguments to examples from fiction that are themselves concerned with the role of the woman author.

Needless to say, the prior task is to read the relevant essays by Barthes and Foucault. Besides the publication details given in the list of works cited at the end of this book, you will find these essays elsewhere – Barthes's essay, in particular, has been frequently anthologized. Both are included in: David Lodge (ed.), *Modern Criticism and Theory: A Reader*. Both are also often discussed in introductions to critical theory. For accessible summaries of the chief ideas, see: Maurice Biriotti and Nicola Miller (eds), *What is an Author?* (Biriotti's 'Introduction' gives a useful over-view) and Roger Webster, *Studying Literary Theory: An Introduction* pp. 18–21. Especially useful is: Seán Burke, *Authorship from Plato to the Postmodern: A Reader* which not only includes the essays of Barthes and Foucault but several important essays by feminists on questions of authorship and excellent introductions by Burke to the whole area.

Barthes and Foucault

1 Barthes's and Foucault's essays make strange reading at first if you are not used to the context and style in which they are writing. However, pick out what ideas you can understand about the meaning of 'author', or hazard a guess at some possibilities. Equally, note the points that seem inexplicable so that you can return to these at later stages and, hopefully, clarify them. Here are what strike me as some of the important ideas about the author in the two essays. I list these in no particular order:

- What is the function of the author? How did this figure come about? What is its significance?
- The author as hero with status and privilege
- The author as unique, intuitive, displaying special insights, a more refined sensibility
- Authoring as linked to ownership and appropriation
- The author gives unity to a body of writing, authenticates it
- The author as source of meaning, able to explain the work, knowing the essence of the work
- The author as regulator and controller of the text, defining the limits of it
- The author as origin of the text, father of the text, god-like creator of the text
- As the author dies, the reader is born.

Amend my list as you think best. Add your own points and queries. Can you go back to the texts and find some short quotes from the essays to exemplify the points that together we've listed?

2   Looking at different aspects of contemporary culture, would you support Barthes's and Foucault's claims about the meaning of 'author'?

➤ What view of the author do we get from popular biographies of writers, magazine articles or from late night Channel 4 discussions?

➤ Think of the tourist industry that has formed around certain literary names – Shakespeare, the Brontës, Lawrence. What sense of the author is created here?

➤ Think of film versions of the author (whether in writing, painting or music). For example, *My Left Foot*, *Prick Up Your Ears*, *Dead Poets' Society*, Ken Russell's film *Mahler*, Robert Altman's *Vincent and Theo* (on Van Gogh), Hollywood's version of Michelangelo, *The Agony and the Ecstasy* – (the title says it all).

➤ What view of the author is held by the apocryphal 'person in the street'?

➤ If you sign yourself author – say on your passport or your tax form – how does that differ from signing yourself 'electrician', 'nurse', 'business consultant'? What connotations and associations are operating?

➤ Why do so many people have aspirations to be an author? What is attractive about that role? If you have such aspirations, what is prompting you?

When you have collected your responses, see if they relate to your list of points from the two essays. For example, it seems to me that many literary fans, myself included, who visit writers' birth places do so, in part, because, in some confused way, we hope to gain access to a source of meaning, a hidden clue. Thus, if we walk the Yorkshire Moors or sit in Lawrence's house in Eastwood, then we will 'really know' what inspired the books and 'really know' what the books mean. As Foucault writes, '... what part of his deepest self did he express in his discourse?

3   In her earlier comment on the author, Spivak looks to dictionary definitions of 'author' and related terms. Can you develop this approach? Using the *Oxford English Dictionary*, if you have easy access, or any good dictionaries, find as many meanings as you can for 'author', 'authorize', 'authority', 'authentic'. Itemize the definitions which relate to notions of:

• origin

• control

• legal power.

Return to the list of ideas from Barthes and Foucault. See, once more, how your new information links to their material. For instance, the first two meanings of 'author' given in the OED are, 'the person who originates or gives existence to anything' and 'one who begets; a father, an ancestor'. Evidently the etymology supports the view that authors are the origin of their works.

4   Though Barthes and Foucault do not consider the relevance of their theories for feminism, we can. The passages that follow are from Nancy Miller and

Maurice Biriotti. In each case, the first passage mentions the liberatory potential of Barthes's and Foucault's view while the second points out the dangers for women and other oppressed groups. Biriotti summarizes part of Miller's argument in his second passage:

> It may also be the case that having been killed off along with 'man', the author can now be rethought beyond traditional notions of biography, now that through the feminist rewritings of literary history the adequacy of a masculine identify to represent the universal has been radically questioned.
>
> Nancy Miller, 'The Text's Heroine: A Feminist Critic and Her Fictions' (1982) p. 71

> The postmodernist decision that the Author is Dead and the subject along with him does not, I will argue, necessarily hold for women, and prematurely forecloses the question of agency for them. Because women have not had the same historical relation to identity to origin, institution, production that men have had, they have not, I think (collectively) felt burdened by *too much* Self, Ego, Cogito etc. Because the female subject has been juridically excluded from the polis, hence decentred, 'disoriginated', deinstitutionalized etc., her relation to integrity and textuality, desire and authority, displays structurally important differences from that universal position.
>
> Nancy Miller, 'Changing the Subject: Authorship, Writing and the Reader' (1986) p. 106

> Traditionally, Western thinking has constructed the subject as white, male and bourgeois. Subjectivity, and indeed authorship itself, have been denied for huge portions of the population: those oppressed on the grounds of race, gender, and sexuality. The death of the author, an attack on the humanist subject, with his implications in racism, sexism and imperialism, can therefore be seen as part of a strategy of political liberation.
>
> Maurice Biriotti, 'Introduction: Authorship, Authority, Authorisation' (1993) p. 4

> With the demise of the male, humanist Author (lionised, canonised, anthologised) new possibilities for challenging the male-dominated literary canon emerge. But ironically, just at the time when different voices were being heard (black voices, women's voices, the voices of those in the margins), the Author's death denied authorship precisely to those who had only recently been empowered to claim it. Miller argues that the Death of the Author, therefore, should not apply to those subjects to whom subjectivity had, historically and traditionally, been denied.
>
> Ibid. pp. 5–6

To paraphrase the first extracts of Miller and Biriotti, both indicate how the characteristics/functions of the author as defined by Barthes and Foucault – origin, control, status, delimitation of meaning – are invested largely in white, bourgeois males. To 'kill' the author is to unsettle the power of this privileged group and to open possibilities, in writing and elsewhere, for marginal groups – women, Blacks, gays and (though Biriotti curiously omits this group) the working class. Perhaps now we can create new meanings and functions for the author which empower new voices.

To this extent, as both Miller and Biriotti indicate, feminism has worked in tandem with post-structuralist and postmodernist thought. All three critical perspectives have questioned the authority of the author; all have had a subversive and undermining impact on canonical views of literary history. Moreover, many contemporary women writers have employed techniques of self-reflexivity, pastiche and irony common in the postmodernist novel. But in introducing issues specific to the *woman* author, feminism has been led to a more questioning position. There may be opportunities for women in 'killing' the author but there may also be losses.

➤ Looking at Millers' and Biriotti's second passages, what doubts and qualifications do they introduce? As I have done above, try to rewrite their comments in your own terms so as to make them comprehensible to you.

5 If you would like to think further about this debate, see the discussion between Peggy Kamuf and Nancy Miller anthologized in my *Feminist Literary Criticism* (1991). Here the importance of the female author is discussed in terms of the significance of the female signature. Kamuf wants to focus on the writing rather than the author; Miller finds a greater importance in the person of the female author. Refer also to the comments of Trinh T. Minh-ha in the section on Creating a Matrilineage for a different interpretation of the author and literary history.

Fictional debates on the woman author

6 I should like us to look at some fictional examples that enable us to question further the death of the woman author. As with Mark Twain, the report of her death may be an exaggeration. The first extract is from Margaret Atwood's *The Handmaid's Tale*. If you have not read the novel you need to know that the book is a dystopia, set in a fundamentalist and totalitarian regime, named Gilead, sometime in the not-too-distant future. A woman narrates an account of her life as a 'handmaid' (the surrogate for a barren wife) to one of the new republic's commanders. At the end of her story the reader is not sure whether she is doomed or about to be saved. The woman's account is followed by a section entitled 'Historical Notes on *The Handmaid's Tale*'. We are some time further in the future and a lecture is being given at an academic conference. The subject of the lecture is a taped account of what appears to be the handmaid's life that we have just read. Professor Pieixoto begins his lecture:

Thank you. I am sure we all enjoyed our charming Arctic Char last night at dinner, and now we are enjoying an equally charming Arctic Chair. I use the word 'enjoy' in two distinct senses, precluding, of course, the obsolete third. (*Laughter.*)

But let me be serious. I wish, as the title of my little chat implies, to consider some of the problems associated with the *soi-disant* manuscript which is well known to all of you by now, and which goes by the title of *The Handmaid's Tale*. I say *soi-disant* because what we have before us is not the item in its original form. Strictly speaking, it was not a manuscript at all when first discovered, and bore no title. The superscription 'The Handmaid's Tale' was appended to it by Professor Wade, partly in homage to the great Geoffrey Chaucer; but those of you who know Professor Wade informally, as I do, will understand when I say that I am sure all puns were intentional, particularly that having to do with the archaic vulgar signification of the word *tail*; that being, to some extent, the bone, as it were, of contention, in the last phase of Gileadean society of which our saga treats. (*Laughter, applause.*)

This item – I hesitate to use the word *document* – was unearthed on the site of what was once the city of Bangor, in what, at the time prior to the inception of the Gileadean regime, would have been the State of Maine. We know that this city was a prominent way-station on what our author refers to as 'The Underground Femaleroad', since dubbed by some of our historical wags 'The Underground Frailroad'. (*Laughter, groans.*) For this reason, our Association has taken a particular interest in it.

The item in its pristine state consisted of a metal foot-locker, U.S. Army issue, *circa* perhaps 1955. This fact of itself need have no significance, as it is known that such foot-lockers were frequently sold as 'army surplus' and must therefore have been widespread. Within this foot-locker, which was sealed with tape of the kind once used on packages to be sent by post, were approximately thirty tape cassettes, of the type that became obsolete sometime in the eighties or nineties with the advent of the compact disc.

I remind you that this was not the first such discovery. You are doubtless familiar, for instance, with the item known as 'The A. B. Memoirs', located in a garage in a suburb of Seattle, and with 'The Diary of P.', excavated by accident during the erection of a new meeting house in the vicinity of what was once Syracuse, New York.

Professor Wade and I were very excited by this new discovery. Luckily we had, several years before, with the aid of our excellent resident antiquarian technician, reconstructed a machine capable of playing such tapes, and we immediately set about the painstaking work of transcription.

There were some thirty tapes in the collection altogether, with varying proportions of music to spoken word. In general, each tape begins with two or three songs, as camouflage no doubt: then the music is broken off and the speaking voice takes over. The voice is a woman's and, according to our voice-print experts, the same one throughout. The labels on the cassettes were authentic period labels, dating, of course, from some time before the inception of the early Gilead era, as all such secular music was banned under the regime. There were, for instance, four tapes entitled 'Elvis Presley's Golden Years', three of 'Folk Songs of Lithuania', three of 'Boy George Takes It Off', and two of 'Mantovani's Mellow Strings', as well as some titles that sported a mere single tape each' 'Twisted Sister at Carnegie Hall' is one of which I am particularly fond.

Although the labels were authentic, they were not always appended to the tape with the corresponding songs. In addition, the tapes were arranged in no particular order, being loose at the bottom of the box; nor were they numbered. Thus it was up to Professor Wade and myself to arrange the blocks of speech in the order in which they appeared to go; but, as I have said elsewhere, all such arrangements are based on some guesswork and are to be regarded as approximate, pending further research.

Once we had the transcription in hand – and we had to go over it several times, owing to the difficulties posed by accent, obscure referents, and archaisms – we had to make some decision as to the nature of the material we had thus so laboriously acquired.

Margaret Atwood, *The Handmaid's Tale* (1985) pp. 313–4

Pieixoto appears to be constructing the author, establishing the coherence and 'classificatory function' of the author in a way reminiscent of Foucault's essay. For example, Pieixoto places the handmaid's story in relation to other discovered memoirs and his colleague, Professor Wade, has situated it in relation to Chaucer's tales. As Barthes describes, Pieixoto is also interested in sources, origins, circumscribing the meaning of the material. Refer to the essays of Barthes and Foucault and note the links you can make with the Atwood extract.

7   With Barthes's and Foucault's work in mind, how might a feminist respond to Atwood's material? I am going to suggest some ideas and queries to which you can add your own:

- Who is the author of this text? Pieixoto and Wade have organized and transcribed the material. It may now be in a form quite different from the handmaid's account – 'what we have before us is not the item in its original form'. What, then, is the status of the female author?

- Have the male academics now become 'authorities' on the female author? Could feminism return that authority to the woman?

- The sexist jokes and the smutty innuendo of Pieixoto lead us to doubt the validity of his analysis. We need to find this woman author through/despite Pieixoto's prejudice.

- Later in this lecture, Pieixoto comments:

  Supposing it to be correct – supposing, that is, that Waterford was indeed the 'Commander' – many gaps remain. Some of them could have been filled by our anonymous author, had she had a different turn of mind. She could have told us much about the workings of the Gileadean empire, had she had the instincts of a reporter or a spy. What would we not give, now, for even twenty pages or so of printout from Waterford's private computer! (p.322)

The woman author Pieixoto constructs is, in his terms, minor and inadequate: the male power relations of the Gileadean empire are of more interest to Pieixoto than the daily life and musings of a powerless woman. Feminism would want to reconstruct that woman author as central.

- The handmaid has no name; she is merely 'Offred' (that is 'of Fred', belonging to Fred). Researching female Romantic poets, J. R. de J. Jackson writes:

  The headnotes have presented great difficulties. Anyone who has tried to pursue the lives of women through standard reference works will be familiar with them. Excluded as they were throughout the period in question from all public offices, from universities, from the armed services, and from the professions, one is deprived of the usual hooks and eyes of biographical history ... This exclusion they shared with many men who did not belong to the social or political establishment. But to it is added a further complication that they did not share with the men, the change of surname on marriage, sometimes more than once in a lifetime.

J. R de J. Jackson, *Romantic Poetry by Women: A Bibliography 1770–1835* (1993) pp. xvi–xvii

Faced with this historical silence, the feminist reader and critic may want to trace origins and sources.

• Foucault, as we noted, asks:

What difference does it make who is speaking?

Foucault wants to move on from this question; Pieixoto is locked in to this question but one has no faith in his answers; feminism still needs to ask the question so as to find the lost women of history.

8   Here is another example of a fictional debate about the woman author. Try working on this material in the way I have above. You may find it helpful to produce your own set of notes on relevant issues as I have done. The passages are from J. M. Coetzee's *Foe*. It is the early years of the eighteenth century. A woman called Susan Barton has been shipwrecked on an island with a white man, named Cruso, and a Black, male slave, Friday. Rescued and back in London, she approaches a writer, Daniel Foe, to tell her story. The first passage comes from Susan's recollected conversation with the ship's captain as she returns to England, the second and third are from her discussion with Foe about the nature and demands of writing:

So I sat with the captain in his cabin and ate a plate of salt pork and biscuit, very good after a year of fish, and drank a glass of Madeira, and told him my story, as I have told it to you, which he heard with great attention. 'It is a story you should set down in writing and offer to the booksellers,' he urged – 'There has never before, to my knowledge, been a female castaway of our nation. It will cause a great stir.' I shook my head sadly. 'As I relate it to you, my story passes the time well enough,' I replied; 'but what little I know of book-writing tells me its charm will quite vanish when it is set down baldly in print. A liveliness is lost in the writing down which must be supplied by art, and I have no art.' 'As to art I cannot pronounce, being only a sailor,' said Captain Smith; 'but you may depend on it, the booksellers will hire a man to set your story to rights, and put a dash of colour too, here and there.' 'I will not have any lies told,' said I. The captain smiled. 'There I cannot vouch for them,' he said: 'their trade is in books, not in truth.' 'I would rather be the author of my own story than have lies told about me,' I persisted – 'If I cannot come forward, as author, and swear to the truth of my tale, what will be the worth of it? I might as well have dreamed it in a snug bed in Chichester.'...

I am not, do you see, one of those thieves or highwaymen of yours who gabble a confession and are then whipped off to Tyburn and eternal silence, leaving you to make of their stories whatever you fancy. It is still in my power to guide and amend. Above all, to withhold. By such means do I still endeavour to be father to my story....

I am not a story, Mr Foe. I may impress you as a story because I began my account of myself without preamble, slipping overboard into the water and striking out for the shore. But my life did not begin in the waves. There was a life before the water which stretched back to my desolate searchings in Brazil, thence to the years when my daughter was still with me, and so on back to the day I was born. All of which makes up a story I do not choose to tell. I choose not to tell it because to no one, not even to you, do I owe proof that I am a substantial being with a substantial history in the world. I choose rather to tell of the island, of myself and Cruso and Friday and what we three did there: for I am a free woman who asserts her freedom by telling her story according to her own desire.

J. M. Coetzee, Foe (1986) pp. 40, 123, 131

You might want to consider the following questions among your notes;
➤ What are Susan's anxieties about telling her story?
➤ How do these anxieties relate to the arguments of Barthes and Foucault?
➤ Two men are involved in the telling of Susan's story – Daniel Foe and J. M. Coetzee. What are the issues in each case?

To find out whether Susan tells her own story, whether the professional author, Mr Foe, tells her story and whether, crucially, Friday ever gets to tell his story – you'll have to read the book.

9 If you wish to pursue this question of the birth, death and, sometimes, tremulous life of the woman author, two further fiction texts of interest are:

Ursula Le Guin, 'Sur' (1982)	In this story a group of middle-class ladies of the early years of the century discover the South Pole before any male explorers. Concerned about appearing unfeminine and about the sensibilities of their male counterparts, they neglect to tell anyone abut their achievement and leave no trace along the journey. The only record is an account stored in an attic trunk for grandchildren to discover.
Alice Walker, 'Nineteen Fifty-five' (1981)	The title refers to the date when Gracie Mae Still, a Black blues singer, sells the rights of one of her songs to the manager of an up-and-coming white, male singer, Traynor. Traynor records his version of Gracie Mae's song and becomes a hugely famous and wealthy, but troubled, star. (The links with Elvis are all evident.) A complex relationship develops between Gracie Mae and Traynor.

10 If you do have an opportunity to read the novels and stories mentioned here, you can study them in relation to the ideas from Barthes and Foucault we put together at the start of this section (see point 1). For example:

- Like Barthes, Susan Barton in *Foe* talks of 'fathering' a text. What is the significance of a potential *woman* author using this term?

- Spivak mentions the notion of 'moral or legal supremacy' inherent in the term 'author'. Could one argue that a central dilemma in Walker's story is that Traynor holds the legal supremacy (he has bought up the copyright), while Gracie Mae retains the moral supremacy? Part of Traynor's angst is that at some deep and barely articulated level he realizes that this is not 'his' song.

- At the same time, one would want to question from the perspective of Gracie Mae, a poor, Black woman, that concept of 'legality' and rename it an act of expropriation.

- Traynor doesn't understand the song he sings and looks to Gracie Mae for the source of meaning. Walker seems to suggest that Gracie Mae does, indeed, have this knowledge as a product of a profound cultural experience.

- The concept of 'ownership', discredited by Barthes and Foucault, has a different meaning for Gracie Mae, Offred and Susan who have such a tenuous grasp on their stories. As Susan points out emphatically, to control the story is to retain a sense of selfhood.

- For Gracie Mae, Offred and Susan, the problem is not that they function as authors who control and regulate the text; rather the problem is that they do not. Traynor's manager controls Gracie Mae's; Pieixoto and Wade control Offred's; and Foe *may* control (the story is open on this point) Susan's.

- Operating within codes of middle–class femininity and a workaday anti-heroism, the women of *Sur* reject authorial privilege and status but, in so doing, risk historical obscurity.

I put these ideas in note form and, if you do research the texts further, they need amplification. What is clear, though, is that once one marries the views of Barthes and Foucault with the historical and cultural situation of women, the relationship becomes uneasy. Concepts of ownership, origin, genius, meaning, control etc. operate differently for women.

11   Nancy Miller reminds us of this fact at the end of her essay, 'The Text's Heroine: A Feminist Critic and Her Fictions'. Returning to Foucault's question, which in the edition Miller uses is translated as 'What matter who's speaking?', she answers:

> This sovereign indifference, I would argue, is one of the 'masks ... behind which phallocentricism hides its fictions'; the authorizing function of its own discourse authorizes the 'end of woman' without consulting her. What matter who's speaking? I would answer it matters, for example, to women who have lost and still routinely lose their proper name in marriage, and whose signature – not merely their voice – has not been worth the paper it was written on; women for whom the signature – by virtue of its power in the world of circulation – is *not* immaterial. Only those who have it can play with not having it.

Nancy Miller, 'The Text's Heroine: A Feminist Critic and Her Fictions' (1982) p. 75

➤ Can you give some specific examples, from contemporary society or from history, of what Miller is here claiming? In what ways have women/do women struggle to establish the authority of their name? For instance, the married woman who retains her maiden name can still encounter problems and confusions. What examples can you offer?

➤ Think back also to the research problems mentioned by J. R. de J. Jackson. To be named and recorded is to establish an historical authority.

12 A way forward? In his introduction to his Reader on the figure of the author in film theory, John Caughie likens the dismissal of the author to the rejection of a teenage infatuation and suggests that theory ought to try harder to find a place for the author:

> ... in its reaction against a teenage romance with the *auteur*, much recent discussion of film (and teaching of film) has tended to deny its former attachment by leaving the author (or *auteur*, or director) without an adequate place in theory: if the author is not at the centre, he is nowhere; if the romance is over, I will reject him utterly.

John Caughie (ed.), Theories of Authorship (1981) p. 3

Feminism does not want to establish the woman author as an icon. Yet, since the woman author has barely entered literary history, feminism cannot risk losing her. How, then, do we know and value the woman writer without deifying her? (You could link here with the section The Woman Writer: Lost and Found.)

The sharp-eyed reader will have noticed a response to Miller embedded within Spivak's earlier comment. Miller writes:

> The postmodernist decision that the Author is Dead and the subject along with him does not, I will argue, necessarily hold for women, and prematurely forecloses the question of agency for them.

Spivak replies:

> Barthes is writing here not of the death of the writer (though he *is* writing, quite copiously, of writing) or of the subject, or yet of the agent, but of the *Author*.

'The author', 'the subject', 'the agent'/agency feature in both quotes; 'the writer' also in Spivak's. Is Spivak suggesting that there is a way for feminism to discover the name, biography, writing, activity of the woman author, without reinstating the privileged, controlling function of 'Author'? That would be an interesting question to work on.

References and further reading

Margaret Atwood, *The Handmaid's Tale*

Roland Barthes, 'The Death of the Author' in *Image-Music-Text*

Maurice Biriotti and Nicola Miller (eds), *What is an Author?* Biriotti's essay, 'Introduction: Authorship, Authority, Authorisation' and Nancy Miller's, 'The Text's Heroine: A Feminist Critic and Her Fictions' are both anthologized in this collection.

Seán Burke, *Authorship from Plato to the Postmodern: A Reader*

John Caughie (ed.), *Theories of Authorship*

J. M. Coetzee, *Foe*

Mary Eagleton (ed.) *Feminist Literary Criticism*. A dialogue between Nancy Miller and Peggy Kamuf on the significance of the woman author is contained in this collection of essays. Miller's contribution is 'The Text's Heroine: A Feminist Critic and Her Fictions'. Here it can be seen in its original format as a response to Peggy Kamuf.

Michel Foucault, 'What Is an Author?' in Josué V. Harari (ed.) *Textual Strategies: Perspectives in Post-Structuralist Criticism*

J. R. de J. Jackson, *Romantic Poetry by Women: A Bibliography* 1770–1835

Ursula Le Guin, 'Sur', *The Compass Rose: Short Stories* anthologized in Sandra M. Gilbert and Susan Gubar (eds), *The Norton Anthology of Literature by Women: The Tradition in English*

Reina Lewis, 'The Death of the Author and the Resurrection of the Dyke' in Sally Munt (ed.), *New Lesbian Criticism: Literary and Cultural Readings*. Lewis ponders the problem of being asked to write as a lesbian while wanting to deconstruct that identity.

David Lodge (ed.), *Modern Criticism and Theory: A Reader*

Nancy Miller, *Subject to Change: Reading Feminist Writing*. Both Miller's essays mentioned in this section are included in this collection of her work. Page references in this section are taken from this text. In 'Changing the Subject: Authorship, Writing and the Reader', Miller also discusses Charlotte Brontë's *Villette* as a further example of the problems of female authorship.

Gayatri Chakravorty Spivak, 'Reading *The Satanic Verses*' in Biriotti and Miller (1993)

Alice Walker, 'Nineteen Fifty-five', *You Can't Keep a Good Woman Down*

Roger Webster, *Studying Literary Theory: An Introduction*

Gender and Genre

Introduction

The terms 'gender' and 'genre' come from the same Greek root. Both have in common the concept of classification; in fact the *Oxford English Dictionary* lists 'kind' and 'sort' as meanings for both words. Dictionaries of literary terms find the word 'genre' difficult to pin down. It used to have a more specific usage. Now, for many readers and critics, 'genre' seems to be interchangeable with 'literary form' and, even, 'mode'. The major contemporary genres are the novel, drama and poetry, but within these large groupings are numerous sub-genres – the realist novel, kitchen-sink drama, the sonnet, for example.

From feminist criticism's discussion of genre I'd like us to consider the following issues:

- How does genre relate to gender? Are certain forms of writing more associated with women, others more with men? How are such associations to be explained?

- Women's special relationship with the novel. Why did/do women become novelists more frequently than poets or dramatists?

- Should the novel be referred to as a *female* form or a *feminized* form? How do we understand those different terms?

Throughout I shall be stressing a double approach – that certain forms are associated with a particular sex but also that a closer examination may reveal for some literary forms a more complex and ambiguous relation between gender and genre. I want us to notice also the changes brought about by history: not only do literary forms themselves change but also the degree of participation by women. So, for instance, women's involvement in poetry has increased considerably in the post-war period.

But, first, if you are not used to the term 'genre' investigate it further. Look up its meaning in a range of dictionaries of literary terms and introductions to literary studies. See:

Chris Baldick, *The Concise Oxford Dictionary of Literary Terms*

Roger Fowler (ed.), *A Dictionary of Modern Critical Terms*

John Peck and Martin Coyle, *Literary Terms and Criticism*.

Make a list of as many different genres as you can think of. Consider not only our own period but forms of writing more common in the past – the writing of philosophical essays or theological tracts. Remember writing for other media – scriptwriting, journalism. Link these genres to relevant authors or titles. Think about how authors sometimes mix genres or deliberately change the conventions. Two helpful introductions are:

Alan Durant and Nigel Fabb, *Literary Studies in Action*, chapter 5

Martin Montgomery, Alan Durant, Nigel Fabb, Tom Furniss and Sara Mills, *Ways of Reading*, unit 17

Gender and Genre

1 How would you feel if, in surveying a shelf of books, you came across the following two titles.

A Mother's Guide to Breastfeeding John Smith

The Theory of Advanced Nuclear Physics Jane Smith

I expect you might wonder why a man is writing a guide to breastfeeding since, self-evidently, he cannot have experienced either motherhood or breastfeeding. But, then, you might think of the number of obstetricians and general practitioners who are male and who must have gathered some knowledge through their daily work of the experience of breastfeeding. You might consider further the impact in recent years of women's health groups and the campaigning they have done amongst male medics for more awareness of women's needs. Perhaps this book is a product of that activism. On the second title, you might be surprised at a woman writing a science textbook since we all know from media reports and from general observation that women are under-represented in science and particularly under-represented in physics. If you think of women as usually more pacifist than men, you might be concerned at the involvement in specifically *nuclear* physics and associate it with nuclear weapons; if you think of women as usually less abstract and theoretical than men, you might wonder at the academic approach. On the other hand, you might remember that there always have been women trail-blazers in the most unlikely areas and you might decide that recent national initiatives to encourage women into science are finally paying off.

I have laboriously enumerated here the kind of thoughts which in reality would rapidly flash through your mind as you moved from one part of the bookshop to another. What these thoughts indicate is how extensively and, often, unconsciously we associate forms of writing with a specific sex. Hence, in this case there is a presumption that

birth, children, the domestic = female

science, technology, the public = male

emotions, the experiential = female

rationality, the theoretical = male.

When we look at the titles from 'John Smith; and 'Jane Smith' the conventions are overturned and we have to readjust our responses to take account of that difference.

The random thoughts indicate also how the development of genres may be affected by factors outside the actual practice of writing:

Changing patterns of education and employment	Women are now gaining more access to science, and, thus, may become science authors.
The creation of new markets	For example, there is now a demand for user-friendly science textbooks for girls and self-help medical manuals for women.
The influence of other cultural forms	As conventional stereotypes are challenged in one medium and one area of the culture, this may open up possibilities within others. So a TV drama about a woman senior police officer leads to the magazine articles, the film, official investigations into opportunities for women in the police force, revised careers advice for girls, and so on.
Wider debates in the culture about the construction of gender	Why does one assume that the book on nuclear physics is likely to be written by a man? Are women *innately* more pacifist, or more emotional, or more experiential than men or is it that our culture imbues women with such attributes? The activities of the women's peace movement would be an important contribution to the debate.

All these factors can challenge both the prevailing gender ideology, what is felt to be 'appropriate' writing for men and women, and the writer's own sense of self as a writer, what s/he feels is within her/his capabilities.

2 Let's try to apply these comments to a different set of examples. In the lists below, replace the term, 'the author', with what seems to you an apt pronoun, 'his', 'her', or both. Of course, we know that both men and women are capable of writing in all these forms, but which is the pronoun that most readily comes to mind when thinking of each of these forms?

the author's screen-play	the author's novel
the author's moral tales	the author's household manual
the author's sermons	the author's poem
the author's etiquette book	the author's political pamphlet

➤ Do you find some genres easier than others to ascribe to a particular sex?

➤ I presume that your likely pronoun for 'household manual' was 'her' on the basis of women's traditional involvement with domesticity and the organization of the home. Look at your other choices and work out why you made the association between a particular sex and a particular form of writing.

➤ At what points do you find contradictions emerging where a genre may have both masculine and feminine associations and, thus, seem in some ways an attractive form to women and in some ways not? For example, Helen Carr comments on poetry:

> Poetry is regarded in our culture in very contradictory ways, and those contradictions seem intimately bound up with gender. It is seen both as a prestigious élite and esoteric form, and as a private, intimate, intensely subjective one. And whilst considered in the

former way women may feel intimidated, in the latter they, and less privileged men, can read poetry as a place in which they are enfranchised. Women writing poetry won't necessarily see it only in one of these ways: more often both at once, or both at different times.

Helen Carr, 'Poetic Licence' (1989) p. 136

➤ Could you produce a similar 'contradictory' analysis for some other literary forms?

3 Some forms seem to be particularly problematic for women. In Antonia Byatt's *Possession* an imaginary Victorian woman poet, Christabel La Motte, writes to an imaginary male poet, Randolph Henry Ash:

> But I write – like a Sermon-Preacher – which we Women are not – it is Decreed – fitted to be – and tell you no more than you must have endlessly – in your wisdom – already cogitated.

Antonia Byatt, *Possession: A Romance* (1991) p. 166

The heroine of Jeanette Winterson's *Oranges Are Not the Only Fruit* faces the same dilemma, though with a sardonic humour impossible for Byatt's nineteenth-century character:

> The days lingered on in a kind of numbness, me in ecclesiastical quarantine, them in a state of fear and anticipation. By Sunday the pastor had word back from the council. The real problem, it seemed, was going against the teachings of St Paul, and allowing women power in the church. Our branch of the church had never thought about it, we'd always had strong women, and the women organised everything. Some of us could preach, and quite plainly, in my case, the church was full because of it. There was uproar, then a curious thing happened. My mother stood up and said she believed this was right: that women had specific circumstances for their ministry, that the Sunday School was one of them, the Sisterhood another, but the message belonged to the men. Until this moment my life had still made some kind of sense. Now it was making no sense at all. My mother droned on about the importance of missionary work for a woman, that I was clearly such a woman, but had spurned my call in order to wield power on the home front, where it was inappropriate. She ended by saying that having taken on a man's world in other ways I had flouted God's law and tried to do it sexually. This was no spontaneous speech. She and the pastor had talked about it already. It was her weakness for the ministry that had done it ...
>
> So there I was, my success in the pulpit being the reason for my downfall. The devil had attacked me at my weakest point: my inability to realise the limitations of my sex.

Jeanette Winterson, *Oranges Are Not the Only Fruit* (1985) pp. 133–4

➤ Byatt self-consciously plays on a tone of anxious deference in Christabel's speech; Winterson's heroine is sharper, cheeky even, and shrewdly aware of sexual politics. Yet both realize that, in taking on the role of 'Sermon-Preacher', they have challenged something fundamental. What is it about sermons and preaching, whether in oral or written form, that render them a difficult area for women?

The article from the *Church Times* of 1892 below suggests that lecturing also was contentious. To modern ears it is a wonderful example of damning with faint praise; this so-called defence of 'lady lecturers' is almost as offensive as any attack.

100 YEARS AGO
Permission for women to speak
From the Church Times of 16 December 1892

IT IS announced that the Liberation Society has engaged the services of two lady lecturers, and some of our contemporaries have been making merry over the fact. We hardly-see why. If the ladies are to address their own sex only, there is surely no reason against. The Church Defence Institution has, we believe, a number of very useful lady secretaries, and one at least has proved an acceptable lecturer in her own neighbourhood.

from the Church Times *18 December 1992*

➤ Could we think of literary forms, whether written or spoken, as open to women, relatively open to women and largely closed to women – or are such demarcations too sweeping?

➤ Could we trace a changing historical pattern with respect to any genre, sometimes more, sometime less open to women?

➤ If women taking on male-dominated forms become over-reachers (this seems to be the suggestion in Byatt and Winterson) one would imagine that men taking on female-dominated forms would be seen as effeminate. Is this the case? Select various forms traditionally associated with women and describe the characteristic public response to male authors of that form.

Women and the novel

2 Virginia Woolf's narrator in *A Room of One's Own* surveys several shelves of works by women and asks:

But why ... were they, with very few exception, all novels?

Virginia Woolf, *A Room of One's Own* (1929; 1993) p. 60

Woolf highlights what has been a particular concern in studies of gender and genre. Why should women be associated more with the novel than any other form of writing?

➤ Jot down your immediate reactions to that question. Think of the contemporary situation and of the position of women in the past. What factors might have encouraged women towards the novel? Have determining factors changed, or changed in emphasis over time?

5 Below is a series of comments on this issue from feminist critics. In the first, Jane Spencer is discussing an eighteenth-century article which, in considering writing by women, commends only one novelist. This is the bias to which Spencer refers in her first sentence:

> This bias in the list suggests the relatively low status of the novel rather then any dearth of women novelists. In fact it was the novel which more than any other literary form attracted large numbers of women into the male-dominated world of publishing. The market for novels, like the market for newspapers, magazines, tracts and pamphlets, expanded enormously during the century. From reviewing perhaps three or four novels a month in its early years, the *Monthly Review* (begun in 1749) soon found itself inundated with ten or a dozen, and the reviewers foresaw that their early plan of describing every book published would not be feasible much longer. 'The most we can do,' explained one writer in 1759, 'with respect to those numerous novels, that issue continually from the press, is to give rather a character than an account of each. To do even this, however, we find no easy task; since we might say of them, as Pope, with less justice, says of the *ladies*, "Most *novels* have no character at all."' It is interesting to note that while gallantly repudiating Pope's low opinion of women, the reviewer implies that ladies and novels belong together. This was a common belief. Critics (mostly male) presented themselves as upholders of cultural standards, bewailing the popularity of such a low (and, they believed, female) amusement as fiction. 'So long as our British ladies continue to encourage our hackney Scriblers, by reading every Romance that appears, we need not wonder that the Press should swarm with such poor insignificant productions', they sighed. The debasement of literature in the marketplace was made even worse when women were successful sellers, and 'this branch of the literary trade', sniffed one reviewer (meaning novel-writing), 'appears, now, to be almost entirely engrossed by the Ladies'.

> Jane Spencer, *The Rise of the Woman Novelist: From Aphra Behn to Jane Austen* (1986) pp. 3–4

Just as Carr indicated the ambiguity of the link between women and poetry, we can see in Spencer's extract several ways in which the novel might be both attractive to women and a problem for women. For example:

- the low status of the early novel might make it seem attainable for women, though, at the same time, it relegates women's literary efforts to a minor category
- the expansion of the literary market offers opportunities for women and yet, again, those opportunities could be interpreted as an unfeminine involvement in 'trade'
- the development of a female readership gives the woman author an audience
- the market for, specifically, romance was one for which the female author could cater but at the risk of being judged 'insignificant'.

Examine the following extracts and see what they add to your understanding of both the possibilities and problems of the novel as a form for women:

> From the beginning there had been an association of women with the sentimental novel, both as readers and writers. As Michael Danahy suggests, this association relied upon stereotypes of what is the feminine. In France, it stemmed from the assumption that women are authorities on love, an emotion that played a central role in the French novelistic tradition. In England too vast numbers of sentimental novels were written and read by women, especially in the eighteenth century.
>
> Mrs Eliza Haywood, one of the most popular of these sentimental novelists of the early eighteenth century, explained why as a writer she was drawn to the new form:
>
>> But as I am a Woman, and consequently depriv'd of those Advantages of Education which the other Sex enjoy, I cannot ... imagine it in my Power to soar to any Subject higher than that which Nature is not negligent to teach us.
>>
>> Love is a topick which I believe few are ignorant of; there requires no aids of Learning ...
>
> Haywood's statement suggests that it was lack of education rather than any particular affinity with sentiment that led women to dwell upon feeling in their fiction.
>
> But there is another reason why women writers should have gravitated to the novel. It was a new form, not known in antiquity. Therefore, there were really no classical models nor critical rules that one would have to know in order to practise its writing....
>
> Women had in letter-writing, and the autobiography or memoir, genres which were not subject to critical censure, because they were not published. The emergence of the novel, in part from these semi-private genres, gave women a non-traditional form with which to work and relieved them of the fear of not living up to classical doctrine.

Josephine Donovan, 'The Silence is Broken' (1990) pp. 44–45, 48

> Even at its lower levels, fiction offered a better financial return than, say, fancywork, for the time invested. A typical level of earning was exemplified by Adeline Sergeant, who wrote about seventy-five novels, none of which ever became a best seller. Sergeant averaged about one hundred pounds a book and turned out up to five books a year. In 1902, her best year, she made 1,500 pounds. The usual system of publication was the outright sale of copyright for three-volume novels suitable for circulating libraries. Authors received flat sums, the size of which depended upon their reputations and the publishers' estimates of sales. This system had many advantages for women authors, who could earn a steady income by writing a certain number of novels per year.

Elaine Showalter, *A Literature of Their Own: British Women Novelists from Brontë to Lessing* (1978) p. 49

> Despite late twentieth-century pieties, women are still very far from attaining that level of socio-cultural, educational, and economic advantage enjoyed by

men. They are also still under pressure to conform to traditional concepts of womanly behaviour, to be self-effacing, supportive, and unjudging, and to invest all their efforts in their man's success rather than their own. Writing a novel is a far less assertive act than making a play. It calls for no further action or input from others to realise it, while the drama by contrast is a collaborative act and a public medium. The act of making a play is a deliberate laying-claim to enjoying visibility and taking up space. As a further obstacle, access to this space has always been in the hands of men, who have shown as much enthusiasm for admitting women as they have for any other challenge to male hegemony. Novel writing, however, is compatible with the conventional requirement of women that they should keep their heads down.

Rosalind Miles, *The Female Form: Women Writers and the Conquest of the Novel* (1987) p. 4

It would help to underline the key points from the extracts above or to make two checklists of the factors which aided and hindered the woman novelist.

➤ I deliberately chose extracts that referred to different historical periods – eighteenth century (Donovan); late nineteenth and early twentieth centuries (Showalter); late twentieth century (Miles). What do you see as the position of the woman novelist at the end of the twentieth century? Which factors, from the many suggested in these passages, are still operational, either encouraging or obstructing the potential woman novelist?

➤ Miles makes a useful comparison between the contemporary woman novelist and the contemporary woman dramatist. Extend this further. Are there ways in which their situations approximate, ways in which they differ? Also, what about the woman poet? Do the factors that help or hinder the woman novelist work in the same way with the woman poet?

➤ The quotations above mention 'romance' and the 'sentimental' novel. One of the passages to follow discusses 'domestic' fiction. Elsewhere critics have written about women's involvements with 'Gothic' fiction. Is there evidence that certain forms of the novel are more approachable for women? If so, why? Can one answer this question without resorting to the stereotypes of which Donovan speaks? Conversely, can you think of novelistic forms where women have made little impression?

Female and/or feminized

6 The first paragraph of the blurb to Rosalind Miles's *The Female Form: Women Writers and the Conquest of the Novel* reads:

Women have found a powerful and authentic voice in the novel above all other literary forms. Indeed, Rosalind Miles asserts that women have achieved supremacy in the writing of fiction, capturing the height of a traditional male stronghold. But what does this victory amount to? Do women writers today, enjoying possession of the citadel, still find that they have to re-invent in every generation their right to speak out as women?

The second paragraph ends with the following questions:

> Is it true to say that women write a different *kind* of novel from men: the woman's novel rather than a novel by a woman? Have the rules been re-written with the supremacy of the woman novelist in our own day?

Some of the claims here are very open to dispute:

- The word 'supremacy' is mentioned twice. Is this to indicate that women are numerically the dominant group as novelists or is it to indicate that women's novels are critically valued more than men's and, if so, how would one prove that?

- 'traditional male stronghold': Are we to take from this that male authors proliferated in the early novel and then women novelist took over?

- The question at the end of the first paragraph seems leading. Is the intimation that women's 'supremacy' in the novel is actually insecure and has to be repeatedly re-established? If that is so then 'supremacy' doesn't seem to be the correct word. The question is made more difficult by a non sequitur. Women today 'enjoying possession of the citadel' can't, also, be agitating 'in every generation' for 'their right to speak out as women' – not unless, that is, they've entered some kind of time warp.

- The question at the start of the second extract suggests that women write a different kind of novel from men. Is it that *all* women novelists differ from *all* male novelists? Moreover, does this suggestion shift the centre of the debate from the person of the author to the nature of the novel?

What is needed to answer these questions is:

Statistical data about women novelists	How many women were publishing novels, in specific periods, and in what proportion to male authors?
An understanding of what is meant by 'the woman's novel'	Is this a form which confirms women's accepted social place or a form which pursues women's interests (in both sense – what women are interested in and what is in their interests) or a form which revalues the common experiences of women's lives or …?

There is little possibility of adequately answering here these two large problems but we can look at some material that sets the context of the issue.

Statistical data abut women novelists

7 Consider the two following passages:

> The preponderance of women among eighteenth-century novelists, combined with the low status of this 'literary trade', suggests that at this period of the novel's first expansion, novel-writing might have become a feminized occupation with all the characteristics of such occupations – low pay and low status. Certainly the commoditization of literature seems to

have provided unprecedented opportunities for the entry of women into literary production. But this feminization of literature was resisted. Men were never less than a substantial minority of its producers, possibly around one third. As fiction provided popular and profitable, and as it won its literary credentials, so men moved back into a position of numerical dominance. By the 1840s the proportion of women producers of fiction had been reduced to about 20 per cent. Did men turn increasingly to fiction because it had become respectable from a literary point of view, or did it become respectable because it had ceased to be a feminine form? Either way we may hazard a confident guess that the participation of men was a necessary condition of the genre being taken seriously as literature. But as men had resisted its feminization in the eighteenth century, so women succeeded in resisting its subsequent masculization. The figure of 20 per cent is actually high, and marks the novel in particular and the writing of literature in general with a distinct gender-ambiguity which it has never lost.

Terry Lovell, *Consuming Fiction* (1987) pp. 42–3

The second passage is the product of Gaye Tuchman's research in the archives of Macmillan and Company. Note that she is considering data concerning the submission of manuscripts, not their publication:

Rather than presenting a literary scene increasingly open to women, the Macmillan archives tell of a literary world closing its gates to them. Firstly, in all three of the periods we examined (the period of invasion, 1866 and 1877; the period of redefinition, 1887 and 1897; and the period of male institutionalization, 1907 and 1917), women submitted the same proportion of all the manuscripts Macmillan and Company received – 30 per cent. Second, especially in the 1860s and 1870s, the Macmillan records show, women constituted a very high proportion of all those trying to publish fiction – 62 per cent. Third, as the novel became even more established, men increasingly tackled the genre. During the 1880s, the very decade when women were supposedly the queens of the circulating library, men such as those described by George Gissing in *The New Grub Street* (1891) besieged Macmillan with fiction manuscripts. Fourth, when the three-decker disappeared and the 'modern' novel emerged, women authors were edged out.

Gaye Tuchman, *Edging Women Out: Victorian Novelists, Publishers, and Social Change* (1989) p. 55

➤ Compare the issues raised and the interpretations offered in the Lovell and Tuchman passages. Do their comments in any way help to elucidate some of the uncertainties of the Miles blurb?

➤ Probably very few of us are in possession of sufficient detailed knowledge or accurate data to dispute much of the above. However, we can make judgements on the appropriateness of material. If you were to do a full-scale study of women's authorship of the novel, what would be the issues you would need to consider; what kind of data would you need to collect; what likely problems would you encounter? Produce a rough schema for such a study.

What is meant by 'the woman's novel'

8 To repeat Lovell's term, women's access to the novel constituted a 'feminization' of culture. As novelists, bourgeois women found an authority, a public voice and a legitimization of their private thoughts and their familial and community activities. Below is a passage from Nancy Armstrong presenting such a view and one from Mary Poovey which, to a certain extent, takes issue with it:

> Domestic fiction mapped out a new domain of discourse as it invested common forms of social behaviour with the emotional values of women. Consequently, these stories of courtship and marriage offered their readers a way of indulging, with a kind of impunity, in fantasies of political power that were the more acceptable because they were played out within a domestic framework where legitimate monogamy – and thus the subordination of female to male – would ultimately be affirmed. In this way, domestic fiction could represent an alternative form of political power without appearing to contest the distribution of power that it represented as historically given.
>
> Nancy Armstrong, *Desire and Domestic Fiction: A Political History of the Novel* (1987) p. 29

> But even if literary discourse did acquire its moral authority by its (putative) distance from the 'masculine' sphere of alienation and market relations, what effect did this 'feminization' have on actual women who did or wanted to write? The answer to this question is obviously complex, and it is not my aim to enter now into those discussions feminists have already undertaken in order to address it. I simply want to point out that the same process that helped clear the way for women to write and publish also erected barriers against all but limited access to such 'self-expression'. If the feminization of authorship derived its authority from an idealized representation of woman and the domestic sphere, then for a woman to depart from that idealization by engaging in the commercial business of writing was to collapse the boundaries between the spheres of alienated and nonalienated labor. A woman who wrote for publication threatened to collapse the ideal from which her authority was derived and to which her fidelity was necessary for so many other social institutions to work.
>
> Mary Poovey, *Uneven Developments: The Ideological Work of Gender in Mid-Victorian England* (1988) p. 125

Once again we discover the woman novelist in a difficult position, caught between conformism and a progressive potential. These are densely written passages so try to clarify the points they make. Answering these questions could help:

➤ What does Armstrong mean by the comment that 'domestic fiction could represent an alternative from of political power'. Is it too large a claim or, generally, sound?

➤ One could believe that Armstrong sees in the feminization of culture a distinctly feminist potential. What evidence is there of this view in her comments? Would you agree?

➤ Poovey wonders about the effect of feminization on 'actual women' and the suggestion is that the effect is not entirely beneficial. Would you agree? Is the position of the contemporary woman novelist as unresolved?

Further research:

9 Our attention here has been largely on the novel. In the following section we shall be looking at generic fiction. That still leaves many aspects of form and genre unexplored. Here, then are a few pointers to possible future areas of research (full publication details are in the list of Works Cited at the end of the book):

On women's rewriting of myth, see:

Patricia Duncker, *Sisters and Strangers: An Introduction to Contemporary Feminist Fiction* (1992), chapter 5

Rachel Blau DuPlessis, *Writing Beyond the Ending: Narrative Strategies of Twentieth-Century Women* (1985), chapter 7

Carolyne Larrington (ed.), *The Feminist Companion to Mythology* (1992)

Alicia Suskin Ostriker, *Stealing the Language: The Emergence of Women's Poetry in America* (1987), chapter 6

On women's autobiography:

Shari Benstock (ed.), *The Private Self: Theory and Practice of Women's Autobiographical Writings* (1988)

Shoshana Felman, *What Does A Woman Want? Reading and Sexual Difference* (1993)

Nicole Ward Jouve, *White Woman Speaks with Forked Tongue: Criticism as Autobiography* (1991)

Sidonie Smith, *Subjectivity, Identify and the Body: Women's Autobiographical Practices in the Twentieth Century* (1993)

Liz Stanley, *The Auto/biographical I: The Theory and Practice of Feminist Auto/biography* (1992)

On debates between women's use of realism and the avant-garde:

Penny Boumelha, 'Realism and the Ends of Feminism' in Susan Sheridan (ed.), *Grafts: Feminist Cultural Criticism* (1988)

Rita Felski, *Beyond Feminist Aesthetics: Feminist Literature and Social Change* (1989)

Laura Marcus, 'Feminist Aesthetics and the New Realism' in Isobel Armstrong (ed.), *New Feminist Discourse: Critical Essays on Theories and Texts* (1992)

On debates concerning epic and lyric verse:

Elizabeth Heslinger, Robin Lauterbach Sheets, William Veeder, *The Woman Question: Literary Issues, 1837–1883* (1983), chapter 2

Cora Kaplan's Introduction to Elizabeth Barrett Browning, *Aurora Leigh and Other Poems* (1977); anthologized in Judith Newton and Deborah Rosenfelt (eds), *Feminist Criticism and Social Change* (1985)

See also references in Kerry McSweeney's Introduction to the World's Classics edition of Elizabeth Barrett Browning, *Aurora Leigh* (1993)

Poor Christabel La Motte (see point 3) worried not only about the feminine impropriety of sermonizing but also about her inadequacy as a writer of epics:

... I have it in my head to write an epic – or if not an epic, still a Saga or Lay or great mythical Poem – and how can a poor breathless woman with no *staying-power* and only a Lunar Learning confess such an ambition to the author of the Ragnarök? (p. 161)

Those who haven't read Byatt's novel will be pleased to know that Christabel eventually writes her epic and that twentieth-century feminist critics bring it into literary prominence.

References and further reading

Nancy Armstrong, *Desire and Domestic Fiction; A Political History of the Novel*

Chris Baldick, *The Concise Oxford Dictionary of Literary Terms*

Ros Ballaster, 'Romancing the Novel: Gender and Genre in Early Theories of Narrative' in Dale Spender (ed.), *Living By the Pen: Early British Women Writers*

Antonia Byatt, *Possession: A Romance*

Helen Carr, 'Poetic Licence' in Helen Carr (ed.), *From My Guy to Sci-fi: Genre and Women's Writing in the Postmodern World*

Church Times, The, 'Permission for Women to Speak', 18 December 1992

Josephine Donovan, 'The Silence Is Broken' in Deborah Cameron (ed.) *The Feminist Critique of Language: A Reader*

Alan Durant and Nigel Fabb, *Literary Studies in Action*

Mary Eagleton (ed.), *Feminist Literary Theory: A Reader* (second edition)

Roger Fowler (ed.), *A Dictionary of Modern Critical Terms*

Cora Kaplan, Introduction to Elizabeth Barrett Browning, *Aurora Leigh and Other Poems*, anthologized in Judith Newton and Deborah Rosenfelt (eds), *Feminist Criticism and Social Change*

Terry Lovell, *Consuming Fiction*

Rosalind Miles, *The Female Form: Women Writers and the Conquest of the Novel*

Martin Montgomery, Alan Durant, Nigel Fabb, Tom Furniss and Sara Mills, *Ways of Reading*

John Peck and Martin Coyle, *Literary Terms and Criticism*

Mary Poovey, *Uneven Developments: The Ideological Work of Gender in Mid-Victorian England*

Elaine Showalter, *A Literature of Their Own: British Women Novelists from Brontë to Lessing*

Jane Spencer, *The Rise of the Woman Novelist: From Aphra Behn to Jane Austen*

Dale Spender, *Mothers of the Novel: 100 Good Writers Before Jane Austen.* As Spender's title illustrates, her aim here is to explore the importance of women in the early novel.

Gaye Tuchman (with Nina E. Fortin), *Edging Women Out: Victorian Novelists, Publishers, and Social Change*

Jeanette Winterson, *Oranges Are Not the Only Fruit*

Virginia Woolf, *A Room of One's Own and Three Guineas*, ed. Michèle Barrett

Feminism and Genre Fiction

Introduction

In the preceding section we looked at the meaning of the term 'genre' and its relation to gender. The novel, we saw there, is one genre amongst others and the major literary genre of our period. However, the term 'genre fiction' has a more precise meaning, referring to popular fiction strongly marked with the conventions of a particular form – the thriller, the Mills and Boon or Harlequin romance, sci-fi. Given a hero, a heroine, a balcony and a moonlit night, most people, whether they read romantic fiction or not, would accurately predict the course of that scene. Critic, Anne Cranny-Francis appends another word to the term and discusses 'feminist genre fiction', by which she means:

> ... the feminist appropriation of the generic 'popular' literary forms, including science fiction, detective fiction and romance. This feminist genre fiction is genre fiction written from a self-consciously feminist perspective, consciously encoding an ideology which is in direct opposition to the dominant gender ideology of Western society, patriarchal ideology.
>
> Anne Cranny-Francis, *Feminist Fiction: Feminist Uses of Generic Fiction* (1990) p. 1

Cranny-Francis puts inverted commas round the term 'popular' so as to dispute the traditional hierarchical distinction between 'literature' on the one hand and 'popular fiction' (also known as 'mass-market', 'block-buster', 'pulp') on the other.

I am unsure about the phrase 'self-consciously feminist perspective' as it seems to me that the author (feminist or non-feminist) can create feminist effects without intending to do so, but Cranny-Francis's main points, namely that genre fiction has been taken up by women writers and that the form, particularly its gender ideology, has been dramatically changed in the process, are arguments well worth consideration. The following questions will help us to explore those arguments:

- Why might a woman author become involved in genre fiction?

- Following Cranny-Francis's lead, can we identify elements in genre fiction which are conservative and others which are progressive? Particularly, which elements either confirm or challenge gender norms? We can consider this issue by looking at science fiction and detective fiction.

- Briefly, how might these issues relate to other forms of genre fiction?

The woman author and genre fiction

1 Where do we find the female author – and, indeed, the female reader – in relation to different forms of genre fiction? Below is listed a number of forms. Indicate where you feel male and female authors and readers may feature:

Form	Authors			Readers		
	M	F	Both	M	F	Both
science fiction						
utopian/dystopian fiction						
romance						
detective fiction						
spy thrillers						
family sagas						
westerns						
fairy tales						
gothic horror						
boys' adventure stories						
girls' school stories						
sex and shopping fiction						

➤ As we discussed in the previous section, you will find that some of these forms can be readily ascribed to a particular sex while others are more ambiguously placed. With which genres do you feel sure of the sex of the likely author and reader; with which do you feel uncertain?

➤ Do you believe that some of these forms carry more status than others? For example, I remember when at school that girls' school stories were considered superficial but acceptable reading, while romance comics were confiscated.

➤ Is there any evidence that the higher status forms are more associated with male authors and readers, the low status with female, or is the pattern more mixed?

➤ Terry Lovell suggests in *Consuming Fiction* that it is specifically 'woman-to-woman writing' (p. 160) which is devalued, that a woman writing for a mixed market is more likely to achieve status than a woman writing for a predominantly female audience. Would you agree?

One reason why you might find some of these questions difficult to answer with any certainty is because genre fiction, like other forms of writing, is far more complex than can be represented on a grid. For instance, what does 'detective fiction' include? Certainly the work of Arthur Conan Doyle, Agatha Christie and

Colin Dexter but perhaps, also the work of Wilkie Collins and Joseph Conrad. Why is 'popular romance' Barbara Cartland and not Jane Austen?

Return to the grid and explore the problems and complexities of the categories given, the reasons why neat answers can't always be found:

➤ Think of sub-genres within the categories

➤ Think of hybrid forms: *Twin Peaks* and *Wild Palms*, for instance, move rapidly between different genres.

➤ Think how the genre might have changed over time. The kind of romance novel which critics decried in the late eighteenth and nineteenth centuries (see the section on Gender and Genre) might now be viewed as a 'classic'.

➤ Does the woman author sometimes play a minor role in a genre dominated by men and vice versa?

➤ Does a predominantly female authorship indicate a predominantly female readership or is the readership of these genres diverse?

2 Why might a woman author involve herself in generic fiction rather than – for want of a better word – 'mainstream' and why one particular form rather than another? Here are some responses:

> It took me years to realise that I chose to work in such despised, marginal genres as science fiction, fantasy, young adult precisely because they were excluded from critical, academic, canonical supervision, leaving the artist free ...

> Ursula Le Guin, *Dancing at the Edge of the World* (1992) p. 234

> ... fantastic literature points to or suggests the basis upon which cultural order rests, for it opens up, for a brief moment, on to disorder, on to illegality, on to that which lies outside the law, that which is outside dominant value systems.

> Rosemary Jackson, *Fantasy: The Literature of Subversion* (1981) p. 4

> Given the inferiority afforded to 'formless romance', writing detective fiction was, and is, for many women writers not only a way of claiming the 'unfeminine' qualities of orderliness and control, but also of attempting to avoid the 'stigma' of gender altogether.

> Alison Light, *Forever England: Femininity. Literature and Conservatism between the Wars* (1991) p. 162

Unfortunately there is no 'free' space left for Ursula Le Guin: in recent years these 'marginal' forms have been fully colonized by critics and academics.

➤ What do you think of these arguments? What points would you add?

➤ If you were writing genre fiction, which genre would you choose and why? What opportunities for feminism would that genre offer?

➤ Light's comment suggests not only that different generic forms offer women different possibilities but also that there is a kind of pecking order within genre fiction. How do you respond to Light's ideas?

➤ Review your material and draft possible answers to the two key questions:

> Where are the women authors and readers?

> Why are they there?

Generic fiction: conservative or progressive?

3 The debate that features most frequently in feminist critiques of generic fiction is that between generic fiction as an inherently conservative form and generic fiction as a form open to progressive potential. In these debates 'conservative' is defined as sexist, racist, class-bound, homophobic, obsessed with the values of order, conformity and stability. Certain Agatha Christie texts, for example, manage to embody virtually all these characteristics. On the other hand, 'progressive' texts are viewed as fluid and adaptable, responsive to appropriation by radical and critical political positions such as feminism. One example of a conservative positioning is illustrated in Roz Kaveney's amusing description of the role of women in the science fiction stories of the 1920s and 30s:

> The role of women in these, except when serving as object lessons in lectures by the authors on eugenics or the folly of extending the suffrage, was restricted to standing around having things explained to them by the hero and saying 'Gosh. Wow. How terrific.' Such lectures were often mingled with adventure stories in the manner of Edgar Rice Burroughs in which the role of the heroine was restricted to one, being captured by the space pirates: two, twisting her ankle when being rescued from them: three, mopping sweat and/or blood from the hero's brow: and four, being told how brave she was.

> Roz Kaveney, 'The Science Fictiveness of Women's Science Fiction', (1989) p. 79

I am not sure how prevalent this figure is in contemporary science fiction but she is still irritatingly alive and well, if slightly ruffled, in the Indiana Jones movies. Can such conventions be adapted – the verb most frequently used in the criticism is 'subverted' – to serve women? Can the conservative norms of generic fiction be successfully undermined?

Think of any generic form with which you have some familiarity. It can be fiction but, equally, it might be a film or a TV programme.

➤ Give the title of the text.

➤ Define the genre – western, thriller, romance, soap opera etc.

➤ List what seem to you both the progressive and the conservative elements in your chosen text.

➤ Which elements relate specifically to issues of gender? For example, romantic fiction might seem conservative in its concern over women's appearance but more progressive in its interest in women's feelings.

➤ If you were rewriting or redirecting that text, what new progressive elements could you introduce? Remember you are adapting or stretching the boundaries of the form, but not totally dismantling them. If you find yourself replacing the western gunslinger with a female, organic farmer you've probably strayed too far.

➤ If you can, compare your findings with somebody else's. Does it seem that certain genres are more adaptable than others or that genres are adaptable in different ways?

4 I suspect that science fiction was one of the forms that you had some difficulty categorizing when you were working on the grid. Kaveney's quote above is one indication of how the form has been dominated by a male-centred focus. But the picture is more complicated than that. Women authors have always had at least some presence in science fiction; in recent years there has been a flowering of science fiction with a consciously feminist perspective; and the Women's Press has produced a successful list of women's science fiction, indicating an expanding market. What this illustrates is how a form may:

- resist classification as simply 'a male form' or 'a female form', a 'conservative' form or a 'progressive' form

- offer possibilities for the female author and reader even though the form has been, historically, male-centred (i.e. the province of the male author and the hero, and supportive of masculine norms)

- combine aspects of masculinity and femininity within a single text.

In short, texts are not a set of clear oppositions, conservative versus progressive, masculine versus feminine. What often confronts the reader is conservative *and* progressive values, masculine norms *and* feminine disruptions all operating within the same text.

Let's try to apply this more complex view to both science fiction and detective fiction. In both cases the aim is not to fit aspects of the form into a neat category but rather to see how the form can evade those tidy definitions:

Generic fiction: conservative and progressive

Science fiction

5 List the reasons why this form might appeal to a male author/and or reader:

- Science is more associated with men than women in our culture

- Technology appeals to men

-

-

-

We began to think earlier how the form could also seem attractive to a female author and readership. Collect together the earlier points and add to them these suggestions from Sarah LeFanu:

> Its glorious eclecticism, with its mingling of the rational discourse of science with the pre-rational language of the unconscious – for SF borrows from horror, mythology, fairy tale – offers a means of exploring the myriad ways in which we are constructed as women....
>
> All this leads to a breakdown of the conventional hierarchies between writers and readers, and challenges the conventional authority of the single author. Such an anti-authoritarian style has, potentially, a particular interest for women, for whom writing requires not just self-confidence, but the confidence necessary to break through what can be seen as a male-dominated world of ordered discourse, into a male-dominated world of professionalism....
>
> Unlike other forms of genre writing, such as detective stories and romances, which demand the reinstatement of order and thus can be described as 'closed' texts, science fiction is by its nature interrogative, open. Feminism questions a given order in political terms, while science fiction questions it in imaginative terms.
>
> Sarah LeFanu, *In the Chinks of the World Machine: Feminism and Science Fiction* (1988) pp. 5, 6, 100

Looking back over the quotes in this section concerning women's place in science fiction (Le Guin, Jackson, Kaveney, LeFanu), notice how wide-ranging are the comments. The debate is not only at the level of character or plot – female Martians instead of male Martians or the defeat of the men in some intergalactic war – but entails as well.

- questions of form
- generic conventions
- the production and reception of the writing
- opportunities as a professional writer
- the political potential for women.

6 Hitherto, we have proceeded largely in a theoretical mode and we need to see how both the feminist critiques of and aspirations for science fiction are embodied in practice. Using any science fiction you know test out the ideas we have considered so far. For those unfamiliar with the form, the science fiction short story offers the quickest entrée. See, for example the volumes edited by Pamela Sargent in the list of references at the end of this section.

Does your text largely reinforce the gender norms of our culture; does it, to use the common term, subvert them; or does the text function in some equivocal way *between* codes of masculinity and femininity?

7 'Science fiction and feminism: a happy marriage or worlds apart?' Draft an answer – in note form, if time is pressing – to that question.

Detective fiction

8 You will have noticed that LeFanu dismisses detection fiction as 'closed' texts. Rosalind Coward and Linda Semple see things somewhat differently. In their study of detective fiction they explore the conservative and progressive potential of three major conventions – the law, the sleuth and the country house. Their argument on the law is, roughly:

Conservative   In detective fiction, the law is finally upheld; order is reaffirmed; social hierarchy maintained.

Progressive   In the course of the text the law is challenged. Women are 'clearly drawn to a genre dealing with the transgression of law.' (p. 51)

Can you product a comparable opposition of arguments with reference to the sleuth? What aspects in the character and function of the sleuth confirm the established order and masculine values; what aspects introduce a more feminine perspective? Think of the varied constructions of the sleuth – Sherlock Holmes, Lord Peter Wimsey, Harriet Vane, Miss Marple, Inspector Morse etc. and think, as indicated earlier, of movements *between* gender conventions within the same character. For example, Miss Marple would be no use in a macho, physical confrontation but her intellect and deductive powers consistently outwit the male police officers.

9 On the convention of the country house Coward and Semple write:

It has been said that this convention leans writers towards fixed, closed, unchanging communities – villages, weekend parties at country houses, schools and institutions. The uncovering of the crime is then seen as the restoration of social stability, usually to its previously hierarchical state. But again this assumption of the straitjacket of form tends to neglect what goes on within the form. Women writers appear to have used this convention to extremely interesting effect producing a number of notable detective novels concentrating on a closed community of women. *Gaudy Night*, *Miss Pym Disposes* and *Spotted Hemlock* were all set in women's colleges. Christianna Brand used a hospital and particularly a nurses' home as the focus of suspicions in *Green for Danger*, a novel which prefigures P. D. James's setting for *Shroud for a Nightingale*. Hilda Lawrence sets her highly atmospheric *Death of a Doll* in a women's hostel, a novel paralleled by the Japanese writer Masako Togawa's *The Master Key*, set in an apartment block for single women – another instance of the worldwide appeal of so many aspects of the genre.

    In all these novels, there is a complexity and richness of characterisation; the relationships between women are presented as deep, often passionate, in a way few other novels of the period achieved. Is this perhaps why there is such a high incidence of lesbian relationships portrayed in these novels? It would be possible to argue that both the closed communities of women and lesbianism are presented as 'unhealthy' breeding grounds for criminal acts. But this neglects both the sympathetic portrayal of women's relationships and the interesting handling of lesbianism which often comes through in novels like *Death of a Doll* and *Miss Pym Disposes*. Needless to say, given such precedents, this convention far from being restrictive has been a blessing for new writers. The closed community of women has allowed a fiction which could reflect and explore the full complexities of relationships between women.

Rosalind Coward and Linda Semple, 'Tracking Down the Past:
Women and Detective Fiction' (1989) pp. 52–3

Considering the same convention of the closed community and referring to several of the same texts as Coward and Semple, Cora Kaplan comes to this conclusion:

In *Strong Poison* (1930) Harriet [Dorothy L Sayers' heroine, Harriet Vane] is under suspicion because she has broken social and sexual codes; in *Gaudy Night*, set in an Oxford women's college (Sayers went to Somerville) she is at risk because she attempts to find the culprit, who turns out to be a female servant in the college, in the unnatural enclave of women scholars. While *Gaudy Night* is in many ways a loving portrait of Somerville, the novel ends with Harriet giving up her risky independence and accepting Wimsey. All-women's institutions are similarly used for settings for two other post-war detective novels, Josephine Tey's *Miss Pym Disposes* and P. D. James' *Shroud for a Nightingale*. In each of these books a world where men are excluded breeds envy, jealousy, competition and – worst of all – unnatural attachments. In both books murder and lesbianism are strongly connected, and the negative implications of these female ghettos – a physical training college and a nursing school attached to a country hospital – are fully exploited. It matters little that Tey's detective is another aging spinster writer, Miss Pym, and James's the poet–detective, Adam Dalgleish. Each book uses the setting to celebrate normative heterosexuality, and implies that even the most humble professional occupations for women involve a period of single sex education which breeds unhealthy and dangerous emotions.

Cora Kaplan, 'An Unsuitable Genre for a Feminist?' (1986) p. 18

➤ Get clear in your mind both the common issues and the contrasting interpretations in these two passages.

➤ Where does each critic locate the progressive and conservative elements in the texts discussed? Indeed, does Kaplan find any redeeming factors in this group of novels?

➤ Kaplan's comment

> It matters little that Tey's detective is another aging spinster writer, Miss Pym, and James's the poet–detective, Adam Dalgleish

is curious. One could equally well argue that, in evaluating the gender ideology of detective fiction, such twists to the conventions matter quite a lot. In what ways, do you think?

➤ If you wanted to analyse a specific example, you could look at the source for Kaplan's title, P. D. James's *An Unsuitable Job for a Woman* (1972), in which the detective heroine is repeatedly told that her job is inappropriate.

10 The clash between signs of masculinity and femininity can be vividly and intriguingly expressed in the visual impact of a book's cover. Consider the example on this page. For those of you unfamiliar with Sara Paretsky's heroine, V. I. Warshawski is a sharp, Chicago private detective, well able to look after herself on the mean city streets but also caring and socially minded.

Cover of Sara Paretsky's Blood Shot, *published by Dell, New York, 1988*

How might one interpret the figure?

- The trench coat with the upturned collar and the barely glimpsed, broad brimmed hat could signify masculinity. These aspects of the figure are reminiscent of the 'hard-boiled' or 'Gumshoe' detectives of Raymond Chandler or Dashiell Hammett novels.

- The long hair, the lipstick and the chiffon scarf might signify femininity.

- The intense colour of the lips reminds one of the *femmes fatales* of film noir and of the Chandler and Hammett novels. But the colour is not the blood red that one would expect from the book's title and the association with the 1940s but a deep cerise. Could this signify a more modern assertive femininity?

- Obviously the black garment also connotes femininity – it isn't a shirt and tie – but what is the garment? Is it a leotard suggesting the athleticism and physical capability of modern femininity or is it a little black dress?

- If we interpret the garment as a little black dress, is it to be understood in 1950s mode as a sign of middle-class, feminine respectability or in the revamped 1990s mode of body-clinging lycra and, hence, as a sign of provocative, independent sexuality?

Clearly we could go on and on with this and meanings would proliferate. If you want to follow further an interest in the visual:

➤ put together your own collection of cover images from detective fiction and analyse them as I have done above; if you want to consider the visual representations in feminist detective fiction, the cover design of Deborah Powell's novels (The Women's Press) are worth a close look;

➤ use film and video to consider the varying representations of femininity in detective fiction. Miss Marple, Harriet Vane, V. I. Warshawski, Cagney and Lacey would all furnish excellent material;

➤ for comparison, look at the relevant chapter in Robin Roberts's work on the representation of women on the covers of science fiction, pulp magazines of the 1940s and 1950s.

11 As a way of gathering your thoughts on detective fiction, repeat the exercise suggested for science fiction and draft an essay. You could use Kaplan's title as a focus: 'Detective fiction – an unsuitable genre for a feminist. Discuss.'

Other forms of genre fiction

12 The main considerations of this section have been science fiction and detective fiction but you can apply some of the issues we've discussed here to other forms of genre fiction. Equally other forms raise their own specific problems.

Romance fiction

Patricia Duncker has some questions on romance:

Can a romantic novel in which the woman eventually sinks into the tweed-jacketed, fur-lined or taut-leathered breast of the taller, older, richer man be anything other than capitulation to the very structures feminist women set out to challenge and subvert – and which for Lesbian women constitute nothing less than a complete denial of identity?

Patricia Duncker, *Sisters and Strangers: An Introduction to Contemporary Feminist Fiction* (1992) p. 89

➤ Is romance fiction more intractable than science fiction and detective fiction or could it, too, be adapted to feminism? What about the sub-genre of gay romance fiction? Would that form answer Duncker's questions?

The Western

Is there a female/feminist version of the Western? Surely not *Calamity Jane*? But, maybe, Suzy Amis's film, *The Ballad of Little Jo* or, as we see here, Margaret Walker's folk heroine, *Kissie Lee*. In appropriate style, she dies with her boots on:

> Toughest gal I ever did see
> Was a gal by the name of Kissie Lee;
> The toughest gal God ever made
> And she drew a dirty, wicked blade.
>
> Now this here gal warn't always tough
> Nobody dreamed she'd turn out rough
> But her Grammaw Mamie had the name
> Of being the town's sin and shame.
>
> When Kissie Lee was young and good
> Didn't nobody treat her like they should
> Allus gettin' beat by a no-good shine
> An' allus quick to cry and whine.
>
> Till her Grammaw said, 'Now listen to me,
> I'm tiahed of yoah whinin', Kissie Lee.
> People don't never treat you right,
> An' you allus scrappin' or in a fight.
>
> 'Whin I was a gal wasn't no soul
> Could do me wrong an' still stay whole.
> Ah got me a razor to talk for me
> An' aftah that they let me be.'
>
> Well Kissie Lee took her advice
> And after that she didn't speak twice
> 'Cause when she learned to stab and run
> She got herself a little gun.
>
> And from that time that gal was mean.
> Meanest mama you ever seen.
> She could hold her likker and hold her man
> And she went thoo life jus' raisin' san'.
>
> One night she walked in Jim's saloon
> And seen a guy what spoke too soon;
> He done her dirt long time ago
> When she was good and feeling low.

Kissie bought her drink and she paid her dime
Watchin' this guy what beat her time
And he was making for the outside door
When Kissie shot him to the floor.

Not a word she spoke but she switched her blade
And flashing that lil ole baby paid:
Evvy livin' guy got out of her way
Because Kissie Lee was drawin' her pay.

She could shoot glass doors offa the hinges,
She could take herself on the wildest binges
And she died with her boots on switching blades
On Talladega Mountain in the likker raids.

Margaret Walker, 'Kissie Lee' (1942)

Is Kissie Lee literature's first feminist gunslinger, I wonder?

13 Final queries:

➤ What is the male version of romance? The authors of *Rewriting English* (1985) refer to thrillers and adventure stories as 'masculine romance' (p. 76). Do you find this a valid point?

➤ Or, is pornography a 'masculine romance' and conversely, to follow Ann Snitow's argument (see References), is romance, pornography for women?

➤ In several quotations in this section (Jackson, LeFanu, Kaplan) we have encountered the view that non-realist genres, what Jackson calls 'fantastic literature', are more critical of the dominant social order than realist genres. Return to the list of genres at the start of this section and divide them into realist and non-realist forms. Is there evidence that the non-realist forms are more open and questioning, the realist more closed and conformist?

➤ How can romance fiction be for LeFanu and Duncker the epitome of conformism, yet for Light (1984) and for Kaplan (1986b) the form – or, at least, the particular examples they consider – can offer all manner of questioning and disruptive potential?

➤ The significance of romance fiction for women, as both authors and readers, has found its way into fiction as well as criticism. These fictional renderings would make a good study in themselves or add a different perspective to a critical study. See:

Margaret Atwood, *Lady Oracle* (1982)

Joan Riley, *Romance* (1988)

Fay Weldon, *The Life and Loves of a She-Devil* (1984).

References and further reading

Lucie Armitt (ed.), *Where No Man Has Gone Before: Women and Science fiction*. Part III looks particularly at science fiction as a form of genre fiction.

Janet Batsleer, Tony Davies, Rebecca O'Rourke and Chris Weedon, *Rewriting English: Cultural Politics of Gender and Class*

Helen Carr (ed.), *From My Guy to Sci-Fi: Genre and Women's Writing in the Postmodern World*

Rosalind Coward and Linda Semple, 'Tracking Down the Past: Women and Detective Fiction' in Carr (1989).

Anne Cranny-Francis, *Feminist Fiction: Feminist Uses of Generic Fiction*

Patricia Duncker, *Sisters and Strangers: An Introduction to Contemporary Feminist Fiction*

Gabriele Griffin (ed.), *Outwrite: Lesbianism and Popular Culture*

Carolyn G. Heilbrun, 'Gender and Detective Fiction', *Hamlet's Mother and Other Women: Feminist Essays on Literature*

Joke Hermes, 'Sexuality in Lesbian Romance Fiction'

Rosemary Jackson, *Fantasy: The Literature of Subversion*

P.D. James *An Unsuitable Job for a Woman*

Cora Kaplan, 'An Unsuitable Genre for a Feminist'

Cora Kaplan, '*The Thorn Birds*: Fiction, Fantasy, Femininity' in *Sea Changes: Essays on Culture and Feminism*

Roz Kaveney, 'The Science Fictiveness of Women's Science Fiction' in Carr (1989).

Kathleen Gregory Klein, *The Woman Detective: Gender and Genre*

Donna Landry and Gerald MacLean, *Materialist Feminisms*. The chapter, 'How RC Can a White Girl Be When Her Sisters of Color Can Represent Themselves?' considers feminist and lesbian detective fiction.

Sarah LeFanu, *In the Chinks of the World Machine: Feminism and Science Fiction*

Ursula Le Guin, *Dancing at the Edge of the World*

Alison Light, '"Returning to Manderley" – Romance Fiction, Female Sexuality and Class'

Alison Light, *Forever England: Femininity, Literature and Conservatism between the Wars*

Terry Lovell, *Consuming Fiction*

Susannah Radstone (ed.), *Sweet Dreams: Sexuality, Gender and Popular Fiction*

Sally Rowena Munt, *Murder by the Book? Feminism and the Crime Novel*

Paulina Palmer, *Contemporary Lesbian Writing: Dreams, Desire and Difference*

Sara Paretsky, *Blood Shot*

Robin Roberts, *A New Species; Gender and Science in Science Fiction*, see chapter 2

Pamela Sargent (ed.), *Women of Wonder* and *New Women of Wonder*

Ann Snitow, 'Mass Market Romance: Pornography for Women is Different' in Ann Snitow, Christine Stansell, Sharon Thompson (eds), *Powers of Desire: The Politics of Sexuality*

Margaret Walker, 'Kissie Lee', *For My People*. This poem is anthologized in Sandra Gilbert and Susan M. Gubar (eds), *The Norton Anthology of Literature by Women: The Tradition in English*

Jenny Wolmark, *Aliens and Others: Science Fiction, Feminism and Postmodernism*

Feminist Publishing

Introduction

To many people in Britain feminist publishing means Virago or Virago and the Women's Press – the dark green spines (actually, now, increasingly lighter green spines) and the black and white zebra spines (actually, now increasingly multi-coloured spines). Virago has achieved what is called in the trade 'brand name recognition': readers will talk about 'Viragos' with some belief that they have a common understanding as to what constitutes a Virago title, just as readers have for a far longer time referred to 'Penguins'. The concentration on Virago as Britain's foremost feminist publishing company tends to hide some of the complexity of recent history. There are, of course, more companies than Virago and the Women's Press; in 1993, the Women's Research and Resource Centre in London recorded twenty-one feminist publishing houses. Moreover, on the basis of the evident success of feminist publishing, many mainstream companies have woken up to the potential of this new market and produced their own feminist listings or developed a particular focus on women's writing.

Indeed, we now need to consider what, if anything, *is* distinctly feminist about a feminist publishing company if the same kind of books can be produced by the most traditional and patriarchal publishing house; as ever, the definition of this term 'feminist' proves problematic. In recent years, the volatile state of British publishing with a bewildering number of takeovers and mergers has had consequences for feminist publishing as much as any other area. Pandora, for example, is now under the wing of HarperCollins; the Women's Press is part of the Namara Group. Virago itself was a member of the Chatto Bodley Head and Cape Group from 1982–7 until a management buy-out returned it to independent status. Celebrations for its twentieth birthday in 1993 were rapidly followed by recession, cuts, redundancies, reorganization. At the end of 1995 the company was bought by Little, Brown and the future remains unknown. Other companies found no homes and no financial backing and went out of existence. We need to remember also in our concentration on the publication of books, the considerable amount of work undertaken by feminists in producing journals, magazines, newspapers, newsletters, pamphlets, the work from women's writing groups etc. This small-scale, often short-lived, production is a vital part of our publishing history and of the infrastructure needed to support the woman writer.

These two factors – the volatility of publishing generally and the relative invisibility of many women's publishing endeavours – make it a difficult area to research: relevant information immediately becomes out of date or disappears.

Magazine articles and newspapers – on occasions, even the financial pages – are the best source for keeping up to date with a rapidly changing scene. Surveying is also helpful. You can learn a lot simply by frequent, intelligent browsing through bookshops and publishers' catalogues, and bookshop staff are valuable sources of information about what's published, what sells and why.

Thus, the need in this section is to gather the information in order then to ask the key questions about it. The focus will be on:

- a survey of bookshops
- a survey of publishers' catalogues
- the politics of feminist publishing

and then a closer look at one particular political issue within academic publishing:

- women's studies versus gender studies.

Survey of bookshops

1 Visit a range of bookshops including, if possible, the large, national chains (for example, Dillons, Waterstones); university/academic bookshops (for example, Blackwell's university bookshops, Heffers); alternative/feminist/radical bookshops (see Loulou Brown et al. for relevant addresses) and the high street stores such as W. H. Smith and John Menzies. The aim is to see how feminist publishing is represented in bookshops.

➤ Which feminist publishers do you already know? Do you find their publications represented in the shops you visit?

➤ Where in the shop do these publishers feature? Are they included alongside all the other publishers on the open shelves or do they feature in particular areas of the shelving or on special stands or in a variety of places? Do they feature prominently, extensively, insignificantly?

➤ Are there specialist sections in the shop devoted to women's fiction, poetry, short stories etc.? If so, who are the publishers of these works?

➤ Is there a specialist section devoted to Black and/or Third World authors, including women? Is there a specialist section devoted to lesbian writing? Is this separately located or included with gay writing? Is any particular emphasis given to the writing of working-class women? Which publishers are represented in these various sections?

➤ Is there a section devoted to non-fiction, feminist texts? If so, what is the section called? Where in the shop is it located? Which publishers are represented in this section?

➤ In the specialist sections, the shelves may have shelf strips naming particular authors or categories of writing. If so, who and what gets mentioned?

➤ Can you see any promotional material from publishers you would consider feminist – posters, bookmarks, dump-bins, display materials, free magazines reviewing the new titles etc.? Can you see any such material from publishers you would not term feminist? Does the non-feminist promotional material ever refer to texts you would consider feminist?

➤ Does the shop include other written materials you would describe as feminist: magazines, journals, newsletters, posters advertising feminist events, flyers etc.?

➤ In surveying the shop, have you found publishers you did not know of previously who seem to you to be feminist publishers? Have you found publishers whom you thought disinterested in feminist material or in focusing on women's writing who are involved in this kind of publication?

➤ What do you notice about the visual appeal of books from feminist publishing companies? Is there a house style, or several house styles? What do you notice about the size of the books, the nature of the covers, the use of colour, the use of logos, styles of typography, graphics etc.?

Survey of publishers' catalogues

2 Because of restricted budgets publishers' catalogues are not always available to the general public though you could be lucky if you write and explain the research needs for which you are using the material. Old catalogues are equally interesting for our purposes and publishers may be more liberal in that respect. Academic libraries and university teachers will have copies since we use them for ordering purposes. Bookshops will also have copies. With a bit of begging, borrowing and no stealing you should be able to put together a collection and, obviously, if you are working with others on this it will be easier. Again, try to cover both companies which you identify as feminist and those which you see as more mainstream; try to represent both the large and the small though, in the latter case, budgets for such material will be even more limited and the 'catalogue' may be, at best, a leaflet; try to give coverage to both academic publishers (Blackwell, Routledge, Macmillan etc.) and those aiming for the widest readership. The aim is to see how feminism is being constructed in publishers' catalogues.

➤ What kind of feminist titles do you find in the catalogues of academic publishers? Are all subject disciplines represented in these titles or do the feminist titles seem to be coming from particular disciplines?

➤ Under what heading are feminist titles placed in academic catalogues? For example, would a book of feminist literary criticism appear under 'Literature' or might it appear under another category? Does 'Feminism' feature as a category in the academic catalogues or is it called something else?

➤ Again, as you considered in the bookshop survey, is there particular representation of the work of Black women, lesbians and working-class women? If so, in what categories and under what headings?

➤ Some catalogues are simply listings of titles but others are carefully produced with a high level of visual appeal. How does feminist work feature in this respect? What images are being used to promote feminist writing?

➤ Consider the names of companies you define as feminist. Do these names carry particular significance?

➤ In the descriptive blurbs, what elements of books are being selected as their most interesting and saleable aspects?

➤ Catalogues of larger publishers contain specialist lists or series (for example, the Livewire Books for Teenagers in the Women's Press catalogue or the Lesbian Landmarks series from Virago or the Women Writers series from Macmillan). What areas are being chosen for specialist focus? What markets are being targeted?

➤ Do you feel some potential feminist markets are being overlooked? Can you anticipate future developments in feminist publishing? What might be the growth areas for the twenty-first century? (Should you think of good ideas here I am sure lots of publishers would be delighted to hear from you!)

➤ If you manage to get a set of catalogues covering a period of years from a particular publisher, what changes do you notice in the way feminism and/or women's writing is being represented? On the other hand, you might want to compare a range of catalogues from different publishers for one particular year.

3 What conclusions are possible on the basis of these two surveys?

➤ Can you say that publishing clearly demarks into those companies interested in promoting women's writing and feminist ideas and others which are not, or is the situation more complicated than that?

➤ What similarities and distinctions do you notice between different feminist publishers and between feminist and non-feminist publishers in terms of the kind of titles they promote?

➤ What similarities and distinctions do you notice between different feminist publishers and between feminist and non-feminist publishers in terms of the marketing strategies employed?

➤ What similarities and distinctions do you notice between different feminist publishers and between feminist and non-feminist publishers in terms of the targeted markets? Do you feel publishers are appealing to a range of feminist markets or to a single feminist market? How would you characterize the market(s)?

➤ Taking into account the quantity and variety of published material devoted to women's writing and feminist discourse, how are publishers sub-dividing that area; into what categories; under what classifications?

➤ Does feminist publishing, however characterized, feature more prominently with particular publishers and in particular types of bookshops?

➤ What impression of feminism is created through the material you have considered? Is it an area of radical commitment and political activism; is it about self-fulfilment and individual achievement; is it about academic study?

➤ Lennie Goodings, at that time Publishing Director of Virago, has said that Virago's role is 'to inspire, to inform, to entertain, to surprise'. On the basis of your research, is that how you would describe the role of Virago and/or of other feminist publishing companies or do you see them undertaking a different role? What, if anything, is specifically 'feminist' about the roles they adopt?

The politics of feminist publishing

4 I suspect that one of the problems you might have found in doing the surveys was that of definition. You may have started the surveys thinking you knew, roughly, what would constitute a feminist publishing company and then found that definition undermined. Was the material you found about feminist publishing what you expected? For example, did you anticipate the involvement of mainstream non-feminist companies in what you might identify as feminist projects? Could you point to distinctive characteristics of feminist publishing companies?

One way you could pursue these questions further is to refer to the section on Defining a Feminist Text. The issues raised there about definition are equally applicable to defining a feminist publishing company. Also, consider the two following passages, both from publishers describing aspects of their publishing policy:

[Feminism] underlies the diversity and inclusiveness of the list, the passionate concern to publish the best, and the belief that women's writing and issues could be the foundation of an inspirational, financially viable list. We have published across many disciplines and in each, taking the woman's part has brought us to the very heart of the matter. Women may not yet have equal power or influence, but we certainly have the talent.

Those talents have provided us with the six hundred titles we currently have in print and the hundred new titles and re-issues we publish each year. They have enabled us publish the voices of women from all over the world, women who recall their lives with devastating intensity, women who tell stories, create fictions and conjure up images of extraordinary power, and women who make us laugh. We publish the work of writers with the all-important ability to find ways of looking at things differently, to make new connections and provide unexpected insights. These are revealed in novels and poetry; in the exciting juxtaposition of poems or stories in an anthology; in a critique of some unexamined aspect of our culture; in an unputdownable thriller, a revealing biography or a work of illuminating literary criticism. (p. vi)

... have always been committed to publishing ground breaking non-fiction for women; Sheila Rowbotham's *Woman's Consciousness Man's World*, Juliet Mitchell's *Psychoanalysis and Feminism* and Ann Oakley's *Housewife* have been in print with us for over 20 years. We have a selection of books which cover a whole range of women's issues from health to history, psychology to sociology and gender to spirituality. This year we are particu-larly proud of biographies about Edith Wharton, Virginia Woolf, Henrietta Moraes and Dora Jordan. Jill Tweedie's autobiography *Eating Children* including her unfinished memoir *Frightening People* cannot fail to move even people coming to her writing for the first time. We are adding to our already strong list of anthologies which highlight the strength of women's writing. *The _____ Book of Women's Lives* edited by Phyllis Rose brings together twentieth-century writing from a disparate group of women from Virginia Woolf to Maxine Hong Kingston. *Chloe plus Olivia* and *The _____ Book of Lesbian Short Stories* makes available some of the best lesbian writing from the seventeenth century to the present. We are also especially proud of a striking new book from Kate Millett *The Politics of Cruelty* and updating editions of two classic pieces of research, *The Sceptical Feminist* and *Just Like A Girl*.

One of these publishers would describe itself as a feminist publisher and the other would not. Don't rack your brains trying to think who is the publisher of the texts listed in the second passage, rather try to discern any differences and similarities in the way each describes its activities. The similarities are much easier to list, though I think there are a couple of telling phrases which might point to distinctions. Can you say which company would happily take on the appellation 'feminist'? (The publishers names are given at the end of the section.)

5 If it is sometimes difficult to distinguish feminist and non-feminist publishing companies on the basis of their publicity, should we look to other categories?

- the centrality of the feminist publications to the company as a whole;

- the sense of a political commitment to feminism on behalf of the company;

- the way the company is financed and structured;

- its working methods;

-

-

Add to this list and think further about these points. In what ways could these factors be relevant to feminist publishing? What evidence to support or question these points have you found in your surveys?

6 In 1984 Gillian Hanscombe described feminist publishing as 'a two-fold phenomenon, of which the commercial factor is only one part, and that the least important. Its essential feature is that it is a political activity. Between the two lies a grey area of uneasy definition'. Since then the relation in feminist publishing between economic and politics has been much debated and with less sureness than Hanscombe could indicate in 1984. Not only does the grey area remain but the economic element has loomed larger as the survival of companies continues to be threatened, and aspirations towards political principle have often given way to pragmatism and the demands of marketing.

Compare these two responses. Joan Scanlon and Julia Swindells refer to Virago as the 'bad apple' of feminist publishing; Gaby Naher is equally emphatic in her condemnation of Scanlon and Swindell's viewpoint.

If, as Harriet Spicer insists, Virago's conscious strategy, was to be 'specialist and mainstream, and to widen the definition of what is perceived to be mainstream', then they can certainly be said to have succeeded in the latter aim. The question remains, though, what do they mean now in the '90s by 'specialist', and what readership are they referring to when they speak of 'brand loyalty'?

The new-format Virago hard-back fiction, while clearly designed to move away from the historical associations of the elegant green spines, is scarcely a radical departure, but a further bid for recognition as a publisher of literary excellence. These little hard backs, not dissimilar to the Bodley Head fiction list, urge you to recognise their craft manship (sic), and come with the hallmark of liberal male academic approval, with quotes from Oxford literary professors such as John Bayley to reassure us that we are all sophisticated enough in the 1990s to know that women write novels in The Great Tradition too.

The very marketability that 'women's ideas' and 'women's lives' of a certain kind have achieved through the women's presses should lead us at least to enquire about the relationship now between a successful publishing house such as Virago and a generally beleaguered women's movement. In Britain at least, throughout the 80s and 90s, the women's movement has been struggling against wave after wave of state opposition, implicit and explicit, and a media which for the most part insisted that we have moved beyond the need for feminism. And yet, women's lists in mainstream publishing and women's studies courses in the academy appear to have boomed. It is also significant that Virago's list is difficult to distinguish from many of the women's (or gender) studies lists of mainstream publishers, such as Routledge or Blackwell. One reason for this may well be that, from the beginning, Virago's non-fiction list has on the whole been dictated by the concerns of academic feminism, rather than activist feminism, and the split between the academic feminism and the women's movement has widened enormously during the last fifteen years. Moreover, unlike The Women's Press, Virago has almost exclusively published work by socialist feminists, and has consequently found itself with a large number of post-feminist (not to mention post-socialist) writers on their hands – in spite of the fact that many of these same women were active in the women's movement in the 70s.

Joan Scanlon and Julia Swindells, 'Bad Apple' (1994) p. 44

In Australia they call it the 'tall poppy syndrome': an irrepressible desire to strike down and discredit the successful. At a time when feminist publishing is looking like one of the real success stories of the recession, two voices from the radical feminist magazine *Trouble & Strife* whinge that the feminist press, especially Virago, are no longer as 'oppositional and unpopular' as they used to be. American imports Naomi Wolf and Susan Faludi have been criticised on similar grounds, for playing too much to the media, for being too photogenic. The *Trouble & Strife* article quotes Ursula Owen, one of Virago's founding directors, as saying 'one forgets how disturbing and unmarketable feminism was in the early seventies', as if the authors mourn that lack of marketability, as if they mourn the ghettos.

Gaby Naher, 'Spreading the Word' (1994) p. 20

➤ If the accusation of 'sell-out' hangs heavily over the first extract, a complaint of 'sour grapes' is present in the second. Go carefully through each passage. What precisely are the objections? What validity do they have for you?

➤ Two of the complaints of the first passage are that Virago is attached to a traditional and privileged view of aesthetics and, secondly, the company has favoured the academic over the activist. Would you agree with either or both of those remarks? What is your evidence? Use data from your bookshop and catalogue surveys and your own reading of Viragos.

➤ I am interested in two phrases quoted in the Naher passage – 'oppositional and unpopular', 'disturbing and unmarketable'. The problem seems to be that feminism as a politics should, *necessarily*, be 'oppositional' and 'disturbing'; however, if it is also 'unpopular' and 'unmarketable', feminist publishing companies will go out of business. Can you find a way round this difficulty? Can one be both 'oppositional' and 'popular', 'disturbing' and 'marketable'? What kind of feminist list would you design to cover both needs? Does feminist publishing also have a role as 'imaginative', 'inspirational', 'encouraging', 'joyous'; is there a specifically feminist inflection to these attributes?

➤ Controversially, Naher suggests that Scanlon and Swindells 'mourn the ghetto'. In your view, is it that which they mourn or is it something else?

Ursula Owen's response to such debates, ostensibly a matter-of-fact realism, seems to me to raise more issues than it solves. What do you think?

> Ursula Owen sees Virago as 'a very broad church. The idea always was to reach women who weren't feminist as well as those who were. We are trying to be aware of what's going on in the margins and at the centre. We are not necessarily preaching. Of course,' she adds, 'for that we get flak from the left and right, but I'm fairly resigned to that.'

> Hilary Macaskill, 'From Nowhere to Everywhere', (1990) p. 434

7 In 1995

● Virago decided to publish male writers

● Lennie Goodings, at that time Publishing Director of Virago, said that 'a dialogue between men and women is appropriate to the 1990s

● Carmen Callil, founder of Virago, said that feminist publishing was no longer needed and the new need was for 'fine writing' on political ideas.

How do you respond to these changes and comments? As we approach the millenium, is there a need for feminist publishing companies devoted exclusively to writing by women? If so, what is their role? Could you produce a kind of short, sharp 'mission statement' that such publishers could distribute to explain their aims, markets and the needs they hope to address?

8 We have considered so far chiefly the reader's response to feminist publishing strategies; what about the author's? The three authors below are not referring to specific publishers, rather to an indeterminate, loose sense of 'market' as something constructed between readers, publishers, publicists, the media etc. None finds her market an easy road to creative or political expression.

Of Course When They Ask for Poems
About the 'Realities' of Black Women

What they really want
at times
is a specimen
whose heart is in the dust

A mother-of-sufferer
trampled, oppressed
they want a little black blood
undressed
and validation
for the abused stereotype
already in their heads

Or else they want
a perfect song

Extract from Grace Nichols, 'Of Course When They Ask for
Poems About the "Realities" of Black Women' (1989) p. 52

But more importantly there is no need to despair because no novel, or other literary work is every going to fulfil the aspirations that women seem to have. This must be grasped. We must demand and respond to more novels and better novels, but we cannot demand that any one novel can be simultaneously:

(a) satisfying to our sense of the complexities of our lives
(b) a paradigm of orthodox feminism
(c) an evangelizing document to convert the unconverted
(d) the bearer of a whole new language and symbol structure and world model
(e) a good read – witty, inspiring, identifiable with
(f) able to provide us with mythological heroines
(g) an exposition of the fullness of women's oppression.

hmmm....

we'd like something light and humourous, but deep and meaningful, which says everything about women's oppression, o.k.? I've had this marvellous idea, see, you have this woman standing there, looking kept down but dignified, right, and she's wearing an apron to show she's working class, and one leg is shackled to the kitchen sink and the other leg is attached by a great heavy chain to a pram with ten kids in it and one arm is being twisted behind her back by a man who looks like a capitalist, you know, a bowler hat and a cigar, and there are three men on her back, symbolising the working, middle and upper class male establishment, but.... you'll love this bit.... she's got her other arm raised and her fist clenched to show she's still struggling..... actually, we were going to have her crucified on a clothes horse, and crowned with nappy pins, but we didn't want it to be too heavy....

Cartoon by Jo Nesbitt, Spare Rib

113

I had thought I was perhaps paranoid and defensive about all this until I saw Jo Nesbitt's cartoon: it is not fair in a sense to snatch this cartoon from its context which is a visual essay of affection for the women's movement; but it does make, wittily and quickly, the point I am labouring over. If we want fictions at all; then we must be clear about what we want them for and what we expect them to do.

Sara Maitland, 'Novels are Toys not Bibles, but the Child is Mother to the Woman' (1979) p. 207

How should I describe myself? I am Black; I am a woman; I am a writer. I am all these things and more. But at the moment I am defined, by others, as a 'Black woman writer', one of the sources of something called 'Black women's writing'.

Now, I define myself as a Blackwoman writer, and for me the difference is at once subtle and vital. But my writing, out there on its own, is classified by others into the ethnocentric, at the moment radically chic, genre of Black women's writing. Because the precise specifications of this genre are not mine, it is being used to define me and my creativity – both from within my culture and from outside it – in a way that is stifling and ultimately deadly.

Barbara Burford, 'The Landscapes Painted on the Inside of My Skin' (1987) p. 37

➤ What are the issues that each writer raises?

➤ Each sees herself as in some ways constrained; her writing is determined to an extent by forces over which she has little control. Can you explain and account for this response?

➤ Return to the data you have collected. Is there evidence to support their comments? The blurbs on back covers and in catalogues could be particularly useful here in indicating how the writing is being marketed.

➤ You can find relevant material also in the section on The Woman Writer: Lost and Found.

Women's studies versus gender studies

10 Look back to your data from the surveys concerning the naming and categorizing of feminist writing. In the bookshop survey, you were asked to discover the varied names given to the sections of non-fiction feminist texts; in the catalogue survey, you were asked to list the headings under which feminist texts featured in the publishers' catalogues. Here is how Diane Richardson and Victoria Robinson have characterized the categorization in academic publishers' catalogues:

There are four main categorizations used by publishers in their catalogues:

(a) Gender studies

Women's studies   Men and masculinity/men's studies

(b) Gender studies/Men's studies

Women's studies

(c) Gender studies/Women's studies

(d) Gender and Women's studies

The term gender studies may then be used as a catch all/superordinate category incorporating women's studies and, in some cases, men's studies and/or 'men and masculinity' (a). Books on sexuality, including women and sexuality, are also sometimes placed under gender studies. An example of this is the situating of books in lesbian and gay studies under 'Gender Studies' in the 1993 Harvester Wheatsheaf *Women's Studies* catalogue. (Although some publishers are now developing separate gay and lesbian studies lists, for example Sage.)

Interestingly, where women's studies is submerged under gender studies, men's studies may still be distinguished (for example, Sage) (b). Alternatively, gender studies may be a separate category from women's studies. For example, in the 1992 Harvester Wheatsheaf catalogue gender theory is distinct from feminism and women's studies (c). Finally, the two may be amalgamated into gender and women's studies as in the case of the Routledge list (d).

Diane Richardson and Victoria Robinson, 'Publishing Feminism:
Redefining the Women's Studies Discourse' (1994) p. 92

➤ How do Richardson and Robinson's comments relate to the data you have collected? You may have catalogues from other publishers where categories differ.

➤ What about the bookshop headings? Do these correlate in any way to what is in the catalogues or to Richardson and Robinson's schema above?

11 The import of Richardson and Robinson's comments is that classification systems are not neutral; they carry with them meanings and associations. There is no single, correct placing for any text but, at the same time, how you classify a text determines to some extent both the priority given to a text and how a reader may interpret it. The political implications of this can be significant as Virginia Woolf's narrator in *A Room of One's Own* learns when trying to look up the category 'women' in the British Museum. You might want to research this aspect of Woolf's text and, subsequently, the classification systems of libraries you know. Robinson and Richardson remark earlier in their article:

> It could be argued that the shift towards the use of the term gender in preference to 'woman' poses a threat to women's studies (for a fuller discussion see Richardson and Robinson, 1993). For example, the backcover of Harry Brod's book *The Making of Masculinities: the New Men's Studies* (1987) states that:
>
> > There has been a marked trend in feminist scholarship during the last few years away from a focus exclusively on women to a broader conception of gender. The study of men is a fundamental part of this trend.

The emphasis on gender has been criticized by some feminists, for example Mary Evans, who argues that the category gender is a neutral term which implies that the 'interests of the sexes have now converged and that the differences in life changes (not to mention economic rewards) that exist between women and men are matters of choice' (Evans, 1991, p. 73). She argues for the necessity of using the name women's studies as it allows the focus to remain on sexual difference. The concern with the use of gender is that sexual inequalities/power relationships between women and men are no longer central. (p. 91)

➤ How do you respond to this view? Does the term 'gender' depoliticize the debate and render women invisible?

➤ Would 'feminist studies' be a better term or does that bring its own range of problems?

➤ Do the terms 'women's studies' and 'feminist studies' suggest that feminism is primarily an academic pursuit?

➤ Should 'lesbian studies' be part of 'feminist studies' or 'women's studies' or 'gay studies' or 'sexuality' or 'queer studies' or separately located? What would be the implications for lesbianism of these different locations?

➤ Here is the contents page of the 1995 Routledge *Gender and Women's Studies* catalogue. What meanings do these classifications have for you? What issues do they raise?

1	Lesbian and Gay Studies
6	Feminist Theory and Philosophy
16	Masculinity
18	Sexuality
19	Cultural and Media Studies
22	Film and Performance
25	Literature
32	History
36	Race and Ethnicity
38	Anthropology
39	Health and Social Policy
42	Family
43	Psychology
44	Law and Criminology
45	Women and Development
48	Education
49	Reference
50	Index

The Routledge Gender and Women's Studies
Catalogue, 1995

I notice, for instance, the absence of class as a category and I suspect that in your surveys of bookshops and catalogues you found explorations of race, ethnicity and sexuality linked to gender far more frequently than issues of class. Why do you think this is so?

References and further reading

Barbara Burford, 'The Landscapes Painted on the Inside of My Skin'

Carmen Callil. The comments of Carmen Callil were made at a conference, 'Literature: A Woman's Business', Sheffield Hallam University, 10–11 March, 1995.

Patricia Duncker, *Sisters and Strangers: An Introduction to Contemporary Feminist Fiction*

Mary Evans, 'The Problem of Gender for Women's Studies' in Jane Aaron and Sylvia Walby (eds), *Out of the Margins: Women's Studies in the Nineties*

Nicci Gerrard, *Into the Mainstream*

Lennie Goodings. The comments of Lennie Goodings were made at a conference, 'Literature and the Marketplace', the University of York, 10 May, 1995.

Gill Hanscombe, 'Reaching the Parts Other Books Can't Reach'

Susanne Kappeler, 'What is a Feminist Publishing Policy?' in Gail Chester and Julienne Dickey (eds), *Feminism and Censorship: The Current Debate*

Hilary Macaskill, 'From Nowhere to Everywhere'

Sara Maitland, 'Novels are Toys not Bibles, but the Child is Mother to the Woman', *Women's Studies International Quarterly*

Gaby Naher, 'Spreading the Word'

Grace Nichols, 'Of Course When They ask for Poems About the "Realities" of Black Women' in *Lazy Thoughts of a Lazy Woman*

Peter Owen (ed.), *Publishing Now*

Diane Richardson and Victoria Robinson (eds), *Introducing Women's Studies: Feminist Theory and Practice*

Diane Richardson and Victoria Robinson, 'Theorizing Women's Studies, Gender Studies and Masculinity: The Politics of Naming'

Victoria Robinson and Diane Richardson, 'Publishing Feminism: Redefining the Women's Studies Discourse. These two articles cover, substantially, the same content.

Joan Scanlon and Julia Swindells, 'Bad Apple'

Susan Sellers (ed.), *Taking Reality by Surprise: Writing for Pleasure and Publication*

Women in Publishing, *Twice as Many, Half as Powerful*

On related aspects of the publishing industry see:

Loulou Brown et al., *The International Handbook of Women's Studies*. Lists details of bookshops, journals, magazines etc.

Eileen Cadman et al., *Rolling Our Own: Women as Printers, Publishers and Distributors*

Jane Cholmeley, 'A Feminist Business in a Capitalist World: Silver Moon Women's Bookshop' in Nanneke Redclift and M. Thea Sinclair, (eds), *Working Women: International Perspectives on Labour and Gender Ideology*

Margaret Cooter et al., (Women in Publishing), *Reviewing the Reviews: A Woman's Place on the Bookpage*

Cath Jackson, 'A Press of One's Own'. Cath Jackson interviews founder members of Onlywomen Press on aspects of print production.

Specifically on publishing for lesbians see:

Joanna Briscoe, 'Books'

Rose Collins, 'Out on the Shelves'

Veronica Groocock, 'Lesbian Journalism: Mainstream and Alternative Press' in Liz Gibbs (ed.), *Daring to Dissent: Lesbian Culture from Margin to Mainstream*

In point 4, 'spot the difference', the first passage was from *A Virago Keepsake: To Celebrate Twenty Years of Publishing* (1993) and the second from the introduction to the Penguin catalogue, *Women's Reading* (1994).

Feminist Reading

Introduction

One of the observations which feminism has brought to theories of reading is the obvious but oft-forgot awareness that the reader is gendered; s/he is not a neutral, impersonal interactive machine but an entity encumbered with all the baggage of daily life, likes and dislikes, prejudices, histories, other reading experiences, various knowledges and gaps of knowledge, needs, aspirations ... and on and on. Somewhere within all this will be the experience of a sexed body, a sexual identity and socialization in which gender plays an important part. In short, 'the reader' is a highly complex individual. We have to resist any simplistic view that men and women read with fixed group identities and that the way women read is utterly distinct from the way men read. At the same time, underpinning all recent debates in reading theory – feminist or otherwise – is the belief that the reader plays a crucial and active role in the production of meaning: s/he is not merely a passive recipient of ideas and imaginative projections created by the author. Thus, for our purposes in this section we need to remember that gender is important in both the construction of the reader and the process of reading.

To give you a sense of the area, below are some of the issues which have been debated in feminist engagements with reading. Not all can be discussed fully here though we shall touch further on some of these points.

- Is a woman reading the same thing as a feminist reading?

- Does a feminist reading have to be produced by a woman or could it be produced by a man?

- Is a feminist reading linked with the experience of being a woman?

- But can we define what *is* 'the experience of being a woman'? Women's experience varies greatly according to age, race, class, sexuality, nationality etc. and the very category 'woman' is itself disputed in some critical theories.

- Even if women's experience is a problem concept, can we afford to dispense with it entirely in our explorations of feminist reading?

- What is the distinctiveness of a feminist reading; how would it differ from other modes of reading?

- How is a feminist reading produced; what happens to make it possible; what determinants are involved?

Note down your initial response to these questions. Are there some that you can answer more readily than others? None, of course, has a simple answer but think of the issues, problems, queries which would need to be addressed in exploring these questions. Some of these questions we shall return to as we consider these three points:

- The experience of women reading texts in which the implied reader is male.

- The debate between feminist reading as a reading strategy open to all readers and feminist reading as related to female experience.

- A consideration of some imaginative texts which particularly connect with issues of gendered reading.

The woman reader and the male implied reader

1 The term 'implied reader' is most associated with the work of Wolfgang Iser. It would be helpful to research this term by looking in dictionaries of literary terms or the many introductions to literary theory, nearly all of which make reference to this concept and/or include extracts from Iser's work. Of particular use is the relevant section in Martin Montgomery et al., *Ways of Reading* since this looks at the implied reader in the context of gender. As another starting point here is Chris Baldick's definition of the implied reader as

> the hypothetical figure of the reader to whom a given work is designed to address itself. Any text may be said to presuppose an 'ideal' reader who has the particular attitudes (moral, cultural, etc.) appropriate to that text in order for it to achieve its full effect. This implied reader is to be distinguished from *actual* readers, who may be unable or unwilling to occupy the position of the implied reader: thus most religious poetry presupposes a god-fearing implied reader, but many actual readers today are atheists.

Chris Baldick, *The Concise Oxford Dictionary of Literary Terms* (1990) p. 108

Let us try to understand this definition by applying it to a story about reading, Alice Walker's 'Porn'. In this story the male character introduces the female character to his porn collection. In the first passage the narrator recounts one of the pornographic stories read by the female character; in the second, we learn of one of the consequences of this reading:

> *A young blonde girl from Minnesota* (probably kidnapped, she thinks, reading) *is far from home in New York, lonely and very horny. She is befriended by two of the blackest men on the East Coast.* (They had been fighting outside a bar and she had stopped them by flinging her naïve white self into the fray.) *In their gratitude for her peacemaking they take her to their place and do everything they can think of to her. She grinning liberally the whole time. Finally they make a sandwich of her: one filling the anus and the other the vagina, so that all that is visible of her body between them is a sliver of white thighs.* (And we see that these two pugilists have finally come together on something.)...

Now, when he makes love to her, she tries to fit herself into the white-woman, two–black-men story. But who will she be? The men look like her brothers, Bobo and Charlie. She is disgusted, and worse, bored by Bobo and Charlie. The white woman is like the young girl who, according to the *Times*, *was* seduced off a farm in Minnesota by a black pimp and turned out on 42nd Street. She cannot stop herself from thinking: *Poor: Ignorant: Sleazy: Depressing*. This does not excite or stimulate.

Alice Walker, 'Porn' (1981) pp. 80, 83

We have two sets of implied and actual readers here. There is the implied reader of Walker's complete story and the actual reader – you, me, anyone – who really reads it. But within Walker's story is narrated another, pornographic story which itself has an implied reader and an actual reader, the female character of whose reactions we hear.

➤ The female character is one of the actual readers of the pornography described in the story within a story. Who is the implied reader? How do you know?

➤ Baldick comments that the actual reader 'may be unable or unwilling to occupy the position of the implied reader'. What is the textual evidence that the actual female reader in the pornographic story is *both* unable and unwilling to adopt the position of the implied reader? Think not only of explicit comments but of style and tone. Why is she both unable and unwilling?

➤ Can you deduce from these two short passages who is Walker's implied reader for the story as a whole? Then read the complete story to get a clearer idea and to consider whether you, the actual reader, are able and willing to adopt the position of the implied reader.

2 Pornography is a particularly extreme example of writing and visuals which, with the exception of lesbian erotica, nearly always posit a male implied reader and which create particular problems for the female actual reader. However, Judith Fetterley is one among a number of feminists critics who would claim that difficulties for the female reader occur also in widely respected, canonical texts. Though Fetterley does not use the vocabulary and concepts of Iser, the textual issues she explores are in some ways similar. Here is Fetterley's comment on Washington Irving's famous story 'Rip Van Winkle' in which the termagant wife, Dame Van Winkle nags and harries the affable Rip:

... the real rub is the fact that the story forces the female reader to enact its definition of her sex. A woman reading 'Rip Van Winkle' becomes perforce one of Irving's 'good wives', taking Rip's side and laying all the blame on Dame Van Winkle; that is the way the story is written. The consequence for the female reader is a divided self. She is asked to identify with Rip and against herself, to scorn the amiable sex and to act just like it, to laugh at Dame Van Winkle and accept that she represents 'woman', to be at once both repressor and repressed, and ultimately to realise that she is neither. Rip's words upon returning home after his twenty-year evasion are ironically appropriate to her: 'I'm not myself – I'm somebody else – that's me yonder – no – that's somebody else ... I can't tell what's my name or who I am'.

Judith Fetterley, *The Resisting Reader: A Feminist Approach to American Fiction* (1978) p. 11

It is important to note that Fetterley is not tritely complaining about negative portrayals of women and insisting that all female characters should be laudable. What she does complain about is a narrative structure which presents women as limitations on the creativity, progress and expansiveness of men and which, consequently, offers little or no place for the female reader; this narrative pattern Fetterley sees as a frequent one in American culture.

➤ You may not be familiar with this specific story but, hopefully, the above gives you the gist of Fetterley's argument about it. Can you relate Fetterley's comments to any texts with which you are familiar? Think of texts or sections of texts with which you have found it difficult to connect. There may well be a hundred and one reasons for such a reaction but could it be that an aspect of the difficulty lay in the fact that you were not the implied reader?

➤ Fetterley talks here of one particular narrative – woman as the obstacle to man's freedom; elsewhere she mentions another common narrative – woman as the scapegoat for all ills. Can you give examples of these narratives from your own reading or suggest other traditional narratives which are problematic for the female reader? Think, for example, of the difficulties raised for any modern production of Shakespeare's *The Taming of the Shrew*. Or consider this extract from Christine de Pizan, clear evidence that we are not dealing here with a new problem. She wonders why

> ... I could hardly find a book on morals where, even before I had read it in its entirety, I did not find several chapters or certain sections attacking women, no matter who the author was ... Like a gushing fountain, a series of authorities, whom I recalled one after another, came to mind, along with their opinions on this topic. And I finally decided that God formed a vile creature when He made woman ...
>
> Christine de Pizan, *The Book of the City of Ladies* (1405) p. 291

➤ Conversely, can you name texts where you feel you do approximate the position of the implied reader? This doesn't mean you have to agree with everything in the text; rather, as Baldick remarks, the implied reader 'has the particular attitudes (moral, cultural etc.) appropriate to that text in order for it to achieve its full effect'.

➤ What is it in specifically the gender ideology of these texts that enables you to take up the position of the implied reader?

3 Consider this passage from Wolfgang Iser:

> Text and reader no longer confront each other as object and subject, but instead the 'division' takes place within the reader himself. In thinking the thoughts of another, his own individuality temporarily recedes into the background, since it is supplanted by these alien thoughts which now become the theme on which his attention is focused. As we read, there occurs an artificial division of our personality, because we take as a theme for ourselves something that we are not. Consequently when reading we operate on different levels. For although we may be thinking the thoughts

of someone else, what we are will not disappear completely – it will merely remain a more or less powerful virtual force. Thus, in reading there are these two levels – the alien 'me' and the real, virtual 'me' – which are never completely cut off from each other. Indeed, we can only make someone else's thoughts into an absorbing theme for ourselves, provided the virtual background of our own personality can adapt to it.

Wolfgang Iser, 'The Reading Process' (1974) p. 293

Despite Iser's user of the generic 'he', we can see how this extract usefully elucidates both Fetterley and Walker. All three writers present the reader as divided:

➤ Compare Fetterley and Iser in terms of their comments on this figure of the divided reader. Have you had experience of 'divided' readings?

➤ One could say that Fetterley relates Iser's general observation on the process of reading to the specific issues of gender. Would you agree with that statement? How would you illustrate it from Fetterley's and Iser's extracts?

➤ How would you apply the concept of the divided reader to Walker's story?

➤ Look again at Iser's final sentence. Why is the female reader in Walker and Fetterley unable to make this adaptation?

➤ The tone of Iser's writing suggests that the divided reader is for him an interesting phenomenon in the process of reading, a discussion point. How would you describe the perspectives of Fetterley and Walker? They both seem to me more impassioned than Iser. In what ways? Why?

4 It is perfectly possible to enjoy and learn from a text even if you are not, in some respects, the implied reader. To take up Baldick's comment about religious belief, many an atheist would happily read *Paradise Lost* or the religious verse of Gerard Manley Hopkins. But what Fetterley is discussing is of a different order; she suggests that the female reader has real problems in adopting a satisfactory reading position with regard to significant, canonical texts. What, then, should she do?

Clearly, then, the first act of the feminist critic must be to become a resisting rather than an assenting reader and, by this refusal to assent, to begin the process of exorcizing the male mind that has been implanted in us. The consequence of this exorcism is the capacity for what Adrienne Rich describes as re-vision – 'the act of looking back, of seeing with fresh eyes, of entering an old text from a new critical direction'. And the consequence, in turn, of this re-vision is that books will no longer be read as they have been read and thus will lose their power to bind us unknowingly to their designs. While women obviously cannot rewrite literary works so that they become ours by virtue of reflecting our reality, we can accurately name the reality they do reflect and so change literary criticism from a closed conversation to an active dialogue.

Judith Fetterley, *The Resisting Reader: A Feminist Approach to American Fiction* (1978) p. xxii–xxiii

Many feminist critics would question Fetterley's view that literature is a reflection of a known reality and the suggestion that men and women have separate, discernible realities. But the nub of Fetterley's argument, that many women have to find some way of reading against the grain of these canonical texts, is undoubtedly true.

➤ As a longer project, research some examples of 'resisting' reading and produce your own resisting reading of a text which you earlier named as one you found difficult to read. For research purposes, Fetterley's own text obviously offers examples. The Adrienne Rich essay to which she refers is: 'When We Dead Awaken: Writing as Re-Vision' in *On Lies, Secrets, and Silence: Selected Prose 1966–1978*. See also:

Kate Millett, *Sexual Politics*

Martin Montgomery et al., *Ways of Reading*

Raman Selden, *Practising Theory and Reading Literature: An Introduction*.

➤ Which kind of reading do you most enjoy – that in which you are the resisting reader or that in which you are the implied reader – or are your responses too complicated to make that kind of distinction?

➤ I find it difficult to think of a text throughout which I have remained in the same reading position. An alert attention to your own responses can indicate that your reading position changes, sometimes rapidly. Can you think of reading experiences where you have moved between different reading positions within the same text? How would you characterize those changing positions?

➤ Can you think of texts which you might generally condemn as anti-women but which at certain moments offer you pleasurable reading experiences? How would you account for this? Are there texts, or parts of texts, which *as a woman* you find impossible to read, despite the most resisting reading? Can you explain what is happening in your attempted reading of such texts?

As/like/man/woman/feminist

5 In trying to explain this curious sub-heading I hope to take you a little further into the questions with which I started the section. A moment ago I asked you to respond to a text 'as a woman': what does that mean? Jonathan Culler has suggested that there is no fixed reading identity 'as a woman' since that identity, as all others, is constantly being formulated and re-formulated: there is no ur version. (For further guidance on this point see the section on Finding the Subject.) Culler writes:

> For a woman to read as a woman is not to repeat an identify or an experience that is given but to play a role she constructs with reference to her identity as a woman, which is also a construct, so that the series can continue: a woman reading as a woman reading as a woman.
>
> Jonathan Culler, 'Reading as a Woman' (1983) p. 64

Culler would argue that a woman reading reads not 'as a woman', since there is no such essential self, but 'like a woman'; she assumes, for a lesser or greater period of time, a particular reading identity. She might, at another stage in the text, read 'like a man'. Robert Scholes replies to this hypothesis:

> ... is there any difference between reading as a woman and reading *like* a woman? Can Mary actually read *as* a woman because she *is* a woman, or can she only read *like* a woman because no individual can ever be a woman? To put the questions still another way, can John read *as* a woman or only *like* a woman? If neither John nor Mary can really read *as* a woman, and either can read *like* a woman, then what's the difference between John and Mary?

Scholes's belief is that there *is* a difference and that it lies in the unequal gender experience of men and women. He continues:

> My own feeling is that until no one notices or cares about the difference we had better not pretend it isn't there. Above all, I think no man should seek in any way to diminish the authority which the experience of women gives them in speaking about that experience, and I believe that women should be very wary of critical systems that deny or diminish that authority.

> Robert Scholes, 'Reading Like a Man' (1987) pp. 217, 217–8

Could the disagreement between Culler and Scholes be avoided by a reformulation of the problem? What if we considered not reading 'as/like a woman' or 'as/like a man' but reading 'as/like a feminist'? Is feminist reading a mode of reading open to all readers irrespective of sexual identity or gender history? Here are two comments on feminist reading, both of which seek to include the male reader:

> 'Feminist reading', then, would be the reception and processing of texts by a reader who is conceived of not only as possibly female, but also as conscious of the tradition of women's oppression in patriarchal culture. The feminist reader – whether in fact male or female – is committed to breaking the pattern of that oppression by calling attention to the ways some texts can perpetuate it.

> Robyn R. Warhol and Diane Price Herndl, *Feminisms: An Anthology of Literary Theory and Criticism* (1991) p. 489

Reading as a feminist, I hasten to add, is not unproblematic; but it has the important aspect of offering male readers a way to produce feminist criticism that avoids female impersonation. The way into feminist criticism, for the male theorist, must involve a confrontation with what might be implied by reading as a man and with a questioning or a surrender of paternal privileges.

> Elaine Showalter, 'Critical Cross-Dressing' (1987) pp. 126–7

Three observations strike me about these two passages:

- In both extracts there is a sense of caution and uncertainty. Showalter is explicit about this; men's entry into feminist reading is 'not unproblematic' and entails at least two prerequisites, contained in Showalter's second sentence. I am interpreting Warhol and Price Herndl's awkward phraseology as also a sign of uncertainty. The feminist reader is described in two phrases – 'not only as possibly female' and 'whether in fact male or female'. Does the first phrase suggest that the feminist reader is more likely to be female than male or are Warhol and Price Herndl referring at that point to the implied reader and in the second phrase referring to the actual reader? I am really not sure.

- Neither passage mentions the issue of female experience. Indeed, Showalter sees feminist reading as a strategy for male critics to avoid female impersonation, that is to avoid having to claim for themselves female experience. They don't have to read 'like a woman'; the male critic can read, as Showalter suggests of Culler, 'as a man and a feminist' (p. 126). Similarly, Warhol and Price Herndl's feminist reader should be 'conscious' of women's oppression and 'committed to breaking the pattern of that oppression' but need not have personal experience of that oppression. Are we to deduce, then, that feminist reading has no relation to female experience, or no necessary relation?

- To extrapolate from that point, if the male reader can produce a feminist reading as effectively as the female we could envisage feminist courses or feminist listings from publishers composed entirely or predominantly of male readings. Should female feminists be perturbed by that or happy that feminism is extending its catchment?

6 There is a lot of material here. Take your time to think it through, look up references and jot down your own responses.

➤ It might help to organize your thoughts if you focus on the key concepts:

man

woman

feminist

as/like

experience

reading position

and see how different arguments use and explain these terms.

➤ Though the concept of female experience is, undoubtedly, a difficult one, the idea that a feminist reading can be distinct from female experience is one that I find troubling. Would you agree? How would you argue the case for a link between feminist reading and female experience?

➤ Stephen Heath writes:

> This is, I believe, the most any man can do today: to learn and so to try to write or talk or act in response to feminism, and so try not in any way to be anti-feminist, supportive of the old structures. Any more, any notion of writing a feminist book or being a feminist, is a myth, a male imaginary with the reality of appropriation and domination right behind.

Stephen Heath, 'Male Feminism' (1984; 1986) p. 9

If I take the liberty of adding 'or producing a feminist reading' to the listing in Heath's second sentence, how would you compare his sentiments to Showalter's? Clearly Heath believes that men *cannot* produce feminist readings. Why? With which critic do you agree? What, then, are men doing when they read 'in response to feminism'?

Readings – feminist or otherwise

7 Let us try to apply the theory we have looked at to some literary examples. I suggest that we might want to keep to the fore of our minds these four problem areas that we have considered:

- the concepts of the implied reader, the actual reader and the resisting reader;
- a sensitivity to our own reading process; how we read; how gender might influence that reading process;
- the difference between reading like a man, like a woman, like a feminist;
- the significance of female experience in a feminist reading.

The extracts I am including focus on dramatizations of sexual violence, an issue which, unsurprisingly, often provokes readings that polarize along lines of gender. The first is from D. H. Lawrence's short story 'Tickets Please' in which a group of female tram conductors, led by Annie, take their revenge on the philandering inspector, John Thomas, who has courted and then rejected every one of them:

'Come on!' cried Annie, looking him in the eye. 'Come on! Come on!' He went forward, rather vaguely. She had taken off her belt and swinging it, she fetched him a sharp blow over the head with the buckle end. He sprang and seized her. But immediately the other girls rushed upon him, pulling and tearing and beating him. Their blood was now thoroughly up. He was their sport now. They were going to have their own back, out of him. Strange, wild creatures, they hung on him and rushed at him to bear him down. His tunic was torn right up the back, Nora had hold at the back of his collar, and was actually strangling him. Luckily the button burst. He struggled in a wild frenzy of fury and terror, almost mad terror. His tunic was simply torn off his back, his shirt-sleeves were torn away, his arms were naked. The girls rushed at him, clenched their hands on him and pulled at him: or they rushed at him and pushed him, butted him with all their might: or they struck him wild blows. He ducked and cringed and struck sideways. They became more intense.

At last he was down. They rushed on him, kneeling on him. He had neither breath nor strength to move. His face was bleeding with a long scratch, his brow was bruised.

Annie knelt on him, the other girls knelt and hung on him. Their faces were flushed, their hair wild, their eyes were all glittering strangely. He lay at last quite still, with face averted, as an animal lies when it is defeated and at the mercy of the captor. Sometimes his eye glanced back at the wild faces of the girls. His breast rose heavily, his wrists were torn.

'Now, then, my fellow!' gasped Annie at length. 'Now then – now – '

At the sound of her terrifying, cold triumph, he suddenly started to struggle as an animal might, but the girls threw themselves upon him with unnatural strength and power, forcing him down.

'Yes – now, then!' gasped Annie at length.

And there was a dead silence, in which the thud of heartbeating was to be heard. It was a suspense of pure silence in every soul.

D. H. Lawrence, 'Tickets Please' (1922) p. 51

The second example is a poem from Joan Larkin, entitled 'Rape'.

> After twenty years I want to call it that, but was it?
> I mean
> it wasn't all his fault, I mean
> wasn't I out there on 8th Street,
> wandering around looking for someone to fill the gap
>   where my center would have been?
> Didn't I circle the same block over & over until he saw me?
> Wasn't I crying when he came along & said *Don't do*
>   *that, cops see me with a white girl crying* –
> *I'm sorry.* Didn't I say *I'm sorry*, & didn't I smile?
> Didn't I walk with him, dumb, to the Hotel Earle,
> didn't I drink with him in his room,
> didn't I undress myself in the stare of a yellow bulb?
> Didn't I drink – what was it I drank?
> Didn't I drink enough to be numb for a long time?
> Didn't I drink myself into a blackout?
>
> Was it rape, if when I lay there letting him fuck me & I started to feel
> sore & exhausted & said *Stop*,
> first softly, then screaming
> *Stop*, over & over?
> And if he was too drunk to hear me,
> or if he heard me but thought, *Girls never mean it when they say stop*,
> was that rape? Was it rape if he meant well
> or was too drunk to hear me, was it rape
> if he kept repeating *Girl, you can fuck*
> & not really meaning any harm?
> I think I remember that the room was green & black,
>
> the small bulb dangling from a cord,
> the bed filthy.
> I don't exactly remember.
> I know I had no pleasure, but lay there; I don't think he forced me.
> It was just that he wouldn't stop when I asked him to.
> He didn't take my money.
> It may have been his booze I drank.
> It may have been sort of a date.
> He wrote his number on half a matchbook & said
> *Call Joe if you need him* – I guess he was Joe.

Did I walk home?
Did I have any money?
Was it me who bought the booze?
Maybe I took a cab.
Was it 2:0 a.m., or safe daylight
when I climbed the five flights,
spent, feeling the tear tracks & pounded cervix,
the booze still coating me, my nerves not yet awake,
    stripped & screaming.
I climbed to my place, five flights,
somehow satisfied,
somehow made real by the pain.

Was it rape, then?

Joan Larkin, 'Rape' (1986)

➤ With the Lawrence we need to remember the caution about making general statements on the basis of an extract. However, can you make some deductions as to who are the implied readers in these two texts? What factors lead you to these deductions? At what points do you, the actual reader, accord with the implied reader?

➤ Are there parts when you become a resisting reader of these texts? Where? For what reasons?

➤ In Lawrence's story we see women portrayed as the violent aggressors. Is this extract open to a feminist reading? You might want to compare with the film *Thelma and Louise* where women, again, take the law into their own hands, though be careful about too-easy comparisons between very different texts, in different media, from different periods.

➤ In what ways might experience – female or male – influence reading of these texts? If you are studying this section in a mixed sex group, do you notice points in the discussion where the group seems to divide, male/female, in its interpretation of the texts? You may prefer to divide the group into single sex sub-groups to study these textual examples. Why might that be necessary or preferable?

➤ Larkin's poem actually invites discussion of how one reads: the narrator repeatedly asks the reader to 'read' the incident, to interpret it and contrasting views are presented to the reader for assessment. Although the poem is written in the voice of the woman, Larkin often suggests how the man might have read the scene. Can you construct three readings of this incident – like a man, like a woman, like a feminist? In what ways would these three readings differ or be the same?

➤ Diana Fuss comments:

I read this piece *like* a feminist; what it means to read as or even like a woman I still don't know.

Diana Fuss 'Reading Like a Feminist' (1989) p. 26

Can you distinguish in your readings of Lawrence and Larkin between reading like a woman and reading like a feminist? Do you find one easier than the other? Does one do something the other does not? Or do the two readings in some ways blur?

➤ Compare Larkin's poem with this newspaper article. In what ways does this article invite polarized readings of the incident?

Girl says night out ended in rape

A HAIRDRESSER'S night out with her girlfriends ended with her being raped by a man she had fancied, a jury was told.

She was 'chatted up' by the stranger in a night club and after her friends took separate taxis home the woman agreed to join the defendant for coffee in his flat.

But the York Crown Court jury heard that she had expected some thing more palatial than the bed sitter containing a single bed, chair, wardrobe and a tiny kitchen area.

It wasn't clean and the coffee cup was dirty and she only took a tiny sip. She hadn't gone there for sex – although she admitted it was in the back of her mind there was a possibility it could be on the agenda if the flat had been more comfortable.

K_____ B_____, a 25-year-old self-employed window cleaner of Fernbank, Acomb Road, York, denies rape in April last year.

Nicholas Campbell, prosecuting, said they met in Toffs night club, York, when she bought him a couple of drinks at the bar. They went into a quieter area to talk about their jobs, holidays and families before taking a taxi to his flat for coffee shortly after 2.20 a.m.

Inside the bed sitter she made it clear she didn't want sex and although she responded briefly to his kisses B_____ lifted her from her chair to his bed.

She was frightened and burst into tears and continued sobbing as he peeled off her jeans and body suit. He did not use a condom.

The alleged victim told Elizabeth O'Hare, defending, that she hadn't made the complaint because she was frightened of what she had done and the consequences of her best friend and boyfriend finding out.

She admitted that no force was used and that she had had plenty of opportunity to leave the flat.

'It would have been rude and ill-mannered if I had left soon after arriving because he had invited me for coffee.' she said.

She stayed one and a half hours and froze with fear when he started to undress her after pushing her on to the bed.

She said she liked him but lost interest when she thought he had lied to her. She saw a document which indicated he was on state benefits, the flat wasn't as he described and she felt 'dirty' and 'uncomfortable'.

She went on: 'I didn't know what would happen if I left suddenly without talking to him.'

She said she had given him no assistance to take off her clothes nor had she undressed him and made the running from buying him drinks in the club.

She was unaffected by drink although she admitted having 'quite a lot of money' on her and drinking up to 13 Bacardi and Cokes throughout the evening.

The trial continues today.

from The Yorkshire Evening Press *22 July 1994*

8 I noted at the beginning of this section that one of the reasons why notions of female experience are difficult to use, though not impossible, is because a sense of a common, unifying experience is hard to locate; other differences may cut into the desired unity. Remember Larkin's lines:

> Wasn't I crying when he came along & said *Don't do*
> *   that, cops see me with a white girl, crying* –
> *I'm sorry*. Didn't I say *I'm sorry*, & didn't I smile?

No politically aware reader in the States could read those lines without bringing to mind the tortured history of racism, the abused women under slavery, inter-racial rapes, the lynching of Black men. Should we be talking about reading like a woman or reading like a *Black* woman or like a *white* woman?

➤ How does the Black woman read Larkin's poem? A companion text would be to consider Alice Walker's 'Advancing Luna and Ida B. Wells' (1981) which also focuses on the politics and interpretation of an inter-racial rape.

➤ Similarly, consider the following poem, riven with problems of class difference. Should we also be talking about reading like a *working-class* woman or a *middle-class* woman? How is this poem read by the Ivy League, rape survivor? (Note, 'the Ivy League' is a group of prestigious colleges in the States; the British equivalent would be 'Oxbridge'.)

> if she's born
> and educated ivy league
>
> and if the ivy
> grows in her hair
>
> without any of
> her roots showing
>
> and if her hair
> blows in the wind
>
> and if the wind
> resonates like a cash register
>
> and if the cash register
> is full, fuller than her breast
>
> or her lips
> and some individual
>
> rapes her
> getting involved in her ivy
>
> and her cash flow
> busting up her register
>
> then, by all means
> we have a case on our hands
>
> a crime, an old fashioned
> news story to sink teeth into

> otherwise, folks
> it's a mere screw, bound to happen

Safiya Henderson-Holmes, 'Rape, A Class Act' (1990)

➤ As yet a further example, Larkin's poem is anthologized in a collection called *Naming the Waves: Contemporary Lesbian Poetry* (1988) edited by Christine McEwen. Should we be reading her poem like a lesbian? Would that be different to reading it like a woman or like a feminist? Could the male readers whom Showalter, and Warhol and Price Herndl suggest might read like feminists, read also like lesbians?

9 In conclusion I can only reinforce what you have, doubtless, already realized – namely, the complexities, subtleties and distinctions of this issue. You can see how defining yourself as a reader becomes increasingly involved and how the relation between reading positions and one's lived experience as a sexed, gendered being is loaded with problems about authenticity and power. I suggested under point 5 that it could help to look at the section on Finding the Subject to clarify the arguments about identity. Review also the section on The Politics of Location. What is said there about the need to develop a precise awareness of the place from which one is speaking is equally relevant to an understanding of the place from which one is reading. Finally, to consider this section alongside the one on Feminine Writing and Reading could lead to a fascinating comparative study of the meanings and potential of both the feminist and the feminine.

There are other literary texts, like the Larkin poem and the Alice Walker stories, which raise, as a central part of the narrative, problems of gendered reading. These texts could be the basis for a longer comparative study. See, for instance:

Charlotte Perkins Gilman, 'The Yellow Wallpaper'

Susan Keating Glaspell, 'A Jury of Her Peers'

Isak Dinesen, 'The Blank Page'.

References and further reading

Chris Baldick, *The Concise Oxford Dictionary of Literary Terms*

Jonathan Culler, 'Reading as a Woman', *On Deconstruction: Theory and Criticism after Structuralism*

Christine de Pizan, *The Book of the City of Ladies* (1405) in Alcuin Blamires (ed.), *Woman Defamed and Woman Defended: An Anthology of Medieval Texts*. Discussion of this passage features also in Carolyne Larrington, *Women and Writing and Medieval Europe: A Sourcebook*

Judith Fetterley, *The Resisting Reader: A Feminist Approach to American Fiction*

Diana Fuss, 'Reading Like a Feminist', *Essentially Speaking: Feminism, Nature and Difference*

Stephen Heath, 'Male Feminism' in Alice Jardine and Paul Smith (eds), *Men in Feminism*

Safiya Henderson-Holmes, 'Rape, A Class Act', *Madness and a Bit of Hope*, also published in *Spare Rib*

Wolfgang Iser, *The Implied Reader: Patterns of Communication in Prose Fiction from Bunyan to Beckett*

Joan Larkin, 'Rape', *A Long Sound*, anthologized in Christine McEwen (ed.), *Naming the Waves: Contemporary Lesbian Poetry*

D.H. Lawrence, 'Tickets Please' in *England, My England*

Kate Millett, *Sexual Politics*

Martin Montgomery, Alan Durant, Nigel Fabb, Tom Furniss, Sara Mills, *Ways of Reading*

Adrienne Rich, 'When We Dead Awaken: Writing as Re-Vision' in *On Lies, Secrets, and Silence: Selected Prose 1966–1978*

Robert Scholes, 'Reading Like a Man' in Alice Jardine and Paul Smith (eds), *Men in Feminism*

Raman Selden, *Practising Theory and Reading Literature: An Introduction*

Elaine Showalter, 'Critical Cross-Dressing: Male Feminists and the Woman of the Year' in Alice Jardine and Paul Smith (eds), *Men in Feminism*

Alice Walker, 'Porn' and 'Advancing Luna and Ida B. Wells' both in *You Can't Keep a Good Woman Down*

Robyn R. Warhol and Diane Price Herndl (eds), *Feminisms: An Anthology of Literary Theory and Criticism*

The Yorkshire Evening Press, 'Girl Says Night Out Ended in Rape'

For further study on gender and reading, see:

Isobel Armstrong, 'Christina Rossetti: Diary of a Feminist Reading' in Sue Roe (ed.), *Women Reading Women's Writing*

Kate Flint, *The Woman Reader 1837–1914*

Elizabeth A. Flynn and Patrocinio P. Schweickart (eds), *Gender and Reading: Essays on Readers, Texts and Contexts*

Sara Mills (ed.), *Gendering the Reader*

Tania Modleski, 'Feminism and the Power of Interpretation: Some Critical Readings' in Teresa de Lauretis (ed.), *Feminist Studies/Critical Studies*

Susan Sellers, 'Learning to Read the Feminine' in Helen Wilcox, Keith McWatters, Ann Thompson, Linda R. Williams (eds), *The Body and the Text: Hélène Cixous, Reading and Teaching*

For specific study on lesbian reading, see:

Nicki Hastie, 'Lesbian BiblioMythography' in Gabriele Griffin (ed.) *Outwright: Lesbianism and Popular Culture*

Alison Hennigan, 'On Becoming a Lesbian Reader' in Susannah Radstone (ed.) *Sweet Dreams: Sexuality, Gender and Popular Fiction*

Jean E Kennard, 'Ourself behind Ourself: A Theory for Lesbian Readers' in Flynn and Schweickart (eds) *Gender and Reading: Essays on Readers, Texts and Contexts*

Feminist Criticisms

Introduction

You will notice the use of the plural in the title to this section. There is no single feminist criticism, rather an ever-growing practice of plural, though frequently interrelating, feminist criticisms. Thus, 'feminist criticism' should be seen as a collective term embracing many different critical perspectives. This situation is, to some extent, the produce of the historical span of feminist literary criticism. If we take Virginia Woolf as the starting point for contemporary feminist literary criticism (though many feminists before her have spoken about writing), then we are considering a history of, approximately, seventy years and within that period the production of the last twenty-five years has been intense. Feminism has also established links with other critical discourses; we can talk of Marxist-feminist criticism or psychoanalytic-feminist criticism or postcolonial-feminist criticism. These links have led to new ways of redefining feminism itself. Furthermore, white western feminism has begun, belatedly, to listen to the voices of feminists elsewhere in the world and the feminist communities unheard within western cultures and marginalized within feminism itself. The consequence is a network of different feminist criticisms, offering diverse contacts and dialogues, varying modes of interpretation – though with beliefs in common. All forms of feminist criticism will recognize the under-representation of women in published writing, will want to challenge that and will see in writing a space of both imaginative and political potential for women. In these ways the struggle around writing and representation is connected to other feminist struggles.

A point which I want to stress in this section is how in our writing and reading of feminist criticism we are at the same time constructing it and defining what constitutes feminist criticism. This is not an irrevocable process – the pattern is constantly changing and being reformed – but it is evident from surveys of feminist literary criticism that priority has been given to certain forms of feminist criticism and others have been underplayed or excluded. That process of selection and prioritizing needs careful examination since, even though it is a process rather than a rigid and doctrinaire imposition, it is not without inequalities. Because certain forms of feminism have more influence, more institutional space, greater access to publishing than others, hierarchies emerge within feminism itself.

I should like us to question three aspects of the issue:

• In what ways is feminist criticism being constructed and categorized? How is that mass of material systematized and organized?

- Processes of categorization, grouping, ordering material are in many ways helpful, but what are their problems and limits?

- What happens to a text if you read it through the filters of different feminist criticisms?

In investigating these questions it would be helpful to look at the collections and surveys of feminist criticism listed in the Introduction to this book since these texts are often a reader's first contact with feminist criticism. If you don't have access to the actual texts on a regular basis, try to get photocopies of the contents pages.

Post Political Cards No. 8 by Ray Lowry, Leeds Postcards

How is feminist criticism being constructed?

1 Collect together as many as you can of the introductions to feminist criticism listed in the Introduction to this book. Add any other introductions, surveys, Readers, collections of key essays which I haven't listed. Add also, if you wish, the feminist sections from general introductions to critical theory. What impression do you get of feminist criticism from this material? Here are some questions you could usefully ask:

➤ How is the material organized in each text – historically; on the basis of certain authors and/or essays; on the basis of important topics and issues; divided into different modes of feminist criticism etc.? What are the chapter/section headings?

➤ Do certain authors, essays, and topics recur? If so, who, which and with what kind of frequency? Is it possible to produce a 'top ten' or 'top five' of names, essays and topics that seem to appear everywhere?

➤ Do you notice any texts which are mentioning names, essays, topics that do not appear frequently and which seem to you to offer a different kind of input?

➤ In the texts which categorize feminist literary studies into different kinds of feminist criticism, which forms are mentioned? Again, do you find certain forms of feminist criticism featuring frequently, others less often?

➤ Can you see any patterns of historical change operating; that is, do names, forms of feminist criticism and issues feature in the later texts that don't feature in the earlier ones and, conversely, emphases in earlier texts that disappear in later ones?

➤ What is the geographical spread of these texts? Where are they published? Do you have any information as to their distribution? Where do the authors mentioned or included in these texts come from? Are they all from English-speaking countries? Are these texts open to feminist literary ideas from all parts of the world or certain parts? Do the texts recognize the range of cultural differences within a single country?

➤ Do the texts make clear how material was selected and the basis on which choices were made? If so, what aims, reasons and problems are discussed?

Having collected all this data –

➤ What conclusions do you come to? Is it possible to summarize the material or indicate major trends and demarcations? What seem to you the advantages and disadvantages in the ways feminist criticism has, so far, been constructed?

➤ How would you characterize the different kinds of feminist criticism you have encountered? Do you see similarities and dissimilarities? Do the varied forms of criticism approach literary texts or ideas in diverse ways or produce different interpretations?

If you have read little feminist criticism and are encountering these ideas for the first time you may well feel you don't have enough experience on which to draw to answer these questions. If that is so, keep these questions in mind as you learn and read more. Be aware that every text, this one included, has emphases and exclusions, particular ways of seeing things; nobody can simply 'tell it like it is'. Try to work out the determining factors in any feminist criticism: why does this idea gain currency but not that one; why is this feminist critic seen as so central; why has this particular critical approach become so popular etc.? In a sense one doesn't need to know all the answers. It is just as important to be conscious of the process at play.

Problems of categorization

Perhaps I am wrong to start here with the word 'problems' since, on the one hand, there is no escape from categorization – we can't inhabit a world of complete undifferentiation – and, on the other hand, categorization is extremely useful as a way of rendering more approachable and intelligible large amounts of varied and/or complex ideas. The introductions to feminist literary thought which you have considered have become popular precisely because readers, especially readers new to feminist criticism, find them helpful. However, as I have just suggested, no way of ordering or systematizing material is innocent and we need to look at some of the issues which I am sure will have been raised already in your own collecting of data. Firstly, the problem of geography.

2 Between 1987 and 1993 the publishers of this volume, Blackwell, produced a series of texts on feminist thought generally, not only feminist *literary* thought, which took nationality as its organizing principal:

1987   *French Feminist Thought: A Reader* (ed.) Toril Moi

1990   *British Feminist Thought: A Reader* (ed.) Terry Lovell

1991   *Italian Feminist Thought: A Reader* (eds) Paolo Bono and Sandra Kemp

1993   *American Feminist Thought at Century's End: A Reader* (ed.)
       Linda S. Kauffman.

Terry Lovell begins her Introduction to *British Feminist Thought: A Reader* in the following way:

NATIONAL FEMINISMS

As woman, I have no country. As a woman I want no country. As a woman my country is the whole world.

Virginia Woolf, Three Guineas

What are we doing, then, in constructing 'national feminisms'? The problem presents itself with particular force when it is British feminism which is in question. The term 'British' carries such a heavy weight of accumulated meaning, generated over the long history of internal and external imperialisms, that it inevitably serves as a negative reference point in left thought. Black feminists, already smarting under the affront of a white middle–class movement which has systematically disregarded the situation and circumstances of black women might well feel that the national label merely compounds the injury. Feminists in the north of Ireland have additional and equally compelling reasons for rejecting it. 'English' on the other hand is too exclusive, unless we use it to refer to language users, in which case it encompasses too much. National labels being so problematic, then, why not discard them, in favour of alternative lines of intellectual demarcation within Woolf's international community of women?

➤ How would you respond to Lovell's question? Do you find national feminisms problematic in the ways she does; do you have additional reservations? What do you think are the issues that might arise concerning the other national feminism indicated above – French, Italian, American? Is Woolf's internationalism less problematic, more feminist? How would one produce a genuinely international introduction to feminist criticism?

➤ On the other hand, is it possible to present a case in favour of structuring feminism in terms of nationality?

Lovell goes on to answer her own question:

The denial of national differences carries difficulties of its own.
International movements such as feminism and socialism develop along
significantly differentiated lines which can be related to specific historical,
political and intellectual contexts. Black feminist thought in Britain arises
from and addresses a different history and a different situation than does
black feminist thought in America. Moreover there is a danger of slipping
into patronizing postures: 'we' (first-world, white, middle-class feminists)
may create for ourselves an 'imaginary' international community that knows
no territorial boundaries; 'you' (third-world, black feminists) may be
conceded your more parochial national imaginings, only provided that they
are of a progressive nature ... Moreover, the very tone and terms of Woolf's
discourse undermine her internationalist claims. They are instantly recognizable in terms of class, place, and historical time.

Terry Lovell, *British Feminist Thought: A Reader* (1990) pp. 3–4

3 With the publication of *Italian Feminist Thought: A Reader*, Bono and Kemp
raise further issues about national feminisms:

In her recent book *Subject to Change*, Nancy Miller highlights a general
current recognition of the need for 'a more international geo-graphics in
feminist writing' (N. Miller 1988: 17). She argues that 'as feminist critics
we do ourselves in by playing the old Franco-American game of binary
oppositions (theory and empiricism, indifference and identify) as though it
were the only game in town ... as though there weren't also Italians, for
instance'. Her example, as she herself remarks, is arbitrary – 'Italians'
because here the reference is to Teresa de Lauretis and Rosi Braidotti,
influential Italian-born theorists who live and work outside Italy. But what
of Canadians, Spaniards, Germans, Asians?

Paolo Bono and Sandra Kemp (eds), *Italian Feminist Thought: A Reader* (1991) p. 1

➤ Bono and Kemp mention some 'missing' feminisms – Canadian, Spanish,
German, Asian. Look back at the data you collected in researching introductions to feminist criticism. From which countries was the material coming? Are
there 'missing' feminisms you would like to know more about? Why is French
feminist thought and Italian feminist thought translated for the English-
speaking market but not other feminisms? Even within English-speaking
feminism, where are the Canadians, as Bono and Kemp ask; the Australians too
are not represented in great numbers.

➤ The quotation from Nancy Miller in Bono and Kemp speaks of a 'Franco-
American game of binary oppositions'. Miller refers here to the way in which
literary feminism has been conceptualized in recent years as a dialogue (indeed,
often as something much more static and antagonistic than a dialogue) between
American feminist thought and French feminist thought. Did you find
evidence of this in the introductions you considered? Did you find evidence
that the opposition is being questioned?

➤ Frequently, this opposition between French and American feminisms is
referred to as an opposition between French and *Anglo*-American feminist
thought. What is the significance of the 'Anglo' element? Is there, in Lovell's

term, something 'distinctive' in British feminist thought; does that distinctiveness feature in the introductions? Is the work of British critics discussed in
this construction of French/Anglo-American?

To research further debates on how French and Anglo-American feminisms
have been constructed in opposition, see Rachel Bowlby in 'References and
further reading'. You could also relate this discussion on feminism and
nationalism to material in the section on the Politics of Location.

➤ We need to remember that there is a difference between the nationality of the
critic and the 'nationality' of the critical ideas. Obviously no idea 'belongs' to a
country but ideas can be linked with particular historical and cultural traditions
and be developed within specific geographical contexts. Did you get a sense in
your research of cross-connections between different cultures?

➤ We have considered here some of the problems of organizing feminist literary
thought within national categories. Would any of the other methods of
structuring material that we noted – by author, by key essays, by topics, by
particular forms of feminist criticism, through history – be more successful?
Select one of these methods and consider the pros and cons. Or choose one or
two of the introductions to feminist criticism with which you have been
working and review it in terms of its selection and organisation of material.

4 Do we come to the conclusion that *any* method of organizing and systematizing
material brings with it its own set of problems? For instance, Chela Sandoval,
considering the work of American, predominantly white, feminism from the
perspective of a 'U.S. third world feminist' comments:

> During the 1980s, hegemonic feminist scholars produced the histories of
> feminist consciousness which they believed to typify the modes of exchange
> operating within the oppositional spaces of the women's movement. These
> feminist histories of consciousness are often presented as typologies, systematic
> classifications of all possible forms of feminist praxis. These constructed
> typologies have fast become the official stories by which the white women's
> movement understands itself and its interventions in history. In what follows I
> decode these stories and their relation to one another from the perspective of
> U.S. third world feminism, where they are revealed as sets of imaginary
> spaces, socially constructed to severely delimit what is possible within the
> boundaries of their separate narratives. Together they legitimize certain modes
> of culture and consciousness only to systematically curtail the forms of experi-
> ential and theoretical articulations permitted U.S. third world feminism.

> Chela Sandoval, 'U.S. Third World Feminism: The Theory and Method of Oppositional
> Consciousness in the Postmodern World' (Spring, 1991) pp. 5–6

Donna Haraway, discussing the work of both Sandoval and Katie King, makes a
similar point:

> King criticizes the persistent tendency among contemporary feminists from
> different 'moments' or 'conversations' in feminist practice to taxonomize the
> women's movement to make one's own political tendencies appear to be the
> telos of the whole. These taxonomies tend to remake feminist history to
> appear to be an ideological struggle among coherent types persisting over time,
> especially those typical units called radical, liberal, and socialist feminism.

Literally, all other feminisms are either incorporated or marginalized, usually
by building on explicit ontology and epistomology. Taxonomies of feminism
produce epistemologies to police deviation form official women's experience.

Donna Haraway, 'A Manifesto for Cyborgs: Science, Technology
and Socialist Feminism in the 1980s' (1985; 1989) p. 181

Paradoxically, both these passages are talking about exclusions from feminism in a
style which itself excludes all but a limited set of readers. However, the points
made are important so try to clarify them. Sandoval complains about 'the official
stories by which the white woman's movement knows itself' as they are stories
which have little or no place for other feminist interventions. Isn't that a
legitimate criticism of what I wrote in the first paragraph of this section? My
feminist literary history starts with Woolf, a white, upper-middle-class English
woman, situates literary feminism amidst a range of *academic* discourses and
mentions third world feminisms only in relation to the dominant mode of white,
western feminism. This was not a ploy on my part; I had not deliberately 'set up'
the first paragraph with the intention of deconstructing it later in this section. It
was not until *after* I had written that paragraph and was re-reading the Sandoval
essay to choose an appropriate quotation that I realized that I had, yet again,
slipped into the old narratives, the old hierarchies.

➤ Once more, return to your own data. Do you see feminism as producing a
rather rigid system of classification from which many perspectives are
excluded? Are certain texts more open and inclusive in content and approach?

➤ Haraway talks of the division between 'radical, liberal, and socialist feminist'.
Do you find this mode of classification operating in the introductions you are
considering? Do you find other modes of classification at work?

➤ Sandoval mentions a number of feminist literary critics in her essay – Elaine
Showalter, Toril Moi, Alice Jardine, Gayle Greene, Coppélia Kahn, Cora Kaplan,
Judith Kegan Gardiner. Despite their differences, Sandoval affirms 'that this
comprehension of feminist consciousness is hegemonically unified, framed, and
buttressed with the result that the expression of a unique form of U.S. third
world feminism, active over the last thirty years, has become invisible outside of
its all-knowing logic' (p. 9). As a longer-term project, begin to familiarize yourself
with the work of one or two of these critics as they appear in the introductions to
feminist criticism and in their own writings. Is Sandoval's point proven – that
U.S. third world feminism is 'invisible' within the work of these major critics?

➤ How can we relate these comments to the British context or to other national
contexts in which you are interested? For example, return to Lovell's *British
Feminist Thought: A Reader* and to the introductions to feminist literary
thought produced in this country. Can one see specifically *British* exclusions
operating? As we noted earlier, in Lovell's introduction, Black feminism in
Britain developed in different circumstances from Black American feminism.
Why, then, do the introductions to feminist literary criticism produced in
Britain focus more on Afra–American feminist writing than on Black British
feminist writing? Are there other anomalies you can notice?

5 How should we respond to the problem of exclusion within feminism? Could
feminism aim to become all-embracing, open to diversity? Consider this passage from
Judith Butler. She is talking here about identity but I think the comment is equally

relevant if we relate it to our focus, the construction of feminist literary criticism:

> The theories of feminist identify that elaborate predicates of color, sexuality, ethnicity, class, and able-bodiedness invariably close with an embarrassed 'etc.' at the end of the list. Through this horizontal trajectory of adjectives, these positions strive to encompass a situated subject, but invariably fail to be complete. This failure, however, is instructive: what political impetus is to be derived from the exasperated 'etc.' that so often occurs at the end of such lines? This is a sign of exhaustion as well as of the illimitable process of signification itself. It is the *supplément*, the excess that necessarily accompanies any effort to posit identity once and for all.
>
> Judith Butler, *Gender Trouble: Feminism and the Subversion of Identity* (1990) p. 143

Butler's point is that there is always an *et cetera*, indeed, always many *et ceteras*: all-inclusiveness escapes us.

Cartoon by Angela Martin

As this poem from Marsha Prescod indicates, the problem is not only one of inclusion or exclusion but of the very categories themselves:

> For us to be free
> we have to know we
> don't let anyone 'ethnicize' us,
> into them marginal categories.
>
> Our positive self cannot be,
> through negative definition,
> saying, 'Well, we're not them'
> to work out own position.
>
> Don't look to *his*-tory,
> to discover our existence.
> Don't hide in another's ideasology,
> to develop our own resistance.

> For us to be free,
> *we* have to know we.
> Our own truth
> our own strength,
> And our
>
> black,
> black,
> black,
> *black*
>
> creativity!

Marsha Prescod, 'Untitled' in Ngcobo (1988) pp. 119–20

Who does the defining, the nature and status of the definitions, the discourses within which the definitions are formulated are all shown by Prescod to be issues of power and subordination. Prescod's final reference to 'creativity' indicates how this power struggle over naming and specifying has relevance also for literature, representation and literary criticism.

6 What is to be done? Aware of all these difficulties we still have to tell our history; we still have to make sense of the material which is produced, understand it and, hence, form it in some respects. What is the most just, the most feminist and the most flexible way of doing this?

➤ Imagine you are writing an introduction to feminist literary criticism for a sixth-form group or as a seminar paper, or imagine you are about to teach a course introducing feminist literary thought. How would you tell the story? What would you want to include? How would you organize your material? On what basis would you make your selection as to what to put in and what to leave out? What guidelines would you give to your readers/students? How would you answer the inevitable and justifiable complaints about omitting significant perspectives?

Different feminist readings

7 In *A Reader's Guide to Contemporary Feminist Literary Criticism*, Maggie Humm organizes her survey, partly, historically – the 'Introduction' reviews feminist criticism from the 1960s to the 1990s and the final chapter is entitled 'Feminist Futures' – and, partly, in terms of different modes of feminist criticism. Her classification and chapter headings are as follows:

1 Second wave: de Beauvoir, Millett, Friedan, Greer

2 Myth criticism

3 Marxist/socialist-feminist criticism

4 French feminist criticism

5 Psychoanalytic criticism

6 Poststructuralism/deconstruction/postmodernism

7 Black feminism: the African diaspora

Maggie Humm, *A Reader's Guide to Contemporary Feminist Literary Criticism* (1994) pp. v–vii

As we have already seen, the ways in which feminist criticism is divided and named and the priority given to different feminist perspectives is highly disputed. However, I am listing Humm's categories here merely to illustrate my first point in this section, namely the variety of literary feminisms that have emerged. From your own studies you may be able to add others to this list.

These multiple critical perspectives have provided feminists with numerous ways of reading texts and one of the interests of feminist criticism is to see how different critical modes may illuminate disparate aspects of a text or produce a number of readings of one particular aspect. But the situation is not always one of happy pluralism. Sometimes one feminist perspective may be seriously at odds with another: it may spring from a markedly different political conviction or expose political inadequacies in an earlier commentary.

To help you research this area, here is some suggested reading:

- Gill Frith, 'Women, Writing and Language: Making the Silences Speak' (1993). In this essay Frith considers Charlotte Brontë's *Jane Eyre* in the context of a number of feminist approaches – the experiential, gynocriticism, feminist genre studies, plus many of those listed by Humm.

- Mary Jacobus, 'An Unnecessary Maze of Sign-Reading' (1986). Jacobus's psychoanalytic reading of Charlotte Perkins Gilman's 'The Yellow Wallpaper' begins by taking issue with two earlier feminist interpretations.

- Sara Mills, Lynne Pearce, Sue Spaull, Elaine Millard, *Feminist Readings/ Feminists Reading* (1989). Several texts – Emily Brontë's *Wuthering Heights*, Alice Walker's *The Color Purple*, Margaret Atwood's *Surfacing*, Angela Carter's *The Magic Toyshop* – are discussed with reference to different feminist critiques.

- Su Reid, *The Critics Debate: To The Lighthouse* (1991). Reid provides a number of feminist interpretations of Woolf's novel.

- Gayatri Chakravorty Spivak, 'Three Women's Texts and a Critique of Imperialism' (1985). Spivak's analysis of *Jane Eyre* strongly critiques the implicit imperialism of earlier feminist readings.

You could collect a variety of feminist critical readings of some favourite text of your own, compare the readings and think how different readings produce, in a sense, different texts.

References and further reading

Paola Bono and Sandra Kemp (eds), *Italian Feminist Thought: A Reader*

Rachel Bowlby, *Still Crazy After All These Years: Women, Writing and Psychoanalysis*

Judith Butler, *Gender Trouble: Feminism and the Subversion of Identity*

Mary Eagleton, 'Who's Who and Where's Where: Constructing Feminist Literary Studies'

Gill Frith, 'Women, Writing and Language: Making the Silences Speak' in Diane Richardson and Victoria Robinson (eds), *Introducing Women's Studies: Feminist Theory and Practice*

Jane Gallop, *Around 1981: Academic Feminist Literary Theory*. Gallop examines some of the key texts of American literary feminism.

Donna Haraway, 'A Manifesto for Cyborgs: Science, Technology and Socialist Feminism in the 1980s' in Elizabeth Weed (ed.), *Coming to Terms: Feminism, Theory, Politics*. The essay is available also in Linda J. Nicholson (ed.), *Feminism/Postmodernism*.

Maggie Humm, *A Reader's Guide to Contemporary Feminist Literary Criticism*

Maggie Humm, *Practising Feminist Criticism: An Introduction*. Humm's companion volume to *A Reader's Guide to Contemporary Feminist Literary Criticism* uses the same categories and applies them to a variety of imaginative texts but doesn't look at a single text through different perspectives.

Mary Jacobus, 'An Unnecessary Maze of Sign-Reading', *Reading Woman: Essays in Feminist Criticism*

Linda S. Kauffman (ed.) *American Feminist Thought at Century's End: A Reader*

Katie King, *Theory in Its Feminist Travels: Conversations in U.S. Women's Movements*. Haraway refers to King's work in the extract included in this section.

Terry Lovell (ed.), *British Feminist Thought: A Reader*

Sara Mills, Lynne Pearce, Sue Spaull, Elaine Millard, *Feminist Readings/Feminists Reading*

Chandra Talpade Mohanty, 'Under Western Eyes: Feminist Scholarship and Colonial Discourses' in Mohanty, Ann Russo, Lourdes Torres (eds), *Third World Women and the Politics of Feminism*. Like Sandoval, Mohanty discusses how the third world woman and third world feminism has been constituted by Western feminism.

Toril Moi (ed.), *French Feminist Thought: A Reader*

Marsha Prescod, 'Untitled', *Land of Rope and Tory*, and anthologized in Ngcobo (ed.), *Let It Be Told: Black Women Writers in Britain*

Sue Reid, *The Critics Debate: To The Lighthouse*

Chela Sandoval, 'U.S. third World Feminism: The Theory and Method of Oppositional Consciousness in the Postmordern World'

Gayatri Chakravorty Spivak, 'Three Women's Texts and a Critique of Imperialism' in Henry Louis Gates, Jr. (ed.) *'Race,' Writing, and Difference*

Tulsa Studies in Women's Literature vol. 12, no. 2 (Fall 1993). The focus of this volume is the question 'Is There an Anglo-American Feminist Criticism?'

═══*Patriarchal Binary Thought*═══

Introduction

In recent years contemporary theory has explored the concept of binary thinking, that is the predilection in our culture to construct the world in terms of oppositions – good/evil, individual/society, knowledge/ignorance etc. As Hélène Cixous (pronounced 'Six-oo') writes, 'Thought has always worked through opposition' (p. 63). How these oppositions are constructed, the meanings they contain, what is revealed or hidden by such oppositions, how to separate these couples are important considerations. In literary circles discussions about canonical versus non-canonical texts, high culture versus popular culture, the imaginative versus the theoretical are all examples of debates related to binary thinking. The literary critic will also look at the binary oppositions operating within a text – sometimes consciously employed by the author, sometimes not. These oppositions may both structure the text and be integral to its ideological concerns. Feminists have found this subject relevant because of their belief that binary thinking upholds patriarchy: thus feminists have a vested interest in understanding and dismantling the processes of binary thought.

This section explores three aspects:

- It looks at the views on binary thinking of French theorist, Hélène Cixous and explores her ideas by applying them to a passage from the nineteenth-century essayist and art critic, John Ruskin.

- It takes up Cixous's assertion that feminists should challenge patriarchal binary thought and considers how that might be done through the practice of deconstructive criticism.

- Finally, Elma Mitchell's poetic response to Ruskin is discussed in the context of deconstructing binary oppositions.

The main location for Cixous's views on patriarchal binary thought is her essay, 'Sorties: Out and Out: Attacks/Ways Out/Forays' which is in a book jointly written with Catherine Clément called *The Newly Born Woman* (1975; 1986). References in this section to the essay are from this text. Extracts from her essay can also be found in Elaine Marks and Isabelle de Courtivron (eds), *New French Feminisms: An Anthology (1981)* and Catherine Belsey and Jane Moore (eds), *The Feminist Reader: Essays in Gender and the Politics of Literary Criticism (1989)*.

In the synopsis of Cixous's ideas from Toril Moi, below, the references are from the original French version, *La Jeune Née* (1975); for your convenience I have included, after the French, the page references to the English translation.

Cixous and Ruskin

1 Cixous's comments on patriarchal binary thought are summarized here by the critic Toril Moi:

> One of Cixous's most accessible ideas is her analysis of what one might call 'patriarchal binary thought'. Under the heading 'Where is she?', Cixous lines up the following list of binary oppositions:
>
> > Activity/Passivity
> >
> > Sun/Moon
> >
> > Culture/Nature
> >
> > Day/Night
> >
> > Father/Mother
> >
> > Head/Emotions
> >
> > Intelligible/Sensitive
> >
> > Logos/Pathos
>
> (*JN*, 115/*NBW*, 63)
>
> Corresponding as they do to the underlying opposition man/woman, these binary oppositions are heavily imbricated in the patriarchal value system: each opposition can be analysed as a hierarchy where the 'feminine' side is always seen as the negative, powerless instance. For Cixous, who at this point is heavily indebted to Jacques Derrida's work, Western philosophy and literary thought are and have always been caught up in this endless series of hierarchical binary oppositions that always in the end come back to the fundamental 'couple' of male/female.
>
> > Nature/History
> >
> > Nature/Art
> >
> > Nature/Mind
> >
> > Passion/Action
>
> (*JN*, 116/*NBW*, 64)
>
> These examples show that it doesn't much matter which 'couple' one chooses to highlight: the hidden male/female opposition with its inevitable positive/negative evaluation can always be traced as the underlying paradigm.
>
> In a typical move, Cixous then goes on to locate *death* at work in this kind of thought. For one of the terms to acquire meaning, she claims, it must destroy the other. The 'couple' cannot be left intact: it becomes a general battlefield where the struggle for signifying supremacy is forever re-enacted. In the end, victory is equated with activity and defeat with passivity; under patriarchy, the male is always the victor. Cixous passionately denounces such an equation of femininity with passivity and death as

147

leaving no positive space for women: 'Either woman is passive or she doesn't exist' (*JN*, 118/*NBW*, 64). Her whole theoretical project can in one sense be summed up as the effort to undo this logocentric ideology: to proclaim woman as the source of life, power and energy and to hail the advent of a new, feminine language that ceaselessly subverts these patriarchal binary schemes where logocentrism colludes with phallocentrism in an effort to oppress and silence women.

Toril Moi, Sexual/Textual Politics: Feminist Literary Theory (1985) pp. 104–5

The opposition intelligible/sensitive, sometimes translated as intelligible/palpable, isn't very comprehensible in English. What Cixous is getting at here is the opposition between an intellectual, rational mode on the one hand and the order of feeling and senses on the other. So it approximates the previous opposition, head/emotions, sometimes translated as head/heart, and it is reminiscent of Jane Austen's opposition of sense/sensibility, though one always has to be cautious about making too ready comparisons with different historical periods or cultural contexts.

Can you list the key points from this passage to ensure that they are clear. For example:

- Cixous sees our processes of thinking as fundamentally binary.

- For Cixous the basic opposition is male/female.

- Binary opposition supports patriarchal values

-

-

-

You might like to pool your list with someone else's or annotate it when you have sorted out the points. With which ideas do you agree; which need further clarification; for which could you offer an illustrative example?

2 Why does Cixous maintain that the *basic* couple is man/woman? Could class or race or sexuality be as fundamental a determinant?

➤ Using the oppositions Black/white, middle-class/working-class, heterosexual/gay as your headings, construct lists of appropriate binary oppositions which are widely accepted in our culture.

➤ Is a hierarchy operating in these oppositions also?

➤ Are there notable similarities and differences between the different listings? For example, is the subordinate term always seen as more problematic or less acceptable than the dominant?

➤ Is Cixous right to emphasize a masculine/feminine dichotomy? Would you put the emphasis elsewhere? For example, you might like to read some of the essays of Monique Wittig which indicate to me that the couple, straight/gay is equally fundamental to dominant modes of binary thought.

3 The following passage from one of John Ruskin's essays makes deliberate use of

binary oppositions as a way of structuring the roles of men and women. The crucial distinction to stress here is that Ruskin is offering this model as an ideal of social harmony; Cixous, we remember, characterizes such an arrangement as 'death':

> Now their separate characters are briefly these. The man's power is active, progressive, defensive. He is eminently the doer, the creator, the discoverer, the defender. His intellect is for speculation and invention; his energy is for adventure, for war, and for conquest, wherever war is just, wherever conquest necessary. But the woman's power is for rule, not for battle, – and her intellect is not for invention or creation, but for sweet ordering, arrangement, and decision. She sees the qualities of things, their claims, and their places. Her great function is Praise: she enters into no contest, but infallibly adjudges the crown of contest. By her office, and place, she is protected from all danger and temptation. The man, in his rough work in open world, must encounter all peril and trial: – to him, therefore, the failure, the offence, the inevitable error: often he must be wounded, or subdued, often misled, and always hardened. But he guards the woman from all this; within his house, as ruled by her, unless she herself has sought it, need enter no danger, no temptation, no cause of error or offence. This is the true nature of home – it is the place of Peace: the shelter, not only from all injury, but from all terror, doubt, and division.
>
> John Ruskin, 'Of Queens' Gardens' (1864; 1907) p. 59

➤ List the binary oppositions operating in this passage. For instance, Cixous's opposition 'activity/passivity' is clearly there at the start of the Ruskin passage.

➤ What views of man and woman are thus constructed by Ruskin? Consider the intellectual differences he posits between men and women, issues of spirituality, geographical scope, spheres of influence etc.

➤ Can you think of other texts or cultural debates which follow Ruskin's system of gender values or which dispute it? If you know any nineteenth-century novels they may well furnish examples. Do Ruskin's oppositions still have currency in our own time? What evidence can you find in newspaper/magazine articles, TV programmes, general conversation that some/all of Ruskin's views are still with us? It strikes me, as one example, that in recent discussions about 'family values', many right-wing comments on the role of the family, the mother, the home, have a distinctly Ruskinesque ring about them.

➤ Though Cixous makes no reference to Ruskin, the situations she poses as problems are very similar to the ones he advocates as socially desirable. For example, in what ways could you see this passage from Cixous as a response to the one we have just considered from Ruskin?

> Woman's voyage: as a *body*. As if she were destined – in the distribution established by men (separated from the world where cultural exchanges are made and kept in the wings of the social stage when it is a case of History) – to be the nonsocial, nonpolitical, nonhuman half of the living structure. On nature's side of this structure, of course, tirelessly listening to what goes on inside – inside her belly, inside her 'house'. In direct contact with her appetites, her affects.
>
> And, whereas he takes (after a fashion) the risk and responsibility of

being an agent, a bit of the public scene where transformations are played out, she represents indifference or resistance to this active tempo; she is the principle of consistency, always somehow the same, everyday and eternal.

Hélène Cixous, 'Sorties: Out and Out: Attacks/Ways Out/Forays' (1975; 1986) pp. 66–7

4 Ostensibly, Ruskin's claim is that gender opposition is equal and complementary: man and woman have separate roles which interlock to make an harmonious whole, a kind of gender apartheid. Cixous's belief is that the opposition is hierarchical and that, as Moi comments, 'the "feminine" side is always seen as the negative, powerless instance'.

➤ Look again at the list of Ruskin oppositions you drew up. Has he constructed a set of complementary pairings or has he constructed a hierarchy? If you think it is a hierarchy, do you agree with Cixous that the masculine side is always privileged?

➤ Do you find yourself identifying with some of Ruskin's subordinated terms and, in a sense, reversing the hierarchy? For example, you might feel that the domestic space he associates with women is just as important or more important than the public space he associates with men. What other examples need consideration?

➤ Are there points where your preferences are at odds with what you believe to be the dominant view in our culture? Thus, *you* could value the home but you feel that generally in our culture more emphasis is given to the work-place.

It might help to tabulate the above material so you can see more easily the points of agreement and disagreement:

Ruskin's opposition	Contemporary view	Personal view
active = male passive = female public = male domestic = female etc.		

5 Later in her essay, 'Sorties', Cixous discusses some of the other binary oppositions she has felt operating in her own life. As a French Algerian Jew, experiencing on a daily basis, colonialism and anti-Semitism, she remembers:

So I am three or four years old and the first thing I see in the street is that the world is divided in half, organized hierarchically, and that it maintains this distribution through violence.

Hélène Cixous, 'Sorties: Out and Out: Attacks/Ways Out/Forays' (1975; 1986) p. 70

In a television interview, Cixous comments:

I was born in Algeria and at a very early age I experienced racism, exclusion, colonialism, etc. When I was jut three or four years old I was already aware of it because I lived it daily in the streets. But it was a complex situation because although I was supposed to be French, I was not French. I was born in Algeria but my father was a Jew of Spanish origin and my mother had fled Hitler, just in time: she was a German Jew. So I had no tie with France at all but we were considered historically French. We had French nationality, although we nearly lost it because of Vichy. So I saw how the French colonial settlers lived in Algeria, behaving as if Algeria belonged to them and treating the Arab population as if they were non-existent. It was taken to be quite normal that they had absolutely no rights at all. I couldn't bear this. I felt it very strongly, as did my family. But on the other hand, I was a Jew and the Arabs at that time were extremely anti-Semitic and I experienced their anti-Semitism daily. I was called a Jew the moment I came out of the house, I had stones thrown at me. Yet at the same time, it was such a complex political situation, I know that I had no hatred towards the Arabs because I felt with them. But I could not identify with them.

So I discovered that racism is general. You're hated and in turn you hate someone else. It's like a chain. So as far as going through the French education system is concerned, it wasn't something that I deliberately formulated, but I wanted to live with books, because books had saved me during my childhood. In a hellish political and ethical climate, I escaped through books ... But when I arrived in France, as soon as I set foot in the university I went away again because I realized immediately that it was just the same system but with different data. I wasn't a Jew any more, I wasn't called a Jew and wasn't spat on as a Jew, but instead as a woman. But I didn't want to give up books just because university professors were just as rotten as French colonialists. So I kept the books, threw away the professors, and worked on my own.

From a series of Channel 4 interviews, *Talking Liberties* (1992) p. 30

➤ Which binary oppositions is Cixous discussing here?

France/Algeria

colonizer/colonized (*Continue the list*)

➤ What has been your experience of the functioning of binary oppositions in your own life? Can you think back and reinterpret your childhood, as Cixous does? You could discuss or write an account of an incident or a relationship, from the past or the present, which you want to examine in the light of an understanding of binary oppositions.

6 Returning to Moi's summary of Cixous, what response do you now want to make to Cixous's major claims?

	Agree	Disagree	Debatable
Our thought is structured by binary oppositions.			
The fundamental pairing is male/female.			
There is an on-going battle between the two sides.			
The battle is one of meaning and interpretation.			
The battle is also a power struggle.			
In a patriarchal culture, the masculine side is dominant.			
Femininity must dislodge the patriarchal structure.			

The grid allows only a brief response. You might want to think out more fully some of these points, particularly those you find debatable.

Challenges to patriarchal binary thought: deconstructive criticism

7 Here are some descriptions of deconstructive practice:

> Such a reading [a deconstructive reading] begins by noting the hierarchy, proceeds to reverse it, and finally resists the assertion of a new hierarchy by displacing the second term from a position of superiority too ... A deconstructive reading would go on to recognize that the couplet cannot be hierarchised in either direction without 'violence' ... Deconstruction can begin when we locate the moment when a text transgresses the laws it appears to set up for itself. At this point texts go to pieces, so to speak.
>
> Raman Selden, *A Reader's Guide to Contemporary Literary Theory* (1989) p. 90

> A deconstructive reading tries to bring out the logic of the text's language as opposed to the logic of the author's claims. It will tease out the text's implied presuppositions and point out the (inevitable) contradictions in them.
>
> Ann Jefferson and David Robey (eds), *Modern Literary Theory: A Comparative Introduction* (1986) p. 118

> It [deconstructive criticism] proceeds by the careful teasing out of the warring forces of signification within the text itself.
>
> Barbara Johnson's Introduction to Jacques Derrida, *Dissemination* (1972; 1981)

> The aim is to locate the point of contradiction within the text, the point at which it transgresses the limits within which it is constructed, breaks free

of the constraints imposed by its own realist form. Composed of contradictions, the text is no longer restricted to a single, harmonious and authoritative reading. Instead it becomes plural, open to re-reading, no longer an object for passive consumption, but an object of work by the reader to produce meaning.

Catherine Belsey, Critical Practice (1980) p. 104

We can draw some conclusions from these quotes:

- It would seem from Selden's quote that deconstruction would find reversing the hierarchy – for example, valuing the personal and the domestic cover the public – insufficient. Such a reversal is still locked in to binary thinking. Deconstruction, on the other hand, involves itself in an endless dismantling of hierarchies.

- The term 'contradictions' is mentioned twice and Johnson talks of 'warring forces'. The text does not compose a unified entity. Whereas some forms of criticism would see these textual contradictions as 'faults' or examples of a loss of control by the author, deconstruction would see these moments as points of greatest interest, avenues of access for the reader.

- In deconstructive criticism, the pattern of binary oppositions (consciously and/or unconsciously formulated) can be dismantled in the act of reading. We see in the quotes the interest in the concept of 'transgression', when the text, in a sense, evades the structure designed for it.

- You might want to refer to the related section, The Death of the Woman Author? and to other sections concerned with reading. Deconstruction is part of that critical school which seeks to remove power from the author and invest it in the reader. Belsey, in her quote above, particularly stresses the idea of the active reader.

Let's relate this deconstructive process to examples from Cixous and Ruskin. The first example concerns national identity; the second class difference.

8 Cixous indicates how in each binary opposition the 'inferior' term functions to maintain and support the 'superior' term:

> There has to be some 'other – no master without a slave, no economico-political power without exploitation, no dominant class without cattle under the yoke, no 'Frenchmen' without wogs, no Nazis without Jews, no property without exclusion – an exclusion that has its limits and is part of the dialectic. If there were no other, one would invent it. Besides, that is what masters do: they have their slaves made to order. Line for line. They assemble the machine and keep the alternator supplied so that it produces all the oppositions that make economy and thought run.

Cixous aims to unlock these hierarchical couples. For instance, having acknowledged the oppressive force of colonial power (France versus Algeria) and anti-Semitism (Arab versus Jew), she then speaks of her national identity in the following terms:

But I was born in Algeria, and my ancestors lived in Spain, Morocco, Austria, Hungary, Czechoslovakia, Germany; my brothers by birth are Arab. So where are we in history? I side with those who are injured, trespassed upon colonized. I am (not) Arab. Who am I? I am 'doing' French history. I am a Jewish woman. In which ghetto was I penned up during your wars and your revolutions? I want to fight. What is my name? I want to change life. Who is this 'I'? Where is my place? I am looking. I search everywhere. I read, I ask. I begin to speak. Which language is mine? French? German? Arabic?

Hélène Cixous, 'Sorties: Out and Out: Attacks/Ways Out/Forays' (1986) p. 71

Cixous's aim here is not to establish binary oppositions, 'x' versus 'y', but to create a 'feminine' practice of open and proliferating meaning. So nationality cannot be pinned down to one single identity – she is French; I am English – but becomes a more complex and fluctuating state.

➤ In what ways does this passage resist binary definitions?

➤ Why are so many sentences in the form of questions?

➤ What do you think is meant by the sentence, 'I am (not) Arab'?

➤ How can one be both on the side of the oppressed against the exploiters *and* dismantling binary oppositions?

➤ Again, can you try to apply Cixous's approach to an aspect of your own biography? You do not have to consider issues of national identity. You might prefer to explore your own complex experience of an aspect of class, race, ethnicity, sexual identity, gender, religious difference ...

9 A second example of deconstructive practice relates to the passage from Ruskin. What happens to Ruskin's neat oppositions when we introduce, alongside gender difference, class difference? Thus, according to Ruskin:

middle–class male = public sphere

middle–class female = private sphere

but where do we place the working–class female? Is she a guardian of the private sphere, or a worker in the public sphere, or both? If she is a worker in the public sphere, how can she ensure, as Ruskin suggests, the separate sanctity of her home? Is the sanctity of the middle–class home maintained, in part, on the basis of working–class, female labour? After all, during the period in which Ruskin is writing, it is the working–class woman who carries coal from the cellar to the top bedrooms while the middle–class woman in the drawing-room provides solace for the middle–class man. Or is the working–class woman a threat to the middle–class home, contaminating it with a corrupting public world? For example, bourgeois and patriarchal ideology of the period would tell us that middle–class men were sometimes led astray by scheming working–class women who duped them within their own homes.

As Selden remarks, 'At this point texts go to pieces, so to speak.' It is no longer possible to maintain the clear oppositions with which we started or even to reverse those oppositions; it has all become much more involved.

Following the above example, try to tease out some of the ambiguities in one or two of the other major oppositions you may have noted in Ruskin. For example:

public violence v. private pacifism

male promiscuity v. female purity, etc.

Elma Mitchell's 'Thoughts After Ruskin'

10 Though Ruskin's oppositions are still recognizable in our culture, other views on the meaning and relationship of man and woman are also now available. Consider Elma Mitchell's reply to Ruskin:

> Women reminded him of lilies and roses.
> Me they remind rather of blood and soap,
> Armed with a warm rag, assaulting noses,
> Ears, neck, mouth and all the secret places.
>
> Armed with a sharp knife, cutting up liver,
> Holding hearts to bleed under a running tap,
> Gutting and stuffing, pickling and preserving,
> Scalding, blanching, broiling, pulverising,
> – All the terrible chemistry of their kitchens.
>
> Their distant husbands lean across mahogany
> And delicately manipulate the market,
> While safe at home, the tender and the gentle
> Are killing tiny mice, dead snap by the neck,
> Asphyxiating flies, evicting spiders,
> Scrubbing, scouring aloud, disturbing cupboards,
> Committing things to dustbins, twisting, wringing,
> Wrists red and knuckles white and fingers puckered,
> Pulpy, tepid. Steering screaming cleaners
> Around the snags of furniture, they straighten
> And haul out sheets from under the incontinent
> And heavy old, stoop to importunate young,
> Tugging, folding, tucking, zipping, buttoning,
> Spooning in food, encouraging excretion,
> Mopping up vomit, stabbing cloth with needles,
> Contorting wool around their knitting needles,
> Creating snug and comfy on their needles.
>
> Their huge hands! their everywhere eyes! their voices
> Raised to convey across the hullabaloo,
> Their massive thighs and breasts dispensing comfort,
> Their bloody passages and hairy crannies,
> Their wombs that pocket a man upside down!
>
> And when all's over, off with overalls,
> Quick consulting clocks, they go upstairs,

> Sit and sigh a little, brushing hair,
> And somehow find, in mirrors, colours, odours,
> Their essences of lilies and rose.

Elma Mitchell, 'Thoughts After Ruskin' (1976)

➤ In what ways does Mitchell confirm Ruskin's oppositions; in what ways does she change them? Again it might help to tabulate the material. For example:

Ruskin male	Ruskin female	Mitchell male	Mitchell female
public	private	public	private
aggressive	pacifist	?	aggressive

The question mark indicates that it is not always possible to be as absolutist as Ruskin aspires to be. Does the delicate manipulation of the market by Mitchell's man suggest refinement and pacifist leanings or does it indicate a sublimation of violence into the economic sphere?

11 It seems that even when Mitchell is confirming a Ruskin opposition, she is still challenging his basic philosophy. Thus the domesticity of Mitchell's woman has little to do with being the Angel in the House and a lot to do with a brutal wrestling with material reality. Using the comparative data you collected on Ruskin and Mitchell, produce an argument for Mitchell's poem as a radical re-writing of Ruskin.

12 Final queries

➤ Would it ever be to women's advantage to *agree* with some of Ruskin's oppositions; for example, for women to be thought more pacifist than men? Would we wish to claim pacifism as a female attribute, on the grounds that the military machinery is, largely, in the hands of men or, in so doing, would we merely be colluding with patriarchal, binary thought?

➤ Is there an advantage in *reversing* the oppositions, as Mitchell does at certain stages of her poem? Thus Ruskin's passive and pacifist woman becomes, in Mitchell's' scenario, active and aggressive. Or are such reversals only partial gains that leave patriarchal, binary thought substantially intact? (Remember Selden's comment in point 7.)

➤ As with the extract from Ruskin, Mitchell's poem also seems to be disturbed by the intrusion of class. Men who 'delicately manipulate the market' across mahogany desks don't usually have wives who scrub and wring or attend to the basic needs of the old and the young; this is the work of the cleaner, the nanny and the nursing home – again, largely female, working-class labour. Is this a contradictory point at which one can begin a deconstruction of Mitchell's poem?

References and further reading

Danny J. Anderson, 'Deconstruction: Critical Strategy/Strategic Criticism' in G. Douglas Atkins and Laura Morrow (eds), *Contemporary Literary Theory*. This essay is a clear introduction to ideas from deconstruction.

Catherine Belsey, *Critical Practice*. Belsey's chapter, 'Deconstructing the Text' contains two useful examples of deconstructive practice – with reference to Sherlock Holmes stories and Arnold's 'Scholar-Gipsy'.

Catherine Belsey and Jane Moore (eds), *The Feminist Reader: Essays in Gender and the Politics of Literary Criticism*

Hélène Cixous interviewed, Broadcasting Support Services, *Talking Liberties*

Hélène Cixous, 'Sorties: Out and Out: Attacks/Ways Out/Forays' in Hélène Cixous and Catherine Clément, *The Newly Born Woman*

Jonathan Culler, *On Deconstruction: Theory and Criticism after Structuralism*. Culler's final chapter, 'Deconstructive Criticism' explores examples of deconstruction at work. His section which most fully relates to feminism, 'Reading as a Woman' is better read in conjunction with the section in this book on Feminist Reading.

Jacques Derrida, *Dissemination* Trans. Barbara Johnson

Ann Jefferson and David Robey (eds), *Modern Literary Theory: A Comparative Introduction*. This collection contains also an earlier version of Moi on Cixous.

Elaine Marks and Isabelle de Courtivron, *New French Feminisms: An Anthology*

Elma Mitchell, 'Thoughts After Ruskin', *The Poor Man in the Flesh*. The Ruskin poem is also anthologized in Carol Rumens, *Making For The Open: Post-Feminist Poetry*.

Toril Moi, *Sexual/Textual Politics: Feminist Literary Theory*. Chapter 6 discusses the word of Cixous.

John Ruskin, 'Of Queens' Gardens', *Sesame and Lilies*

Raman Selden, *A Reader's Guide to Contemporary Literary Theory*

Raman Selden, *Practising Theory and Reading Literature: An Introduction*. Chapter 7 offers an accessible introduction to the concept of 'binary oppositions', though Selden relates the concept to feminism only in passing.

Monique Wittig, *The Straight Mind and Other Essays*

Gender
Play

Introduction

One relatively straightforward definition of the term 'gender' is: the social construction of our concepts of masculinity and femininity. This definition makes clear that there is no inevitable, 'natural' link between one's identity as 'a man' or 'a woman' and one's social behaviour. Not only may a man behave in a way that is deemed 'feminine' and a woman behave in a 'masculine' manner, but our very understanding of what constitutes 'masculine' and 'feminine' changes constantly in time and between different cultures and social groups. As illustration, consider Alice Walker's replacement of the term 'feminist' with 'womanist' because she wants to give expression to a specifically Black femininity which she does not see reflected in an American feminism dominated by white women. In Black folk idioms Walker finds a construct of femininity different in important ways to the white norms:

> **Womanist** 1. From *womanish*. (Opp. of 'girlish', i.e., frivolous, irresponsible, not serious.) A black feminist or feminist of color. From the black folk expression of mothers to female children, 'You're acting womanish,' i.e. like a woman. Usually referring to outrageous, audacious, courageous or *willful* behaviour. Wanting to know more and in greater depth than is considered 'good' for one. Interested in grown-up doings. Acting grown up. Being grown up. Interchangeable with another black folk expression: 'You're trying to be grown.' Responsible. In charge. *Serious.*
>
> Alice Walker, Preface to *In Search of Our Mothers' Gardens* (1983) p. xi

To make the distinction between the biological category of sex and the social possibilities of gender definition has been vital to feminists. For instance, such a distinction means that being born a woman does not automatically equip one for motherhood or imply that one *ought* to become a mother. Some women may wish to mother; some may not; some may wish to but be unable; some may not wish to mother but find themselves mothers despite; some may wish to bear children but not care for them and vice versa; some may have children only through medical intervention; some may mother, but not their own biological children and on and on. Which of these, then, is 'the maternal woman'? Of course, some men may wish to be the primary carers of children also; are they, then, 'maternal'?

I said above that this was a 'relatively straightforward' definition of gender though, self-evidently, there is more than enough even in this definition to keep us occupied. For example, I have referred to the biological categories 'male' and

158

'female' as if there was no debate about these terms, whereas, in fact, the belief that the world can be neatly divided into two distinct sexes is much disputed in feminism. The definition of gender, above, is but a starting-point. The continuing work on the concept by feminists and gay theorists has rendered it an increasingly complex category. Indeed, my reference to the concept of 'construction' – meaning that our understanding of feminine and masculine behaviour is something that we create rather than something given in nature – is questioned by Judith Butler in the following ways:

> When feminist theorists claim that gender is the cultural interpretation of sex or that gender is culturally constructed, what is the manner or mechanism of this construction? If gender is constructed, could it be constructed differently, or does its constructedness imply some form of social determinism, foreclosing the possibility of agency and transformation? Does 'construction' suggest that certain laws generate gender difference along universal axes of gender difference? How and where does the construction of gender take place? What sense can we make of a construction that cannot assume a human constructor prior to the construction?
>
> Judith Butler, *Gender Trouble: Feminism and the Subversion of Identity* (1990) pp. 7–8

To this we can add Jane Flax's equally provocative set of questions:

> What is gender? How is it related to anatomical sexual differences? How are gender relations constituted and sustained (in one person's lifetime and, more generally, as a social experience over time)? How do gender relations relate to other social relations such as class or race? Do gender relations have a history (or many)? What causes gender relations to change over time? What are the relationships between gender relations, sexuality, and a sense of individual identity? What are the relationships between heterosexuality, homosexuality, and gender relations? Are there only two genders? What are the relationships between forms of male dominance and gender relations? Could/would gender relations wither away in egalitarian societies? Is there anything distinctively male or female in modes of thought and social relations? If there is, are these distinctions innate or socially constituted? Are gendered distinctions socially useful or necessary? If so, what are the consequences for the feminist goal of attaining gender justice?
>
> Jane Flax, 'Postmodernism and Gender Relations in Feminist Theory' (1987) p. 43

To address any one of these questions would give us pause for lengthy thought but you might select one or two that particularly intrigue you and begin to think of some of the issues raised. If, as suggested in my Introduction to this book, you have been collecting definitions of and references to gender, this could be a good moment to review and collate that material.

One of Butler's questions is 'where does the construction of gender take place?' and one on the many answers to that question is – 'in writing'. Writing is a rich location for exploring the political meanings and imaginative potential of gender, for testing its boundaries, for thinking the unthinkable in terms of changing and shifting gender definitions. What I should like to concentrate on in this section are two aspects:

- Some activities which will help you to appreciate the fluidity of gender categories. In so doing we can better understand Flax's queries about how gender norms can change – in one's own life, throughout history, in reference to race and class, different cultural or regional localities etc.

- To examine some of the wonderful literary effects gained by writers who challenge gender norms by questioning the relationship between gender and biological categories, gender and sexual identity, gender and the choice of sexual object.

The fluidity of gender

1 Let us try to define what is 'a woman' and what is 'a man' in late-twentieth-century British culture. Think of those figures which we all readily recognize as female or male. (Of course, I am making a presumption there which you might want to question.) I'll start the lists; you continue for as long as you like:

What is 'a woman'?	What is 'a man'?
the little woman	the new man
(the) Madonna	the Chippendales
the page-three girl	the city gent
the lesbian	the lad

Based on my own examples, I suggest the following questions:

➤ Can we summarize from my lists what constitutes femininity and/or masculinity or is it difficult to pin down the characteristics?

➤ Do my female figures all embody femininity and all embody the same femininity? Do my female figures sometimes embody aspects of masculinity? The questions can be reversed, of course, to consider the male figures.

➤ When you read 'Madonna' did you think of the mother of Christ or of an American pop-star with a penchant for wearing interesting underwear? How do those two differing readings relate to your understanding of femininity? (One could say, for example, that Madonna, the pop-star, quite deliberately exploits the contradictory meanings.)

➤ Did you read Madonna's (pop-star) femininity as equivalent to that of the page-three girl or as something different?

➤ Taking into account that both are involved in forms of sexual exhibitionism, do you see the gender identities of the page-three girl and the Chippendales as similar?

➤ Is there a male equivalent to 'the little woman'?

➤ To what extent does class play a part if we compare the masculinity of the city gent and the lad?

➤ If I added the figure 'the bisexual' to both these lists, what would be the difference between the male bisexual and the female bisexual?

➤ If I wanted to add the figure 'the male transsexual', to which list should I look or is the reliance on only two categories becoming an unnecessary restriction?

You can see the number of issues about gender that are raised simply with the few male and female figures I suggested. There is no easy relation between gender and biological categories, or gender and sexuality. I am sure your selection will have generated just as many problems. Produce your own list of queries on the basis of the figures you have noted.

2 To take the matter further:

➤ Look at your list again and consider how adequately it reflects the cultural diversity of our country. All my male categories and, with the exception of the lesbian, all my female categories suggest to me 'whiteness'. I say this even of Madonna (the mother of Christ) since, in western iconography, she is depicted, almost always, as white. As we have seen, Alice Walker, for one, would claim that constructions of femininity based on the life experience of white women are not necessarily relevant to Black women.

➤ What happens to your understanding of gender if you think of a different historical period? As an example, if you chose the mid-nineteenth century your lists might begin with 'the Angel in the house', 'the fallen woman', 'the manufacturer', and 'the ragged boy'. Whether these figures equate with contemporary figures fully, partially, or not at all is debatable. The lesbian could appear in the mid-nineteenth-century list but within a rather different construct of femininity. Try to put your original list in a cross-cultural or trans-historical context. What kinds of agreements, disagreements, juxtapositions, shades of meaning occur?

3 To examine the changing pattern of gender in one's own life is a fascinating, sometimes scary, sometimes hilarious activity. You could assemble a history of your experience of gender by putting together a scrapbook or montage of old photos of yourself and personal written records – diary entries, school exercise books and reports, letters, birthday cards, etc. I find that these personal items carry a weight of memory and sensation: the photo shows you not only what you looked like as a little girl of seven – the significance of the dress, the hairstyle, the pose – but miraculously recreates the feelings of that moment, a sense of 'little girlness'. A later photo is likely, almost inevitable, to give expression to a different sense of femininity. Sometimes between two images or two written pieces of memorabilia we can recognize a significant change in our experience of femininity that could have been prompted by an important life event. In this activity we see something of what Butler refers to as the 'manner or mechanism of (gender) construction', an understanding of the process.

➤ To develop this point further you could look at the section on Finding the Subject where the creation of differing modes of femininity through the adoption of varied physical appearances is discussed.

➤ It would be relevant also to research the work of photographer, Jo Spence, whose therapeutic use of photography was very much linked with recouping a woman's life and with the changing expressions of femininity within that life. See research suggestions in the 'References and further reading'.

Gender play and literary effects

4 In playing with gender and the relations between gender and biology, and gender and sexual identity, writers can achieve some powerful literary effects. When a hero or heroine changes in the course of a novel and becomes a different person by the end, some reconfiguration of gender always plays a part. But what I am more concerned with here is those texts in which the author consciously challenges the expectations of the reader regarding gender. Let us think, firstly, of some of the many devices an author might use to unsettle the reader's preconceptions. I have listed these devices separately though, sometimes, more than one may be operating within the same text:

transvestism/cross-dressing	Caryl Churchill, *Cloud Nine*; Joanna Russ, 'The Mystery of the Young Gentleman'
magical changes of sex and gender identify	Virginia Woolf, *Orlando*; Suniti Namjoshi, *The Conversations of Cow*
narrators of indeterminate sex and gender	Jeanette Winterson, *Written on the Body*; Maureen Duffy, *Love Child*
sci-fi characters with a biology and/or sexual identity unknown to human society	Ursula Le Guin, *The Left Hand of Darkness*
characters whose biology and gender identity has been reconstructed through surgery or technology	in non-realist form: Angela Carter, *The Passion of New Eve* in realist form: Rose Tremain, *Sacred Country*
authors playing on conventions of gender to confound the reader	the children's story: Gene Kemp, *The Turbulent Term of Tyke Tyler*
authors deliberately hiding their own identities	James Tiptree Jr./Raccoona Sheldon/ Alice Sheldon; Rahila Khan/Toby Forward

5 We can look at an example to understand these ideas more clearly. In this passage from Jeanette Winterson, a male character, Jordan, has dressed as a woman:

I have met a number of people who, anxious to be free of the burdens of their gender, have dressed themselves men as women and women as men.

After my experience in the pen of prostitutes I decided to continue as a woman for a time and took a job on a fish stall.

I noticed that women have a private language. A language not dependent on the constructions of men but structured by signs and expression, and that uses ordinary words as code-words meaning something other.

In my petticoats I was a traveller in a foreign country. I did not speak the language. I was regarded with suspicion.

I watched women flirting with men, pleasing men, doing business with men, and then I watched them collapsing into laughter, sharing the joke, while the men, all unknowing, felt themselves master of the situation and went off to brag in bar-rooms and to preach from pulpits the folly of the weaker sex.

This conspiracy of women shocked me. I like women; I am shy of them but I regard them highly. I never guessed how much they hate us or how deeply they pity us. They think we are children with too much pocket money. The woman who owned the fish stall warned me never to try to cheat another woman but always to try and charge the men double or send them away with a bad catch.

'Their noses are dull,' she said. 'They won't be able to mark a day-old lobster from a fresh one.'

And she asked me to remember that a woman, if cheated, will never forget and will some day pay you back, even if it takes years, while a man will rave and roar and slap you perhaps and then be distracted by some other thing.

Jeanette Winterson, Sexing the Cherry (1989) p. 28–9

The fish stall owner then gives Jordan a rule-book, the contents of which aim to prove the pitiful folly of all men. Jordan reads this, inwardly concedes its truth and falls into a depression.

In what ways can such a passage open a debate on gender? Here are some suggestions:

- Transvestism is for Jordan a liberation – 'free of the burdens of their gender' – but, at the same time, uncertain, maybe dangerous, territory – 'I was regarded with suspicion'.

- The play at femininity gives Jordan access to new places and new perceptions but those new perceptions can be an affront to his masculinity. Does Jordan appear like a woman but listen like a man?

- Jordan might superficially appear like a woman but he doesn't seem to act appropriately – 'I did not speak the language' – and he doesn't believe himself to *be* a woman: women are referred to as 'they'; men as 'us'.

- On the other hand, Jordan's masculinity does not ally itself with the masculinity of the bragging bar-room bore or the pontificating cleric. Is the man in petticoats to represent the feminized man, capable of seeing both/many perspectives?

- Jordan is both *ingénu*, the innocent man bewildered in a woman's world and *ingénue*, the unsophisticated young woman advised by the street-wise fish woman.

- Jordan, the man, is playing a role as a woman. For explicit political purposes, all the women he observes play roles in their relations with men. The untransformed men do not even seem to know that a game is taking place, let alone how to take part.

- The woman on the fish stall sees men and women not in terms of gender differences but in terms of immutable sexual differences: women always act like this; men always act like that.

If we bring into the frame the roles of the author and the reader yet more issues emerge:

- Why do I, a female reader, feel sympathetic and indulgent towards Jordan? Why don't I see him as a voyeur? At the same time, I am very familiar with the subversive potential of women's 'private language' and quite happily associate myself with the women joking at men's discomfort.

- Does the author's humorous representation of the fish woman's views – men can't smell properly, women can; men are distracted; women remember – lead the reader to question the logic of sexual difference?

- Does our knowledge that the author is female (some readers may have other knowledge about Jeanette Winterson) influence the way we read the passage?

Just from these few observations on a single passage we have begun to think about:

transvestism

gender definitions as restrictive

gender as performance

gender as constructed

the relation between identity and gender

gender and language

the relation between sexual difference and gender difference

the fluidity of gender

how one reads gender ...

6 Here are some extracts for you to consider in the way I have above. The first two passages are from Joanna Russ's 'The Mystery of the Young Gentleman'. The year is 1885. On a transatlantic voyage all are literally and metaphorically at sea. The 'young gentleman' of the title masquerades at masculinity and femininity, heterosexuality and homosexuality so as to confound the prurient enquiries of a fellow passenger, significantly a medical doctor. In the first passage the 'young gentleman', who narrates the story, convinces the doctor that s/he is a woman dressed as a man. The doctor is titillated and a sexual interlude follows. In the second passage, the 'young gentleman' convinces the horrified doctor not only that s/he is really a man but that the sexual encounter is evidence of the doctor's latent homosexuality. See if you can find your way through the clever gender repositionings and notice how the problems of gender are complicated here by questions of sexual orientation and sexual practice:

'You're a woman!'

I do nothing. I say nothing. I don't have to, you see, I have only to
smile, all sex in my smile. He will do it all himself, from 'My dear girl,
why didn't you tell me!' to 'But you mustn't walk alone, oh dear, no, you
mustn't go alone to your cabin!' He remembers my face on a playbill
(though the name eludes him) – must be an actress, of course, have to be
an actress; we have to learn such things for the stage, don't we? Special
dress, altered voice, dye on the skin – but nothing injurious, he hopes,
nothing that will mar, eh? Don't want to spoil that complexion, not when
one needs it for one's work, not when one's famous for it (still searching).
And what a clever little women, to pull it off, when otherwise they'd all be
about me, spoiling my trip, with their interviews and their publicity.

He babbles: *He* knew. Doctors *know*, you know. Little hands, little feet,
smooth face, delicate features, slender body! Quite obvious. Quite, quite
obvious. Trying to remember what he said to the gentleman that he
oughtn't to have said to the lady – but actresses are different, don't you
know – free-thinking – though nothing indelicate – and he was only playing
along, you understand, being a little free in his language, but nothing
sensible, only gabble, only a lot of nonsense –

And the second passage:

'You are a woman.'

The stupidity. The absolute unconquerable stupidity! Like the best
swordsman in the world beaten by a jackass. I walk round him, searching,
to Maria-Dolores's door. Say, 'Have you heard what happened at cards last
night? Yes, that's me; that is how I get my living; the nonsense about
Colorado helps. Well, I knocked down a man fifty pounds heavier than
myself; ask about it tomorrow.'

Bumble is trembling.

I turn and flip the knife point-first across the cabin and into the door to
the corridor – why is it that acts of manliness always involve damage to the
furniture? – which is, you must understand, something a woman cannot do.
That's faith. I repeat: What a woman cannot do.

Logic also. I say:

'If I am lying now, what is the purpose of my lie? To drive you away?
The little actress would not want to drive you away, not after having gone
to all the trouble of acquiring you! Why confess she's a woman unless she
wanted you? And why should I lie? For fear you'll expose me? I can expose
you. I could blackmail you if I wanted; we were seen, you know. To drive
you away? I don't want to; I like you – although I don't fancy being
attacked and having to knock you down or throttle you as I did to the other
gentleman at the game last night – and why on earth, if I wanted to drive
you away, should I have taken such trouble to – well, we won't name it.
But it's perfect nonsense, my dear fellow, a woman pretending to be a man
who pretends he is a woman in order to pretend he is a man? Come, come,
it won't work! A female invert might want to dress and live as a man, but
to confess she's a woman – which would defeat her purpose – and then be
intimate with you – which she would find impossibly repulsive – in order
to do what, for heaven's sake? Where's the sense to it? No, there's only one

possibility, and that's the truth: that I have been deceiving nobody, including you, but that you, my poor dear fellow, have been for a very long time deceiving yourself. Why not stop, eh? Right now?'

Joanna Russ, 'The Mystery of the Young Gentleman' (1984) pp. 84, 88

A second set of examples comes from Angela Carter's *The Passion of New Eve*. Through massive surgical intervention, Evelyn has become the new Eve. Biologically a woman to the extent of menstruating and becoming pregnant, Eve finds other aspects of the process of transformation – adjusting to gender norms, understanding her changed sexuality, accommodating a new sense of self-hood – less swift than the surgeon's knife:

> But when I looked in the mirror, I saw Eve: I did not see myself. I saw a young woman who, though she was I, I could in no way acknowledge as myself, for this was only a lyrical abstraction of femininity to me, a tinted arrangement of curved lines. I touched the breasts and the mound that were not mine; I saw white hands in the mirror move, it was as though they were white gloves put on to conduct the unfamiliar orchestra of myself. I looked again and saw I bore a strong family resemblance to myself, although my hair had grown so long it hung down to a waist that, on the operating table, had acquired an emphatic indentation. Thanks to the plastic surgery, my eyes were now a little larger than they had been; how blue they were showed more. The cosmetic knife had provided me with a bee-stung underlip and a fat pout. I was a woman, young and desirable. I grasped my tits and pulled out the dark red nipples to see how far they'd go; they were unexpectedly elastic and it did not hurt to tug them sharply. So I got a little more courage to explore myself further and nervously slid my hand between my thighs.
>
> But my over-taxed brain almost exploded, then, for the clitoris transplant had been an unqualified success. The tactile sensation was so well-remembered and gave me so much pleasure, still, I could scarcely believe the cleft was now my own.
>
> Let the punishment fit the crime, whatever it had been. They had turned me into the *Playboy* center fold. I was the object of all the unfocused desires that had ever existed in my own head. I had become my own masturbatory fantasy. And – how can I put it – the cock in my head, still, twitched at the sight of myself.
>
> The psycho-programming had not been entirely successful.
>
> But, where I remembered my cock, was nothing. Only a void, an insistent absence, like a noisy silence.

And the second passage:

> ... when I was at home among the girls, I kept as silent as I could and tried to imitate the way they moved and the way they spoke for I knew that ... I would often make a gesture with my hands that was out of Eve's character or exclaim with a subtly male inflection that made them raise their eyebrows. This intensive study of feminine manners, as well as my everyday work about the homestead, kept me in a state of permanent

exhaustion. I was tense and preoccupied; although I was a woman, I was now also passing for a woman, but, then, many woman born spend their whole lives in just such imitations.

However, the result of my apprenticeship as a woman was, of course, that my manner became a little too emphatically feminine. I roused Zero's suspicions because I began to behave *too much* like a woman and he started to watch me warily for signs of the tribade.

Angela Carter, The Passion of New Eve (1977; 1982) pp. 74–5, 100–1

7 I mentioned earlier with reference to Winterson how knowing the sex of the author, and, even more, knowing something of his/her lifestyle or attitudes can influence how one reads the gender play of the text. You might look here at the first part of the section on Gender and Genre where I discuss the responses which occur when the sex of the author seems in some way at odds with the content of the book. On some occasions, however, an author may deliberately disguise his/her sex and this too affects our reading. For instance, how do you feel when you discover that science fiction writer, 'James Tiptree Jr.' is also science fiction writer, 'Raccoona Sheldon' and also 'real person', Alice Sheldon? In 1970 'James Tiptree Jr.' was writing:

Christ but he was tired! Wacked out ... Young cunt, old cunt, soft, sinewy, bouncy, bony, wriggly, lumpy, slimy, lathery, leathery cunt squeaking, shrieking, growling – all of them after him, his furry arms, his golden masculinity, his poor old never-failing poker – Oh Ches I've never oh Ches it's so it's oh Ches oh Darling darling darlingdarlingdarling –

James Tiptree Jr., 'I'm Too Big but I Love to Play' (1970) p. 107

Inevitably the reading of this passage changes when six years after publication it is revealed that 'James Tiptree Jr.' is a woman. What could be seen as the macho pyrotechnics of the male author, crowing about male prowess and female availability, becomes, perhaps, a satiric parody in the hands of the female author.

➤ You could experiment with some passages from Tiptree/Sheldon's work or, indeed, with complete stories. (Sheldon wrote some with one pen name and some with the other.) Try reading the material with a sense of 'James Tiptree Jr.' as the author and then as the work of 'Raccoona Sheldon'. Is there a difference? If so, what is it and why? Are you presuming that the female author will act within one set of gender norms and the male author another? Maybe you need to challenge your own expectations.

Studies of the reviews of pseudonymous texts certainly reveal that reviewers and critics often have very gender specific ideas of what they expect from authors. See, for instance, Showalter and Ohmann in the 'References and further reading'.

Sarah LeFanu comments on the consequences of discovering Tiptree's real identity:

The 'masculine manner' of Tiptree's style is a cunning contrivance that reveals, first, the limitations of a machismo-orientated culture and the limitations of science fiction when that culture is incorporated unquestioningly into its fictive conventions....

The way Tiptree uses male personae to tell her stories is, finally, subversive both of a male-dominated world-view derived from unequal relations of power between the sexes and also of ideas of writing that divide experience, both lived and fictional, into separate spheres of masculine and feminine. Tiptree herself says her so-called 'male writing style' is merely an expression of intensity, of narrative drive, and that such a style is not confined to men.

> Sarah LeFanu, *In the Chinks of the World Machine:*
> *Feminism and Science Fiction* (1988) pp. 126, 129

The point about 'masculine' and 'feminine' styles of writing and how these may be used, or not, by male and female writers is given fuller consideration in the section on Feminine Writing and Reading. After all, a female writer could affect macho pyrotechnics so as to enjoy a vicarious sense of power; a male author might want genuinely to satirize forms of brutish masculinity.

➤ What you could discuss here or prepare as a research topic for an essay or seminar, is LeFanu's claim that Tiptree's gender play about her own identity enhances the subversive potential of her writing. Do you agree with that? If so, what precisely is subverted and how? Or do you merely feel duped and irritated by Tiptree's gender play?

8 The case of Toby Forward/Rahila Khan is another example of the deliberate use of a pseudonym but with rather different consequences:

... in 1987 ... Rahila Khan, author of a Virago Upstart collection of short stories, was unveiled as Toby Forward, Anglican Priest. Virago pulped the book and accused Forward of 'a cruel hoax'. Forward, who has since had twelve books published (including the offending stories), protests that he's intended nothing of the kind, and it was Virago which made a serious error of judgement: 'I felt that if they wanted the book – publishers ought to publish books, not authors'. Half of his Rahila Khan stories, he points out, were written in the third person, about Asian teenage girls, half were about white teenage boys, written in the first person. 'Now they were quite happy for Rahila Khan to write in the first person as a white man, they were not happy for a white man to write in the third person as an Asian woman.' A keen feminist, Forward would still, he says, 'write for them at the drop of a hat, and be very pleased to'.

Catherine Bennett, 'The House that Carmen Built' (1993) p. 10

Forward's point is interesting in itself and interesting also in comparison with Sheldon/Tiptree. Why should Sheldon's assumption of a male pseudonym and a male narrative voice be seen by many critics as a thought-provoking questioning of gender norms but Forward's assumption of new sexual and racial identities be seen as devious? I think there are issues to consider here though I have to say the situation is not quite the easy opposition I have suggested: as LeFanu indicates elsewhere in her chapter on Tiptree, Tiptree's own gender play posed problems for readers and fellow writers. That is another aspect you could research.

9 Two final activities.
➤ Firstly, return to the questions you selected at the beginning from the lists of

Butler and Flax. Add to or revise your notes in the light of what you have learned during this section. Or select another one or two questions which interest you and again try to think through some of the implications of the issue(s). You could also, at this stage, return to the chart of literary devices and exemplary texts and supplement with your own suggestions.

➤ Secondly, enjoy this marvellous send-up of right-wing femininity from the American political/performance group Ladies Against Women. Gail Ann Williams introduces the group as follows:

Ladies Against Women (LAW) travels around the country enacting right-wing fantasies. Bejeweled, well-heeled, bedecked in pink, polka dots, and furs, the Ladies have marched daintily in parades, passed out tasteful Ladyfestos, and held consciousness-lowering sessions since 1980. They've shown up in tasteful picket-reception lines for 'Stop ERA' spokesgal Phyllis Schlafly, the very Right reverends Pat Robertson and Jerry Falwell, and other heart-throbs of the ruling regime.

And here is the Ladyfesto, unfortunately not decorated with lace and pink bows on this occasion:

LADIES AGAINST WOMEN!

Ladyfesto:

We truly tasteful Ladies do hereby ~~demand~~ Request:

★ Weed out Uppity Women! Establish HULA Committee... the House Committee on Unladylike Activities!

★ All true change comes from the outside... amend the U.S. Criminal Code to include a dress code.

★ Abolish the Environment. It takes up too much space, and is far too difficult to keep clean.

★ Free all gals from wage slavery: it is unladylike to accept money for work.

★ Suffering, not suffrage ! A real lady has no opinions, and if one accidentally forms, she certainly doesn't go about voting, petitioning or expressing herself in public.

★ S_x is never supposed to be f_n. Ladies, close your eyes and do your duty.

★ Make America a man again... invade abroad.

★ Protect the unconceived. Sperms are people too, yet millions are murdered every day at the hands of men practicing certain unmentionable male activities.

L.A.W. Headquarters: 1600 Woolsey Street, Berkeley, Ca. 94703

Endorsed By: Millionaire Mommies with Nannies Against Free Daycare, The Rambo Coalition, Another Mother for World Domination, Hysteria in Media, Americans Against Civil Liberties and Unions, The Save the Stoles Foundation, Peace Officers for a Police State (POPS), The Future Dictators of America Clubs, DADD: Democrats Against Drafted Disarmament, National Association for the Advancement of Rich People, Moral Monopoly, Astrologers for Star Wars, Ego Forum, Moms for Bombs, The Sub-Urban League, Students for an Aristocratic Society, Friends of the Foetus, Scientists for Enhanced Military Spending, Federal Bureau of Intimidation, Committee Against Comic Agitators (C A C A) © '88

from Gloria Kaufman (ed.) In Stitches: A Patchwork of Feminist Humor and Satire *(1991), Indiana University Press*

References and further reading

Catherine Bennett, 'The House that Carmen Built'

Judith Butler, *Gender Trouble: Feminism and the Subversion of Identity*

Angela Carter, *The Passion of New Eve*

Caryl Churchill, *Cloud Nine*

Maureen Duffy, *Love Child*

Jane Flax, 'Postmodernism and Gender Relations in Feminist Theory' in Linda J. Nicholson (ed.), *Feminism/Postmodernism*

Gloria Kaufman (ed.), *In Stitches: A Patchwork of Feminist Humor and Satire*

Gene Kemp, *The Turbulent Term of Tyke Tyler*

Sarah LeFanu, *In the Chinks of the World Machine: Feminism and Science Fiction*

Ursula Le Guin, *The Left Hand of Darkness*

Suniti Namjoshi, *The Conversations of Cow*

Carol Ohmann, 'Emily Brontë in the Hands of Male Critics' in Mary Eagleton (ed.), *Feminist Literary Theory: A Reader*

Joanna Russ, 'The Mystery of the Young Gentleman' in *Extra (ordinary) People*

Elaine Showalter, *A Literature of Their Own: British Women Novelists from Brontë to Lessing*, particularly chapter III

James Tiptree Jr., 'I'm Too Big but I Love to Play', *10,000 Light Years from Home*. The passage included here is quoted in LeFanu and the page number refers to LeFanu.

Rose Tremain, *Sacred Country*

Alice Walker, *In Search of Our Mothers' Gardens*

Jeanette Winterson, *Sexing the Cherry*

Jeanette Winterson, *Written on the Body*

Virginia Woolf, *Orlando*

For further research on the work of Jo Spence see:

James Guimond, 'Auteurs as Autobiographers: Images by Jo Spence and Cindy Sherman'

Rosy Martin and Jo Spence, 'New Portraits for Old: The Use of the Camera in Therapy'

Jo Spence, *Putting Myself in the Picture: A Political, Personal, and Photographic Autobiography*

Jo Spence and Patricia Holland, *Family Snaps: The Meanings of Domestic Photography*

Jo Stanley (ed), *Cultural Sniping: The Art of Transgression*

Further studies on gender:

Teresa de Lauretis, *Technologies of Gender: Essays on Theory, Film and Fiction*

Christine Delphy, 'Rethinking Sex and Gender'

Diana Fuss (ed.), *Inside/Out: Lesbian Theories, Gay Theories*. The first section, 'Decking Out: Performing Identities' is relevant to the ideas discussed here about gender play and gender performance.

Linda Nicholson, 'Interpreting Gender'

Mary Poovey, *Uneven Developments: The Ideological Work of Gender in Mid-Victorian England*, see chapter 1.

Joan W. Scott, 'Gender: A Useful Category of Historical Analysis' in Elizabeth Weed (ed.), *Coming to Terms: Feminism, Theory, Politics*. Though Scott's title specifies the discipline of history, the essay has a much wider relevance.

Elaine Showalter, 'The Rise of Gender' in Showalter (ed.) *Speaking of Gender*

Monique Wittig, *The Straight Mind and Other Essays*. See particularly 'The Mark of Gender'.

The easiest way to understand the significance of gender across a range of disciplines, literature included, is to look at the relevant sections in readers on feminist thought: these contain many key essays. For instance:

Linda S. Kauffman (ed.), *American Feminist Thought at Century's End: A Reader*, see particularly part 1.

Terry Lovell, (ed.), *British Feminist Thought: A Reader*, see particularly parts III and V.

The Polity Reader in Gender Studies

Feminine Writing and Reading

Introduction

Like 'gender', feminine' is a term of multiple meanings, a term which feminism has found open to wide debate and new interpretations. The term often carries with it a range of negative connotations – docility, weakness, dependency; it can be associated with the childlike as opposed to a sense of adult capability; it can even be linked to silliness and excessive frivolity. One has only to think of romantic fiction's creation of the 'feminine' heroine to know it is the last thing on earth one would want to be. In her study *Thinking About Women*, Mary Ellmann produces a devastating critique of the 'feminine stereotypes' operating in literature. On the contents page she lists the stereotypes as: 'formlessness, passivity, instability, confinement, piety, materiality, spirituality, irrationality, compliancy, two incorrigible figures: the shrew and the witch'. Self-evidently there is need for a revised thinking of the term 'feminine'.

One feminist response has been to emphasize the value of the feminine. Feminists have researched domesticity, mothering, the female body, for example, with a sense of the significance and worth of these areas. Within the arts, the previously derided female crafts of knitting, needlework, china painting etc. have been given new status and central to this revaluation has been a questioning of the very distinction between 'art' and 'craft': why has so much of women's aesthetic work been categorized as 'mere' domestic crafts? Within the specifically literary, the presumption that women's contribution is provincial, minor, small-scale has also been re-examined.

In the section on Patriarchal Binary Thought we see how in our culture the feminine is frequently defined both in opposition to the masculine and as inferior to the masculine, the negative absence of the feminine against the positive presence of the masculine. However, we have to resist the temptation simply to reverse the hierarchy. Beyond a temporary gratification there is no great advantage in seeing the feminine as the source of all that is fine and the masculine as the source of all that is debased. More important is to expose the limitations and fallacy of binary logic. The need is to break down that restrictive concept, rather than reorder it.

The meanings of 'feminine' which I want us to consider in this section spring from writing first produced about twenty years ago in France and which, by the early eighties, was being discussed in the British and American academies as 'French feminism' and *l'écriture féminine* (feminine writing). Both these terms are unsatisfactory: the first suggests that the feminism produced in France is

172

homogenous, nationally based and completely distinct from other feminisms; the second suggests that there is something identifiable as 'feminine' writing and that this is what all women do. In reality, feminists most associated with feminine writing have often proved extremely reluctant to define what feminine writing is (for example, Hélène Cixous); other feminists have been indiscriminately placed in the feminine writing camp even though they have expressed reservations about feminine writing generally and its link to women specifically (for example, Julia Kristeva). The connections between, on the one hand, feminine writing and the repressed elements of our male-dominated culture (the female body, female desire, woman's voice) and, on the other, between feminine writing and innovative, avant-garde writing have been so reductively employed in some cases that every writer who makes even passing mention of a woman's needs in the form of a mildly unusual metaphor is deemed the latest exponent of feminine writing. Perhaps I exaggerate here – then again, perhaps I don't.

Another problem lies in the almost talismatic status which French feminism, and especially the work of Hélène Cixous, Julia Kristeva and Luce Irigaray, has been ascribed within the academic contexts of Britain and America, particularly during the eighties. This is not without irony since much of the writing of these authors is deeply questioning about the construction of knowledge and the play of power within that process. My advice would be to approach these writers with the same kind of open, attentive, interrogative spirit that you would bring to any other; indeed, how to read is a problem we shall actually be considering later in this section.

The three questions I should like us to centre on are:

• What is feminine writing?

• What is feminine reading?

• What is the relation between 'feminine' and 'feminist'?

Before we move on to those questions you might want to familiarize yourself a little more with some of the points I have already raised. On meanings of 'feminine' and 'femininity' see:

Cheris Kramarae and Paula A. Treichler, *Amazons, Bluestockings and Crones: A Feminist Dictionary* (19912). Most of the definitions relate to binary thinking, the feminine in relation to the masculine.

Jane Mills, *Womanwords: A Vocabulary of Culture and Patriarchal Society* (1991). Mills's focus is primarily on etymological and linguistic meanings.

Toril Moi, 'Feminist Literary Criticism' in Ann Jefferson and David Robey (1986).

Elizabeth Wright (ed.), *Feminism and Psychoanalysis: A Critical Dictionary* (1992). See the entries on *l'écriture féminine* and 'feminine economy'. The entry on 'femininity' discusses psychoanalytic interpretations of the construction of femininity.

On the history of French feminism and its entry into British and American academic work see:

Rachel Bowlby, *Still Crazy After All These Years: Women, Writing and*

Psychoanalysis (1992).

Claire Duchen (ed.) *French Connections: Voices from the Women's Movement in France* (1987).

Nicole Ward Jouve, *White Woman Speaks with Forked Tongue: Criticism as Autobiography* (1991).

Susan Sellers, *Language and Sexual Difference: Feminist Writing in France* (1991).

Feminine writing

1 To ask, 'What is feminine writing?' is the kind of question to make the heart sink of any feminist interested in this kind of writing practice and yet it is, almost inevitably, the initial question to be asked by any reader encountering the phrase 'feminine writing' or *l'écriture féminine* for the first time. Here are three extracts from feminists well versed in concepts of the feminine and feminine writing practice and, yet, convinced that they cannot explain what the feminine is:

> In 'woman' I see something that cannot be represented, something that is not said, something above and beyond nomenclatures and ideologies. There are certain 'men' who are familiar with this phenomenon; it is what some modern texts never stop signifying: testing the limits of language and sociality – the law and its transgression, mastery and (sexual) pleasure – without reserving one for males and the other for females, on the condition that it is never mentioned.
>
> Julia Kristeva, 'Woman Can Never Be Defined' (1974) pp. 37–8

> For to speak *of* or *about* woman may always boil down to, or be understood as, a recuperation of the feminine within the logic that maintains it in repression, censorship, nonrecognition.
>
> Luce Irigaray, 'The Power of Discourse and the Subordination of the Feminine' (1975) p. 78

> It is impossible to *define* a feminine practice of writing, and this is an impossibility which will remain, for this practice can never be theorized, enclosed, coded – which doesn't mean that it doesn't exist. But it will always surpass the discourse that regulates the phallocentric system; it does and will take place in areas other than those subordinated to philosophico-theoretical domination. It will be conceived of only by subjects who are breakers of automatisms, by peripheral figures that no authority can ever subjugate.
>
> Hélène Cixous, 'The Laugh of the Medusa' (1976) p. 253

Irigaray puts the point strongly and succinctly: to try to define the feminine is an act of mastery and recuperation, a way of returning the feminine to the known, the manageable, the comprehensible. What, then, should I do – advise you to question no further, draw a line here and end the section? Well, probably not, since that would simply leave you repeating the initial question with growing frustration. So let's continue the exploration, though with Irigaray's caution in our minds and ask, not 'what *is* the feminine?' but 'why is the feminine impossible to represent?' Using the extracts above, how would you respond to that question?

You can see that the feminine considered here is not the same as those definitions of feminine discussed in my Introduction: it is not the feminine in opposition to the masculine; nor the subordinated feminine of docility and inferiority; nor the valorized femininity of women's achievements. All these meanings circulate *within* the dominant order of patriarchal society though, in the third case, not without opposition. The writers above are pointing to a meaning of the feminine which cannot be contained within the dominant order, which is 'testing the limits' of that order (Kristeva) and which will 'surpass the discourse that regulates' (Cixous). The feminine is not a place for the upholders of the social order but for those marginal, 'peripheral figures' – men included, Kristeva suggests – who have no interest in identifying with authority.

2 As Cixous remarks above, being unable – and unwilling – to reduce the feminine to a list of precise characteristics, does not mean that the feminine does not exist. Here are some extracts from two of Cixous's essays, 'The Laugh of the Medusa' and 'Castration or Decapitation?'. I am not saying that these are examples of feminine writing since, like the commentators above, I am not sure I can define feminine writing, but the examples discuss and enact writing in a way that certainly was never part of my education:

> I wished that that woman would write and proclaim this unique empire so that other women, other unacknowledged sovereigns, might exclaim: I, too, overflow; my desires have invented new desires, my body knows unheard-of songs. Time and again I, too, have felt so full of luminous torrents that I could burst – burst with forms much more beautiful than those which are put up in frames and sold for a stinking fortune. And I, too, said nothing, showed nothing; I didn't open my mouth, I didn't repaint my half of the world. I was ashamed. I was afraid, and I swallowed my shame and fear. I said to myself: You are mad! What's the meaning of these waves, these floods, these outbursts? Where is the ebullient, infinite woman who, immersed as she was in her naivety, kept in the dark about herself, led into self-disdain by the great arm of parental-conjugal phallocentrism, hasn't been ashamed of her strength? Who, surprised and horrified by the fantastic tumult of her drives (for she was made to believe that a well-adjusted normal woman has a … divine composure), hasn't accused herself of being a monster? Who, feeling a funny desire stirring inside her (to sing, to write, to dare to speak, in short, to bring out something new), hasn't thought she was sick? Well, her shameful sickness is that she resists death, that she makes trouble.

> Write! and your self-seeking text will know itself better than flesh and blood, rising, insurrectionary dough kneading itself, with sonorous perfumed ingredients, a lively combination of flying colors, leaves, and rivers plunging into the sea we feed. 'Ah, there's the sea', he will say as he holds out to me a basin full of water from the little phallic mother from whom he's inseparable. But look, our seas are what we make of them, full

of fish or not, opaque or transparent, red or black, high or smooth, narrow or bankless; and we are ourselves sea, sand, coral, seaweed, beaches, tides, swimmers, children, waves ... More or less wavily sea, earth, sky – what matter would rebuff us? We know how to speak them all.

Heterogeneous, yes. For her joyous benefits she is erogenous; she is the erogeneity of the heterogeneous: airborne swimmer, in flight, she does not cling to herself; she is dispersible, prodigious, stunning, desirous and capable of others, of the other woman that she will be, of the other woman she isn't, of him, of you.

Hélène Cixous, 'The Laugh of the Medusa' (1976) pp. 246, 260

Let's look not at syntax but at fantasy, at the unconscious: all the feminine texts I've read are very close to the voice, very close to the flesh of language, much more so than masculine texts ... perhaps because there's something in them that's freely given, perhaps because they don't rush into meaning, but are straightway at the threshold of feeling. There's *tactility* in the feminine text, there's touch, and this touch passes through the ear. Writing in the feminine is passing on what is cut out by the Symbolic, the voice of the mother, passing on what is most archaic. The most archaic force that touches a body is one that enters by the ear and reaches the most intimate point. This innermost touch always echoes in a woman-text. So the movement, the movement of the text, doesn't trace a straight line. I see it as an outpouring ... which can appear in primitive or elementary texts as a fantasy of blood, of menstrual flow, etc., but which I prefer to see as vomiting, as 'throwing up', 'disgorging'. And I'd link this with a basic structure of property relations defined by mourning.

And finally this open and bewildering prospect goes hand in hand with a certain kind of laughter. Culturally speaking, women have wept a great deal, but once the tears are shed, there will be endless laughter instead. Laughter that breaks out, overflows, a humor no one would expect to find in women – which is nonetheless surely their greatest strength because it's a humor that sees man much further away than he has ever been seen. Laughter that shakes the last chapter of my LA [Cixous's text of 1976], 'she who laughs last'. And her first laugh is at herself.

Hélène Cixous, 'Castration or Decapitation?' (1981) pp. 54, 55

One uncertainty for me in reading these passages is that I am not sure whether I am reading critical writing or creative. Cixous is, at times, discussing the nature of writing, which we might see as the activity of the critic. She is also, obviously, a theoretician – the references to 'phallocentrism', 'the Symbolic', the 'phallic mother' are all terms from contemporary critical discourse. Yet her conscious use of metaphor and rhythm seems closer to the poetic. In all kinds of ways Cixous breaks the rules about writing that I was taught. She starts sentences with conjunctions; her syntax and punctuation often seem irregular; her mode of arguing doesn't follow the kind of rhetorical forms students are commonly advised to use in their critical essays; moreover, in my experience, references to vomiting, menstruation and the 'stinking' fortunes made by collectors of the art world would elicit a lot of red ink.

Of course all this is intentional on Cixous's part. One aspect of her writing practice is to break down the divisions between critical and creative, the cerebral and the physical, the poetic and the analytic, the measured and the impassioned, the formal and the colloquial.

What are your responses to these extracts? Take Cixous's advice and 'don't rush into meaning'. Don't try to pin down the meaning of every line; don't get tense; don't worry if you can't explain everything. Let's proceed, as Cixous suggests, more through feeling:

➤ What do you like in these extracts? Any phrases, ideas, images that strike you? Why did you connect with Cixous's writing at those points?

➤ Were there any moments when you found yourself thinking, 'Yes, that's right; that's how it is', or 'I've experienced that'. What have been your experiences that connect?

➤ Have you ever experienced the self-censoring that Cixous refers to in one extract? What have you always wanted to say but never said? To whom have you wanted to say these things? (Perhaps now is the time to say it or to write down those hidden words.) You could refer here to the section on Speech and Silence.

➤ Cixous talks of a secret potential in women, under the surface, sometimes breaking through, often repressed – a potential that is powerful, sensuous and creative. Does that ring true for you or does that seem a fanciful idea? If you find credibility in the idea, what have been the glimpses of and clues to that potential which you have noticed?

➤ I particularly like the rhythmic qualities in Cixous's work, the way she changes pace, the way she can quicken the rhythm for stirring and invigorating effects. Try reading the extracts out loud.

➤ What appears different to you about these extracts in comparison with other styles of writing? Don't draw back at the point of difference; the danger is to retreat and simply say you don't understand or you don't have anything to say. There is always *something* to say, some response to make if you listen carefully enough to how you are thinking and feeling.

3 To research further the ideas of Cixous on feminine writing, see:

Pam Morris, *Literature and Feminism: An Introduction* (1993), chapter 5.

You could compare Cixous with the work of Luce Irigaray. See both Morris and:

Elizabeth Grosz, *Sexual Subversions: Three French Feminists* (1989), particularly pp. 126–132.

Mary Jacobus, 'Men of Maxims and *The Mill on the Floss*' (1986).

Feminine reading

4 Think of the many different reading situations in which you might find yourself in the course of a week: reading a set text in preparation for a seminar; reading some criticism in preparation for an essay you have to write; reading a light novel

on the train or before you drop off to sleep; reading a letter from the bank; reading a recipe; reading some poetry to the writing group to which you belong; reading a story to a child … Compile your own list of common reading experiences and then try to identify your characteristic feelings during each of those reading events.

Now focus specifically on reading within an academic context – the first two situations listed above, plus any others you may want to add. In this context, which of the following are frequent reading responses for you:

	YES	NO
anxiety at lack of comprehension	☐	☐
delight in new ideas	☐	☐
laughter	☐	☐
anger/irritation/frustration	☐	☐
revelation	☐	☐
meditation	☐	☐
boredom	☐	☐
feeling you've missed the point	☐	☐
surprise	☐	☐
perplexed	☐	☐
a meeting of minds	☐	☐

Add your own suggestions of possible responses and decide which relate to your experience of reading. Would you say you find academic reading pleasurable – ever? sometimes? mostly? What are your most pleasurable reading experiences now and in the past? Do you find academic reading stressful and, if so, in what ways, for what reasons? Certainly I feel that the languorous, sensuous woman reader seen opposite is unlikely to be reading the latest volume of literary theory.

5 Can you remember the advice you were given on critical reading at school? In English lessons what were you taught to do with texts? Were you advised to look out for particular aspects? Did you learn a technical vocabulary to describe parts/devices/effects within a text? Was it ever suggested to you that your response to a text was inappropriate in some way, that you had made an invalid response?

If you are now in higher education, how has your experience of critical reading developed? Have you been introduced to new ways of reading texts, to critical theories you had not heard of before? Do you now feel more at ease with critical reading, more sure of what you are doing? Or less at ease, less confident? Does reading criticism and critical theory help you to appreciate imaginative texts and vice versa? Are you happy with the distinction between 'imaginative' and 'critical' or would you like to collapse that distinction in some way?

6 Here are four commentators describing the practice of what we might call feminine reading:

I choose to work on the texts that 'touch' me. I use the word deliberately because I believe there is a bodily relationship between reader and text. We work very close to the text, as close to the body of the text as possible; we work phonically, listening to the text, as well as graphically and typographically.

Sometimes I look at the design, the geography of the text, as if it were a map, embodying the world. I look at its legs, its thighs, its belly, as well as its trees and rivers: an immense human and earthly cosmos. I like to work

Young Girl Reclining on Sofa *Lucius Rossi, Fine Art Photographic Library*

like an ant, crawling the entire length of a text and examining all its details, as well as like a bird that flies over it, or like one of Tsvetaeva's immense ears, listening to its music.

We listen to a text with numerous ears. We hear each other talking with foreign accents and we listen to the foreign accents, its strangenesses, and these act like signals, attracting our attention. These strangenesses are our cue. We aren't looking for the author as much as what made the author take the particular path they took, write what they wrote. We're looking for the secret of creation, the same process of creation each one of us is constantly involved with in the process of our lives. Texts are the witnesses of our proceeding. The text opens up a path which is already ours and yet not altogether ours.

Hélène Cixous, 'Conversations with Hélène Cixous and
Members of the Centre d'Etudes Féminines' (1986) p. 148

Virginia Woolf believed that a woman's reading group was revolutionary; and in her edition of Virginia Woolf's *Reading Notebooks*, Brenda Silver describes a lifetime of intellectual and political obsession with reading and notetaking which belies the biographer's portrait of a lady. Woolf's attitude (reading as desire) is perhaps best expressed in this letter to Ethel Smyth:

Sometimes I think heaven must be one continuous unexhausted reading. It is a disembodied trance-like intense rapture that used to seize me as a girl, and comes back now and again down here, with a violence that lays me low ... the state of reading consists in the complete elimination of the *ego*; and its the ego that erects itself like another part of the body I don't dare to name (Letter 2915).

It seems pointless to argue whether women are better readers than men because of their receptiveness and openness to the text. What is important is that Woolf saw gender as determining the roles of writer, speaker, and reader and privileged the female versions of these acts as more democratic than the male. Given contemporary male critics' descriptions of ravishing the text, Woolf's critical 'still practice' as the enraptured reader, ego-less and open to the text rather than aggressively attacking it, is consistent with the goals of feminist philosophy. The reader's desire to be enraptured by the writer, which Woolf celebrates, is very different from contemporary criticism's assertion of intellectual superiority over writers and books. It is difficult to imagine an American formalist deconstructive critic being laid low by a book. Woolf's imagined embrace of the common reader and the common writer comes from a desire for shared pleasure.

Jane Marcus, 'Still Practice, A/Wrested Alphabet: Toward a Feminist Aesthetic (1987) p. 86

The only reply that can be given to the question of the meaning of the text is: read, perceive, feel ... *Who are you?* would be a pertinent question, provided that it does not collapse into a demand for an identity card or an autobiographical anecdote. The answer would be: *and who are you?* Can we meet? Talk? Love? Create something together? Thanks to which milieu? What between-us [entre-nous]?

We cannot do that without the horizon of sexual difference.

Luce Irigaray, *Sexes et Parentés* (1987; 1991) p. 14

Perhaps the best way to describe a 'feminine' reading is to say that it implies 'opening' the self to what the text is saying, even if this is puz or painful or problematic. It entails reading to see how a text is made exploring all the various resources for meaning a writer has at their disposal: the writer's intended meaning, as well as the 'other' meanings that contradict, complement, unsettle or dislodge this meaning. It involves standing back from the text and looking at its overall construction; it entails reading at the level of the words themselves, at the level of syntax, the syllables and letter-patterns, the rhythm and punctuation. It means asking who and what produced this text: and why? It means acknowledging that I as reader participate in the on-going process of the text's creation; it means recognizing that my reading is itself a product of certain questions, blind-spots, needs and desires, and that these motivations are constantly changing.

Susan Sellers, 'Learning to Read the Feminine' (1990) p. 192

Let's try to understand these extracts and the relations between them:

➤ Both Woolf's comments, quoted in Marcus, and Cixous's suggest a connection between reading and a bodily awareness of sensation. Look particularly at Woolf's and Cixous's use of figurative language. Both are expressing a very physical relation to reading, though in somewhat different ways. How would you characterize their responses?

➤ Woolf's description of reading is like a sexual encounter; Rossi's '*Young Girl Reclining on a Sofa*' also carries erotic overtones. I flippantly mentioned earlier that I thought it unlikely that the female reader was reading literary theory. What is interesting, however, is that many images of women reading are being used at the moment as the cover image for literary books and these are often books of a more general nature, not specifically books about women's reading. With what motivation, do you think? Is the image of a woman reading an effective marketing device and, if so, why?

➤ Both Marcus and Sellers talk of being 'open' to the text; Cixous repeatedly uses the verb to work rather than to read; Irigaray seems to suggest a kind of conversation between text and reader. What do these terms suggest to you about the reading practices being discussed here?

➤ Cixous mentions the 'strangenesses' of a text, its 'foreign accents'. I don't think Cixous is primarily talking here about texts written in languages she does not know, or about texts in translation. What, then, is the point?

➤ Marcus compares Woolf's 'reading as desire' with the reading practices of contemporary critical discourses familiar to American academics and students. What differences does she notice in the relationship of the reader to the text? What is the significance of the ego in this debate?

➤ Cixous says, 'we aren't looking for the author ...'; Irigaray says that she doesn't want 'a demand for an identity card or an autobiographical anecdote'. What is the significance of these cautions? What kind of relationships do Cixous and Irigaray want between readers and authors? It would help at this point if you referred to the material in the section on The Death of the Woman Author.

➤ The reading practices that Sellers lists come from a range of theoretical bases: structuralism, stylistics, materialism, reader-response theories, psychoanalysis.

Surely Sellers cannot be saying that all these are feminine readings. Is she saying that they could be used to produce a feminine reading or that the openness to a range of reading activities is itself feminine or ... what?

➤ Cixous talks of choosing texts that touch her in some way. What if you cannot 'choose' your text; what if it is 'required reading' for a course; what if you don't like the text? Is a feminine reading possible in these constrained circumstances?

➤ Marcus, following Woolf, discusses the 'enraptured reader' and the 'shared pleasure' of the reader and writer. Is it impossible for the feminine reader to be a disenchanted reader, a bored reader, a suspicious reader? Is the 'enraptured reader' the only feminine reading position?

7 Compare your understanding of feminine reading with your analysis of your own reading experiences which you considered under points 4 and 5.

➤ Would you now describe your reading or some aspects of your reading as feminine? If not, would you like to become a feminine reader; does it appeal?

➤ Do you have to make some distinctions between reading for pleasure, reading for information, course-related reading etc.; are some of these readings closer to feminine reading than others?

➤ Do you, like Woolf, have memories of reading in a 'trance–like intense rapture'? Do you still have that experience or did it leave you at a certain age? Have you ever noticed children reading in that way?

➤ Do you sympathize with Marcus's comments about certain styles of reading as 'aggressively attacking' the text and exhibiting an 'intellectual superiority' over the text?

➤ Thinking again of your education in reading at school and elsewhere, has it been an education in feminine reading or, as Marcus describes, in an 'aggressively attacking' reading or in some other kind of reading?

8 With this understanding of feminine reading, do you want to return to the extracts from Cixous you considered earlier? Would you now approach them in a different way? Obviously, feminine reading and feminine writing are not separate activities so review all the extracts in this section to find some common threads. For instance:

• an emphasis on openness

• the multiple rather than the single; the varied rather than the prescriptive

• delighting in 'otherness'

• concern with creativity

• concern with physicality and the body.

In my own review I was struck by the number of ways the body and the relation to the body was described, even within these few extracts. This is an area you could research.

Feminine and/or feminist?

9 In what ways might the *feminine* practices of writing and reading we have considered in this section be seen also as *feminist* practices? Whether we like it or not we inevitably return here to the issue of definition. What is feminist/feminism; how is that similar or dissimilar to the feminine? Two activities which could help – though, as ever, don't look for easy answers – would be:

➤ to refer again to the texts listed in the 'Introduction' to this section and examine the meanings of feminist/feminism. How do they compare with the meanings for feminine?

➤ to refer to the sections on Defining a Feminist Text and Feminist Reading. Is the material there distinct from, interrelating with, overlapping the material on *feminine* texts and *feminine* reading in this section? To compare Judith Fetterley's figure of the 'resisting' female reader with the figure of the feminine reader proffered here would be particularly helpful.

10 At the end of Moi's 'Feminist Literary Criticism' she summarizes the definitions of 'female', 'feminine' and 'feminist' which she has been discussing throughout the essay:

> To sum up this presentation of feminist literary theory today, we can now define as *female*, writing by women, bearing in mind that this label does not say anything at all about the nature of that writing; as *feminist*, writing which takes a discernible anti-patriarchal and anti-sexist position; and as *feminine*, writing which seems to be marginalised (repressed, silenced) by the ruling social/linguistic order. The latter does not (*pace* Kristeva) entail any specific *political* position (no clear-cut feminism), although it does not exclude it either. Thus some feminists, such as Hélène Cixous, have tried to produce 'feminine' writing, and others (Simone de Beauvoir) have not. The problem with the 'feminine' label so far has been its tendency to privilege and/or overlap with existing forms of literary modernism and avant-gardism. This, I think, is only one possible way of being marginal in relation to the dominant order (in this case in relation to the traditional representational or realist forms of writing). 'Marginality' cannot or should not *only* be a matter of form.
>
> Toril Moi, 'Feminist Literary Criticism' (1982) p. 220

Pam Morris comments, as follows, on the political potential of Cixous's feminine writing practice:

> A feminine practice of writing is offered by Cixous as a means of resistance; the word-play, metaphors and punning exemplified in her style challenges (explodes it with laughter) any insistence on unitary meaning, the logic of the same, asserting instead that 'nothing is simply one thing'. Her syntax attempts to track the libidinal pulse of repressed desire; rhythm and sound patterns convey a sensuous tactile immediacy rather than rational mastery of what is other and separate. Identity slips free of a unified 'I' into a

polyvalent play of the multiple possibilities of self: 'I' and 'you' not 'I' or 'you'. Such heterogeneity mocks any authoritative or dominant language which must always insist on its version of 'truth', 'identity' and 'knowledge' as single and unquestionable. The subversiveness of a feminine practice of writing, then, is aiming to undermine the underlying logic, the very perception of reality on which the present structure of cultural order rests. For this reason Cixous likes the metaphor of women as moles tunneling out of the darkness imposed on them: 'We are living in an age where the conceptual foundation of an ancient culture is in the process of being undermined by millions of a species of mole.' When the process is successful, 'all the stories would be there to retell differently, the future would be incalculable'.

Pam Morris, Literature and Feminism: An Introduction (1993) pp. 123–4

Morris summarizes here several aspects of the feminine which we have already noticed in the extracts:

- its questioning of the authority of singular meaning – the party line, the definitive study, the seminal text;

- its interest in the force of repressed desire rather than rational control;

- its attraction to a sense of multiple identities (remember Woolf's remark in Marcus about the 'elimination of the *ego*');

- the suggestive use of metaphor. Morris mentions the metaphor of the mole; in other extracts, the feminine has been likened to a disruptive pressure, an 'insurrectionary dough' or represented as an uncontainable force, flooding, flowing or seeping like water or lava.

- If, for the moment, we accept Moi's definition of feminist writing – that is, writing which takes 'a discernible anti-patriarchal and anti-sexist position', how does this accord, or not, with Morris's description of feminine writing?

11 Finally, I want to return to a problem raised by Irigaray earlier in this section. She said that 'to speak *of* or *about* woman may always boil down to, or be understood as, a recuperation of the feminine within the logic that maintains it in repression, censorship, nonrecognition'. This seems to be a dire position for women: the feminine is unspeakable and what is spoken is readily harnessed by the dominant order. What can women do?

Here are two suggestions from Irigaray herself. Firstly, an attack on patriarchal thinking:

> ... the issue is not one of elaborating a new theory of which woman would be the *subject* or the *object*, but of jamming the theoretical machinery itself, of suspending its pretention to the production of a truth and of a meaning that are excessively univocal ... They (woman) should not put it, then, in the form 'What is woman?' but rather, repeating/interpreting the way in which, within discourse, the feminine finds itself defined as lack, deficiency, or as imitation and negative image of the subject, they should signify that with respect to this logic a *disruptive excess* is possible on the feminine side.

Luce Irigaray 'The Power of Discourse and Subordination of the Feminine' (1975; 1985) p. 78

Secondly, a suggestion as to how feminine and feminist politics may work together:

> Of course, certain things have been achieved for women, in large parts owing to the liberation movements: liberalized contraception, abortion, and so on. These gains make it possible to raise again, differently, the question of what the social status of women might be – in particular through its differentiation from a simple reproductive-maternal function. But these contributions may always just as easily be turned against women. In other words, we cannot yet speak, in this connection, of a feminine politics, but only of certain conditions under which it may be possible. The first being an end to silence concerning the exploitation experienced by women: the systematic refusal to 'keep quiet' practiced by the liberation movements.
>
> Luce Irigaray, 'Questions' (1977; 1985) p. 128

In this second analysis feminist politics seems to be the precursor of feminine politics. How do you respond to Irigaray's suggestions? What are your final thoughts on the feminine and the relationship between the feminine and the feminist?

Conclusion

In what ways does this poem relate to the content of this section?

I Poet

ah was readin
readin all de time
fram book
fram play
fram t.v.
fram life
in odder words
fram yuh all
befo ah was writin
ah was readin
yuh all
neva did know who yuh all was but
ah was full a love
ah give it here
ah give it dere
neva see no harm
in a likkle share of
de warmes ting ah have
sista, bredda,
older, younger
neva matta

185

jus love
like evrybody was preachin
ah was readin
ah was lovin
befo ah was writin

ah read all yuh poems
ah read all yuh plays
ah read all tea leaf, palm,
anyting wid a good story
even if it didn't always have
a happy endin
and evryting ah read, ah sey,
but how come I know dis story already? or
I do dat yesterday
I see dat last night
I live troo dat
so I stap readin fi a while
stap lovin fi a while
jus befo I start writin
I stap evryting
jus fi a moment
and I sey, maybe, (I humble)
I sey, maybe
it was you readin me all de time
so doah I was well hurt inside
wen yuh all did sey
I wasn't no poet
I never mind
cause I sey
I was poet all de time
so I start write
an I tankful
to madda an fadda
dat ah did read an love firs
fah I know
when I writin
I poem
is you
all you

Jean 'Binta' Breeze, 'I Poet' (1992)

References and further reading

Rachel Bowlby, *Still Crazy After All These Years: Women, Writing and Psychoanalysis*

Jean 'Binta' Breeze, 'I Poet', *Spring Cleaning*

Hélène Cixous, 'The Laugh of the Medusa' (1976) in Elaine Marks and Isabelle de Courtivron (eds), *New French Feminisms: An Anthology*. This essay has been widely anthologized. See, for example, Dennis Walder (ed.), *Literature in the Modern World: Critical Essays and Documents*

Hélène Cixous, 'Castration or Decapitation?' in *Signs: Journal of Women in Culture and Society*

Hélène Cixous, 'Conversations with Hélène Cixous and Members of the Centre d'Etudes Féminines' (1986) in Susan Sellers (ed.), *Writing Differences: Readings from the Seminar of Hélène Cixous*

Claire Duchen (ed.), *French Connections: Voices from the Women's Movement in France*

Mary Ellmann, *Thinking About Women*

Kate Flint, *The Woman Reader 1837–1914*. Within this detailed study of women's relation to reading, Flint raises many fascinating points about the visual representation of the woman reader during this period.

Elizabeth Grosz, *Sexual Subversions: Three French Feminists*

Luce Irigaray, 'The Power of Discourse and the Subordination of the Feminine' (1975) and 'Questions' (1997), both included in *This Sex Which Is Not One*

Luce Irigaray, *Sexes et Parentés* (1987). Quoted extract and page reference from Margaret Whitford (ed.), *The Irigaray Reader*

Mary Jacobus, 'Men of Maxims and *The Mill on the Floss*', *Reading Woman: Essays in Feminist Criticism*. Jacobus's discussion of Eliot's novel is in the context of Irigaray's work.

Nicole Ward Jouve, *White Woman Speaks with Forked Tongue: Criticism as Autobiography*

Cheris Kramarae and Paula A. Treichler, *Amazons, Bluestockings and Crones: A Feminist Dictionary*

Julia Kristeva, 'Woman Can Never Be Defined' (1974) in Elaine Marks and Isabelle de Courtivron (eds), *New French Feminisms: An Anthology*

Jane Marcus, 'Still Practice, A/Wrested Alphabet: Toward a Feminist Aesthetic' in Shari Benstock (ed.), *Feminist Issues in Literary Scholarship*

Jane Mills, *Womanwords: A Vocabulary of Culture and Patriarchal Society*

Toril Moi, 'Feminist Literary Criticism' in Ann Jefferson and David Robey (eds), *Modern Literary Theory: A Comparative Introduction*. Extracts from this essay are also available under the title 'Feminist, Female, Feminine, in Catherine Belsey and Jane Moore (eds), *The Feminist Reader: Essays in Gender and the Politics of Literary Criticism*

Pam Morris, *Literature and Feminism: An Introduction*

Susan Sellers, 'Learning to Read the Feminine' in Helen Wilcox, Keith McWatters, Ann Thompson, Linda R. Williams (eds), *The Body and the Text: Hélène Cixous, Reading and Teaching*. See also Jennifer Birkett's essay in this volume, 'The Implications of *Etudes Féminines* for Teaching', for a most useful situating of Cixous's ideas within a British institutional context.

Susan Sellers, *Language and Sexual Difference: Feminist Writing in France*

Elizabeth Wright (ed.), *Feminism and Psychoanalysis: A Critical Dictionary*

Finding the Subject

Introduction

I am going to simplify a complicated argument in feminism about women's subjectivity, about what it means when a woman says 'I'. This has been an important issue for feminist writers, readers and literary critics because of our awareness that writing is one of the locations in which women can construct a sense of self. What a woman writes or reads *about* women can create or limit possibilities *for* women. Thus, questions of representation are at the same time political questions. The debate I am describing is one between humanist and anti-humanist concepts of the subject. The actual term 'subject' is usually employed by the anti-humanist position; the humanist position tends to refer to 'identity' or 'the individual'.

Humanist

The humanist wing of feminism would argue that women are misrepresented under patriarchy and that the images of women which appear in literature, the media and elsewhere are often false and misogynistic. Women find it difficult to give expression to their true selves and can feel invisible or marginal in a male-dominated culture. Part of the struggle of feminism has been to support women in creating new, valid images of themselves, a sense of wholeness and a more authentic representation of what it means to be a woman. In this endeavour emphasis is given to the centrality of personal experience, the need to find one's own voice and to give an account of one's inner self.

Anti-humanist

In its concern with the subject, the anti-humanist wing of feminism has been influenced by a number of theoretical discourses – most notably:

- the psychoanalytical theories of Jacques Lacan

- theories of ideology developed by Louis Althusser

- developments in post-structuralist thought, particularly in the area of language

- the discourse theory of Michel Foucault.

Don't worry if you don't know anything about all these theories; it is enough, at the moment, to be aware of the context in which ideas about subjectivity are operating. If you would like to learn more, introductions can be found in:

Elizabeth Grosz, 'Contemporary Theories of Power and Subjectivity' in Sneja Gunew (ed.), *Feminist Knowledge: Critique and Construct* (1990)

Lois McNay, *Foucault and Feminism: Power, Gender and the Self* (1992)

My *Feminist Literary Theory: A Reader* (second edition), (1996), chapter 6.

Other useful references are at the end of this section.

Anti-humanist feminists would agree that, under patriarchy, women are oppressed and marginalized. Some sense of wholeness is clearly needed for women to remain sane and functioning on a daily basis but there is no such things as a single, coherent identity. They would argue that:

- subjectivity is not single but multiple; there is not one true 'I', but lots of different 'I's';
- subjectivity is not complete and resolved but *in process*, never fully realized;
- the subject does not create the world but is the product, the effect of language and culture;
- the subject does not control his/her world but is *subject* to certain available positions in the culture (N.B. here another meaning of the term 'subject');
- the hope of a unified subject can be seen as a utopian desire for a pre-social state or as a relic of bourgeois humanism. To pursue the former could lead to psychosis; to pursue the latter will confine women to the existing order.

People sometimes feel resistant to this anti-humanist position since it is not the dominant position in our culture and, hence, less familiar. Furthermore, at first glance, it can seem to be suggesting that we are, on the one hand, psychological wrecks, fragmented and unresolved and, on the other, victims of insidious controlling forces – neither of which appears a particularly attractive sense of selfhood. In fact the anti-humanist position does recognize that there are psychological and political reasons why the desire for wholeness and integrity remains strong within us and it does affirm the possibility – indeed, the necessity – of choice. However, it believes that these choices are constrained in a way that the humanist emphasis on 'free choice' does not acknowledge.

To take an extreme example of this last issue, there is little point in my waking up tomorrow and 'choosing' to be a member of the Japanese Royal family; that position is not available to me. But, equally, there is not much point in my deciding to become a member of the British Royal family, although it is, apparently and alarmingly, many people's frequent dream fantasy. Despite Mr Major's protestations about the classless society, despite sharing a common language and certain cultural experiences, we all know that the British Royal family is unlikely to extend its embrace as far as the likes of me. Hence, one aspect of my subjectivity is where I am both placed and place myself in terms of class identity. It is not that I am irrevocably fixed – in fact, through education I have changed my class position – but, on the other hand, I don't have a free choice to place myself anywhere on the greasy pole of class.

You might like to think further about this problem of choice. For example, to what extent do we have a free choice about marrying or not marrying; about career possibilities; about our appearance?

The above not only simplifies the argument but polarizes it: there are many other feminist positions which mediate between and complicate the two here given. Moreover, I do not want to suggest that one position is somehow 'better' than the other. Indeed, I am very aware how in my own thinking and practice I oscillate between positions. However, for the moment, these two arguments can act as a frame to our considerations.

There are four ways in which I suggest we can explore this area:

- looking at some literary representations of women actively constructing and deconstructing themselves

- looking at some poetry which examines women's sense of a fragmented self, a prevalent self-image in women's writing

- considering further the concept of subjectivity *in process*

- considering further the political implications of the debate – which position (or positions) on subjectivity is beneficial for feminism?

Cartoon by Angela Martin, Everywoman, *November 1994*

Lisa Adkins graphics from Trouble & Strife *25, Winter 1992*

Constructing and deconstructing the female subject

1 Read these two passages. The first, from Doris Lessing, describes an adolescent girl on the verge of womanhood; the second, from Sylvia Plath, tells of Esther Greenwood, an American undergraduate of the 1950s, close to psychological breakdown:

> Her first self-portraits ... she had found an old dress, white with sprigs of pink flowers. Parts were stained and worn. These she cut away. Bits of lace and tulle, beads, scarves were added and removed to a kaleidoscope garment that changed with her needs. Most often it was a bride's dress. Then it was a young girl's dress – that ambiguous declaration of naïveté more usually made by a maturer vision than that of the wearer, an eye that sees the fragility of certain types of young girls' clothes as the expression of the evanescence of that flesh. It was nightdress when she wore its transparency over her naked body. It was evening dress, and sometimes when she did not intend this, for a hardness in her, the watchfulness of her defences, took away innocence from anything she wore, so that she might have flowers in her hair, in an attempt at her version of Primavera, yet she had about her

the look of a woman who has calculated the exact amount of flesh she will show at a dinner party. This dress was for me an emotional experience. I was frightened by it. Again, this was a question of my helplessness with her. I believed her capable of going out on the pavement wearing it. Now I judge myself to have been stupid: the elderly tend not to see – they have forgotten – that hidden person in the young creature, the strongest and most powerful member among the cast of characters inhabiting an adolescent body, the self which instructs, chooses experience – and protects.

Doris Lessing, *The Memoirs of a Survivor* (1976) pp. 53–4

It was becoming more and more difficult for me to decide to do anything in those last days. And when I eventually *did* decide to do something, such as packing a suitcase, I only dragged all my grubby, expensive clothes out of the bureau and the closet and spread them on the chairs and the bed and the floor and then sat and stared at them, utterly perplexed. They seemed to have a separate, mulish identity of their own that refused to be washed and folded and stowed.

'It's these clothes,' I told Doreen. 'I just can't face these clothes when I come back.'

'That's easy.'

And in her beautiful, one-track way, Doreen started to snatch up slips and stockings and the elaborate strapless bra, full of steel springs – a free gift from the Primrose Corset Company, which I'd never had the courage to wear – and finally, one by one, the sad array of queerly cut forty-dollar dresses ...

'Hey, leave that one out. I'm wearing it.'

Doreen extricated a black scrap from her bundle and dropped it in my lap. Then, snowballing the rest of the clothes into one soft, conglomerate mass, she stuffed them out of sight under the bed.

Quiet as a burglar in my cornflower-sprigged bathrobe, I crept to the edge of the parapet. The parapet reached almost to my shoulders, so I dragged a folding chair from a stack against the wall, opened it, and climbed onto the precarious seat.

A stiff breeze lifted the hair from my head. At my feet, the city doused its lights in sleep, its buildings blackened, as if for a funeral.

It was my last night.

I grasped the bundle I carried and pulled at a pale tail. A strapless elasticized slip which, in the course of wear, had lost its elasticity, slumped into my hand. I waved it, like a flat of truce, once, twice ... The breeze caught it, and I let it go.

A white flake floated out into the night, and began its slow descent. I wondered on what street or rooftop it would come to rest.

I tugged at the bundle again.

The wind made an effort, but failed, and a batlike shadow sank toward the roof garden on the penthouse opposite.

Piece by piece, I fed my wardrobe to the night wind, and flutteringly, like a loved one's ashes, the gray scraps were ferried off, to settle here, there, exactly where I would never know, in the dark heart of New York.

Sylvia Plath, *The Bell Jar* (1972) pp. 85, 91

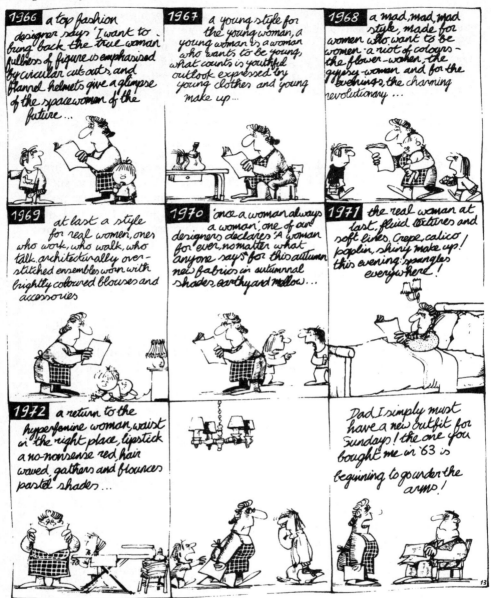

Cartoon by Claire Bretécher, What a Life … *(Frederick Muller Ltd., 1982), from* Salades de Saison, *'Les Petites Femmes de Paris'* © *Dargand*

Take a few minutes to gather together your thoughts about these passages. Obviously the common denominator is the link, frequent in women's writing, between clothes and identity. Trying clothes on, adapting clothes, discarding clothes become metaphors for the creation, transformation and abandonment of a sense of self or a sense of different selves.

➤ As Lessing's character puts on different clothes and as Plath's character sorts through and throws away assorted clothes, varied female identities emerge. How do you respond to these representations of womanhood?

➤ Lessing likens the process to the painting of 'self-portraits'. Do you find that an apt analogy? What other analogies could you use?

➤ Lessing's narrator mentions, 'the self which instructs, chooses experience – and protects'. What do you think that means? In these passages, who is in control; who participates in these constructions and deconstructions of the self? In both passages, there is a sense of wider social forces at work. To what extent are these characters freely choosing their experience?

➤ Are you aware in your own life of choosing clothes to construct a particular definition(s) of femininity? Presumably this is a changing definition of femininity; you wouldn't wear the same clothes for a wedding as you would for cleaning the house. Can you look to earlier periods in your life and see, in retrospect if not at the time, how you were trying to 'assemble' yourself in the way Lessing's character does?

➤ Do you find these movements between different constructions of yourself a pleasurable or a painful experience?

➤ Have you ever used dress as a sign of resistance – feminist or otherwise? Few people get through adolescence without, consciously or unconsciously, using dress in this way. Chris Weedon writes:

> Dress, for example, necessarily signifies and is open to many different readings. The effect intended by the wearer can never be guaranteed, but this does not negate the potential of dress as a site of conscious sexual-political struggle. It is possible, for example, to dress in conventionally feminine ways yet wear women's liberation jewellery, to dress in ways likely to be read as signifying a rejection of current norms of femininity or in accordance with the current conventions of lesbian culture.
>
> Chris Weedon, *Feminist Practice and Poststructuralist Theory* (1987) p. 87

➤ Some women claim that their attitude to clothes is entirely practical and utilitarian – 'I wear whatever is comfortable.' Is such a claim every totally valid?

2 Angela Carter and Jean Rhys are further examples of authors interested in women creating themselves through clothes. Scenes in which women view themselves in mirrors and/or are viewed by others also frequently feature in women's writing as explorations of female subjectivity. You could research these issues further as a longer-term project or a group project.

The fragmented woman

3 One of the most unnerving impressions of the Plath passage we have just looked at is that sense of woman as a mere collection of constituent parts beneath which is – possibly – nothing. What is left once all the visible 'bits' have been shed? In writing by women certain motifs recur as signs of women's feeling of fragmentation and obliteration in patriarchal culture.

Can you find examples of the following? Contemporary women's poetry is a particularly rich source but feel free to refer also to other literary and cultural forms. You might over time put together an anthology or a bibliography of appropriate references:

➤ Woman as falsely represented, distorted images of women
➤ Woman as unable to speak, silent or stumbling over words
➤ Woman as a public persona, a facade or mask behind which is emptiness
➤ Woman as a public persona behind which is anger, revenge
➤ Woman as a public persona behind which is another, secret self
➤ Woman as dismembered, a set of parts or a set of functions
➤ Woman as invisible or insubstantial, gradually disappearing like Alice's Cheshire Cat.

A good example of the last category would be a speech on eating disorders given by Princess Diana in May, 1993 and much reported in the British press, when she spoke of the feeling of dissolving 'like a Disprin';
  or 'I felt myself melting into the shadows like the negative of a person I'd never seen before in my life' (p. 8, *The Bell Jar*);
  or 'She was my patron saint, the one I called on when I felt myself dwindling away through cracks in the floor or slowly fading in the street' (p. 142, Jeanette Winterson, *Sexing the Cherry*).

4 How would you relate the idea of fragmentation to the following poems?

> By chance I was alone in my bed the morning
> I woke to find my body had gone.
> It had been coming. I'd cut off my hair in sections
> so each of you would have something to remember,
> then my nails worked loose from their beds
> of oystery flesh. Who was it got them?
> One night I slipped out of my skin. It lolloped
> hooked to my heels, hurting. I had to spray on
> more scent so you could find me in the dark,
> I was going so fast. One of you begged for my ears
> because you could hear the sea in them.
>
> First I planned to steal myself back. I was a mist
> on thighs, belly and hips. I'd slept with so many men.
> I was with you in the ash-haunted stations of Poland,
> I was with you on that grey plaza in Berlin
> while you wolfed three doughnuts without stopping,
> thinking yourself alone. Soon I recovered my lips
> by waiting behind the mirror while you shaved.
> You pouted. I peeled away kisses like wax
> no longer warm to the touch. Then I flew off.
>
> Next I decided to become a virgin. Without a body
> it was easy to make up a new story. In seven years
> every invisible cell could be renewed

and none of them would have touched any of you.
I went to a cold lake, to a grey-lichened island,
I was gold in the wallet of the water.
I was known to the inhabitants, who were in love
with the coveted whisper of my virginity:
all too soon they were bringing me coffee and perfume,
cash under stones. I could really do something for them.

Thirdly I tried marriage to a good husband
who knew my past but forgave it. I believed in the power
of his penis to smoke out all those men
so that bit by bit my body service would resume,
although for a while I'd be the one woman in the world
who was only present in the smile of her vagina.
He stroked the air where I might have been.
I turned to the mirror and saw mist gather
as if someone lived in the glass. Recovering
I breathed to myself, '*Hold on! I'm coming.*'

Helen Dunmore, 'Three Ways of Recovering a Body' (1994)

Deep in the recesses of my heart hangs a picture of myself
God knows who painted it and when
There it remains hidden from me and my friends
but if ever I glimpse it, even by accident,
My heart shudders at the comparison with myself.

Fahmida Riaz, 'Image' (1991)

I made my head, as I used to,
out of a paper bag,
pull it down to the collarbone,

draw eyes around my eyes,
with purple and green
spikes to show surprise,
a thumb-shaped nose,

a mouth around my mouth
penciled by touch, then colored in
flat red.

With this new head, the body now
stretched like a stocking and exhausted could
dance again; if I made a
tongue I could sing.

An old sheet and it's Halloween;
but why is it worse or more
frightening, this pinface
head of square hair and no chin?

Like an idiot, it has no past
and is always entering the future
through its slots of eyes, purblind

and groping with its thick smile,
a tentacle of perpetual joy.

Paper head, I prefer you
because of your emptiness;
from within you any
word could still be said.

With you I could have
more than one skin,
a blank interior, a repertoire
of untold stories,
a fresh beginning.

Margaret Atwood, 'A Paper Bag' (1978)

In all three poems there is a sense of an identity painfully split between an inner and an outer self. Which, if either, is the 'real' self, the active and creative self? Riaz's poem is translated from Urdu which makes comment on linguistic effects an uncertain activity for me but I am intrigued by the two uses of the word 'myself'. The fact that in neither case can one be sure of the referent is precisely the problem of the poem; where is 'myself'? Atwood's poem plays between a facade and an inner self though the conventions are reversed. It is not the inner self that provides profound meaning but the blank facade that offers possibilities of 'untold stories' and 'a fresh beginning'. Dunmore, like Sylvia Plath, explores the disjunction between self and body, the body becoming a kind of interesting project to be regarded quizzically and disarmingly. In selecting these poems I deliberately left out the most obvious choices, namely the poetry of Plath and Anne Sexton but do refer to these authors too if you want to investigate this area.

➤ You could take up some of these points to produce a reading of one or more of the poems above. Consider:

the self as split

the body as object

an absence of a tangible sense of self, a vacuum

the construction of a self

facades, masks, disguises.

➤ To what extent do you think these poems also show an aspiration towards wholeness? Rosemary Jackson comments:

> A fantasy of physical fragmentation corresponds, then, to a breakdown of rational unity. That linguistic order which creates and constitutes a whole self, a total body, is un–done.

Rosemary Jackson, *Fantasy: The Literature of Subversion* (1981) p. 90

➤ As I indicated in the 'Introduction' to this section, the problem could be phrased in two ways. Is this 'wholeness' a wish for a coherent, unified self who can function admirably in the social world; or is it an alluring but dangerous desire for a state of undifferentiation that preceded the creation of the subject, a fantasy of completeness?

Obviously the answer to that question needs to be pondered upon.

The subject in process

5 Julia Kristeva who, as both a critical theorist and a psychoanalyst, has worked extensively on the concept of the subject, uses the phrase 'subject in process'. She explains the phrase thus:

> Anyone who reads Artaud's texts will realize that all identities are unstable: the identity of linguistic signs, the identity of meaning and, as a result, the identity of the speaker. And in order to take account to his de-stabilization of meaning and of the subject I thought the term 'subject in process' would be appropriate. 'Process' in the sense of process but also in the sense of a legal proceeding where the subject is committed to trial, because our identities in life are constantly called into question, brought to trial, over-ruled.

> Julia Kristeva, 'A Question of Subjectivity', (1986) p. 19

There are several points in even this short quotation which you may want to consider further. For example, we could link Kristeva's sense of legal process with one of the meanings of subject considered earlier, that is 'subject to'. Both suggest that identity is not entirely freely chosen or independently created. What other comments would you want to clarify?

Pam Morris glosses Kristeva's explanation of 'subject in process' in the following way:

> Meaning remains shareable but always in a state of generative instability. Similarly, identity is constructed on this intertextuality of boundary between the unconscious drives and the social; self is thus a dialogic interaction of these two dispositions and produces a subject always 'in process' – a pluralized identity never fixed or finished.

> Pam Morris, *Literature and Feminism: An Introduction* (1993) p. 146

Thus the subject is, in several ways, in flux:

- It is 'destablilized', formed between/across the unconscious and the social.

- The subject precariously relies on the repression of the unconscious; in the Plath passage we saw that Esther's sense of subjectivity was threatened by unconscious forces.

- It is subject to different ideological pressures, constituted in constantly varying discursive formations.

Let's consider some concrete examples of a de-stable subjectivity:

➤ Have you ever bumped into an old friend and discovered that you no longer have anything in common? The person you were then is not the person you are now.

➤ If I went out for a riotous Saturday night with my friends and for a job interview on the Monday morning would I present myself in the same way on both occasions? (Not if I wanted the job is the simple answer to that.) Would this be an illustration of a changing 'me'?

➤ Do you know people who swore they would never have children and then, when the situation arose, turned into doting parents? Which was the genuine conviction – pre-children, post-children, both?

➤ Do you know people with strong beliefs – political, religious etc. – who then dramatically changed those views? For example, I have known numerous trainee-teachers who were liberal and egalitarian before the first teaching practice and somewhat to the right of Ghengis Khan at the end.

➤ To return to our thinking on appearance, why do women open their wardrobes, look at rows and shelves of clothes and say, 'I haven't a thing to wear'? Obviously the comment is factually incorrect; what, then, does it signify?

In all these transformation, it is not that subjectivity is so changed as to render the person unrecognizable. If my friends were flies on the wall at my interview they would recognize that it was me, albeit on my best behaviour. Nor is it simply a case of saying we all have many aspects to our personality. At the interview I shall construct myself differently so as to fulfil the demands of the situation and, conversely, the situation will, in a sense, require of me my best behaviour if I am to perform appropriately. One of the very distressing aspects of severe mental illness or conditions such as Alzheimer's is that the subject *is* so transformed as to be barely recognizable.

6 Whether you see yourself as 'multiple' or 'fragmented' indicates radically different positions. The former is more positive, suggesting diversity, variety, flexibility; the latter is negative, suggesting a loss of selfhood, a breakdown into atomized parts. How do you respond to the subjectivities outlined below? The first passage, from Wendy Mulford, explores a specifically writing subject; the second and third, from Donna Haraway and Gloria Anzaldúa, create new concepts of subjectivity appropriate, the authors believe, for the postmodern age:

> My writing, however, still works restlessly within the unreconstructed domain of the passions. This implies for me continuing to work with a subject, and 'I', despite or through its rifts, absences, contradictions, yet an 'I' which carries links with the Coleridgean 'I' in its perception of itself as moral agent and as in part imaginative creator of its world. Corkscrewing between this space of the 'I' and the actual world is that force we call love, creating its desired visionary world, in a relentless twisting to and fro of energy I map as a triangle. And what is transformative for me in this traditional mapping, even in our contemporary bleakness, is 'I' as active and desiring subject, that 'I' being specifically gendered.
>
> Wendy Mulford, 'Notes on Writing' (1982) p. 39

> The cyborg is resolutely committed to partiality, irony, intimacy, and perversity. It is oppositional, utopian, and completely without innocence. No longer structured by the polarity of public and private, the cyborg defines a technological polis based partly on a revolution of social relations in the *oikos*, the household. Nature and culture are reworked; the one can no longer be the resource for appropriation or incorporation by the other. The relationship for forming wholes from parts, including those of polarity and hierarchical domination, are at issue in the cyborg world. Unlike the

hopes of Frankenstein's monster, the cyborg does not expect its father to save it through a restoration of the garden; i.e., through the fabrication of a heterosexual mate, through its completion in a finished whole, a city and cosmos. The cyborg does not dream of community on the model of the organic family, this time without the Oedipal project. The cyborg would not recognize the Garden of Eden; it is not made of mud and cannot dream of returning to dust. Perhaps that is why I want to see if cyborgs can subvert the apocalypse of returning to nuclear dust in the manic compulsion to name the Enemy. Cyborgs are not reverent; they do not re- member the cosmos. They are wary of holism, but needy for connection – they seem to have a natural feel for united front politics, but without the vanguard party. The main trouble with cyborgs, of course, is that they are the illegitimate offspring of militarism and patriarchal capitalism, not to mention state socialism. But illegitimate offspring are often exceedingly unfaithful to their origins. Their fathers, after all, are inessential.

Donna Haraway, 'A Manifesto for Cyborgs: Science, Technology
and Socialist Feminism in the 1980s' (1985; 1989) pp. 175–6

The new *mestiza* copes by developing a tolerance for contradictions, a tolerance for ambiguity. She learns to be an Indian in Mexican culture, to be Mexican from an Anglo point of view. She learns to juggle cultures. She has a plural personality, she operates in a pluralistic model – nothing is thrust out, the good the bad and the ugly, nothing rejected, nothing abandoned. Not only does she sustain contradictions, she turns the ambivalence into something else.

She can be jarred out of ambivalence by an intense, and often painful, emotional event which inverts or resolves the ambivalence. I'm not sure exactly how. The work takes place underground – subconsciously. It is work that the soul performs. That focal point of fulcrum, that juncture where the mestiza stands, is where phenomena tend to collide. It is where the possibility of uniting all that is separate occurs. This assembly is not one where severed or separated pieces merely come together. Nor is it a balancing of opposing powers. In attempting to work out a synthesis, the self has added a third element which is greater than the sum of its severed parts. The third element is a new consciousness – a mestiza consciousness – and though it is a source of intense pain, its energy comes from continual creative motion that keeps breaking down the unitary aspect of each new paradigm.

Gloria Anzaldúa, 'La Conciencia de la Mestiza/Towards a New Consciousness' (1987) pp. 79–80

➤ Mulford's 'I' and Anzaldúa's 'mestiza' are gendered; Haraway's 'cyborg' is genderless. Do you find that the subjectivities that are gendered as female relate more readily to yourself and to the project of feminism; or do you find that a genderless subjectivity suggests its own range of possibilities for feminism? If so, what are they?

➤ Mulford and Anzaldúa, in particular, talk in terms of movement; all three make use of spatial relationships in exploring these particular subject positions; all three refer to the concept of transformation. Illustrate these aspects in the passages and consider the significance of them.

➤ Haraway's cyborg is 'wary of holism, but needy for connection'; what sense do you make of this distinction? Anzaldúa talks of the struggle for 'synthesis';

Mulford of a connecting 'force we call love'. These authors are not looking, naively, for some simple resolution for the subject. What, then, are they looking for; what do they see as the issues here?

➤ All three are unwilling to construct the subject in absolute terms. Can you illustrate and account for this?

➤ All three ground their subjects in specific historical/cultural/geographical contexts. Can you explain these and why the authors see it necessary to so do?

➤ Mulford and Anzaldúa make some reference to the role of the unconscious in the creation of the subject. In what ways? Could the unconscious have part to play in Haraway's cyborg or is this view of the subject too firmly linked to the technological?

Subjectivity and the politics of feminism

7 You may not fully understand Mulford's reference to Coleridge and to do so you need to read Coleridge's 1817 essay, 'Biographia Literaria' or consult critical works on the role of the poet; these would act as introductions to Coleridge's thought. My understanding is that Mulford is trying to formulate her position as a writer. She is aware that this identity is subject to 'rights, absences, contradictions', but also – and here lies the evocation of Coleridge – she is conscious of both the transformative power and the moral responsibility of the writer. This leads to our final problem in this section. Which concept of the subject is most productive for feminism? Or, are different concepts productive in different ways?

➤ Should the destabilized subject be seen by feminists as an opportunity for transformation or a further alienation and marginalization of women?

➤ Should feminists reject the coherent, rational subject as a product of humanism or claim it as a basis for political action?

➤ To return to Mulford's comment, does the feminist subject have to take up a moral and ethical position or continually warn against the dangers of dogmatism?

➤ Thinking again of Haraway's extract, should feminism be embracing the cyborg, the subject of the technological, computer age or fighting against it as the manifestation of 'militarism and patriarchal capitalism, not to mention state socialism'?

➤ And so on ... Consider also that none of these options are really straight-forward either/ors but examples from a range of possibilities.

8 Listed below, ordered simply on the basis of publication date, is a series of responses to this issue:

Isn't the 'death of the subject/author' position tied by mere reversal to the very ideology that invariably glorifies the artist as genius, whether for marketing purposes or out of conviction and habit? Hasn't capitalist modernization itself fragmented and dissolved bourgeois subjectivity and authorship, thus making attacks on such notions somewhat quixotic? And, finally, doesn't poststructuralism, where it simply denies the subject altogether, jettison the chance of challenging the *ideology of the subject* (as male, white, and middle-class) by developing alternative and different notions of subjectivity.

Andreas Huyssen, 'Mapping the Postmodern' (1984) p. 264

I would rather see subjectivity as always in process and contradiction, even female subjectivity, structured, divided and denigrated through the matrices of sexual difference. I see this understanding as part of a more optimistic political scenario than the ones I have been part of, one that can and ought to lead to a politics that will no longer overvalue control, rationality and individual power, and which, instead, tries to understand human desire, struggle and agency as they are mobilized through a more complicated, less finished and less heroic psychic schema.

Cora Kaplan, *Sea Changes: Essays on Culture and Feminism* (1986) p. 227

The truth of the matter is: one cannot deconstruct a subjectivity one has never been fully granted; one cannot diffuse a sexuality which has historically been defined as dark and mysterious. In order to announce the death of the subject one must first have gained the right to speak as one; in order to demystify metadiscourse one must first gain access to a place of enunciation.

Rosi Braidotti, 'Envy: or With Your Brains and My Looks' (1987) p. 237

To deconstruct [the subject] is not to negate or to dismiss, but to call into question and, perhaps, most importantly, to open up a term, like the subject, to a reusage or redeployment that previously had not been authorized.

Judith Butler, 'Feminism and the Question of Postmodernism' (1990) p. 172

I am very interested in black women's struggles right now for self-actualisation because, while I don't want to place so much emphasis on narcissistic individual change, I also know that when Paulo Freire (author of *Pedagogy of the Oppressed*) tells us we cannot enter the struggle as objects, only later to become subjects, that we can't be revolutionaries if we don't have a sense of our own subjectness. And that, to me, means that there is a certain stage in a revolutionary process where it is important for individuals to know who they are and where they are going and what they dream about.

bell hooks in interview with Grace Evans, 'To Live Long and Deep and Well', (1991) p. 13

Indeed, it is because subjecthood has become so difficult, has been so deconstructed, that there is need to work towards it. This is particularly so for women. It has often been pointed out in recent years that women's autobiographies carry a sense of their being somehow 'unfinished' human beings. The awareness of being 'different', pain arising from that sense of being somehow incomplete, unable to add up, to see your existence as related to, let alone symbolic of, the world at large.

Nicole Ward Jouve, *White Woman Speaks With Forked Tongue: Criticism as Autobiography* (1991) p. 11

At this point, I will take the risk of acting as critic of my own work. In writing my recent study of lesbian fiction from 1969 to 1989, I found myself constantly falling into that trap of generalising a lesbian subject, even when I situated that lesbian subject in a specific historical context and even as I attempted to show the failures of such generalisation. Pulled between the desire to affirm a historical lesbian collective identity and to 'de-stabilise' (another popular term today) that identity by introducing the discourses of differences within, I did not entirely satisfy either goal. Hence I am personally interested in ways of theorising how lesbians in different historical and cultural contexts develop a sense of themselves as lesbians, or whatever terms and categories are present in each specific situation.

Bonnie Zimmerman, 'Lesbians Like This and That' (1992) p. 8

This is dense material and you will need to spend some time going through it. All the listed critics are fully aware of debates about the subject but respond with varying degrees of support/doubt/enthusiasm/qualification to the anti-humanist concept of the subject. Don't be concerned about understanding every word and don't feel that you have to come to some final position on all the material. Select the phrases or sentences with which you do connect, either in agreement or disagreement. As you consider the comments, let me remind you of the central political questions:

➤ Which concept(s) of the subject is most helpful to feminism?
➤ Are different concepts helpful in different ways?

Checklist

9 Here is the start of a checklist of the key ideas covered in this section. These ideas are not intended to cohere as a final definitive statement; rather, I suggest compiling a list simply as an *aide-mémoire*.

If you want to supplement your list, jot down a short summary of your thoughts on each point or on the points which most interest you. Note where you need to do more research:

• Feminists have debated both the construction and significance of the female subject.

• Under patriarchy women experience a feeling of fragmentation. Thus, they desire a sense of wholeness and authenticity.

• Women writers have often explored issues of female subjectivity through metaphors – for example, of masks, clothes and mirrors.

•

•

•

Further discussion of the female subject as, specifically, *writer* can be found in the section on The Death of the Woman Author?.

WO-MAN
WOMAN'

Lisa Adkins graphics from Trouble & Strife 25, *Winter 1992*

References and further reading

Lisa Adkin's visuals, reproduced in this section, accompany an informative and combative article on feminism and postmodernism which, in part, refers to issues of the subject. See Stevi Jackson, 'The Amazing Deconstructing Woman', *Trouble & Strife*

Gloria Anzaldúa, 'La Conciencia de la Mestiza/Towards a New Consciousness' in *Borderlands/La Frontera: The New Mestiza.* The chapter from which the section included here comes is available also in Linda S. Kauffman (ed.), *American Feminist Thought at Century's End: A Reader.*

Margaret Atwood, 'A Paper Bag', *Two-Headed Poems*

Rosi Braidotti, 'Envy: or With Your Brains and My Looks' in Alice Jardine and Paul Smith (eds), *Men in Feminism*

Judith Butler, 'Feminism and the Question of Postmodernism' (1990). An unpublished conference paper. The quote was taken from Diane Elam, *Romancing the Postmodern.*

Jane Caputi, 'On Psychic Activism: Feminist Mythmaking' in Carolyne Larrington (ed.), *The Feminist Companion to Mythology*. See particularly pp. 436–8 for discussion of new, mythic identities of women.

Samuel Taylor Coleridge, 'Biographia Literaria', extracts available in *Selected Poetry and Prose*

Helen Dunmore, 'Three Ways of Recovering a Body', *Recovering a Body*

Donna Haraway, 'A Manifesto for Cyborgs: Science, Technology and Socialist Feminism in the 1980s' in Elizabeth Weed (ed.), *Coming to Terms: Feminism, Theory, Politics* (Routledge, 1989). The essay is available also in Linda J. Nicholson (ed.), *Feminism/Postmodernism*.

bell hooks (in interview with Grace Evans), 'To Live Long and Deep and Well', in *Everywoman*

bell hooks, *Yearning: Race, Gender, and Cultural Politics*, see especially 'Postmodern Blackness'

Avril Horner and Sue Zlosnik (eds), *Landscapes of Desire: Metaphors in Modern Women's Fiction*. As the sub-title indicates, this study considers metaphor in women's fiction. The mirror, the mask and clothes are among the metaphors discussed.

Andreas Huyssen, 'Mapping the Postmodern' in Linda J. Nicholson (ed.), *Feminism/Postmodernism*.

Rosemary Jackson, *Fantasy: The Literature of Subversion*

Nicole Ward Jouve, *White Woman Speaks With Forked Tongue: Criticism as Autobiography*

Cora Kaplan, *Sea Changes: Essays on Culture and Feminism*

Julia Kristeva (in interview with Susan Sellers), 'A Question of Subjectivity', *Women's Review*. Anthologized in Philip Rice and Patricia Waugh (eds), *Modern Literary Theory: A Reader*

Ursula Le Guin, 'The Writer on, and at, Her Work' in Janet Sternburg (ed.), *The Writer on Her Work*. Le Guin's poem, in part an exploration of the multiple selves of the writer, makes a good comparison with the Mulford extract.

Doris Lessing, *The Memoirs of a Survivor*

Pam Morris, *Literature and Feminism*, see on this issue chapter 6

Wendy Mulford, 'Notes on Writing: A Marxist/Feminist Viewpoint', in Michelene Wandor (ed.), *On Gender and Writing*

Alicia Suskin Ostriker, *Stealing the Language: The Emergence of Women's Poetry in America*. Chapter 2 contains lots of useful poetic references on explorations of women's identity.

Sylvia Plath, *The Bell Jar*

Fahmida Riaz, 'Image' in Rukhsana Ahmad (ed.), *We Sinful Women*

Chris Weedon, *Feminist Practice and Poststructuralist Theory*, see particularly chapter 4.

Jeanette Winterson, *Sexing the Cherry*

Bonnie Zimmerman, 'Lesbians Like This and That' in Sally Munt (ed.), *New Lesbian Criticism: Literary and Cultural Readings*

For further research on the theoretical aspects of this issue see:

Catherine Belsey, *Critical Practice*, especially chapter 3. A revised version of this material is available in Judith Newton and Deborah Rosenfelt (eds), *Feminist Criticism and Social Change* and Robyn R. Warhol and Diane Price Herndl (eds), *Feminisms: An Anthology of Literary Theory and Criticism.*

Judith Butler, *Gender Trouble: Feminism and the Subversion of Identity.* Butler's work is very densely written but you might try pp. 1–6, 142–9 as the beginning and end of her argument.

Teresa de Lauretis, 'Eccentric Subjects: Feminist Theory and Historical Consciousness', *Feminist Studies.* De Lauretis's 'eccentric subject', like Haraway's 'cyborg' and Anzaldúa's 'mestiza', suggests a new critical position and sense of subjectivity.

Mary Eagleton (ed.), *Feminist Literary Theory: A Reader*, see chapter 6.

Rita Felski, *Beyond Feminist Aesthetics: Feminist Literature and Social Change*, see particularly chapter 2.

Diana Fuss, *Essentially Speaking: Feminism Nature and Difference.* With reference to the issues of this section, see particularly pp. 97–105.

Elizabeth Grosz, *Sexual Subversions: Three French Feminists*

Elizabeth Grosz, 'Contemporary Theories of Power and Subjectivity' in Sneja Gunew (ed.), *Feminist Knowledge: Critique and Construct.* See also Grosz's entry on 'the subject' in Elizabeth Wright (ed.), *Feminism and Psychoanalysis: A Critical Dictionary*

Lois McNay, *Foucault and Feminism: Power, Gender and the Self.* A very clear introduction to the significance for feminism of Foucault's thought.

Tania Modleski, *Feminism Without Women: Culture and Criticism in a 'Postfeminist' Age*, see especially chapter 1, 'Postmortem on Postfeminism'

Toril Moi (ed.), *The Kristeva Reader*

Gayatri Chakravorty Spivak, *The Post-Colonial Critic: Interviews, Strategies, Dialogues* (ed. Sarah Harasym)

Patricia Waugh, *Practising Postmodernism/Reading Modernism*

Monique Wittig, *The Straight Mind and Other Essays.* Wittig's focus is the radical political importance of the lesbian subject.

Susan Wolfe and Julia Penelope (eds), *Sexual Practice, Textual Theory: Lesbian Cultural Criticism.* Wolfe and Penelope's introductory essay relates the issues we have discussed in this section to lesbian identity.

The Politics
of Location

Introduction

Rosi Braidotti describes the politics of location as follows:

> But this recognition of a common condition of sisterhood in oppression
> cannot be the final aim; women may have common situations and
> experiences, but they are not, in any way, *the same*. In this respect, the idea
> of the politics of location is very important. This idea, developed into a
> theory of recognition of the multiple differences that exist among women,
> stresses the importance of rejecting global statements about all women and
> of attempting instead to be as aware as possible of the place from which
> one is speaking. Attention to the *situated* as opposed to the universalistic
> nature of statements is the key idea.

Rosi Braidotti, *Nomadic Subjects: Embodiment and Sexual*
Difference in Contemporary Feminist Theory (1994) p. 163

At the beginning of her essay, 'Notes Toward a Politics of Location', one of the
fundamental texts in this debate, Adrienne Rich remembers the childhood game
in which she used to address herself as:

Adrienne Rich
14 Edgevale Road
Baltimore, Maryland
The United States of America
The Continent of North America
The Western Hemisphere
The Earth
The Solar System
The Universe

A couple of pages later she writes:

> I wrote a sentence just now and x'd it out. In it I said that women have
> always understood the struggle against free-floating abstraction even when
> they were intimidated by abstract ideas. I don't want to write that kind of
> sentence now, the sentence that begins 'Women have always ...' We started
> by rejecting the sentences that began 'Women have always had an instinct
> for mothering' or 'Women have always and everywhere been in subjugation
> to men.' If we have learned anything in these years of late twentieth-

century feminism, it's that 'always' blots out what we really need to know: When, where, and under what conditions has the statement been true?

Adrienne Rich, 'Notes Toward a Politics of Location' (1984) pp. 211–2, 214

Both Braidotti and Rich focus on two central points:

- the danger of generalizing about women or, putting it another way, the failure to recognize differences between women

- the importance of situating oneself and one's words. I do not speak/act simply as a 'human being' but as a human being of particular identities and experiences, speaking at a particular historical moment from a particular culture.

Rich's childhood game raises a third point which she describes as

- 'the arrogance of believing ourselves at the center'. (p. 223)

Thus, a politics of location is important both in understanding the commonalties and differences between women and in contributing to one's own sense of selfhood. On this second aspect it would help to look at the section on Finding the Subject in conjunction with this one. For the feminist writer and reader an understanding of the politics of location is essential. We need, in Braidotti's words, 'to be as aware as possible of the place from which one is speaking' – we might add, or reading, or writing. Equally, we need to be as aware as possible of the locations of the other women taking part in those speaking, reading, writing interactions. You can appreciate how informing Braidotti's and Rich's remarks is a deep anxiety about the dangers of speaking *for* other women or of presuming that one's own needs and experiences are common to all women. At the same time, there is an equal urgency for feminists to speak together – in both senses of that phrase, to speak to each other to enhance understanding and to speak with a collective voice to combat those reactionary forces which would happily divide and conquer.

To examine further the politics of location we can ask three questions:

- Who am 'I'?

- Where am 'I' located?

- Who are 'we'?

Who am 'I'?

1 The following three passages are attempts by writers to express a sense of who they are, what it means for them to say 'I'. Audre Lorde embraces the task with challenging directness, Gloria Anzaldúa with poetic verve, Rachel Blau DuPlessis with some reservations:

> I am a Black feminist lesbian warrior poet mother doing my work. Who are you and how are you doing yours?

Audre Lorde, quoted in Teresa de Lauretis (1993) p. 402

> I am a wind-swayed bridge, a crossroads inhabited by whirlwinds ... You say my name as ambivalence? Think of me as Shiva, a many-armed and

legged body with one foot on brown soil, one on white, one in straight society, one in the gay world, the man's world, the women's, one limb in the literary world, another in the working class, the socialist, and the occult worlds. A sort of spider woman hanging by one thin strand of web.

Who, me confused? Ambivalent? Not so. Only your labels split me.

Gloria Anzaldúa, 'La Prieta' (1983) p. 205

'I' can be said to be an off-white feminist, resisting even 'enlightenment' Judaism, a radical but middle-class US inhabitant in a professional job category. A person mainly gendered female, who maintains an imaginary bisexuality, and a polygynous curiosity about the feminisms I and others have traversed. Who benefits from many world-economic interests which I abhor. I am a non-biological real mother. Am a heterosexual married property owner. Poet, critic and essayist. My writing space is saffron orange with a light blue ceiling. I use a Mac Plus …

My tone is turning arch. Also compressed. I am already leaving things out. Memoir is already seduction, not the least is self-seduction. I am both pleased and uncomfortable to be telling you all this.

Rachel Blau DuPlessis, 'Reader, I Married Me: A Polygynous Memoir' (1993) pp. 97–8

➤ Evidently, locating the self is not the easiest of undertakings. Could you attempt you own description of 'I'? Would you be using the same categories as these authors or would you be defining yourself in different terms or with different priorities? Were you surprised by any of the ways in which these authors situated themselves?

➤ DuPlessis is conscious that she is leaving things out, perhaps making herself more noble or politically right-on or coherent than she feels she is: 'memoir is already seduction, not the least is self-seduction'. Review your self-analysis. Did you deliberately censor yourself at any point; can you detect moments where you evaded problems, trimmed the interpretation? Did you, unexpectedly, define yourself in new ways you hadn't really thought of before?

➤ Aware of the duplicity of memory and self-analysis, DuPlessis tries to contain herself, scrupulously, within the precise and factual. Anzaldúa invokes metaphorical and mythic modes: the bridge, the crossroads, the multi-limbed Hindu god, Shiva and the Spider Woman of Native American mythology convey her sense of the manifold. Do you prefer one of the approaches over the other? What further images can you think of – from literature, mythology or, perhaps, of your own making – to suggest the varied, complex ways in which we are all situated? If you were expressing diagrammatically or with some visual image this sense of your situation, what would it look like – concentric circles, a web, building blocks …?

➤ I described Lorde's comment as 'challenging'. Situating oneself leads to certain awareness, responsibilities and task, she suggests. How would you answer her? What is the work of your situation?

Where am 'I' located?

2 Let us look more closely at two particular locations and their implications for feminism and for writing. The first concerns Trinh T. Minh-ha's situation as a writer; the second, Rich's expression of herself as a body:

> Neither black/red/yellow nor woman but poet or writer. For many of us, the question of priorities remains a crucial issue. Being merely 'a writer' without doubt ensures one a status of far greater weight than being 'a woman of color who writes' ever does. Imputing sex or race to the creative act has long been a means by which the literary establishment cheapens and discredits the achievements of non-mainstream women writers. She who 'happens to be' a (non-white) Third World member, a woman, and a writer is bound to go through the ordeal of exposing her work to the abuse of praises and criticisms that either ignore, dispense with, or overemphasize her racial and sexual attributes. Yet the time has passed when she can confidently identify herself with a profession or artistic vocation without questioning and relating it to her color-woman condition .... On the one hand, no matter what position she decides to take, she will sooner or later find herself driven into situations where she is made to feel she must choose from among three conflicting identities. Writer of color? Woman writer? Or woman of color? Which comes first? Where does she place her loyalties? On the other hand, she often finds herself at odds with language, which partakes in the white-male-is-norm ideology and is used predominantly as a vehicle to circulate established power relations.

> Trinh T. Minh-ha, *Woman, Native, Other: Writing Postcoloniality and Feminism* (1989) p. 6

> Perhaps we need a moratorium on saying 'the body'. For it's also possible to abstract 'the' body. When I write 'the body', I see nothing in particular. To write 'my body' plunges me into lived experience, particularity: I see scars, disfigurements, discolorations, damages, losses, as well as what pleases me. Bones well nourished from the placenta; the teeth of a middle-class person seen by the dentist twice a year from childhood. White skin, marked and scarred by three pregnancies, an elected sterilization, progressive arthritis, four joint operations, calcium deposits, no rapes, no abortions, long hours at a typewriter – my own, not in a typing pool – and so forth. To say 'the body' lifts me away from what has given me a primary perspective. To say 'my body' reduces the temptation to grandiose assertions.
>
> This body. White, female; or female, white. The first obvious, lifelong facts. But I was born in the white section of a hospital which separated Black and white women in labor and Black and white babies in the nursery, just as it separated Black and white bodies in the morgue. I was defined as white before I was defined as female.

> Adrienne Rich, 'Notes Toward a Politics of Location' (1984) p. 215

➤ Remember Braidotti's comment: '... to be as aware as possible of the place from which one is speaking'. In what ways do these extracts fulfil that requirement? What sense do you get of both the intimate and the larger forces that situate the individual writer and the individual body?

➤ Do you find your relation to writing or reading as complex as Trinh's? She entitles the section from which I quoted 'The Triple Bind'. What phrase would summarize your position?

➤ Could you write a passage based on Rich's about your own body? What story does your body tell?

➤ Trinh feels strongly that there are pressures upon her to prioritize aspects of her identity, to select one location above others. The same issue arises in Rich's extract. Have you had similar experiences of finding yourself, somehow, caught between gender or race or class or religion or sexuality or ... Can you think of occasions when you might, unwittingly, have put such a pressure on another?

3 Rich's childhood game could raise a range of responses and queries. For instance:

➤ As Rich herself says, 'the arrogance of believing ourselves at the center'. Hence, *my* experience is the definitive experience; the experience of others is secondary or has meaning only when related to mine.

➤ If we reject that notion, does it mean that all experiences, all knowledges, all ways of understanding the world are equally true and, especially, equally true for feminism?

➤ Can I speak only from my own situation? Is there no way that I can speak 'on behalf of' other women? What are the problems if I, as a white woman, speak sympathetically on behalf of Black women? What are the problems if I, as a white woman, *don't* speak sympathetically on behalf of Black women? Have you ever felt indignant at someone speaking on your behalf or, equally, have you ever felt grateful?

➤ If we can speak only for ourselves, what happens to the idea of the collective, of sisterhood, of solidarity? Does the concept of 'the universal' and of 'global sisterhood' retain any credibility? Do concepts of unity connect individuals across differences or obliterate important differences?

➤ Rich now rejects the 'Women have always ...' sentences. We could add as well the 'Women are ...' and 'Men are ...' comments. What remarks along these lines have you ever made or heard others making: for example, 'Women have always had to pick up the pieces' or 'Women are better at inter-personal relations' or 'Men are hopeless about their bodies'. Add your own examples. How do you now feel about such statements? Do they retain a measure of validity? Is there any space for the generalized comment? Or do you agree with Rich that every such remark has to be followed with the questions: 'When, where, and under what conditions has the statement been true?'

➤ Another way of interpreting Rich's litany would be to see the child positioning herself, not at the centre of the universe, but as an insignificant speck within the universe, lost amidst these greater configurations. In such circumstances the politics of location could help women to feel more situated and grounded, could give them a base from which to make links.

4 You might want to pause at this point, to think about these ideas and formulate your own. Look back at preceding passages to help you and, then, relate your

thoughts to the three following extracts, each exploring further the relevance to feminism of 'the universal'. The first is Adrienne Rich's irritated response to a particular reading of her sequence of lesbian love poems:

Two friends of mine, both of them artists, wrote to me about reading *Twenty-One Love Poems* with their male lovers, assuring me how 'universal' the poems were. I found myself angered, and when I asked myself why, I realized that it was anger at having my work essentially assimilated and stripped of its meaning, 'integrated' into heterosexual romance. That kind of 'acceptance' of the book seems to me a refusal of its deepest implications. The longing to simplify, to defuse feminism by invoking 'androgyny' or 'humanism', to assimilate lesbian existence by saying that 'relationship is really all the same, love is always difficult' – I see that as a denial, a kind of resistance, as refusal to read and hear what I've actually written, to acknowledge what I am ... We're not trying to become part of the old order, misnamed 'universal', which has tabooed us; we are transforming the meaning of universality.

Adrienne Rich, Interview with Elly Bulkin (1977) p. 166

The second extract is Rosi Braidotti's comment on Rich's essay, 'Notes Toward a Politics of Location':

This is no relativism but rather a topological approach to discourse where positionality is crucial. The feminist defences of 'situated knowledges', to quote Donna Haraway, clashes with the abstract generality of the classical patriarchal subject. What is at stake is not the specific as opposed to the universal, but rather two radically different ways of conceiving the possibility of legitimating theoretical remarks. For feminist theory the only consistent way of making general theoretical points is to be aware that one is actually located somewhere specific.

Rosi Braidotti, *Nomadic Subjects: Embodiment and Sexual Difference in Feminist Theory* (1994) p. 238

The third passage contains Gayatri Chakravorty Spivak's remarks, in discussion with Elizabeth Grosz, on the strategic use of the concept of the universal:

GROSZ: ... I am interested in how *use* universalism, essentialism etc., strategically, without necessarily making an overall commitment to these kinds of concepts.

SPIVAK: You see, you *are* committed to these concepts, whether you acknowledge it or not. I think it's absolutely on target not to be rhetorically committed to it, and I think it's absolutely on target to take a stand against the discourse of essentialism, universalism as it comes in terms of the universal – of classical German philosophy or the universal as the white upper-class male ... etc. But *strategically* we cannot. Even as we talk about *feminist* practice, or privileging practice over theory, we are universalising – not only generalising but universalising.

Gayatri Chakravorty Spivak. *The Post-Colonial Critic: Interviews, Strategies, Dialogues* (1990) p. 11

Obviously, Rich's remarks are more immediately accessible and there are certain terms in the Braidotti and Spivak you may need to research. But let's see how far we can get in comparing these three extracts:

➤ How does Rich explain her anger? Were you surprised at her response? Are you convinced by her explanation?

➤ Evidently, Rich's friends thought they were complimenting her; certainly, I can remember from my own education how often I was told that 'great' literature was 'universal'. All three commentators feel that the term 'universal' has been misappropriated and has been used in support of the interests of a very particular group. Can you explain their arguments?

➤ Both Braidotti and Spivak suggest that universalism is a dangerous concept but that it can be used by feminism if it is used carefully. Try to understand what they are saying in this respect: what are the dangers; how and why is universalism still useful?

➤ Spivak's key term is 'strategically'. What do you think she means by this?

Who are 'we'?

We (?) need to consider more closely the political implications for feminism of the arguments so far. Authors like those we are discussing here are trying to position themselves in a specific, focused way, to be aware of the determinants in their own lives, careful not to generalize from their life experience to all women. The process requires honesty about oneself and an attention towards other women: 'this is me; I want to hear who you are; are there points at which we meet?' This last question is vital if women are to work together in feminism. Ann Snitow talks of feminists who 'question the eternal sisterhood'. Note also how she, like Spivak, employs the concept of the 'strategic':

> It may be a pleasure to be 'we', and it may be strategically imperative to struggle as 'we', but who, they ask, are 'we'?

> Ann Snitow, 'A Gender Diary' (1990) p. 10

'We women' is not a self-evident given but an identity which has to be created, sometimes with difficulty, and which has to recognize the differences between and within women.

5 Here are two extracts concerned with differences. The first, from Audre Lorde, describes the experience of entering a crowded room; the second, from Caryl Churchill, features two sisters, joined by gender and biology, separated by class. For those unfamiliar with Churchill's work, her use of the slash [/] is a production direction to indicate where a character interrupts another or speaks at the same time as another:

> Once when I walked into a room
> my eyes would seek out the one or two black faces

for contact or reassurance or a sign
I was not alone
now walking into rooms full of black faces
that would destroy me for any difference
where shall my eyes look?
Once it was easy to know
who were my people.

Audre Lorde, 'Between Ourselves' (1978)

MARLENE:	... I think the eighties are going to be stupendous.
JOYCE:	Who for?
MARLENE:	For me./ I think I'm going up up up.
JOYCE:	Oh for you. Yes, I'm sure they will.
MARLENE:	And for the country, come to that. Get the economy back on its feet and whoosh. She's a tough lady, Maggie. I'd give her a job./ She just needs to hang in there. This country
JOYCE:	You voted for them, did you?
MARLENE:	needs to stop whining./ Monetarism is not stupid.
JOYCE:	Drink your tea and shut up, pet.
MARLENE:	It takes time, determination. No more slop./ And
JOYCE:	Well, I think they're filthy bastards.
MARLENE:	who's got to drive it on? First woman prime minister. Terrifico. Aces. Right on./ You must admit. Certainly gets my vote.
JOYCE:	What good's first woman if it's her. I suppose you'd have liked Hitler if he was a woman. Ms Hitler. Got a lot done, Hitlerina./ Great adventures.
MARLENE:	Bosses still walking on the workers' faces? Still Dadda's little parrot? Haven't you learned to think for yourself? I believe in the individual. Look at me.
JOYCE:	I am looking at you.
MARLENE:	Come on, Joyce, we're not going to quarrel over politics.
JOYCE:	We are though.
MARLENE:	Forget I mentioned it. Not another word about the slimy unions will cross my lips.

Caryl Churchill, *Top Girls* (1982) pp. 83–4

A third extract is preoccupied with the possibility of a female collectivity as something that has to be worked towards – strenuously and with a realistic sense of potential:

Coalition work is not work done in your home. Coalition work has to be done in the streets. And it is some of the most dangerous work you can do. And you shouldn't look for comfort. Some people will come to a coalition and they rate the success of the coalition on whether or not they feel good when they get there. They're not looking for a coalition; they're looking for a home! They're looking for a bottle with some milk in it and a nipple, which does not happen in a coalition. You don't get a lot of food in a coalition. You don't get fed in a coalition. In a coalition you have to give, and it is different from your home. You can't stay there all the time. You go to the coalition for a few hours and then you go back and take your bottle wherever it is, and then you go back and coalesce some more.

Bernice Johnson Reagon 'Coalition Politics: Turning the Century' (1983)

The final text, 'Naming the Waves', wants differences to be named but, intriguingly, uses a metaphor which undermines any sense of fixity:

> We are done with feeling all the same –
> done with that blind joy
> of sudden recognition:
> womanness alone will not get us through.
>
> Our differences are like oceans –
> all bodies of water, yes
> but take me, eyes bound, to any shore;
> remove the blindfold and I recognize the sea.
>
> Atlantic grey is not
> Pacific green-grey is not
> Aegean clear-green, though we hardly know
> the words to describe the differences.
>
> There are places, though
> where patterns in the water
> guiding sailors
> have names in certain languages.

Judith Barrington, 'Naming the Waves' (1985).

➤ Both Reagon and the earlier quote from Lorde refer to 'work'. How do you understand the term in this context?

➤ Reagon makes metaphorical use of 'street' and 'home' and images of nurture; Barrington develops a comparison between differences and 'oceans'. Explore the meanings operating here.

➤ Reagon's view of the collective is very different from the 'eternal sisterhood' Snitow mentions. In what ways? Similarly, the 'blind joy/ of sudden recognition' described by Barrington and the certain knowledge of 'my people' in Lorde are *past* recollections. How would you describe their *present* perceptions?

➤ '... womanness alone will not get us through', says Barrington. Do you agree? Have you found situations where 'womanness alone' has been inadequate? Certainly Joyce's views on Mrs Thatcher would suggest that for her 'womanness alone' is not enough. How would you explain the argument in the scene from *Top Girls*?

➤ How would you summarize your thoughts on this issue – which, of course, does not mean to solve all the inherent problems? How can one recognize difference *and* work together with common understandings and goals?

Problems with pronouns

6 As a way of drawing together the material in this section we could relate the issues specifically to our understandings of the two pronouns 'I' and 'we'. I'll start to list some suggestions. Add your own possibilities from the extracts included here or from other things you've read, other discussions in which you've taken part. Try to link my suggestions and your own to concrete examples, textual or otherwise:

- finding the courage to say 'I'
- 'The difficulty of saying "I"' (Christa Wolf)
- the arrogance of 'I'
- 'we' versus 'they'; 'us' versus 'them'
- the intimacy of 'we'
- the false unity of 'we'
- saying 'we' when we really mean 'I'
- the tyranny of 'we' ...

Let's think again of those original questions: Who am 'I'? Where am 'I' located? Who are 'we'? And also, can we now add – What is the relation between 'I' and 'we'?

References and further reading

Gloria Anzaldúa, 'La Prieta' in Cherríe Moraga and Gloria Anzaldúa (eds), *This Bridge Called My Back: Writings by Radical Women of Color*. There are many other texts in this volume which relate to the politics of location. See, for example, Cherríe Moraga's 'La Güera' and Rosario Morales' 'I Am What I Am'

Judith Barrington, 'Naming the Waves' (1985); anthologized in Christine McEwen (ed.), *Naming the Waves: Contemporary Lesbian Poetry*

Rosi Braidotti, *Nomadic Subjects: Embodiment and Sexual Difference in Contemporary Feminist Theory*

Elly Bulkin, Minnie Bruce Pratt, Barbara Smith, *Yours in Struggle: Three Feminist Perspectives on Anti-Semitism and Racism*. This study is an excellent example of a politics of location in practice.

Caryl Churchill, *Top Girls*

Teresa de Lauretis, 'Eccentric Subjects: Feminist Theory and Historical Consciousness', *Feminist Studies*. De Lauretis discusses here Reagon's comments on the meaning of 'home'.

Rachel Blau DuPlessis, 'Reader, I Married Me: A Polygynous Memoir' in Gayle Greene and Coppélia Kahn (eds), *Changing Subjects: The Making of Feminist Literary Criticism*

Audre Lorde. Comment spoken before a poetry reading. Quoted in Teresa de Lauretis, 'Feminist Genealogies: A Personal Itinerary', *Women's Studies International Forum*

Audre Lorde, 'Between Ourselves', *The Black Unicorn*, quoted in Bulkin et al., p. 191

Biddy Martin and Chandra Talpade Mohanty, 'Feminist Politics: What's Home got to Do With It?' in Teresa de Lauretis (ed.), *Feminist Studies/Critical Studies*

Chandra Talpade Mohanty, 'Under Western Eyes: Feminist Scholarship and Colonial Discourses' in Mohanty, Ann Russo, Lourdes Torres (eds) *Third World Women and the Politics of Feminism*

Chandra Talpade Mohanty, 'Feminist Encounters: Locating the Politics of Experience' in Michèle Barrett and Anne Phillips (eds), *Destbabilizing Theory: Contemporary Feminist Debates*. Mohanty discusses Reagon's concept of 'coalition' in this essay and meanings of universalism. See also Mohanty's other work.

Bernice Johnson Reagon, 'Coalition Politics: Turning the Century' in Barbara Smith (ed.) *Home Girls: A Black Feminist Anthology*, quoted in Bulkin et al., p. 190

Adrienne Rich, 'Notes Toward a Politics of Location; in *Blood, Bread, and Poetry: Selected Prose 1979–1985*

Adrienne Rich, Interview with Elly Bulkin, *Conditions: Two* (1977), quoted in Jan Montefiore, *Feminism and Poetry: Language, Experience, Identity in Women's Writing*. If you would like to read this sequence of poems, see Adrienne Rich, *The Dream of a Common Language: Poems 1974–1977*

Ann Snitow, 'A Gender Diary' in Marianne Hirsch and Evelyn Fox Keller (eds), *Conflicts in Feminism*

Gayatri Chakravorty Spivak, *The Post-Colonial Critic: Interviews, Strategies, Dialogues* (ed. Sarah Harasym)

Trinh T. Minh-ha, *Woman, Native, Other: Writing Postcoloniality and Feminism*

Christa Wolf, *The Quest for Christa T.* (1968). This novel is centrally concerned with problems of identity. The particular phrase, 'the difficulty of saying "I"' occurs on pp. 170 and 174 and with different inflections throughout the book.

Conclusion

I don't know how or where you have read this book. The likelihood is that the place of reading has been within an educational institution as part of a course or as supplementary reading, though the nature of the course may be varied – women's studies, literature, critical theory, cultural studies. What is also uncertain is how you have read it. You could have worked through all fifteen sections as course material; you could have dipped in; you could have scanned; you could have selected. I only hope you haven't done what I confess I sometimes do, namely to turn directly to the Conclusion in the hope of finding a quick summary of the book's major argument. If you do that in this case you're in trouble since this book has not been about proving a thesis but about attending to a process, a process of familiarizing yourself with and deepening your understanding of feminist literary ideas. Along the way, I hope you've learned something, generally, about how to study. Though I started the book by listing lots of useful resources and included in every section advice about further reading, my major concern was with the resource that is in your own head and heart. I've tried to raise issues which encourage you to think, evaluate, connect, dispute (the head) but also I've wanted to focus on material that might move you, hopefully seem important to you and validate what you may have oft felt but not expressed (the heart). In both cases I am concerned with self-confidence, not as some kind of ego-tripping, but as a necessary part of feminist literary and political work.

Where do you go from here?

Finally, let me draw together some of the study advice from earlier in the book; this might help you to continue your engagement with this subject-matter and to respond to new, developing areas in feminist literary thinking.

➤ If you have worked through the book or through a good measure of it, this is the time to take stock. Where have you got to; what do you still need to do; what's worked; what hasn't; what would be the way forward over, say, the next three months?

➤ On the practical side, try to establish some kind of group support (if you're not taking a course) or even to work alongside an official course programme. Women's reading/writing/study groups will extend and stimulate your own thinking.

➤ Think also of keeping your own written record as an adjunct to any course requirements: a reading diary or journal, a common-place book, a note-book of favourite quotes or your own random thoughts and impressions.

➤ You know by now not to expect immediate illumination or immediate inspiration. It *may* work like that but if it doesn't there's nothing wrong. Be prepared to return to material and re-evaluate.

➤ Keep questioning. Your first response is important but it isn't the only possible response. Try playing devil's advocate with your own arguments. Don't dodge the awkward questions; relish them.

➤ Keep thinking about those key relationships which we have come across so often in so many different ways: the differences between women and the commonality of women; the relationship between your understanding of yourself and your understanding of other women or between self and the political movement of feminism. How do literature and writing help with these issues?

➤ Related to that is Lillian Robinson's wonderfully sardonic remark that 'the revolution is simply not going to be made by literary journals' (*Sex, Class, and Culture* p. 52). How can feminist literary study promote political change? If you are committed to feminism everything you do has to be tested against that question – though not necessarily as a simple cause and effect.

➤ Resist, resist and resist again the pressures to fatalism – 'things never change'; 'it's all down to human nature' – and, equally, the pressures to naive optimism or the reactionary masquerading as optimism – 'it's all different now'; 'we're in a post-feminist age'; 'but we've got Equal Opportunities legislation'.

➤ We started with the idea of pleasure related to Roland Barthes's title *The Pleasure of the Text*. Barthes actually uses the term 'pleasure' in a specific and theoretically inflected way. He probably wouldn't be much impressed with my commonsensical use of the term. But a sense of enjoyment in what you are doing is important. Indeed, I would say that any point of pressure is the way in to a creative response. So whatever you feel when you read feminist literary ideas – pleasure, anger, curiosity, identification – follow that lead.

Works
Cited

Abel, Elizabeth (1990), 'Race, Class, and Psychoanalysis?'. In Hirsch and Keller (1990).

Abelove, Henry, Barale, Michèle Aina, Halperin, David M. (eds) (1993), *The Lesbian and Gay Studies Reader*. London: Routledge.

Anderson, Danny J. (1989), 'Deconstruction: Critical Strategy/Strategic Criticism'. In G. Douglas Atkins and Laura Morrow, (eds), *Contemporary Literary Theory*. London: Macmillan.

Angelou, Maya (1970; 1984), *I Know Why the Caged Bird Sings*. London: Virago.

Anzaldúa, Gloria (1983), 'La Prieta'. In Moraga and Anzaldúa (1983).

Anzaldúa, Gloria (1987), *Borderlands/La Frontera: The New Mestiza* San Francisco: Spinsters/Aunt Lute.

Arkin, Marian and Shollar, Barbara (1989), *Longman Anthology of World Literature by Women: 1875–1975*. White Plains, New York: Longman Inc.

Armitt, Lucie (ed.) (1991), *Where No Man Has Gone Before: Women and Science Fiction*. London: Routledge.

Armstrong, Isobel (1987), 'Christina Rossetti: Diary of a Feminist Reading'. In Sue Roe, (ed.), *Women Reading Women's Writing*. Brighton, Sussex: The Harvester Press Ltd.

Armstrong, Isobel (ed.) (1992), *New Feminist Discourses: Critical Essays on Theories and Texts*. London: Routledge.

Armstrong, Nancy (1987), *Desire and Domestic Fiction: A Political History of the Novel*. Oxford: Oxford University Press.

Atwood, Margaret (1976; 1982), *Lady Oracle*. London: Virago.

Atwood, Margaret (1978), *Two-Headed Poems*. New York: Simon and Schuster.

Atwood, Margaret (1987), *The Handmaid's Tale*. London: Virago.

Baldick, Chris (1990), *The Concise Oxford Dictionary of Literary Terms*. Oxford: Oxford University Press.

Ballaster, Ros (1992), 'Romancing the Novel: Gender and Genre in Early Theories of Narrative'. In Dale Spender, (ed.), *Living By the Pen: Early British Women Writers*. New York: Teachers College Press.

Ballou, Patricia K. (1980), *Women: A Bibliography of Bibliographies*. London: G.K. Hall & Co.

Barnstone, Aliki and Barnstone, Willis (eds) (1980), *A Book of Women Poets from Antiquity to Now*. New York: Schoken Books.

Barrett, Michèle (1982), 'Feminism and the Definition of Cultural Politics'. In Rosalind Brunt and Caroline Rowan, (eds), *Feminism, Culture and Politics*. London: Lawrence and Wishart Ltd.

Barrington, Judith (1985), 'Naming the Waves'. In McEwen (1988).

Barthes, Roland (1968; 1977), 'The Death of the Author'. In *Image–Music–Text*. Trans. Stephen Heath. London: Fontana.

Barthes, Roland (1973; 1990), *The Pleasure of the Text*. Trans. Richard Miller. Oxford: Blackwell.

Batsleer, Janet, Davies, Tony, O'Rourke, Rebecca, Weedon, Chris (1985), *Rewriting English: Cultural Politics of Gender and Class*. London: Methuen.

Bell, Maureen, Parfitt, George, Shepherd, Simon (eds) (1990), *A Biographical Dictionary of English Women Writers, 1580–1720*. Hemel Hempstead, Hertfordshire: Harvester Wheatsheaf.

Works Cited

Belsey, Catherine (1980), *Critical Practice*. London: Methuen.

Belsey, Catherine and Moore, Jane (eds) (1989), *The Feminist Reader: Essays in Gender and the Politics of Literary Criticism*. London: Macmillan.

Bennett, Catherine (14 June 1993), 'The House that Carmen Built', *The Guardian*.

Benstock, Shari (ed.) (1988), *The Private Self: Theory and Practice of Women's Autobiographical Writings*. London: Routledge.

Bernikow, Louise (1979), *The World Split Open: Four Centuries of Women Poets in England and America, 1552–1950*. London: The Women's Press.

Biriotti, Maurice and Miller, Nicola (eds) (1993), *What Is an Author?* Manchester: Manchester University Press.

Birkett, Jennifer (1990), 'The Implications of Etudes Féminines for Teaching'. In Wilcox, McWatters, Thompson and Williams (1990).

Blain, Virginia, Clements, Patricia, Grundy, Isobel (1990), *The Feminist Companion to Literature in English: Women Writers from the Middle Ages to the Present*. London: Batsford.

Bono, Paolo and Kemp, Sandra (eds) (1991), *Italian Feminist Thought: A Reader*. Oxford: Blackwell.

Boumelha, Penny (1988), 'Realism and the Ends of Feminism'. In Susan Sheridan, (ed.), *Grafts: Feminist Cultural Criticism*. London: Verso.

Bowlby, Rachel (1992), *Still Crazy After All These Years: Women, Writing and Psychoanalysis*. London: Routledge.

Braidotti, Rosi (1987), 'Envy: or With Your Brains and My Looks'. In Jardine and Smith (1987).

Braidotti, Rosi (1994), *Nomadic Subjects: Embodiment and Sexual Difference in Contemporary Feminist Theory*. New York: Columbia University Press.

Breeze, Jean 'Binta' (1992), *Spring Cleaning*. London: Virago.

Briscoe, Joanna (7 September 1993), 'Books'. *The Guardian*.

Brown, Loulou, Collins, Helen, Green, Pat, Humm, Maggie, Landells, Mel (eds) (1993), *The International Handbook of Women's Studies*. Hemel Hempstead, Hertfordshire: Harvester Wheatsheaf.

Bryan, Sharon (ed.) (1993), *Where We Stand: Women Poets on Literary Tradition*. New York: W.W. Norton.

Buck, Claire (ed.) (1992), *Bloomsbury Guide to Women's Literature*. London: Bloomsbury.

Bulkin, Elly, Pratt, Minnie Bruce, Smith, Barbara (1984), *Yours in Struggle: Three Feminist Perspectives on Anti-Semitism and Racism*. Brooklyn, New York: Long Haul Press.

Burford, Barbara (June, 1987), 'The Landscapes Painted on the Inside of My Skin'. *Spare Rib* no. 179.

Burke, Seán (1995), *Authorship from Plato to the Postmodern: A Reader*. Edinburgh: Edinburgh University Press.

Butler, Judith (1990), *Gender Trouble: Feminism and the Subversion of Identity*. London: Routledge.

Butler, Judith (1990), 'Feminism and the Question of Postmodernism'. Unpublished conference paper. Quoted in Diane Elam (1992), *Romancing the Postmodern*. London: Routledge.

Byatt, Antonia (1991), *Possession: A Romance*. London: Vintage.

Cadman, Eileen, Chester, Gail, Pivot, Agnes (1981), *Rolling Our Own: Women as Printers, Publishers and Distributors*. London: Minority Press Group.

Cameron, Deborah (ed.) (1990), *The Feminist Critique of Language: A Reader*. London: Routledge.

Cameron, Deborah (1995/6), 'Lost in Translation: Non-Sexist Language'. *Trouble & Strife* 32.

Capek, Mary Ellen S. (1987), *A Women's Thesaurus: An Index of Language Used to Describe and Locate Information By and About Women*. New York: Harper & Row.

Caputi, Jane (1992), 'On Psychic Activism: Feminist Myth Making'. In Larrington (1992).

Carr, Helen (ed.) (1989), *From My Guy to Sci-Fi: Genre and Women's Writing in the Postmodern World*. London: Pandora.

Carter, Angela (1977: 1982), *The Passion of New Eve*. London: Virago.

Carter, Sarah and Ritchie, Maureen (1990), *Women's Studies: A Guide to Information Sources*. London: Mansell.

Caughie, John (ed.) (1981), *Theories of Authorship*. London: Routledge & Kegan Paul.

Childers, Mary and hooks, bell (1990), 'A Conversation about Race and Class'. In Hirsch and Keller (1990).

Churchill, Caryl (1979), *Cloud Nine*. London: Pluto Press Ltd.

Churchill, Caryl (1982), *Top Girls*. London: Methuen.

Church Times, The, 'Permission for Women to Speak' (18 December 1892).

Cholmeley, Jane (1991), 'A Feminist Business in a Capitalist Word: Silver Moon Women's Bookshop'. In Nanneke Redclift and M. Thea Sinclair, (eds), *Working Women: International Perspectives on Labour and Gender Ideology*. London: Routledge.

Cixous, Hélène (1976), 'The Laugh of the Medusa'. Trans. Keith Cohen and Paula Cohen. In Marks and de Courtivron (1981).

Cixous, Hélène (Autumn, 1981), 'Castration or Decapitation?'. Trans. Annette Kuhn. *Signs: Journal of Women in Culture and Society* vol. 7, no. 1.

Cixous, Hélène and Clément, Catherine (1975; 1986), *The Newly Born Woman*. Trans. Betsy Wing. Manchester: Manchester University Press.

Cixous, Hélène (1986), 'Conversations with Hélène Cixous and Members of the Centre d'Etudes Féminines'. Trans. Susan Sellers. In Sellers (1988).

Cixous, Hélène (1992) Interview recorded by Broadcasting Support Services, *Talking Liberties*. London: Channel 4 Television.

Coetzee, J.M. (1986), *Foe*. Harmondsworth, Middlesex: Penguin.

Coleridge, Samuel Taylor (1957), *Selected Poetry and Prose*. Harmondsworth, Middlesex: Penguin.

Collins, Rose (24 June 1994), 'Out on the Shelves'. *Bookseller*.

Cook, Tim (1992), 'Canon Survey Report'. In *Pace Newsletter* issue 5. Plymouth University: SCEPCHE.

Cooter, Margaret et al. (Women in Publishing) (1987), *Reviewing the Reviews: A Woman's Place on the Bookpage*. London: Journeyman Press.

Coward, Rosalind (1980), 'Are Women's Novels Feminist Novels?'. In Elaine Showalter (1986).

Coward, Rosalind and Semple, Linda (1989), 'Tracking Down the Past: Women and Detective Fiction'. In Carr (1989).

Cranny-Francis, Anne (1990), *Feminist Fiction: Feminist Uses of Generic Fiction*. Cambridge: Polity Press.

Crawford, Anne et al. (1983), *Europa Biographical Dictionary of British Women*. London: Europa.

Culler, Jonathan (1983; 1989), *On Deconstruction: Theory and Criticism after Structuralism*. London: Routledge.

Daly, Mary and Caputi, Jane (1988), Webster's *First New Intergalactic Wickedary*. London: The Women's Press.

Davis, Gwenn and Joyce, Beverly (1989), *Personal Writings by Women to 1900: A Bibliography of American and British Writers*. London: Mansell.

Davis, Gwenn and Joyce, Beverly (1991), *Poetry by Women to 1900: A Bibliography of American and British Writers*. London: Mansell.

Davis, Gwenn and Joyce, Beverly (1992), *Drama by Women to 1900: A Bibliography of American and British Writers*. London: Mansell.

de Lauretis, Teresa (1987), *Technologies of Gender: Essays on Theory, Film and Fiction*. Bloomington: Indiana University Press.

de Lauretis, Teresa (Spring, 1990), 'Eccentric Subjects: Feminist Theory and Historical Consciousness'. *Feminist Studies* 16, no. 1.

de Lauretis, Teresa (1993), 'Feminist Genealogies: A Personal Itinerary'. *Women's Studies International Forum* vol. 16, no. 4.

de Pizan, Christine (1405), *The Book of the City of Ladies*. In Alcuin Blamires (ed.), *Woman Defamed and Woman Defended: An Anthology of Medieval Texts*. Oxford: Clarendon Press.

Delphy, Christine (1992), 'Rethinking Sex and Gender'. *Women's Studies International Forum* vol. 16, no. 1.

Derrida, Jacques (1972; 1981), *Dissemination*. Trans. Barbara Johnson. Chicago: University of Chicago Press.

Dinesen, Isak (1957; 1990), 'The Blank Page'. *Last Tales*. Harmondsworth, Middlesex: Penguin.

Donovan, Josephine (1990). 'The Silence Is Broken'. In Cameron (1990).

Doyle, Margaret (1995), *The A–Z of Non-Sexist Language*. London: The Women's Press.

Duchen, Claire (ed.) (1987), *French Connections: Voices from the Women's Movement in France*. London: Hutchinson.

Duffy, Maureen (1971; 1994), *Love Child*. London: Virago.

Duncker, Patricia (1992), *Sisters and Strangers: An Introduction to Contemporary Feminist Fiction*. Oxford: Blackwell.

Dunmore, Helen (1994), *Recovering a Body*. Newcastle upon Tyne: Bloodaxe Books.

DuPlessis, Rachel Blau (1985), *Writing Beyond the Ending: Narrative Strategies of Twentieth-Century Women*. Bloomington and Indianapolis: Indiana University Press.

DuPlessis, Rachel Blau (1993), 'Reader, I Married Me: A Polygynous Memoir'. In Greene and Kahn (1993).

Durant, Alan and Fabb, Nigel (1990), *Literary Studies in Action*. London: Routledge.

Eagleton, Mary (ed.) (1991), *Feminist Literary Criticism*. London: Longman.

Eagleton, Mary (ed.) (1996), *Feminist Literary Theory: A Reader*. Second Edition. Oxford: Blackwell.

Eagleton, Mary (Summer, 1996), 'Who's Who and Where's Where: Constructing Feminist Literary Studies. *Feminist Review* no.53.

Ellmann, Mary (1968), *Thinking about Women*. New York: Harcourt Brace Jovanovich.

Evans, Mary (1991), 'The Problem of Gender for Women's Studies'. In Jane Aaron and Sylvia Walby, (eds), *Out of the Margins: Women's Studies in the Nineties*. London: Falmer Press.

Felman, Shoshana (1993), *What Does A Woman Want? Reading and Sexual Difference*. Baltimore: The Johns Hopkins University Press.

Felski, Rita (1989), *Beyond Feminist Aesthetics: Feminist Literature and Social Change*. Cambridge, Mass: Harvard University Press.

Fetterley, Judith (1978), *The Resisting Reader: A Feminist Approach to American Fiction*. Bloomington: Indiana University Press.

Flax, Jane (1987) 'Postmodernism and Gender Relations in Feminist Theory'. In Nicholson (1990).

Flint, Kate (1993), *The Woman Reader 1837–1914*. Oxford: Clarendon Press.

Flynn, Elizabeth A. and Schweickart, Patrocinio P. (eds) (1986), *Gender and Reading: Essays on Readers, Texts and Contexts*. Baltimore: The Johns Hopkins University Press.

Foucault, Michel (1969; 1979), 'What Is an Author?'. Trans. Josué V. Harari. In Josué V. Harari, (ed.), *Textual Strategies: Perspectives in Post-Structuralist Criticism*. Ithaca, New York: Cornell University Press.

Fowler, Roger (ed.) (1987), *A Dictionary of Modern Critical Terms*. London: Routledge.

Frith, Gill (1993), 'Women, Writing and Language: Making the Silences Speak'. In Richardson and Robinson (1993).

Fuss, Diana (1989), *Essentially Speaking: Feminism, Nature and Difference*. New York: Routledge.

Fuss, Diana (ed.) (1991), *Inside/Out: Lesbian Theories, Gay Theories*. London: Routledge.

Gallop, Jane (1992), *Around 1981: Academic Feminist Literary Theory*. London: Routledge.

Gerrard, Nicci (1989), *Into the Mainstream*. London: Pandora.

Gilbert, Sandra M. and Gubar, Susan (1979), *The Madwoman in the Attic: The Woman Writer and the Nineteenth-Century Literary Imagination*. New Haven: Yale University Press.

Gilbert, Sandra M. and Gubar, Susan (eds) (1985), *The Norton Anthology of Literature by Women: The Tradition in English*. New York: W.W. Norton and Co.

Gilbert, Sandra M. and Gubar, Susan (1988), *No Man's Land: The Place of the Woman Writer in the Twentieth Century* (vol. 1, 'The War of the Words'). New Haven: Yale University Press.

Gilman, Charlotte Perkins (1892; 1981), *The Yellow Wallpaper*. London: Virago.

Glaspell, Susan Keating (1917; 1973), 'A Jury of Her Peers'. In Lee R. Edwards and Arlyn Diamond, (eds), *American Voices, American Women*. New York: Avon Books.

Godwin, Gail (28 April 1985), 'One Woman Leads to Another'. *The New York Times Book Review*.

Graham, Alma (1975), 'The Making of a Nonsexist Dictionary'. In Barrie Thorne and Nancy Henley, (eds), *Language and Sex: Difference and Dominance*. Rowly, Mass: Newbury House.

Greene, Gayle and Kahn, Coppélia (eds) (1993), *Changing Subjects: The Making of Feminist Literary Criticism*. London: Routledge.

Griffin, Gabriele (ed.) (1993) *Outwrite: Lesbianism and Popular Culture*. London: Pluto Press.

Groocock, Veronica (1994), 'Lesbian Journalism: Mainstream and Alternative Press'. In Liz Gibbs, (ed.), *Daring to Dissent: Lesbian Culture from Margin to Mainstream*. Poole, Dorset: Cassell.

Grosz, Elizabeth (1989), *Sexual Subversions: Three French Feminists*. St Leonards, New South Wales: Allen and Unwin.

Grosz, Elizabeth (1990), 'Contemporary Theories of Power and Subjectivity'. In Sneja Gunew, (ed.), *Feminist Knowledge: Critique and Construct*. London: Routledge.

Guimond, James (Fall, 1994), 'Auteurs as Autobiographers: Images by Jo Spence and Cindy Sherman'. *mfs* vol. 40, no. 3.

Hanscombe, Gill (8 June, 1984), 'Reaching the Parts Other Books Can't Reach'. *New Statesman*.

Haraway, Donna (1985), 'A `Manifesto for Cyborgs: Science, Technology and Socialist Feminism in the 1980s'. In Weed (1989) and Nicholson (1990).

Harrison, Tony (1987), *Selected Poems*. Harmondsworth, Middlesex: Penguin.

Heath, Stephen, (1984; 1986) 'Male Feminism'. In Jardine and Smith (1987).

Heilbrun, Carolyn G. (1991), 'Gender and Detective Fiction'. *Hamlet's Mother and Other Women: Feminist Essays on Literature*. London: The Women's Press.

Henderson-Holmes, Safiya (1990), 'Rape, A Class Act'. *Madness and a Bit of Hope*. New York: Harlem River Press. Published in *Spare Rib* no. 232, (March, 1992).

Hermes, Joke (Autumn 1992), 'Sexuality in Lesbian Romance Fiction'. *Feminist Review* no. 42.

Heslinger, Elizabeth, Sheets, Robin Lauterbach, Veeder, William (1983), *The Woman Question: Literary Issues, 1837–1883*. Manchester: Manchester University Press.

Hinds, Hilary (1992), 'Oranges Are Not the Only Fruit: Reaching Audiences Other Lesbian Texts Cannot Reach'. In Munt 1992.

Hirsch, Marianne (1989), *The Mother/Daughter Plot: Narrative, Psychoanalysis, Feminism*. Bloomington and Indianapolis: Indiana University Press.

Hirsch, Marianne and Keller, Evelyn Fox, (eds) (1990), *Conflicts in Feminism*. London: Routledge.

hooks, bell (in interview with Grace Evans) (May, 1991), 'To Live Long and Deep and Well'. *Everywoman*.

hooks, bell (1991), *Yearning: Race, Gender, and Cultural Politics*. London: Turnaround.

Horner, Avril and Zlosnik, Sue (eds) (1990), *Landscapes of Desire: Metaphors in Modern Women's Fiction*. Hemel Hempstead, Hertfordshire: Harvester Wheatsheaf.

Humm, Maggie (ed.) (1992), *Feminisms: A Reader*. Hemel Hempstead, Hertfordshire: Harvester Wheatsheaf.

Humm, Maggie (1994), *A Reader's Guide to Contemporary Feminist Literary Criticism*. Hemel Hempstead, Hertfordshire: Harvester Wheatsheaf.

Humm, Maggie (1995), *The Dictionary of Feminist Theory*. Second Edition. Hemel Hempstead, Hertfordshire: Prentice Hall/Harvester Wheatsheaf.

Humm, Maggie (1995), *Practising Feminist Criticism: An Introduc*tion. Hemel Hempstead, Hertfordshire: Prentice Hall/Harvester Wheatsheaf.

Huyssen, Andreas (1984), 'Mapping the Postmodern'. In Nicholson (1990).

Irigaray, Luce (1977; 1985), *This Sex Which Is Not One*. Trans. Catherine Porter. Ithaca, New York: Cornell University Press.

Iser, Wolfgang (1974), *The Implied Reader: Patterns of Communication in Prose Fiction from Bunyan to Beckett*. Baltimore: The Johns Hopkins and University Press.

Jackson, Cath (Summer, 1993), 'A Press of One's Own'. *Trouble & Strife* 26.

Jackson, J.R. de J. (1993), *Romantic Poetry by Women: A Bibliography 1770–1835*. Oxford: Clarendon Press.

Jackson, Rosemary (1981), *Fantasy: The Literature of Subversion*. London: Methuen.

Jacobus, Mary (1986), *Reading Woman: Essays in Feminist Criticism*. London: Methuen.

James, P.D. (1972), *An Unsuitable Job for a Woman*. London: Faber.

Jardine, Alice and Smith, Paul (eds) (1987), *Men in Feminism*. London: Methuen.

Jardine, Alice (1989), 'Notes for an Analysis'. In Teresa Brennan, (ed.), *Between Feminism and Psychoanalysis*. London: Routledge.

Jefferson, Ann and Robey David (eds) (1982), *Modern Literary Theory: A Comparative Introduction*. London: Batsford.

Jouve, Nicole Ward (1991), *White Woman Speaks with Forked Tongue: Criticism as Autobiography*. London: Routledge.

Kaplan, Cora (1977), Introduction to Elizabeth Barrett Browning, *Aurora Leigh and Other Poems*. London: The Women's Press.

Kaplan, Cora (June, 1986), 'An Unsuitable Genre for a Feminist?'. *Women's Review* no. 8.

Kaplan, Cora (1986), *Sea Changes: Essays on Culture and Feminism*. London: Verso.

Kappeler, Susanne (1988), 'What Is a Feminist Publishing Policy?'. In Gail Chester and Julienne Dickey, (eds), *Feminism and Censorship: The Current Debate*. Bridport, Dorset: Prism Press.

Kauffman, Linda S. (ed.) (1993), *American Feminist Thought at Century's End: A Reader*. Oxford: Blackwell.

Kaufman, Gloria (ed.) (1991), *In Stitches: A Patchwork of Feminist Humor and Satire*. Bloomington and Indianapolis: Indiana University Press.

Kaveney, Roz (1989), 'The Science Fictiveness of Women's Science Fiction'. In Carr (1989).

Keller, Evelyn Fox and Moglen, Helen (1987), 'Competition and Feminism: Conflicts for Academic Women'. In *Signs: Journal of Women in Culture and Society* vol. 12, no. 3.

Kemp, Gene (1979), *The Turbulent Term of Tyke Tyler*. Harmondsworth, Middlesex: Puffin.

Kennedy, Angus J. (1995), *The Internet & World Wide Web: The Rough Guide*. London: Rough Guides Ltd.

Kenyon, Olga (1992), *800 Years of Women's Letters*. Stroud, Gloucestershire: Alan Sutton Publishing.

King, Katie (1994), *Theory in Its Feminist Travels: Conversations in U.S. Women's Movements*. Bloomington and Indianapolis: Indiana University Press.

Kingston, Maxine Hong (1981), *The Woman Warrior: Memoirs of a Girlhood among Ghosts*. London: Picador.

Klein, Kathleen Gregory (1988), *The Woman Detective: Gender and Genre*. Urbana and Chicago: University of Illinois Press.

Kramarae, Cheris and Treichler, Paula A. (1992), *Amazons, Bluestockings and Crones: A Feminist Dictionary*. London: Pandora. (Originally published by Pandora in 1985 as *A Feminist Dictionary*.)

Kristeva, Julia (1974), 'Woman Can Never Be Defined'. Trans. Marilyn A. August. In Marks and de Courtivron (1981).

Kristeva, Julia (in interview with Susan Sellers) (October 1986), 'A Question of Subjectivity'. *Women's Review* issue 12.

Landry, Donna and MacLean, Gerald (1993), *Materialist Feminisms*. Oxford: Blackwell.

Larkin, Joan (1986), 'Rape'. *A Long Sound*. Granite Press. In McEwen (1988).

Larrington, Carolyne (ed.) (1992), *The Feminist Companion to Mythology*. London: Pandora.

Larrington, Carolyne (1995), *Women and Writing in Medieval Europe: A Sourcebook*. London: Routledge.

Lauter, Paul (1982), 'Working-Class Women's Literature: An Introduction to Study'. In Warhol and Price Herndl (1991).

Lawrence, D.H. (1922; 1962), 'Tickets Please'. In *England, My England*. Harmondsworth, Middlesex: Penguin.

LeFanu, Sarah (1988), *In the Chinks of the World Machine: Feminism and Science Fiction*. London: The Women's Press.

Le Guin, Ursula (1969), *The Left Hand of Darkness*. New York: Ace Books.

Le Guin, Ursula (1982), 'Sur'. *The Compass Rose: Short Stories*. New York: Harper and Row. In Gilbert and Gubar (1985).

Le Guin, Ursula (1992), *Dancing at the Edge of the World*. London: Paladin.

Le Guin, Ursula (1992), 'The Writer on, and at, Her Work'. In Janet Sternburg (ed.), *The Writer on Her Work*. London: Virago.

Lessing, Doris (1976), *The Memoirs of a Survivor*. London: Picador.

Lewis, Reina (1992), 'The Death of the Author and the Resurrection of the Dyke'. In Munt (1992).

Light, Alison (Summer, 1984), '"Returning to Manderley" – Romance Fiction, Female Sexuality and Class'. *Feminist Review* no. 16.

Light, Alison (1991), *Forever England: Femininity, Literature and Conservatism between the Wars*. London: Routledge.

Lochhead, Liz (1985), *True Confessions and Clichés*. Edinburgh: Polygon Books.

Lodge, David (ed.) (1988), *Modern Criticism and Theory: A Reader*. London: Longman.

Lorde, Audre (1978), *The Black Unicorn*. New York: W.W. Norton and Co.

Lorde, Audre (1984), *Sister Outsider: Essays and Speeches*. New York: The Crossing Press.

Lorde, Audre (1988), *A Burst of Light*. London: Sheba.

Lovell, Terry (1987), *Consuming Fiction*. London: Verso.

Lovell, Terry (ed.) (1990), *British Feminist Thought: A Reader*. Oxford: Blackwell.

Lurie, Alison (1988), *The Truth about Lorin Jones*. London: Michael Joseph

Macaskill, Hilary (July, 1990), 'From Nowhere to Everywhere'. *British Book News*.

Maggio, Rosalie (1992), *The Beacon Book of Quotations by Women*. Boston: Beacon Press.

Maggio, Rosalie (1992), *The Bias-Free Word Finder: A Dictionary of Nondiscriminatory Language*. Boston: Beacon Press.

Magill, Frank M. (ed.) (1994), *Great Women Writers: The Lives and Works of 135 of the Worlds' Most Important Women Writers from Antiquity to the Present*. London: Robert Hale.

Mainiero, Lina (1979), *American Women Writers: from Colonial Times to the Present*, vols. 1–4. New York: Frederick Ungar.

Maitland, Sara (1979), 'Novels are Toys not Bibles, but the Child is Mother to the Woman'. *Women's Studies International Quarterly* vol. 2, no. 2.

Maitland, Sara and Wandor Michelene (1987), *Arky Types*. London: Methuen.

Malcolm Janet (1994), *The Silent Woman: Sylvia Plath and Ted Hughes*. London: Picador.

Marcus, Jane (1987), 'Still Practice' A/Wrested Alphabet: Toward a Feminist Aesthetic'. In Shari Benstock, (ed.), (1987) *Feminist Issues in Literary Scholarship*. Bloomington: Indiana University Press.

Works Cited

Marcus, Laura (1992), 'Feminist Aesthetics and the New Realism'. In Armstrong 1992.

Marks, Elaine and de Courtivron, Isabelle (eds) (1981), *New French Feminisms: An Anthology*. Brighton: Harvester Press.

Martin, Biddy and Mohanty, Chandra Talpade (1986), 'Feminist Politics: What's Home Got to Do With It?'. In Teresa de Lauretis, (ed.), *Feminist Studies/Critical Studies*. Bloomington: Indiana University Press.

Martin, Rosy and Spence, Jo (Spring, 1985), 'New Portraits for Old: The Use of the Camera in Therapy'. *Feminist Review* no. 19.

McDowell, Deborah E. (1980), 'New Directions for Black Feminist Criticism'. In Showalter (1986).

McEwen, Christine (ed.) (1988), *Naming the Waves: Contemporary Lesbian Poetry*. London: Virago.

McNay, Lois (1992), *Foucault and Feminism: Power, Gender and the Self*. Cambridge: Polity Press.

McSweeney, Kerry (1993), Introduction to Elizabeth Barrett Browning, *Aurora Leigh*. Oxford: Oxford University Press.

Medbh, Máighréad (Summer, 1993), 'Easter 1991'. *Feminist Review* no. 44.

Miles, Rosalind (1987), *The Female Form: Women Writers and the Conquest of the Novel*. London: Routledge.

Miller, Casey and Swift, Kate (1981), *The Handbook of Non-Sexist Writing for Writers, Editors and Speakers*. London: The Women's Press.

Miller, Nancy (1988), *Subject to Change: Reading Feminist Writing*. New York: Columbia University Press.

Millett, Kate (1972), *Sexual Politics*. London: Abacus.

Mills, Jane (1991), *Womanwords: A Vocabulary of Culture and Patriarchal Society*. London: Virago.

Mills, Sara, Pearce, Lynne, Spaull, Sue, Millard, Elaine (1989), *Feminist Readings/Feminists Reading*. Hemel Hempstead, Hertfordshire: Harvester Wheatsheaf.

Mills, Sara (ed.) (1994), *Gendering the Reader*. Hemel Hempstead, Hertfordshire: Harvester Wheatsheaf.

Milner, Valerie (1982), *Murder in the English Department*. London: The Women's Press.

Mitchell, Elma (1976), 'Thoughts After Ruskin'. *The Poor Man in the Flesh*. Calstock, Cornwall: Peterloo Poets.

Modleski, Tania (1988), 'Feminism and the Power of Interpretation: Some Critical Readings'. In Teresa de Lauretis, (ed.), *Feminist Studies/Critical Studies*. London: Macmillan.

Modleski, Tania (1991), *Feminism Without Women: Culture and Criticism in a 'Postfeminist' Age*. London: Routledge.

Mohanty, Chandra Talpade (1991), 'Under Western Eyes: Feminist Scholarship and Colonial Discourse'. In Chandra Talpade Mohanty, Ann Russo, Lourdes Torres, (eds), *Third World Women and the Politics of Feminism*. Bloomington: Indiana University Press.

Mohanty, Chandra Talpade (1992), 'Feminist Encounters: Locating the Politics of Experience'. In Michèle Barrett and Anne Phillips, (eds), *Destabilizing Theory: Contemporary Feminist Debates*. Cambridge: Polity Press.

Moi, Toril (1982), 'Feminist Literary Criticism'. In Jefferson and Robey (1982).

Moi, Toril (1985), *Sexual/Textual Politics: Feminist Literary Theory*. London: Methuen.

Moi, Toril (ed.) (1986), *The Kristeva Reader*. Oxford: Blackwell.

Moi, Toril (ed.) (1987), *French Feminist Thought: A Reader*. Oxford: Blackwell.

Montefiore, Jan (1987), *Feminism and Poetry: Language, Experience, Identity in Women's Writing*. London: Pandora.

Montgomery, Martin, Durant, Alan, Fabb, Nigel, Furniss, Tom, Mills, Sara (1992), *Ways of Reading*. London: Routledge.

Moraga Cherríe and Anzaldúa, Gloria (eds) (1983), *This Bride Called My Back: Writings by Radical Women of Color*. New York: Kitchen Table Press.

Morris, Pam (1993), *Literature and Feminism: An Introduction*. Oxford: Blackwell.

Mukherjee, Bharati (1994), *The Holder of the World*. London: Virago.

Mulford, Wendy (1983), 'Notes on Writing: A Marxist/Feminist Viewpoint'. In Michelene Wandor (ed.), *On Gender and Writing*. London: Pandora.

Munt, Sally (ed.) (1992), *New Lesbian Criticism: Literary and Cultural Readings*. Hemel Hempstead, Hertfordshire: Harvester Wheatsheaf.

Munt, Sally (1992), 'Is There a Feminist in This Text? Ten Years (1979–1989) of the Lesbian Novel: A Retrospective'. *Women's Studies International Forum* vol. 15, no. 2.

Munt, Sally Rowena (1994), *Murder by the Book? Feminism and the Crime Novel*. London: Routledge.

Naher, Gaby (June 1994), 'Spreading the Word'. *Everywoman*.

Namjoshi, Suniti (1985), *The Conversations of Cow*. London: The Women's Press.

Nasta, Susheila (ed.) (1991), *Motherlands: Black Women's Writing from Africa, the Caribbean and South Asia*. London: The Women's Press.

NATE Language and Gender Committee (1988), *Gender Issues in English Coursework*. London: National Association of Teachers of English.

Newton, Judith and Rosenfelt, Deborah, (eds) (1985), *Feminist Criticism and Social Change*. London: Methuen.

Ngcobo, Lauretta (ed.) (1988), *Let It Be Told: Black Women Writers in Britain*. London: Virago.

Nichols, Grace (1989), 'Of Course When They Ask for Poems About the "Realities" of Black Women'. In *Lazy Thoughts of a Lazy Woman*. London: Virago.

Nicholson, Linda J. (ed.) (1990), *Feminism/Postmodernism*. London: Routledge.

Nicholson, Linda (Autumn, 1994), 'Interpreting Gender', *Signs: Journal of Women in Culture and Society* vol. 20, no. 1.

Olsen, Tillie (1978), *Silences*. New York: Dell Publishing.

Ohmann, Carol (1971), 'Emily Brontë in the Hands of Male Critics'. In Eagleton (1996).

Ostriker, Alicia Suskin (1987), *Stealing the Language: The Emergence of Women's Poetry in America*. London: The Women's Press.

Owen, Peter (ed.) (1993), *Publishing Now*. London: Peter Owen Ltd.

Palmer, Paulina (1993), *Contemporary Lesbian Writing: Dreams, Desire and Difference*. Buckingham: Open University Press.

Paretsky, Sara (1988) *Blood Shot*. New York: Dell.

Partnow, Elaine (ed.) (1993), *The New Quotable Woman: From Eve to the Present Day*. New York: Headline.

Peck, John and Coyle, Martin (1984), *Literary Terms and Criticism*. London: Macmillan.

Plath, Sylvia (1963; 1972), *The Bell Jar*. New York: Bantam.

Polity Press (1994), *The Polity Reader in Gender Studies*. Cambridge: Polity Press.

Poovey, Mary (1988), *Uneven Developments: The Ideological Work of Gender in Mid-Victorian England*. Chicago: the University of Chicago Press.

Prescod, Martha (1985), 'Untitled', *Land of Rope and Tory*. In Ngcobo (1988).

Radstone, Susannah (ed.) (1988), *Sweet Dreams: Sexuality, Gender and Popular Fiction*. London: Lawrence & Wishart.

Reagon, Bernice Johnson (1983), 'Coalition Politics: Turning the Century'. In Barbara Smith, (ed.), *Home Girls: A Black Feminist Anthology*. New York: Kitchen Table Press.

Reid, Su (1991), *The Critics Debate: To The Lighthouse*. London: Macmillan.

Register, Cheri (1975), 'American Feminist Literary Criticism: A Bibliographical Introduction'. In Josephine Donovan, (ed.), *Feminist Literary Criticism: Explorations in Theory*. Lexington: University Press of Kentucky.

Riaz, Fahmida (1991), 'Image'. Trans. Rukhsana Ahmad. In Rukhsana Ahmad (ed.) *We Sinful Women*. London: The Women's Press.

Rice, Phillip and Waugh, Patricia (eds) (1989), *Modern Literary Theory: A Reader*. London: Edward Arnold.

Rich, Adrienne (1977), Interview with Elly Bulkin. *Conditions: Two.*

Rich, Adrienne (1978), *The Dream of a Common Language: Poems 1974–1977.* New York: W.W. Norton and Co.

Rich, Adrienne (1979), *On Lies, Secrets, and Silence: Selected Prose 1966–1978.* New York: W. W. Norton and Co.

Rich, Adrienne (1987), *Blood, Bread and Poetry: Selected Prose 1979–1985.* London: Virago.

Richardson, Diane and Robinson, Victoria (eds) (1993), *Introducing Women's Studies: Feminist Theory and Practice.* London: Macmillan.

Richardson, Diane and Robinson, Victoria (1994), 'Theorizing Women's Studies, Gender Studies and Masculinity: The Politics of Naming'. *The European Journal of Women's Studies* vol. 1, issue 1.

Riley, Joan (1988), *Romance.* London: The Women's Press.

Ritchie, Maureen (1980), *Women's Studies; A Checklist of Bibliographies.* London: Mansell.

Roberts, Robin (1993), *A New Species: Gender and Science in Science Fiction.* Illinois: University of Illinois Press.

Robinson, Lillian S. (1979; 1986), *Sex, Class and Culture.* New York and London: Methuen.

Robinson, Victoria and Richardson, Diane (1994), 'Publishing Feminism: Redefining the Women's Studies Discourse'. *Journal of Gender Studies* vol. 3, no. 2.

Rose, Jacqueline (1991), *The Haunting of Sylvia Plath.* London: Virago.

Rumens, Carol (ed.) (1985), *Making for the Open: Post-feminist Poetry.* London: Chatto and Windus.

Ruskin, John (1864; 1907), 'Of Queens' Gardens'. *Sesame and Lilies.* London: J. M. Dent & Sons.

Russ, Joanna (1984), *Extra (ordinary) People.* New York: St Martin's Press.

Ruthven, K.K. (1984), *Feminist Literary Studies: An Introduction.* Cambridge: Cambridge University Press.

Sadoff, Dianne F. (Autumn 1985), 'Black Matrilineage: The Case of Alice Walker and Zora Neale Hurston'. *Signs: Journal of Women in Culture and Society* vol. 11, no. 1.

Sandoval, Chela (Spring, 1991), 'U.S. Third World Feminism: The Theory and Method of Oppositional Consciousness in the Postmodern World'. *Genders* No. 10.

Sargent, Pamela (ed.) (1978), *Women of Wonder.* Harmondsworth, Middlesex: Penguin.

Sargent, Pamela (ed.) (1979), *New Women of Wonder.* Harmondsworth, Middlesex: Penguin.

Sarton, May (1974), *Collected Poems 1930–1973.* New York: W.W. Norton and Co.

Scanlon, Joan and Swindells, Julia (Spring, 1994), 'Bad Apple'. *Trouble & Strife* 28.

Schipper, Mineke (ed.) (1985), *Unheard Words: Women and Literature in Africa, the Arab World, Asia, the Caribbean and Latin America.* London: Allison and Busby.

Schlueter, Paul, and Schlueter, June (eds.) (1988), *An Encyclopaedia of British Women Writers.* London and Chicago: St James Press.

Schockley, Ann Allen (1988), *Afro-American Women Writers, 1746–1933: An Anthology and Critical Guide.* London: Macmillan.

Scholes, Robert (1987), 'Reading Like a Man'. In Jardine and Smith (1987).

Scott, Joan W. (1986), 'Gender: A Useful Category of Historical Analysis'. In Weed (1989).

Scott, Mary (June, 1994), 'Making Faces'. *Everywoman.*

Searing, Susan (1985), *Introduction to Library Research in Women's Studies.* Boulder, Colorado: Westview Press.

Selden, Raman (1989), *A Reader's Guide to Contemporary Literary Theory.* Second Edition. Hemel Hempstead, Hertfordshire: Harvester Wheatsheaf.

Selden, Raman (1989), *Practising Theory and Reading Literature: An Introduction.* Hemel Hempstead, Hertfordshire: Harvester Wheatsheaf.

Sellers, Susan (ed.) (1988), *Writing Differences: Readings from the Seminar of Hélène Cixous.* Milton Keynes: Open University Press.

Sellers, Susan (1990), 'Learning to Read the Feminine'. In Wilcox, McWatters, Thompson and Williams (1990).

Sellers, Susan (1991), *Language and Sexual Difference: Feminist Writing in France*. London: Macmillan.

Sellers, Susan (ed.) (1994), *Taking Reality by Surprise: Writing for Pleasure and Publication*. London: The Women's Press.

Sharpe, Tom (1976), *Wilt*. London: Secker and Warburg.

Shattock, Joanne (1993), *The Oxford Guide to British Women Writers*. Oxford: Oxford University Press.

Showalter, Elaine (1978), *A Literature of Their Own: British Women Novelists from Brontë to Lessing*. London: Virago.

Showalter, Elaine (1983), 'Critical Cross-Dressing: Male Feminists and the Woman of the Year'. In Jardine and Smith (1987).

Showalter, Elaine (ed.) (1986), *The New Feminist Criticism: Essays on Women, Literature and Theory*. London: Virago.

Showalter, Elaine (ed.) (1989), *Speaking of Gender*. London: Routledge.

Smith, Sidonie (1993), *Subjectivity, Identity and the Body: Women's Autobiographical Practices in the Twentieth Century*. Bloomington and Indianapolis: Indiana University Press.

Snitow, Ann (1979), 'Mass Market Romance: Pornography for Women is Different'. In Ann Snitow, Christine Stansell, Sharon Thompson, (eds) (1983), *Powers of Desire: The Politics of Sexuality*. New York: Monthly Review Press.

Snitow, Ann (1990), 'A Gender Diary'. In Hirsch and Keller (1990).

Spence, Jo (1987), *Putting Myself in the Picture: A Political, Personal, and Photographic Autobiography*. London: Camden Press.

Spence, Jo and Holland, Patricia (1991), *Family Snaps: The Meanings of Domestic Photography*. London: Virago.

Spencer, Jane (1986), *The Rise of the Woman Novelist: From Aphra Behn to Jane Austen*. Oxford: Blackwell.

Spender, Dale (1980), *Man Made Language*. London: Routledge and Kegan Paul.

Spender, Dale (1986), *Mothers of the Novel: 100 Good Writers Before Jane Austen*. London: Pandora.

Spender, Dale (1995), *Nattering on the Net: Women, Power and Cyberspace*. Melbourne: Spinifex.

Spender, Dale and Todd, Janet (1989), *Anthology of British Women Writers: From the Middle Ages to the Present*. London: Pandora.

Sprengnether, Madelon (1993), 'Generational Differences: Reliving Mother–Daughter Conflicts'. In Greene and Kahn (1993).

Spivak, Gayatri Chakravorty (1985), 'Three Women's Texts and a Critique of Imperialism'. In Henry Louis Gates Jr. (ed.), *'Race,' Writing, and Difference*. Chicago: The University of Chicago Press.

Spivak, Gayatri Chakravorty (ed. Sarah Harasym) (1990), *The Post-Colonial Critic: Interviews, Strategies, Dialogues*. London: Routledge.

Spivak, Gayatri Chakravorty (1993), 'Reading *The Satanic Verses*'. In Biriotti and Miller (1993).

Stanley, Jo (ed.) (1995), *Cultural Sniping: The Art of Transgression*. London: Routledge.

Stanley, Liz (1992), *The Auto/biographical I: The Theory and Practice of Feminist Auto/biography*. Manchester: Manchester University Press.

Steedman, Carolyn (1986), *Landscape for a Good Woman: A Story of Two Lives*. London: Virago.

Stevenson, Anne (1985), 'Re-reading Jane'. *The Fiction-Makers*. Oxford: Oxford University Press.

Stevenson, Anne (1989), *Bitter Fame: A Life of Sylvia Plath*. Harmondsworth, Middlesex: Penguin.

Stevenson, Anne (1990), 'Letter to Sylvia Plath'. *The Other House*. Oxford: Oxford University Press.

Stibbs, Anne (ed.) (1992), *Like a Fish Needs a Bicycle ... And Over 3,000 Quotations By and About Women*. London: Bloomsbury.

Works Cited

Sweeney, Patricia E. (1993), *Biographies of British Women: An Annotated Bibliography*. London: Mansell.

Taylor, Helen (March 1986), 'The Cult of the Woman Author'. *Women's Review* issue 5.

Tiptree Jr., James (1970; 1975), 'I'm to Big but I Love to Play'. *10,000 Light Years from Home*. London: Eyre Methuen.

Todd, Janet (ed.) (1987), *A Dictionary of British and American Women Writers 1660–1800*. London: Methuen.

Todd, Janet (ed.) (1989), *Dictionary of British Women Writers*. London; Routledge.

Tremain, Rose (1992), *Sacred Country*. London: Sinclair-Stevenson.

Trinh, T. Minh-ha (1989), *Woman, Native, Other: Writing Postcoloniality and Feminism*. Bloomington and Indianapolis: Indiana University Press.

Tuchman, Gaye (with Nina E. Fortin) (1989), *Edging Women Out: Victorian Novelists, Publishers, and Social Change*. London: Routledge.

Tulsa Studies in Women's Literature, vol. 12, no. 2 (Fall 1993). Tulsa, Oklahoma: University of Tulsa.

Tuttle, Lisa (1986), *Encyclopaedia of Feminism*. London: Longman.

Uglow, Jennifer and Hinton, Frances (1982), *The Macmillan Dictionary of Women's Biography*. London: Macmillan.

Walder, Dennis (ed.) (1990), *Literature in the Modern World: Critical Essays and Documents*. Oxford: Oxford University Press.

Walker, Alice (ed.) (1979) *I Love Myself When I am Laughing …: A Zora Neale Hurston Reader*. New York: The Feminist Press.

Walker, Alice (1981). *You Can't Keep a Good Woman Down*. New York: Harcourt Brace Jovanovich.

Walker, Alice (1983), *In Search of Our Mothers' Gardens*. New York: Harcourt Brace Jovanovich.

Walker, Barbara G. (1983), *The Woman's Encyclopaedia of Myths and Secrets*. San Francisco: Harper & Row.

Walker, Margaret (1942), *For My People*. New Haven: Yale University Press.

Warhol, Robin R. and Herndl, Diane Price (eds) (1991), *Feminisms: An Anthology of Literary Theory and Criticism*. New Brunswick, New Jersey: Rutgers University Press.

Wattman, Francine, Treichler, Frank and Paula A. (1989), *Language, Gender, and Professional Writing*. New York: Modern Language Association.

Waugh, Patricia (1992), *Practising Postmodernism/ Reading Modernism*. London: Edward Arnold.

Webster, Roger (1990), *Studying Literary Theory: An Introduction*. London: Edward Arnold.

Weed, Elizabeth (ed.) (1989), *Coming to Terms: Feminism, Theory, Politics*. London: Routledge.

Weedon, Chris (1987), *Feminist Practice and Poststructuralist Theory*. Oxford: Blackwell.

Weekes, Ann Owens (1993), *Unveiling Treasures: The Attic Guide to the Published Works of Irish Women Literary Writers*. Dublin: Attic Press.

Weldon, Fay (1984), *The Life and Loves of a She-Devil*. London: Coronet.

Whitford, Margaret (ed.) (1991), *The Irigaray Reader*. Oxford: Blackwell.

Wilcox, Helen, McWatters, Keith, Thompson, Ann, Williams, Linda R. (eds) (1990), *The Body and the Text: Hélène Cixous, Reading and Teaching*. Hemel Hempstead, Hertfordshire: Harvester Wheatsheaf.

Williams, Linda R. (1992), 'Feminist Reproduction and Matrilineal Thought'. In Isobel Armstrong (1992).

Williams, Raymond (1976; 1983; 1988), *Keywords: A Vocabulary of Culture and Society*. London: Fontana Press.

Winterson, Jeanette (1985), *Oranges Are Not the Only Fruit*. London: Pandora.

Winterson, Jeanette (1989), *Sexing the Cherry*. New York: Atlantic Monthly Press.

Winterson, Jeanette (1992), *Written on the Body*. London: Jonathan Cape.

Wittig, Monique and Zeig, Sandie (1980), *Lesbian Peoples: Materials For A Dictionary*. London: Virago.

Wittig, Monique (1992), *The Straight Mind and Other Essays*. Hemel Hempstead, Hertfordshire: Harvester Wheatsheaf.

Wolf, Christa (1968), *The Quest for Christa T*. Trans. Christopher Middleton London: Virago.

Wolfe, Susan and Penelope, Julia (eds) (1993), *Sexual Practice, Textual Theory: Lesbian Cultural Criticism*. Oxford: Blackwell.

Wolmark, Jenny (1993), *Aliens and Others: Science Fiction Feminism and Postmodernism*. Hemel Hempstead, Hertfordshire: Harvester Wheatsheaf.

Women in Publishing (1989), *Twice as Many, Half as Powerful*. London: Polytechnic of North London Business School.

Woolf, Virginia (1928; 1992), *Orlando*. Oxford: Oxford University Press.

Woolf, Virginia (1929; 1938; 1993), *A Room of One's Own and Three Guineas*. Michèle Barrett (ed.). Harmondsworth, Middlesex: Penguin.

Woolf, Virginia (1942; 1979), 'Professions for Women'. In Michèle Barrett, (ed.), *Virginia Woolf: Women and Writing*. New York: Harcourt Brace Jovanovich.

Wright, Elizabeth (ed.) (1992), *Feminism and Psychoanalysis: A Critical Dictionary*. Oxford: Blackwell.

Yorkshire Evening Press, 'Girl Says Night Out Ended in Rape' (22 July 1994).

Zimmerman, Bonnie, (1981), 'What Has Never Been: An Overview of Lesbian Feminist Literary Criticism'. In Showalter (1986).

Zimmerman, Bonnie (1982), 'One Out of Thirty': Lesbianism in Women's Studies Textbooks'. In Margaret Cruickshank (ed.), *Lesbian Studies: Present and Future*. New York: The Feminist Press.

Zimmerman, Bonnie (1992), 'Lesbians Like This and That'. In Munt (1992).

Index